An
Archaeological
Companion
to the Bible

An Archaeological Companion to the Bible

Harry Thomas Frank

SCM PRESS LTD · London

Scripture quotations unless otherwise noted are from the
Revised Standard Version of the Bible and are used by
permission.

Selections from *The Legacy of Canaan*, by John Gray, are
used by permission of the publishers, E. J. Brill, Leiden.

Selections from James B. Pritchard, *Ancient Near Eastern
Texts Relating to the Old Testament* (3rd ed. with Supplement,
copyright © 1969 by Princeton University Press, pp. 279,
280, 288 trans. by Leo Oppenheim; p. 320 trans. by W. F.
Albright. Reprinted by permission of Princeton University
Press.

Selections from *Thespis*, by Theodore H. Gaster, copyright
© 1950, 1961 by Theodore H. Gaster; from *The Scriptures
of the Dead Sea Sect*, trans. by Theodore H. Gaster,
copyright © 1956, 1964 by Theodore H. Gaster. Reprinted
by permission of Doubleday & Company, Inc.

334 00051 3

First British edition 1972
published by SCM Press Ltd, 56 Bloomsbury Street, London
© Abingdon Press 1971

Typeset in the United States of America and
printed in Great Britain by
Hazell Watson & Viney Ltd, Aylesbury, Bucks

for
E. M. M. F.
J. L. R. F.
M. M. F.
I. D. F.

PREFACE

The towering magnificence of the Corinthian capitals soared high above us as we stood in awe amid the ruins of Jerash. Deep ruts cut by chariots into the paving stones of the colonnaded streets led into the marketplace, a huge semicircle cupped by fifty-six tall columns. The city's two amphitheaters bore mute evidence of the cultural level of this place in bygone days. To the left, quite near, were the vaulted remains of the long-fallen roofs of the public baths. Far off in the distance to the right, like a sentinel on the horizon, stood the triple gates of the triumphal arch built to celebrate the visit of the Emperor Hadrian in A.D. 129. And in the fountains of this ancient city of Transjordan, where water once bubbled and danced, sand and dust shifted silently as the wind passed along streets and up stairways that in other times had resounded to the hurried footsteps of Roman legionnaires, the slow shuffling of Bedouin shepherds, and the cries of Greek merchants.

All at once my journey into the past was shattered by a companion who remarked, somewhat unappreciatively I thought, "This is all splendid, but what really interests me is under the ground." My archaeologist-friend's remark was apt. What lies beneath the surface is often as important, if not more so, than impressive monuments above ground. With proper excavation such materials can literally write history from the soil. Such had been the case at Jerash which was now partly restored as a tourist site.

This is a book about history written from the soil. Not just any history, but ancient Middle Eastern history with emphasis upon Palestine and the people of the Bible. A century ago a book of this sort was unthinkable; until fairly recently it was not possible. Almost all of man's knowledge of his ancient past was limited to the period and those cultures mentioned in the Bible and in Greek and Roman writings. Archaeology, through use of societal remains as well as newly deciphered languages, has in a brief time nearly trebled the known span of recorded sedentary society. The vastness of preliterary history to which it bears witness is multiplied beyond that. The Bible is no longer a "historical fossil," as a scholar once called it. It can now be situated in a living context. The Hebrews did not live in a vacuum; nor, indeed, did the early Christians. They were parts of larger complexes, and even their religious thought and ways of worship, often common in form with those of other men and cultures of their day, shows this. At the same time, precisely because archaeology places the peoples of the Bible against their backgrounds we are better able than previous generations to understand the uniqueness of the Hebrew-Christian biblical tradition and to appreciate that faith in God which in its higher moments has been "a light to the nations."

Many peoples and institutions, in this country, Europe, and the Middle East, have contributed to this volume. A number of professional colleagues have been kind enough to offer advice and criticism. The list is lengthy, and I hope I will be forgiven if I mention only two to whom I owe a special debt. Paul Lapp, whose untimely death at age thirty-nine is an incalculable loss to archaeology, was a much appreciated tutor in field excavation techniques. Herbert G. May, my esteemed Oberlin colleague and friend, offered valuable criticisms and numerous suggestions. His selfless generosity immeasurably improved this book. Most of all his interest and encouragement prompted me on when, to paraphrase Churchill, this volume had ceased to be my mistress and had become my master.

I must also pay tribute to two other friends, Mrs. Barbara Turek and Mrs. Betty Berman. They accepted the difficult task of typing this manuscript with typical kindness and executed the work with their extraordinary efficiency.

Finally, it hardly needs to be said that this book is in no sense a substitute for the Bible. On the contrary, numerous references are included in the hope that the reader will have a Bible at hand and will read not merely the verses and passages cited, but their contexts as well.

H. T. F.
Oberlin, Ohio

CONTENTS

Joint Expedition to Tell el-Hesi

Joint Expedition to Tell el-Hesi

Joint Expedition to Tell el-Hesi

Archaeologists At Work

Joint Expedition to Tell el-Hesi

Joint Expedition to Tell el-Hesi

I: BIBLE AND ARCHAEOLOGY

1. THE WAY OF ARCHAEOLOGY

ARCHAEOLOGY is usually defined as "the science of the treatment of the material remains of the human past," or as a "systematic and descriptive study of antiquities," or something similar. In one sense adequate, such definitions are all the same misleading. They concentrate too much on the means and not enough on the ends. Sir Mortimer Wheeler was correct in his "insistence that the archaeologist is digging up not *things*, but *people*." [1] Walls, potsherds, inscriptions, and other artifacts are ever the mainstays of archaeology. But they are not for the excavator museum pieces to be treasured in and of themselves. Their importance lies in what they can tell about the men and cultures which produced them. Thus an ordinary cooking pot found crushed under a fallen wall may be of inestimably more value than a vase of the finest materials and highest craftsmanship whose context is not known. The latter may be the premier attraction of a gallery but depend upon the pot for its identification. Furthermore, the crushed pot, blackened by many an evening over an open fire, can date the wall which destroyed it and perhaps fill in a few lines on an otherwise blank page from history.

While the archaeological value of the two objects may be the reverse of what at first appears to be the case, both are important. Each has something to tell about the way men at a certain place and time thought, worked, and lived. And it is the purpose of archaeology to find out from the things man has made how his mind worked and how he translated his ideas into the organizing and functioning of human society.

This all seems obvious enough, yet it hardly occurred to anyone before the eighteenth century, and even in the nineteenth century when so many of the so-called "conquering sciences" came to life it was not pursued systematically. Indeed, until quite recently archaeology has been identified with that function it had during and following the Renaissance: the recovery of art objects for private collectors and museums. There

[1] Sir Mortimer Wheeler, *Archaeology from the Earth* (Penguin Books, 1964), p. 13.

has, of course, been an interest in the remains of older cultures since antiquity. Ashurbanipal, a king of Assyria who was a contemporary of Manasseh of Judah, is reported to have fancied himself something of an interpreter of old inscriptions and to have dispatched scribes to various parts of his far-flung empire to bring copies to him. The sister of Belshazzar is said to have had her own private collection of antiquities. Julius Caesar's fascination with the Sphinx is fabled, while the twin colossi of Memnon of Thebes, once the monumental gateway to the mortuary temple of Amenophis III (*ca.* 1406-1370 B.C.), was a major tourist attraction in Roman times. Yet such interests were little more than a concern for art laced with a good deal of curiosity which, if undisciplined and unsystematized, does little to enhance our knowledge of the past. Instructive is the Imperial Romans' use of such artifacts. They filled their ancient city with relics of still more ancient Egypt. There are more obelisks in Rome than along the Nile. But it was all for decoration.

With the demise of the Roman Empire came a diminuation of the ability of men and nations to pursue even this limited concern. The Renaissance, literally "an awakening" of interest in the past, changed everything. Yet scholars and men of letters were wholly preoccupied with the glories of Rome and the sublimities of Athens. There was a direct literary tradition and an abundance of visible monuments. General interest in the physical remains of the past was high. Artists and architects looked to Phidias, Hadrian, and others for their models. And patrons of the arts, first in Florence, then in Rome, and then more widely, began to collect antiquities to adorn their villas and palaces. Luca Pitti began his collection at this time, and slightly later Cosimo I built a splendid edifice to house another Florentine collection which today is known as the Uffizi. These people and others of similar inclination were *dilettanti*,

"enjoyers of art." Indeed, in England there arose a "Society of the Dilettanti" dedicated to the recovery of the art of the classical civilizations of the Mediterranean. Interest was unfortunately but understandably confined to works of art and buildings of aesthetic importance. Archaeology, as it was then understood, came to be identified with the history of classical art. Nations as well as individuals became involved. It was under this impetus that great collections came to the Louvre, the British Museum, and the German State Museum in Berlin. With greater resources larger works could be moved. Thousands of tons of monuments were taken from the sands of Egypt, the valleys of the Tigris and the Euphrates, and the rocky hills of Greece. Even the marble frieze was stripped from the Parthenon. Over 2,000 pieces of Etruscan ceramics were spirited out of Italy. Today enormous sphinxes stare down at one in London and Paris, and not a few gigantic winged bulls with human heads are blinkingly stared at by relatively tiny school children.

The focus of interest was Greece and Rome. This was, after all, *our* heritage. Moreover, in addition to comprehensive classical texts there was an abundance of inscriptions from monuments. In Greek and Latin these could be read without difficulty. The Athenians and the Romans told us what their lives were like and what they hoped for, accomplished, and in some cases failed to do. But this surfeit of knowledge had its doubters. Not everything—nor perhaps even the main things—about a given time or people is recorded. What is written down is usually seen through the eyes of kings or priests, of poets and politicians. Is there more to be known? If so, by what means?

When Napoleon came to power in France, among his early interests was the capture of Egypt. Like Alexander the Great many years before, the Corsican took with him a retinue of scholars as well as force of arms. The beginnings of modern archaeology can be dated from this time. The French experts were everywhere along the Nile, measuring, drawing, calculating. A systematic attempt was made to catalog the antiquities of Egypt —for their own sake. Furthermore, from bases near Alexandria and Cairo, surveyors under Colonel Jacotin mapped the Nile Delta on forty-two sheets at a scale of 1/100,000. An additional five sheets extended the survey into Palestine, but battle conditions there made it less possible to exercise exacting controls over the work. Although beautifully engraved and with a Gallic sense for detail, these precedent-setting maps were nonetheless little more than a series of magnificent military sketches.

Of more importance was the discovery of the Rosetta Stone. While constructing a fort at Rosetta in the Delta in 1799, French soldiers came upon a black basalt stone nearly four feet high. Broken along the edges, particularly the top, it nonetheless perfectly preserved numerous lines of the same inscription written in three different scripts: hieroglyphic, Demotic, and Greek. By 1822, using this substantial clue, Thomas Young and J. F. Champollion unlocked the secrets of hieroglyphics, the language of ancient Egypt. As the Egyptians had the happy facility of writing all over the sides of their temples and other monuments, this meant that a wealth of information, heretofore held secret by those strange markings, became accessible.

Napoleon's men had dealt only with visible structures. Excavation of subsurface materials in the Middle East grew out of French and British interest in Mesopotamia. Paul Botta became French consul at Mosul in 1842. He let it be known that he was in the market for antiquities. When these came to him he sought to trace their source. On one occasion he was told that some items had come from a large mound where villagers habitually dug brick for their own uses. Botta hired some laborers and sent them to the site. Some days later they reported to him that they had come down on walls covered with paintings, reliefs, and extraordinary color. Botta hurried to the spot on the east bank of the Tigris about twelve miles from Mosul. The place was named Khorsabad, and Botta was sure it was the site of an ancient and splendid palace, perhaps Assyrian. At that time no one could read the cuneiform inscriptions the workers found there. But when they were read it was clear that Botta had discovered nothing less than the palace of Sargon II (722-705 B.C.), conqueror of Samaria and destroyer of the Kingdom of Israel. When fully excavated the ruins covered an area of twenty-five acres.[2]

The Land of the Nile had long been known and had been considered to be the cradle of civilization. Was it not there, after all, that the pharaohs lived in splendor unequaled? To this Botta's work gave a resounding "No." His surprising discoveries rivaled those of Egypt and prompted considerable interest. The French government placed almost unlimited resources at his disposal, and in England a man named Henry Layard decided to go to Mesopotamia to have a look at other mounds.

Layard set off with virtually no financial backing. At Nimrud, twenty miles southeast of Mosul and about a mile and a half east of the Tigris, he decided to attempt a modest dig. The first day portions of an ancient palace were uncovered. The next day another palace. Everywhere were alabaster slabs seven feet high and covered with meticulously crafted reliefs. And then workmen began to find unspeakably beautiful ivory carvings: decoration from walls and furniture (see pp. 164-66). Such was ancient Calah, an Assyrian capital whose main palace was built by Ashurnasirpal II (ca. 884-859 B.C.).

[2] This palace alone was larger than many of the cities of contemporary Palestine.

Examples of the exquisitely carved ivories from Nimrud show both the high standard of workmanship and the mythological subjects which were often the inspiration for this art form. The Egyptian influence is particularly noticeable on the cherubim to the left.

The Nimrud Expedition—Sir Max Mallowan

The Nimrud Expedition

The Nimrud Expedition

The Nimrud Expedition

In 1849 Layard began excavating just across the river from Mosul. Success did not come quite so soon as before, but it proved to be even more spectacular in the long run. After about a month he began to lay bare Nineveh with its magnificent palace of Sennacherib. Nineveh, whose destruction brought forth from Nahum a bitter poem of unrestrained joy, was a truly great city. It was the capital of Assyria for only ninety years, but these were the years of Assyrian greatness and all was lavished upon the city. Double brick walls thirty-two feet thick and seventy-six feet high were further strengthened by fifteen strong gates and a moat of seventy-seven feet. Within this defensive barrier were multicolored buildings of glazed brick and delicate mosaics including white cuneiform lettering set against turquoise blue backgrounds. Here were the forerunners of the familiar Arab decorations from the Koran. Dark blue was a favorite of the architects of Nineveh, and it was set off by various other colors, black and yellow being prominent.

From the palace proper was recovered an extensive library, apparently added by Ashurbanipal, Sennacherib's grandson. Hundreds of cuneiform tablets, still more or less neatly arranged according to subject, contained a broad survey of knowledge in that day. Layard had found not only the palace of the man who besieged Jerusalem in Isaiah's day, but had also provided the means by which modern man could enjoy a then unparalleled view of the content of Assyrian knowledge at the height of imperial power.

Archaeological interest, which to this time had centered on Greece and Italy, expanded to the countries of the eastern Mediterranean. A new set of problems was encountered. Primary among these were the questions of ancient written sources and of multiple occupational layers. There was no Herodotus to guide; no Caesar, no Livy, no Pausanias. As over against the myriad texts available to classical archaeology, there were none, or almost none, for those working in the Middle East. Not that inscriptions and texts did not exist—the languages in which they were written were still undeciphered.

Note has already been taken of the unraveling of Egyptian hieroglyphics. Henry Rawlinson, a contemporary of Botta and Layard, performed the same thing for cuneiform and in much the same way. Twenty-six miles from Kermanshah, where he was a major in the British army assigned to the East India Company, there is a huge bas-relief carved on the cliff face. The figures are surrounded by extensive cuneiform inscriptions in three languages. Hanging from ropes high above the valley floor, Rawlinson managed to copy about 12,000 lines of writing. With arduous labor and great patience he managed to translate some 400 lines of Old Persian. It was an incredibly difficult task. There was unfortunately no Greek to

Cuneiform writing, such as on these tablets from the Babylonian Chronicle, remained a mystery until the nineteenth century when Henry Rawlinson began his monumental work of decipherment. This work, when completed, opened vast libraries of knowledge about the Ancient Near East.

guide him. All the same he made surprising progress. Later, with the discovery of a tablet correlating ideogrammatic script with syllabic materials, it was possible to produce a Babylonian grammar which unlocked the secrets of many inscriptions from Mesopotamia. Yet so difficult was the problem of translation that half a century later the newly established German School of Assyriology was still hard at work developing adequate linguistic and philological methods for cuneiform.

This is but one example of the philological progress which has been a continuing characteristic of Middle Eastern archaeology. One by one inscriptions have been deciphered and grammars written—Egyptian, Accadian, Hittite, Hurrian, Sumerian, Elamite, Lycian, Lydian, Vannic, Lithyanic, Thamudic, Safaitic, etc.—and the task continues. In addition, vast strides have been made in our understanding of Hebrew, Aramaic, Coptic, and other tongues which were known. Comparative Semitics has now advanced to the state where it is possible to reconstruct a hypothetical proto-Semitic.

A little over a hundred years ago the Bible was virtually the only written source for the ancient history of the region. Now many matters merely mentioned or alluded to in the Scriptures are known in some detail. Certain enigmas in history as recorded in the Bible are no longer occasions for puzzlement. Most important, dozens of texts and other archaeological discoveries put the Bible into a living context. While the origin of the Hebrews remains a mystery, the world in which they lived is becoming increasingly well known. Nahum no longer lashes out at a shadowy city, nor is Sennacherib merely a dreaded name trembling on the lips of Isaiah.

The second problem distinguishing classical from Middle Eastern archaeology is that of multiple occupational layers. For the most part excavators in Greece, Italy, Roman Britain, and similar places have to deal with

Ruins of Samaria showing 1st century B.C. foundations above 9th century B.C. walls in foreground.

only one period of occupation by one cultural group. At Bath in England, for example, there is a Roman spa which was built and occupied by one group of people and used for a relatively short time. There are indications of three different phases of construction during that period. While this has its own peculiar difficulties, it is not a matter of numerous peoples over hundreds or even thousands of years—with the evidence compressed into twenty or thirty feet of soil affected by war, erosion, and rebuilding. And here again literature is a factor. The archaeologists who undertook extensive excavations in the Athenian agora knew from contemporary records when it was built, more or less what it looked like, and to a large extent the area it covered. There was much to be learned, all the same, and their splendid work has added immeasurably to our knowledge of classical Athens. Those working at Shechem, on the other hand, were dealing with a site occupied for approximately eighteen centuries, undescribed in literature, and of relatively unknown dimensions.

Although it is not nearly so acute as in Middle Eastern sites, the problem of multiple occupational layers (stratigraphy) does occur in some classical excavations. Indeed, it was at Homeric Troy that this phenomenon was first recognized. A dilettante German-American banker,[3] Heinrich Schliemann, recognized that the town site had an accumu-

[3] Born in Mecklenburg, Germany in 1822, Schliemann became an American citizen in 1850.

lation of successive occupational strata, separated by destruction layers.

Twenty years later, in 1890, Flinders Petrie undertook a stratigraphic excavation at Tell el-Hesi in southwestern Palestine. Paying particular attention to the remains of broken pottery, he developed a method of sequence-dating which through continuous refinement has become one of the cardinal principles of archaeology. He noted that careful observation of the types of artifacts occurring in each layer made it possible to date the occupational strata within reasonable and accepted limits. This is the backbone of archaeological chronology.

Archaeology in Palestine moved slowly but decisively prior to the First World War. Important German work took place at various sites such as Taanach, Shechem, and Jericho; the American School of Oriental Research was founded in 1900 (the British School of Archaeology in Jerusalem, 1910), and there was the Harvard Expedition to Samaria with its recovery of the Samaria ivories (see p. 164). After the war there occurred what might be termed "an archaeological explosion in the Holy Land." Many sites were dug, and advancement in knowledge was astounding. This was due to several factors. The Turkish rule which had actively discouraged outsiders from coming into the region was replaced by a British administration eager to aid the excavator. Not the least manifestation of this was the establishment of the Palestine Department of Antiquities. A number of extremely able men appeared in the field: Reisner, Fisher, Guy, Vincent, Starkey, Alt, Albright, and others. In the main those who made a durable contribution to archaeological technique were those who paid greatest attention to the work of Petrie. Finally, but by no means least, there was money available. The case of the Oriental Institute of the University of Chicago with its sixteen million dollars is unique, but there were limited funds for others as well. Petrie's

insights were modified, refined, expanded. Fisher's work at Megiddo and Albright's classic dig at Tell Beit Mirsim need especially to be mentioned. The latter set a standard which many have sought to emulate.

In more recent years the techniques of archaeology have been significantly advanced by the work of Kathleen Kenyon at Jericho and Jerusalem and G. E. Wright at Shechem. Particularly the former, the director of the British School of Archaeology in Jerusalem, has refined the art of stratigraphic digging in epoch-making proportions.

The Cardinal Principles of Archaeology

The observations of Schliemann and Petrie provided the basis for the two cardinal principles of archaeology: (1) *stratigraphy* and (2) *typology*. When the excavator of Troy suggested that it was a series of cities, one on top of the other, and indeed, that he had found the city of Homer,[4] he became a laughingstock on both counts. In 1870 few people believed that one city could be built on top of another, much less that it had been done repeatedly at the same site or many sites. But the fact has been demonstrated over and over again in various excavations.

(1) The building up of ancient cities occurred in a number of ways. Natural disaster was one. The example of volcanic destruction at Pompeii is well known. Earthquake, particularly in Palestine, has taken its toll. The walls of Jericho may at one time have been constructed so as to localize and thus minimize damage from tremors. Floods were destructive in certain areas, and fire was a constant danger. Woolley discovered that water had brought one culture to an end at Ur and that a silt deposit divided that stratum from another and different one above. Evidence of fire damage has been

[4] Schliemann incorrectly identified the Homeric level. It was not until 1932 that an American scholar named Blegen established that the seventh level, dating from 1185 B.C., was the one known to Homer.

found at many excavated cities; sometimes it was localized near the walls as at Taanach, sometimes it encompassed the whole city as at Lachish. While accidental fire was always a hazard, both these flaming destructions were set by attackers. Humans more than nature have been the great destroyers. No one knows when man first lifted his hand against his neighbor. In telling the story of Cain and Abel (Genesis 4:1-16), the Bible seems to suggest that it is an almost primeval instinct of human nature. However that may be, we cannot say when anger and covetousness produced the initial strife. Yet from the dawning of archaeologically recorded history there is evidence of fighting and wars. With the coming of urban society with its concentration of wealth and increasing spheres of influence, hostilities grew and intensified. No longer were they focused on a passing family or tribe, but upon settled sites with vested interests. The earliest known city, Jericho, has an impressive defense system. Indeed, the story of city-building in the ancient East is a chronology of a continuous arms race. Better offensive weapons produced new forms and combinations of walls which in turn set off a search for more effective offensive weapons. On the whole the tide ran with the offense. By battering ram, by scaling ladder, by starvation and fire, city after city was breached, sacked, dismantled. Roofs fell in, walls collapsed or were pulled down, pottery was crushed, wells were covered, household gods as well as the great altars of the temples lay quietly in the dust and rubble. Suffering was in abundance. "How lonely sits the city that was full of people" (Lamentations 1:1), is a fitting description of what occurred innumerable times in Palestine, land bridge between continents and juncture of hostile interests.

The destruction of ancient cities was awful and sometimes total. Yet there was much to attract men back to the sites. Rebuilding often began immediately. Occasionally years would elapse. In a few instances the location was abandoned. But almost invariably the advantages that had caused a city originally to be built on a certain spot would beckon again. In general these advantages were fourfold. A strategic location near a trade route was often an attraction. Adequate water is a matter of first importance to any concentration of people and even more so in an arid climate. The availability of fertile land for farming and grazing was a third major factor. And, of course, there was always a concern for defense. These last two factors meant that cities were normally to be found on hilltops rather than on the plains. "But none of the cities that stood on mounds [*tells*] did Israel burn, except Hazor only," says Joshua 11:13 in speaking of the conquest of north Palestine by the Hebrews.

Around the middle of the third millennium B.C., awakening urban culture reached one of its high points in Palestine. The cities of this period are examples of various combinations of these four advantages. Megiddo, Taanach, Dothan, Tirzah, and other Bronze Age cities excavated in recent years have revealed hilltop cities of relatively considerable size located beside fertile plains. Each of these also shows a long history of successive destructions and reoccupations.

How were these cities built and rebuilt in such a way as to produce the layer-cake effect encountered by the archaeologist? Today when a contractor begins to build, the first consideration is preparation of the site. The huge machines move in. If the site has been used before, remains of previous buildings are knocked down and removed. Bulldozers then push dirt this way and that. If it is to be a large building, enormous power-driven shovels dig deep into the earth until bedrock is reached or perhaps until the engineers and architects are satisfied the subsoil will bear the weight of the building. This process unfortunately results in the loss or considerable confusion of evidence of previous occupation.

19

How Cities Build Up

The mammoth arches of the Pool of Bethesda, prominent structures of Jerusalem in Jesus' day, were subsequently covered by debris and later construction. Now, thanks to the archaeologists' spades, they can be seen once more (lower left). The model trash pit from Williamsburg (upper left) shows how human habitation leaves its remains in layercake fashion. The same thing can be seen in Rome where the columns of an imperial forum project above present ground level, and at Samaria, where second-century Roman shops have been unearthed.

How very different were the methods of the ancients. First of all there were no machines as we know them. Although block, tackle, and pully eventually came into general use, power was normally provided by the back and arm of man with animals sometimes employed as well. This lack of power limited to a degree the size of structures that could be built, unless, as in the case of the pyramids, slave labor was readily and abundantly at hand. It also meant that the clearing of a site was severely restricted. Moreover, unless the structure were royal or religious, chances are that virtually no site clearance at all was involved. Most houses were of sunbaked mud brick although a large number were of easily available field stones. Usually of one room, the dwellings were square with flat roofs. Heavy winter rains would in time prove disastrous to the mud brick, while earthquakes and wars were equally fatal to brick and stone. When catastrophe struck, the unfortunate householder was not able to call the nearest contractor. With his family and friends he would make the place as level as he could and build again. He thus constructed on top of debris. Moreover, when buildings collapsed they entombed many of the everyday items which had been in use by the family or former inhabitants.[5] Pottery was broken, fire pits covered, implements and jewelry lost. Bowls, beds, and bangles had new floors of earth, straw, and occasionally plaster laid right over the top of them. If a stone wall were to be built, it would be necessary to cut a foundation trench for the lower courses of rocks. Such trenches are readily spotted by the well-trained eye and are extremely valuable in correctly reading the occupational history of a site.

[5] It was not always nor perhaps even usually that the same family built a second time on a site. They almost certainly did not when a city had been overrun in war. Slaughter and slavery would see to that.

In this oversimplified description it is possible to gain an idea of how cities built up as one level of occupation was constructed on top of the debris of another. Cities do not sink down. They grow upward and become what is known as a *tell:* a mound of ruins. The earliest level is nearest the bottom while the top may be a wall built last year by a shepherd or an orchard whose young trees are about to yield their first fruit. It is the task of the field archaeologist not merely to dig through this layer cake, but to understand what he is seeing. His trained eye must be ever alert to changes in the texture and composition of the soil, to the presence of foundation trenches, to the use of "robber stones,"[6] and to literally a hundred and one other clues to the occupational history of the location.

Foremost, this involves the recognition of different strata, the careful extraction of *all* artifacts including *every* potsherd however small or broken, and the accurate compiling of a thorough field notebook complete with numerous and regular three-dimensional diagrams. This is very different from the archaeologist of years ago who sat in his tent —or in Mosul!—coming up the tell only if workers found something interesting.

Strata are not always easily recognized. They can be indicated by a subtle change in the color or texture of the soil; or they can be signified by the appearance of a floor or a charred layer. To make the task more difficult, layers are almost never level. They run this way and that, and one must dig the stratum, not the level. If there is a tremendous trash pit in the stratum, this must be dug in its entirety, for when one finishes, the ground should ideally appear as it was at a given period in history. The pit may penetrate several recognizable layers from other ages, as pits tend to do, but it must be

[6] Stones originally cut for use in one structure but employed in the building of another and later one.

dug out before one proceeds to work on the other strata.

The intention of Reisner and Fisher at Megiddo was to strip that large mound layer by layer until all its occupational periods had been fully explored one by one. Not even the unheard-of resources of the Oriental Institute proved equal to the task. Massive work continued over a number of years (1925-1939), but the original purpose was not realized. It was fortunate. No mound should be stripped. Archaeology is by its nature a destructive undertaking. While field books and published final reports should allow the trained expert to reconstruct all of importance that appeared to excavators, the actual materials can never be studied again once they are dug. Not even a fallen stone can be placed back in a wall in its exact original position. However sure one is of the method employed, areas should be left for future excavators whose approach may be—and probably will be—superior to those being employed. Such has proved to be the case at Megiddo. The correct stratigraphic insight of Reisner and Fisher had a major methodical flaw. The value of vertical cut was not stressed, much less consistently employed. Working mainly with the horizontal plain produced a flat apprehension of the site. The true nature of the various deposits was not

A reconstruction of Megiddo as scholars think it was in Canaanite and biblical times.

Convent de Sion

clear, and as a consequence dating of artifacts and structures was often difficult and, as has been shown by the more recent work of Yadin (1960), sometimes incorrect. Nonetheless, the emphasis was in the right place. In progress toward adequate method, the Megiddo dig was an important contribution.

Not all appreciated Petrie's insight, however. During the 1930s (and sad to say, to an extent even today) some excavators bashed through walls tracing out a building or, still worse, what they thought was a building. But buildings as such are not important. It is their relative position within a given stratum that affords the opportunity for correct interpretation. Preoccupation with buildings is a residue of archaeology's heritage as outlined earlier. W. F. Albright recognized this in his work at Tell Beit Mirsim and sought to correlate all materials which appeared in or came from the earth. Of perhaps greater importance at this point, this meticulous scholar produced a number of students who have continually sought to improve the methods of stratigraphic digging. Foremost among these is G. E. Wright whose excavations at Shechem have produced yet another generation of archaeologists concerned with the importance of method for correct interpretation.

The present generation benefits also from the work of Kathleen Kenyon. Her excavation at Jericho (1952-1958) was epoch-making.[7] Employing skills and knowledge gained from her work on Roman ruins in Britain and North Africa, she demonstrated the extreme accuracy of three-dimensional digging. Her stratigraphic method is to lay out a site on a grid and dig squares, not

[7] Charles Warren sank a number of well-like shafts into the mound at Jericho in 1867. One, it was discovered in Kenyon's excavations, penetrated the Early Bronze Age city wall while another cut into the still earlier pre-Pottery Neolithic levels. Because of inadequate methods he failed to recognize this richest of all known Palestinian sites and reported that there was nothing to be found at the mound.

structures. This means that sections of earth, called "balks," run at right angles to structures. Thus vertical as well as horizontal cuts are made available for interpretation of materials. Structures can then be interpreted in terms of their relationship to the different layers of soil, including any disturbances which might be in them (such as trash pits, burn areas, post holes, and so forth). Unless a building has an inscription or some clearly distinguishing characteristic, it can be dated only with reference to the associated strata. And even the criterion of "clearly distinguishing characteristic" can be misleading. Excavators at Ramat Rahel uncovered a palace strikingly similar in design and decoration to royal Hebrew structures from ninth-century Samaria, Megiddo, and Hazor. On the basis of "distinguishing characteristics" it would be logical to assign this building to Solomon or one of his immediate successors. But evidence from associated levels shows that this palace is from the last days of the Judean monarchy (late seventh century or early sixth century). It seems, in fact, to be remains of the new palace of Jehoiakim which provoked a stinging rebuke from Jeremiah (22:31; see p. 203).

Miss Kenyon has perfected stratigraphic digging to a high state and has justified archaeology's often repeated claim to scientific status. Careful three-dimension digging combined with meticulous and continuous recording in the field has produced a possibility of accuracy undreamed of when Schliemann put forth his seemingly preposterous suggestion that one city was actually built on top of another at Troy.[8]

So far almost nothing has been said about what is in the various layers that allows for the accuracy of interpretation possible through true stratigraphic excavation. This brings us to the second cardinal principle of

archaeology: *typology.*

(2) Typology has to do with the general shape and decoration of artifacts. Style and form might be an equally good designation. One would suspect that something were wrong if a picture claiming historical accuracy showed Martha Washington in a miniskirt or if Clive at Plassey were shown with a submachine gun in his hand. The representations are obviously later, as they picture different styles and techniques. Likewise a person acquainted with ancient technology can tell by the artifacts in a given stratum of soil the age of the level.

By far the most readily available objects for such identification are pieces of pottery, broken and whole. From the late Neolithic Period on, pottery was plenteous and its use universal in the ancient Middle East. It was also fragile. Differing geographical areas and peoples produced local variations of style. But there was an astonishing unity, and in general styles changed chronologically more than regionally. It is thus possible, given the shape of a pot and the technology employed in its manufacture, to identify its date within given margins of error. It is not necessary to have the whole piece to make this judgment. Bases, rims, and handles are often distinctive. Moreover, a grid square is likely to produce quantities of potsherds, not one, two, or a dozen. The accumulation of many provides evidence. As a general rule of thumb, if there are not compelling reasons otherwise, the level is to be dated by the latest artifact found in it. Thus a stratum containing fifty to a hundred Early Bronze sherds and a few from the Iron Age is judged to be Iron Age. Sometimes one sherd is enough to produce a later dating. Whenever there is doubt the later date is always to be preferred.

The implication is obvious. Each stratum must first of all be recognized and then dug thoroughly and completely. Every artifact in it must be preserved, recorded, and kept

[8] See Kathleen Kenyon, *Beginning in Archaeology* (London: J. M. Dent and Sons, 1964), for a thorough and brilliant exposition of her method.

separate from those of other levels until experts have had a chance to "read" it, that is, to determine its age and whatever else it has to tell. Surveyors and artists also employ their skills to augment the square supervisor's field book. An adequate photographic record is kept. Finally the published excavation report should contain drawings and photographs of all types of pottery found. In addition, it is increasingly the practice to save random samples of potsherds to allow others not directly associated with a given excavation to check the judgment of the field experts from actual materials. Typology thus not only provides the means for fairly accurate dating but also provides opportunity for others to check on the conclusions of a given expedition.

Typology also gives substantial clues to cultural influences and the extent of trade in the ancient world. For example, most people are of the impression that Greek influence penetrated Palestine with the coming of Alexander the Great. But the discovery of Mycenaean ware and copies of such pottery in Bronze Age contexts indicate the presence of Greek traders and influence a thousand to fifteen hundred years before Alexander. The influence was, however, of a very different character from that which followed in the conqueror's wake. Or take another example of how typology can write history. The rapid appropriation of Palestinian pottery styles by the Philistines has been interpreted, probably correctly, as evidence of their cultural assimilation into the native ways of the peoples they conquered in the thirteenth century B.C. At the same time, failure to isolate distinctive thirteenth-century Hebrew pottery forms has made the task of determining the character and extent of the "conquest" considerably more difficult.[9]

[9] Pottery has been used in this section as the premier example of typology. There are numerous artifacts as well as distinctive practices which aid in the matter of establishing relative chronology. One of the most important of these is burial habits.

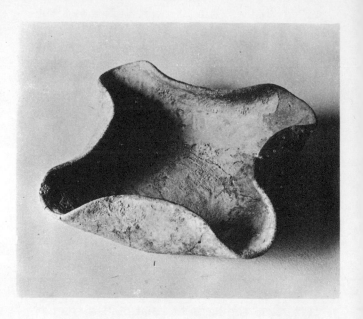

Technological and stylistic changes in pottery manufacture and form afford the archaeologist an opportunity to develop a chronological cultural sequence based upon this relatively indestructible type of artifact. Lamps, which clearly show distinctive forms, are particularly helpful. At upper left is a

four-spouted lamp from patriarchal times, while at lower left is a graceful shell-shaped lamp from the period of the Judges. At upper right is a slipper lamp from the Hellenistic period in Palestine; below it is a Herodian lamp of the type known to Jesus.

Limitations and Possibilities

For a young discipline, archaeology has a spectacular record of achievement. Yet it is not without its limitations, most inherent in the nature of the materials dealt with, but a few due to more human factors. Many of the digs which were carried out previous to the development of adequate stratigraphic method have produced unreliable conclusions. This means that some sites need to be redug, and many excavation reports have to be re-evaluated. Excavation reports, however, are a problem in themselves. While articles indicating the work of a season appear with some regularity, the expense and time involved in a final comprehensive report (often several large volumes) tend to postpone such publications for years. In some cases as long as thirty years have elapsed between the actual field work and the major excavation report. Ten years is by no means unusual. Furthermore, claims are often made which are too broad for the evidence to bear. The field archaeologist, however good, is not necessarily the best prepared to interpret the material he has recovered or to make the kind of synthesis of data which is now becoming possible. The provision of archaeologically recovered material is but the first step in a lengthy and difficult process of historical and cultural reconstruction and appreciation. Many experts in various fields have a contribution to make. At the same time, those best able to make a critical synthesis of the materials are those who, having had some experience in the field, are able to reconstruct the actual dirt situation from reports, and who thus understand clearly the extent of evidence available. Coupled with this must be generous self-criticism, which archaeology possesses in abundance. An excavator may understandably be jealous of his own interpretation carefully arrived at, but he above all understands the possibility of new evidence and new combinations of evidence which the discipline is constantly producing.

Limitations imposed by the nature of the material available are a different matter. Bone, stone, and metal artifacts tend to survive, whereas wood, textiles, and other types of organic substances do not. There have been notable exceptions to this, and the amazing discoveries in the Wilderness of Judea have completely revolutionized our ideas about the survival possibilities of writings on leather, wood, and papyrus. At Ur, Woolley was able to reconstruct an elegant harp from impressions in the soil. At Sutton Hoo in Suxsex, there was a similar but more remarkable recovery of a Saxon funeral ship—eighty feet long with a fourteen-foot beam. Its timbers had all perished, but the damp sand had been discolored by the disintegration. Further, iron nails that had once fixed the ribs and planking were still in place. With infinite care the entire stain layer and thus the hull of the ship itself was laid bare. Even more remarkable, the size and shape of the cabin were recovered by noting the sloped lines of discoloration over the clean sand which had filtered in before the roof collapsed. These are, however, unusual examples.

The general inability to identify individuals is often taken to be a limitation of archaeological interpretation. This problem is, of course, more acute for the preliterary phase of history than for that time after which man began to write and to keep records. Yet even when written materials are available, it is seldom possible, apart from palaces, to tell who the actual families were who once lived in excavated areas. For this reason archaeology has been said to deal with "faceless men." But is there not an element of gain involved? Written records are after all capable of misleading; in any event they are one-sided. This is relatively more true of ancient than modern times; writing was less widespread in those days. The exploits of

rulers (usually exaggerations if not outright lies), rituals and myths of religion, legal documents, and some poetic works (often religious in character) survive. This is certainly an unbalanced view of any society. The "faceless man" may, indeed, be the so-called "average man" of every society, and in the last analysis it is he who provides the sinews of civilization.

The possibilities of archaeology are to be seen in various areas: linguistic, typological, geographical, chronological, historical, and cultural analyses, to mention a few. It is of first importance to bear in mind that judgments can only be drawn from what is at hand. Abstract sets of values or preconceived ideas, whatever their origin and value, can never be the context for valid archaeological understanding. At the same time, interpretation can be made on a wider plane than at first appears possible. One is not bound to mere material remains in themselves. Artifacts are many things: responses to both natural and human environment; expressions of ideas, aesthetic feelings, and religious convictions; as well as a larger range of creativity envisioned by the mind. Patient scholarly endeavor can often produce a fairly complete picture of ancient cultures, including some aspects of the spiritual life. Funerary customs certainly had religious significance. The Middle Bronze Age tombs uncovered at Jericho with their tables, bowls, baskets, and other items of everyday use, including toilet articles, surely point to a conception of afterlife. If we are not able on the basis of the available indications to speak in detail about that conception, we can, nonetheless, point to its considerable importance as evidenced by the elaborate interments. Other types of burial customs—the position and orientation of the body, whether it is disarticulated or not, the kind of tomb, and so forth—also have meaning. And that is the point: artifacts, whether toggle pin or temple, mean something. With a due sense of modesty and a healthy appreciation for the somewhat speculative nature of his work, the synthesizer of archaeological evidence searches for these meanings. What is the social role of certain excavated materials? Do they express art for art's sake or religion? What part did politics or trade or war or natural environment play? These and innumerable other questions arise. All this is in keeping with Wheeler's point about working with people, not things.

In the long run the possibilities of archaeology are to be judged by its achievements. Although scientific archaeology is a relatively new phenomenon, it has opened up not only the vast panorama of preliterary man, but a good deal of what we are accustomed to calling "ancient history." Our knowledge of Greece and Rome has come to us through an unbroken literary tradition. But the documents of Middle Eastern civilizations—Sumer, Assyria, Babylon, Egypt, the Hittites, and the Canaanites—have had to be dug up, deciphered, and made a part of the common storehouse of knowledge. Along with these documents have been palaces, temples, houses, tombs, and literally a thousand and one items of daily life. In the process the best-known document from ancient times, the Bible, has been put into context. As a historical writing it is no longer an isolated fossil, but a living account of people in interaction with their neighbors who are increasingly well known.

Archaeology has had a checkered history. It has been an adjunct to art history, a synonym for thievery under the guise of antique collecting, and an avocation for amateurs. It has been romanticized, doubted, and deified. Today it has earned its place as a scientific discipline, and like any such study has peculiar limitations and possibilities. It has become a prestigious historical tool. But its prestige can be maintained only if those who excavate and interpret continue to give proof of balance of mind and objectivity.

2. BIBLICAL ARCHAEOLOGY IN CONTEXT

Interest in the past is as old as man's ability to relate tales. When writing was developed it was natural to include in those early documents stories of the great deeds of gods and ancestors, of the founding of cities, peoples, and empires. This interest in antiquity has never wavered. Somehow man has suspected all along that he can neither understand his present nor plan his future unless he has a knowledge of the past.

It is not surprising, then, that archaeology, which has been called "history's latest and greatest source," [1] has in recent years become so vital to man's self-understanding. But the value of archaeology scarcely accounts for the vast and continuing public interest, even fascination, with this newest historical tool. The popular mind associates romance and sensationalism with the archaeologist and his work. Stories of men breaking into long-sealed tombs and standing in long-forgotten temples have occasionally reached newspaper and slick magazines. The image of the archaeologist as a daring adventurer braving the wilds for the sake of knowledge is an almost constant accompaniment to the usually misleading popular accounts of buried treasure and dazzling discovery. In particular those who have excavated in the Middle East have had this sort of image attached to them, because on occasion their discoveries have been genuinely sensational, and because almost all their work bears upon the story told in the Bible. It is, after all, not quite fifty years since two Englishmen, Howard Carter and Lord Carnarvon, revealed to an astonished world the discovery—intact! —of the tomb of Pharaoh Tutankhamen, who died about 1344 B.C. Hardly seven years after

[1] H.-P. Eydoux, *History of Archaeological Discoveries*, trans. J. White (London: Leisure Arts, n.d.), p. 7.

the opening of "King Tut's tomb" and the subsequent growth of the legend of "the mummy's curse," another Englishman, Sir Leonard Woolley, announced that at Ur near Baghdad he had found possible evidence of the flood reflected in the story of Noah and the Ark (Genesis 6:5–9:17). More recently, in the late 1940s, in the midst of a terrible if localized war, came the finding of a large number of old manuscripts in caves northwest of the Dead Sea. International intrigue, accusations of theft, and threats of various kinds surrounded the discovery of these writings and added to their interest. They are part of a library of a Jewish sect that lived at Qumran, now a ruined site, and for the most part they date from the three centuries before the birth of Jesus. These are the famous "Dead Sea Scrolls."

The nature of certain discoveries, only three of which have been mentioned, has focused attention on the ancient Middle East, the land of the Bible. It is not mere sensationalism, however, that has been responsible for interest in the relation of Bible and archaeology. There were certainly impressive finds prior to those which are more closely associated with the Bible. Heinrich Schliemann had identified the site of Homer's Troy in 1870, and the recovery of Pompeii, destroyed by an eruption of Mount Vesuvius in A.D. 79, had begun as early as 1594. Moreover, for years British and French conquerors had been populating the British Museum and the Louvre with antiquities of almost every sort. But Troy had nothing directly to do with the story told in Sacred Scripture, nor did Pompeii. Most of the collected items in museums were considered art objects, not clues to some of the less-clear pages of history.

The Historical Dimension of Biblical Archaeology

Biblical archaeology—the discovery and interpretation of the material remains of mankind which bear upon the history and understanding of biblical times—includes a good deal more than was thought at first. Where once we were used to thinking of biblical man confined mainly to tiny Palestine, our increasing knowledge places him in the larger context of the eastern Mediterranean basin. Indeed, the vastness of the vista of ancient Middle Eastern life is perhaps the major discovery of archaeology in the last century and a half. This recovery of ancient cultures of the eastern Mediterranean has, in the words of W. F. Albright, "doubled the span of human history as recorded in contemporary written documents; it has nearly trebled the duration of archaeologically recorded sedentary society." [2] The Old Testament, once thought by many to be mankind's oldest writing, is now seen to have numerous antecedents hundreds, perhaps thousands of years older. Hebrew itself, far from being the oldest language spoken by man, is now shown by recovered documents to be a more or less provincial development of widespread Semitic speech forms which had a long and distinguished history before the time of the patriarchs of Israel. And the Chosen of God —Abraham and those who came after him— were latecomers onto a complex and already hoary international scene. Centuries before that day sometime after 2000 B.C., when Abraham began his fateful and faithful journey from Ur, many generations had witnessed the rise and fall of brilliant cultures and mighty empires in that fertile Mesopotamian plain between the two northern rivers, the Tigris and the Euphrates ("Mesopotamia" means "between the rivers"). Likewise, far to the south across green hills and arid deserts Egypt, the creation of the Nile, had already witnessed perhaps a dozen dynasties. One of the earliest of these built the Great Pyramids of Gizeh, which today as then are

[2] W. F. Albright, *History, Archaeology, and Christian Humanism* (New York: McGraw-Hill, 1964), p. 123.

regarded as one of the wonders of the world. Between these two cradles of antique empire, Mesopotamia in the north and Egypt in the south, lay Palestine. Palestine, the "Holy Land," hallowed by patriarch, prophet, Apostle, and by Jesus himself, is a narrow land bridge bounded by surf and sand. Over this strip flowed the commerce and armies of the superpowers of that era long ago. First one and then the other came, conquered, plundered, ruled, exploited. Palestine was a political, economic, and military football. It was only when the powers of the north and the power of the south were weak that the inhabitants of the land in between enjoyed calm and relative strength. Such was the case at the time of David and Solomon.

Yet it was probably here in Palestine that man began to develop that urban culture which today has become characteristic of human society. Around 8000 B.C., deep in the Jordan Valley just north of the Dead Sea, at Jericho, Mesolithic (Middle Stone Age) hunters built a sanctuary near the spring of Ain-es-Sultan. As they returned to this holy site time and again, some of these hunters constructed more or less permanent dwellings by gradually transforming their light nomadic shelters into mud brick houses. During this slow cultural process which took about a thousand years, Jerichoan man became a food-producer rather than merely a food-gatherer. Only regular crops and the domestication of animals can support a settled population. For these developments perennial water and warmth were needed. Jericho combined both in admirable quantity.

By 7000 B.C. this now Neolithic (New Stone Age) farming community had grown to such size, complexity, and wealth that its inhabitants found it necessary to surround the town with massive fortifications. At least one very large stone tower with a stair through its center was a part of this perhaps first-ever town defense system. This remarkable tower, the bottom of which was some

seventy feet below the present surface level of the ground, was uncovered by Miss Kathleen Kenyon's excavations in 1955-1956. It is still in good condition, and steps cut to the bottom of the trench around it allow the energetic and daring visitor to climb up the inside staircase and stand on top of this astounding achievement of ancient engineering.

Some time before 5000 B.C. a second group of Neolithic farmers, perhaps invading from the north, captured Jericho. These people strengthened the walls and introduced a new style of house architecture. Like their predecessors they apparently did not know how to make pottery. But they were highly skilled in art. From this period at Jericho come the portraits molded in plaster over human skulls. No one is entirely sure of the function of these skulls. But the fact that they have been found associated with burials leads many to think that they are probably evidence of some form of ancestor worship.

As waves of nomadic groups poured into Palestine, not only the portrait skulls disappeared, but also the people who made them and the ancient town which housed them. Living in squalid huts at Jericho as they did elsewhere in Syria and Palestine, these new invaders introduced pottery to the area. Yet they made few if any other known contributions to culture. For almost 2000 years, down until about 3000 B.C., these people destroyed more than they built as they held sway over a large region. During this time Jericho became an important point of entry into Palestine from the arid deserts and fertile uplands of Transjordan. It was so in Jesus' day. The Gospels record that his last journey to Jerusalem was by way of Jericho (Matthew 20:29; Mark 10:46; Luke 19:1). Today one of the major bridges across the Jordan River is located near the same site.

In the Early Bronze Age, about 3000 B.C., Jericho regained some of its former stature. But it was no longer unique. Cities were to be found in many parts of Syria and Palestine as well as in other parts of the Middle East. Although destroyed and refortified several times, Jericho survived as a town of notable size well into the Middle Bronze Age (the time of the Hebrew patriarchs, *ca.* 1900 –1550 B.C.). The recovery by archaeologists of the Middle Bronze town site with its tombs and well-preserved house furnishings allows us to reconstruct what a Palestinian town may have looked like at the time of Abraham, Isaac, and Jacob.

Here our archaeologically substantiated knowledge of ancient Jericho ends. There are no remains at the site later than the Middle Bronze Age. Yet we know from the Bible that Jericho continued to play its dual historic role as a point of entry and as a town coveted by invaders. Joshua 4:19 tells us that Hebrews entering Palestine from the eastern desert "came up out of the Jordan on the tenth day of the first month, and they encamped in Gilgal on the east border of Jericho." Then they laid siege to Jericho. According to Joshua 6, after seven days of marching around the city with the Ark of the Covenant, "the people raised a great shout, and the wall fell down flat." Thus the first of the great Canaanite cities to be destroyed by the invading Hebrews was captured.

Not again until the New Testament period does the town emerge as a place of importance. But then as archaeology has shown us, the town site has been shifted westward away from the river (see pp. 231-3).

Here, then, is our oldest known town. Already ancient in Abraham's time, it had altogether disappeared from its original site by Jesus' day. Yet we would be wrong to think that Jericho is old by Palestinian standards. From Ubaidiya in the Jordan Valley and Khirbet Maskana near Tiberias come the earliest anthropoid remains yet discovered in the Middle East. Skull fragments and crude tools made from potato-shaped pebbles

Herbert G. May

Neolithic Jericho: the fortified tower (above); one of the plastered skulls (below).

Palestine Archaeological Museum

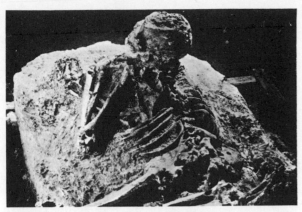

A skeleton from Mount Carmel, one of the first places man began to farm and to domesticate animals.

sharpened on one end are evidence of man in Palestine 300,000 to 600,000 years ago. The three to four inch flake-scarred stones used by these early hunters give the name to this Grand Pluvial "Pebble Culture."

The extent and dimension of this culture are as yet not known to us. But another early culture, unknown until forty years ago, has been brought to light by archaeology and has added much to our knowledge of the development of man from roving hunter to settled farmer. Beginning in April 1929, a joint British and American Expedition under the direction of Miss Dorothy Garrod began a twenty-one-and-a-half-month excavation of caves along the sides of Mount Carmel, that great ridge abruptly breaking the coastal plain of Palestine and jutting out into the Mediterranean. The reader of the Bible will readily identify this area as a part of the mountain on which Elijah hurled taunts and ridicule at the priests of Baal (I Kings 18:17-40).

The Anglo-American enterprise was one of the most lengthy continuous archaeological investigations ever undertaken. But the surprising results more than justified the investment of time, energy, and money. In three caves in the Wadi el-Mughara, Miss Garrod and her associates discovered the skeletal remains and flint instruments of some of the oldest known people of the earth.

Popularly known as *Mount Carmel Man,* these Neanderthal men and women of Palestine had made their homes in these caves as early as 50,000 years ago. Here on the sides of these hills the full range of Paleolithic (Old Stone Age) culture was found followed by the Mesolithic (Middle Stone Age, *ca.* 8000 B.C.) culture which shows some of the earliest known tendencies toward a proto-farming culture. Man was not yet a farmer as he was to become at Jericho and many other places in the Middle East a thousand years later. Nonetheless, at Wadi el-Mughara biologists, botanists, and others working side by side with archaeologists provided our earliest evidence of man ceasing to live solely by hunting animals and collecting wild plants. In his last days Mount Carmel Man stood on the brink of one of the two greatest revolutions in the history of mankind: the Neolithic Revolution. During the Neolithic period (New Stone Age, *ca.* 7000 B.C.–3400 B.C.) man became a farmer. He planted seed, tilled the land, and domesticated animals. This change from food-gatherer to food-producer laid the foundations of civilization. Families began to join together to raise larger crops and to protect against common enemies. Cities such as Jericho appeared, and the need to keep records and to communicate over distances became necessary. Writing, the second great revolution basic to civilization, was inevitable and was not long in coming. Again, so far as we now know, it came from the ancient Middle East.

All our knowledge about Mount Carmel Man and Jericho (except for the biblical narrative) and, indeed, about anything else in Palestine previous to the Hebrew patriarchs was unknown until relatively recently. Because of the ignorance which prevailed until such a short time ago, it was naturally common to speak of Palestinian archaeology as dealing only with the biblical period. We knew of nothing earlier. Now persistent and continuing work over the last one hundred and fifty years has shown that from the perspective of time the period from the patriarchs to the apostles is but one part of the long and continuing story of Palestine and the Middle East. Moreover, it is becoming increasingly clear, as we shall see in subsequent chapters, that the thought and customs of biblical man stand in direct debt to his predecessors and neighbors.

For some people this fact is viewed as a danger to the integrity of the message of the Bible and to personal faith. For them the utter uniqueness of the Bible is related to the validity of its message. Yet to insist that the Bible and its message arose in a vacuum unrelated to the past and to the surrounding cultures is to fail to see the immense richness of biblical thought and of the biblical world. Furthermore, it runs the serious risk of misunderstanding what the Bible has to say. The timeless message of the Eternal God is spoken to man in time, in continuing time. To be different, even unique, is not to be totally new and without debt.

One major contribution of biblical archaeology, then, is to show the antiquity of the historical context of the life and thought found in the Bible. By so doing archaeology not only indicates the continuity between biblical man and his ancestors and neighbors, but also illumines the uniqueness of his confession of faith.

The Geographical Extension of Biblical Archaeology

What archaeology and other studies have shown to be true of the Bible in terms of the continuing story of mankind is equally if not more importantly true of geography and the overlap of cultures. Biblical archaeology cannot be confined to one brief period of time in the developing story of the Middle East. Neither can it be confined to a small area such as Palestine. To define biblical archaeology as the discovery and interpretation of the material remains of mankind which bear upon the history and interpretation of

biblical times means that we must immediately cast a very wide geographical net. Historically biblical archaeology is a part of Palestinian archaeology. Geographically it is a part of a much larger Middle Eastern archaeology.

At the outset of the narrative concerning Abraham we are told that his home was Ur of the Chaldees and that with his family he journeyed to Canaan by way of Haran (Genesis 11:31). In 1854, J. E. Taylor, the British consul at Basra, investigated some ruined sites in southern Mesopotamia on behalf of the trustees of the British Museum. At al Muqayyar, eleven miles west of the Euphrates River and quite near the Persian Gulf, he found cuneiform inscriptions establishing without doubt that this site was the ancient city of Ur-Nammu, known somewhat anachronistically to Genesis as "Ur of the Chaldeans." This, according to Genesis 11:27-28, was Abraham's birthplace. Here, in the 1920's, Woolley's excavations confirmed Taylor's identification and also found evidence of widespread flooding. Many biblical scholars think that the accounts in Genesis 6 through 8 are based upon much earlier Sumerian stories of a great flood. If, as Woolley said, "there could be no doubt that the flood of which we had thus found the only possible evidence was the Flood of Sumerian history and legend," then, many insisted, there was also no doubt that the biblical story was based upon a real deluge.

Ur is on a direct east-west line with Hebron in southern Palestine, the place of Abraham's burial. Yet it is nonetheless separated from "The Promised Land" by over seven hundred miles of trackless desert. It was necessary, therefore, for Abraham to travel northwestward, up the Mesopotamian Valley, in order to come around this vast and almost impenetrable sea of sand. At length he came to Haran, over six hundred miles northwest of Ur. Here Abraham's father, Terah, died. After some time the son, his family, and flocks turned south (Genesis 12:4-5). Days, weeks, and months passed until at last they stood before Shechem, whose proud walls, still there today, had sometimes withstood and occasionally fallen to many an Egyptian battering ram. At this city, one thousand miles from Ur by the route he had to take, Abraham would have seen the great temples of Baal-berith, where several centuries later Joshua declared his loyalty to the God of his Fathers (Joshua 24:1-28).

Abraham, however, is not primarily associated in the Bible with Shechem nor with any other northern Palestinian cities or valleys. It is southern Palestine and particularly the area around Hebron which is identified with this first of the Fathers of Israel. For many centuries tradition has identified a cave at Hebron with the Cave of Machpelah which Abraham bought from Ephron (Gene-

The el-Khalil Mosque at Hebron, traditional site of the Cave of Machpelah where Abraham and Sarah were buried.

sis 23). In this cave he and Sarah and members of their family were buried. Eventually a mammoth building was erected on the site. It has been added to and adorned by Herod the Great (see pp. 237-8) and Suliman the Magnificent among others, for it is sacred both to Jew and Muslim. Today this extraordinary building is a mosque. The Arabs call it *el-Khalil,* "the friend of God." This is the name by which Abraham, spiritual father to Jews, Christians, and Muslims, is known.

But before settling at Mamre near Hebron, Abraham followed a path even farther south, into Egypt. Either because of or in spite of some shameful behavior toward his wife (Genesis 12:10-20), he left Egypt and returned once more to the land of Canaan. On his journeys to and from Egypt he sojourned, passing at length, in the Negeb. Professor Nelson Glueck's remarkable surveys of this semi-barren region, begun in 1932 and completed in 1959, have located numerous sites from the Abrahamic age and confirm the general validity of the background of some of the historical memories underlying Genesis 12 through 24.

If you follow Abraham's route on a map, you will see that he traversed the whole of what James Breasted has called "the fertile crescent." This is certainly an apt name for that thin verdant strip threatened eternally by the hostile sands that form its borders. If you look further at the map, you

Shechem, whose west walls (above) were known to Abraham, and whose monumental east gate (below) from the Patriarchal Era suffered numerous destructions and rebuilds well into the Late Bronze Age.

Bedouin tents on the Plain of Dothan, where Abraham and Lot, living much like the Bedouin of today, agreed to part.

will notice that Abraham traveled over twelve hundred miles through the oldest, most magnificent and most highly developed cultures of his day. There can now be little doubt that the mode of living and many of the customs and practices of this man were indistinguishable from those of his contemporaries and neighbors. The details of his purchase of the Cave of Machpelah, for example, are in keeping with a widespread practice of his day in which ownership of real property was feudal rather than personal (see p. 64). The transfer of ownership from Ephron to Abraham took place in accordance with Hittite, not Hebrew nor Canaanite, law. Why such practice should extend so far south of Hittite territory (modern central Turkey) is not entirely clear. Some have suggested that it was universal law in the ancient East. A clear-cut statement of this law is in the Boghazkoey texts found at the ancient Hittite capital of Hattusha. These fourteenth-century B.C. documents preserve standard customs of earlier generations. An even simpler explanation has been offered for the Hittite dealings of Abraham in the matter of the cave. It has been suggested that Ephron was a Hittite living in a Hittite community at Hebron. Abraham, wishing to do business in this community, found it necessary to abide by Hittite law.

Other recently found texts, particularly those from Nuzi in northern Iraq, throw light upon certain events in the stories of Abraham and other Hebrew patriarchs. According to the Nuzi texts (fifteenth century but embodying earlier tradition), a childless couple could adopt a son who would serve them until their deaths when he would inherit their wealth. This helps to explain Abraham's fear that his slave Eliezer would be his heir (Genesis 15:1-4). Again, at Nuzi a barren wife was to provide her husband with another woman for the purpose of producing an heir. If such a son was born to the slave wife, he was not to be cast out. Thanks to these texts one can better understand Sarah's gift of a concubine to Abraham (Genesis 16:1-4) and his reluctance to send Hagar and Ishmael into the wilderness (Genesis 21:10-14).

These are but a few of many illustrations. Others could be cited from Nuzi and Mari as well which indicate the similarity in laws and customs to those described in the patriarchal narratives. The Hebrews emerged out of the mass of ancient Middle Eastern peoples and cultures and for the most part worked, played, and thought like their ancestors and neighbors. When they came to dwell in the land of Palestine, reciprocal influences between them and their neighbors did not diminish. On the contrary, they increased sharply as the invaders spread out over Canaan and sought to secure a kingdom for themselves. The Hebrew struggle with Canaanite culture was, as we shall see, a significant factor in shaping Israelite life, and in the ninth and eighth centuries was a principal cause of the rise of prophecy among the Hebrews.

To see the extent of the interpenetration of cultures, one need only hear the prophets condemn the foreign beliefs and practices which those strange emissaries of God thought were destroying the nation and corrupting the pure worship of the true God. One need look no further than the geography of Palestine to understand that every influence easily continued to penetrate the area. From time immemorial trade routes criss-crossed the land. Up *The Way of the Sea* on the western coast and along *The King's Highway* in the eastern highlands, down the great valleys and through the land moved the slow trains of donkey-riding caravaneers. Everywhere they brought new goods, new skills, new people—and new ideas. Moreover, invading armies often laid waste the land and ravaged the population as they moved north and south to do battle. Yet soldiers, like traders, brought new ideas and practices with them. They often married and settled down to become a permanent part of the scene.

At least as important as the north-south trade routes was the mammoth northern valley, the Plain of Esdraelon, which slices from the Mediterranean southeast to the Jordan. This breadbasket not only fed the people's stomachs, but their minds as well. It was a highway linking Phoenicia, center of Canaanite culture, with Israel. From their northwestern neighbors the Hebrews adopted not only their language, architecture, and craft skills, but sometimes religious customs as well. The harmful effects of such influences upon Hebrew society and religion can be seen in the conflict between Jezebel, the wife of King Ahab of Israel and daughter of the priest-king of Sidon, and Elijah, who sought to defend the purity of Hebrew worship. The bitterness of this conflict eventually ended in a horrible bloodbath (I Kings 16:29–II Kings 10:28).

Just as examples of interplay between the Hebrews of the *Old* Testament and their neighbors could be multiplied, so the same pattern of cultural and intellectual exchange emerges on almost every page of the *New* Testament. The Roman presence in Palestine is well attested by the story of Jesus told in the Gospels. He was born "when Quirinius was governor of Syria" (Luke 2:2), tried by a Roman governor (Mark 15:1-2; Matthew 27:1-2; Luke 23:1-2; John 18:28-29;) and put to death in the Roman manner (Mark 15:22-26; Matthew 27:33-37; Luke 23:33-34; John 19:17b-27). At various times between his birth, dated by the rule of one Roman governor, and his death, carried out by another Roman governor, Jesus met and understood the ways and thoughts of the conquerors who held sway in the East for over half a millennium.

Before the Romans the Greeks had come to Palestine, and before the Greeks the Persians, and before them the Babylonians, and before them the Assyrians, and before them the Egyptians. But it was, at the time of Christianity at any rate, the Greeks who were the true conquerors. They had won the mind. The rule was Roman, but the language and the foreign ideas were Greek. The first Christian missionaries traveled on Roman-made roads and on seas kept safe by the naval might of the Caesars. Yet the Scriptures these men carried were a Greek translation of the Hebrew Bible; many of their names were Greek, and they spoke the common (*koine*) Greek of the streets which was the only language universally understood. They even called their Master by a Greek title, *Christos*. This is the equivalent of the Hebrew, *Messiah*, meaning "Anointed One." Furthermore, when these first witnesses to God's action in Christ began to write about their experiences and their faith, they wrote in the language they knew best and which could be most readily understood by others. The New Testament was written in Greek.

We have noted that Genesis witnesses to the extensive wanderings of Abraham who traversing the Fertile Crescent moved through ancient splendor and magnificent empire. Living almost all his life as a foreigner among foreigners, he was for the most part indistinguishable from them. In the end he was buried in a cave which he had secured by the usual and probably universal practice of his day. The book of Revelation, on the other hand, focuses upon a lonely old man on a small island in what seemed a vast sea. John, faithful to his heavenly vision, wrote to the mainland churches, so near yet never to be seen again. The accounts in Genesis and Revelation seem to present very different pictures. Yet the essential point about the scope of the biblical world can be seen in the situations of Abraham and John. Neither can be left out of a complete account of the story told in the Bible. Both have associations with lands far from Palestine and both hear and obey a divine call. They are representatives of the ancient and widespread interplay of ideas and customs which weave so rich a fabric upon the pages of the Bible.

3. PALESTINIAN BIBLICAL ARCHAEOLOGY

The period of history covered by the biblical narrative is roughly two thousand years. Scholars usually date the time of Abraham's obedience and journey between 2000 B.C. and 1750 B.C. There are some who say Abraham was earlier than this; there are a few who suggest that he came later. At the other end of the scale is II Peter, probably the latest book of the Bible. This letter shows the young Christian church struggling for its life in the cosmopolitan turbulence of the middle Roman Empire. The time of this writing is generally regarded as mid or late second century A.D., although again some would date it earlier and a few later.

The locale of this extensive biblical narrative is a very wide-ranging one. If we note the Old Testament references to Tarshish in Spain (I Kings 10:22; Jeremiah 10:9; Psalm 72:10; Jonah 1:3; 4:2; and others) and take seriously Paul's desire to preach the Good News in Spain (Romans 15:24, 28), the stage for the divine drama extends from the Persian Gulf in the east (on whose shores Abraham grew up) to the Iberian

Peninsula in the west.[1] In the north it included modern Turkey, Iraq, and southern Russia. To the south it reached present-day Ethiopia and even Somaliland on Africa's east coast (with which Solomon carried on trade and from which came the monkeys that were favored household pets of the rich in Israel; see I Kings 10:22). Almost at the heart of this area—"center-stage," if you wish—is Palestine.

It is here that our focus centers.

We ought to understand, however, that Palestine never really was very much to look at. Seen from the larger perspective, neither the natural landscape nor the adornments of man would attract much attention in and of themselves. Yet it is a land of many contrasts with some magnificent sights. As Moses stood on Mount Nebo (Deuteronomy 34:1-4) and looked out over the Jordan Valley, the lowest spot on earth, he must have seen the calm blue of the Dead Sea to his left, the deep green jungle surrounding the winding Jordan to his right and, beyond both, the golden Judean Hills of the Promised Land. But the gold of these hills is the heat of the sun. Dry, breathlessly hot, and devoid of vegetation for most of the year, these hills are typical of much of the land on both sides of the river. It is not without cause that the Gospels refer to this site of Jesus' temptation as a "wilderness" (Matthew 4:1; Mark 1:12; Luke 4:2). From time immemorial man has had to enter into a life-and-death struggle with this inhospitable country.

It may thus seem strange that the Bible repeatedly (twenty times) refers to Palestine as a "land of milk and honey," giving the impression that it is a bountiful country. The phrase "milk and honey" refers to the products of herds and flocks and to the cultivation of fruit trees and vines, particularly dates and grapes. This description seems originally to have been applied to the area

[1] Esther 1:1 mentions India.

around Hebron by Caleb and the other spies sent out by Moses to explore the south of Canaan (Numbers 13:17-33). Through the centuries Hebron has been known for the fertility of its soil. In late summer, for example, large grapes grow in enormous bunches, and pomegranates and figs are in abundance. It is little wonder that to people fresh from desert wanderings these sights should be reported as a "land flowing with milk and honey." Gradually, this description came to be applied to the entire land, a land which for the most part is rocky, thirsty, and very difficult to farm.

Lack of water is the major problem. Vegetation is dependent upon the morning dew and the winter rains. So heavy is the dew that early in the morning rivulets of water often stream from slanting roofs and the ground is quite wet. By eight or nine o'clock all is dry and puffs of dust accompany each footstep. In powerful and unmistakable imagery Hosea speaks of Israel's love for God as "dew that goes early away" (Hosea 6:4).

The rains of winter, which in high elevations such as Jerusalem can occasionally produce almost as much annual fall as London, unfortunately all tend to come within a few weeks. They run off the hard, dry ground. Water erosion is a common feature of the landscape. Wadis, normally dusty creek beds, can in winter become raging torrents. Flash floods are a constant threat. Only a few years ago a number of French archaeologists and students were drowned in the Siq, the narrow mile-long wadi that forms the entrance to Petra. At many of the excavated sites in Palestine large cisterns and elaborate water systems have been uncovered. Foremost among these are Megiddo, Gezer, Hazor, and Jerusalem where the inhabitants sank deep shafts and then dug long horizontal tunnels to connect with springs outside the city walls. Most of these are Canaanite and from the Late Bronze period. In 1969

a large Early Bronze system was discovered at et-Tell, perhaps biblical Ai. Many other cities, Samaria for example, had their inadequate water supply augmented by cisterns which stored rain water. Not until Roman times did the aqueduct come into use in Palestine.

For the land which you are entering to take possession of it is not like the land of Egypt, from which you have come, where you sowed your seed and watered it with your feet, like a garden of vegetables; but the land which you are going over to possess is a land of hills and valleys, which drinks water by the rain from heaven, a land which the Lord your God cares for; the eyes of the Lord your God are always upon it, from the beginning of the year to the end of the year. Deuteronomy 11:10-12

These words, a part of the blessings and curses which follow the giving of the Ten Commandments, serve to warn the people of two things. First, it is made clear that the land is dependent upon God who "will give the rain for your land in its season, the early rain and the later rain, that you may gather in your grain and your wine and your oil. And he will give grass in your fields for your cattle, and you shall eat and be full" (Deuteronomy 11:14-15). Throughout their history the Hebrews understood that it was God who was the giver of the waters of heaven. Against this background Elijah, as a man of God, was able to threaten Ahab: "As the Lord the God of Israel lives, before whom I stand, there shall be neither dew nor rain these years, except by my word" (I Kings 17:1). This was a threat of famine and starvation. It was to remove from the land both the milk and the honey.

Second, the people are warned that the land into which they are coming is vastly different from Egypt which they have known. In contrast to broad plains annually flooded by the Nile and covered with the natural fertilizer of silt, the people are to expect seemingly endless hills and valleys where flourish and famine are a predictable but irregular cycle. It was a hard land into which the people were coming, hard and uninviting. Yet by the presence and goodness of God it was a land in which a faithful people could prosper.

Many of them did prosper. Through conquest and amalgamation the Hebrews slowly became dominant. Cities, the work of unknown architects and masons of the Bronze Age, fell to the Hebrews. Often, on these carefully chosen sites, new cities arose. As greater wealth came to the kingdom, monuments to the greatness of Israel arose. Jerusalem, an ancient Jebusite fortress captured by David, became "Jerusalem the Golden" as Solomon caused the magnificent Temple and his equally splendid Palace to adorn the crest of Mount Moriah. At Hazor, Megiddo, Lachish, and other places imposing cities were rebuilt. After the division of the kingdom (*ca.* 922 B.C.) Omri founded at Samaria the only major city entirely of Hebrew origin. Like Solomon before him he employed the skill of Phoenician craftsmen whose ivory work at Samaria was much admired and much vilified (Amos 3:15; 6:4). The land has known its great builders. Not the least of these was Herod, justly deserving his title "the Great" (see p. 230). He populated the countryside with vast projects the ruins of which still convey some of their former splendor. The journey south from Jerusalem toward Bethlehem, the birthplace of Jesus, and Tekoa, the home of Amos, is dominated by the Herodion, the mountaintop fortress Herod intended as his tomb. Today looking north and east from here, Jerusalem and Bethlehem can be seen in one view. Commanding all, even from this distance, is the sparkling golden crown of the Dome of the Rock. This mosque, built in the seventh Christian century, is one of the most superb creations of the mind and hand of man. It is not difficult to imagine ancient Jerusalem,

infinitely smaller than today's somewhat small city, even more dominated by the Temple and Palace of Solomon. With its carefully hewn stone covered with cedar and olive wood and its enormous but intricate carvings overlaid with gold, the Temple must indeed have appeared to the people of Israel as a house fit for their God (I Kings 6). It took seven years to build. Solomon's Palace took thirteen (I Kings 7:1). The comparison is instructive. A series of interconnected soaring porches was decorated with carvings and bronze-cast statues by the finest foreign and domestic craftsmen of the day. This forest of columns served as home to the splendid king; it soon became famous. Partly to see this building the Queen of Sheba undertook her perilous journey to Jerusalem (I Kings 10:1-13).

Yet for all the riches attributed to Solomon and for all the work of others, there never was much in Palestine to challenge, much less to equal, the glory of the pharaohs or the splendor of the Mesopotamian kings. Except for its days under Herod Jerusalem was a provincial town, hardly a rival for a Thebes or a Babylon. Yet it is neither splendor nor cosmopolitan urbanity which long captures the attention of men. In his poem, "Ozymandias," Shelley tells of coming across two vast and trunkless legs of stone standing in the desert:

> And on the pedestal these words appear:
> "My name is Ozymandias, king of kings:
> Look on my works, ye Mighty, and despair!"
> Nothing beside remains. Round the decay
> Of that colossal wreck, boundless and bare
> The lone and level sands stretch far away.

Our focus is upon the land of Palestine, undistinguished by nature and relatively unadorned by man. But it was here, in this tiny corner of the earth, where that series of events took place which have had a greater influence upon men's lives than any other. Here the divine drama unfolded. Here God called out his people, commanded them to be "a light to the nations," and in the fullness of time revealed himself in Jesus Christ, born in Bethlehem, reared in Nazareth, crucified in Jerusalem. The stage for this drama changed, shifted, enlarged. Eventually it encompassed the whole world. But at first the names associated with it were primarily Palestinian ones. Hazor, Hebron, Shiloh, Shechem, Bethlehem, Bethany, and Beersheba; these and almost all the others so familiar to readers of the Bible are located in that approximately two-hundred-mile by forty-five-mile strip known as "The Holy Land." Here Joshua commanded, David ruled, Amos preached; and here men walked on the road to Emmaus with the Risen Christ.

It is thus hardly surprising that so much archaeological effort has centered in so small a place. It is also to be expected that interest would concentrate primarily upon those two thousand years from Abraham to the Early Christian Church. Palestinian biblical archaeology deals with this area and with this historical period. It is a highly concentrated undertaking with a specific purpose. We want to know all we can about the life and times of biblical man. Who were these participants in the divine drama? How did they think, work, and live? What were the influences upon them? Surely the more we know about the land, the cities, the culture, and the people of that time and place, the closer we shall be able to draw to the events and lives described in the Bible.

In the larger perspective archaeological efforts of recent decades have removed the Bible from its cultural and historical isolation and have placed its events, peoples, and thought in the living context of ancient Middle Eastern life. More specifically these efforts have illumined many passages of scripture. Until 1912, for example, it was thought that Amos' references to the rich living in houses of ivory (Amos 3:15; 6:4)

while the poor were abused was a heightened form of exaggerated speech common to the Middle East. Then in the royal area at Samaria, archaeologists found evidence of houses richly decorated with ivory. Amos was describing an actual situation which would have been well known to his hearers. His words had real bite in their contemporary setting, a setting now recovered for us by the spade and trowel. This discovery is a matter of some importance. It is one more piece of evidence in an ever-enlarging picture showing just how concrete and to the mark was the prophetic message.

Or take an example from the New Testament. That four of the seven place-names known only to John among the Four Gospels[2] have been identified by archaeologists is likewise of considerable value. At a time when few of these places had been positively identified, many scholars were suggesting that John was unfamiliar with southern Palestine, the location of much of his narrative. Perhaps he had "created" geographical settings for his stories. It was also possible, some said, that his unfamiliarity with the land was matched by his lack of knowledge of its customs and practices. The outcome of such thinking is obvious. Where John was not in complete agreement with the first three Gospels, or where he related stories not found in Matthew, Mark, or Luke, his narrative was regarded with the utmost suspicion. John was said to be a "theological Gospel" while the others were looked to for the outlines of the historical life of Jesus. A number of things have contributed to the correcting of this idea. Not the least among these is the identification in the last forty years of all the so-called Johannine sites. No longer can it be said that John was unfamiliar with southern Palestine. On the contrary,

[2] These are Aenon near Salim (3:23), Sychar (4:5), Bethesda (5:2), and Gabbatha (19:13). The other three (Bethany beyond Jordan, Solomon's Porch, and Ephraim) were known, if somewhat debated.

it is now clear that his Gospel betrays intimate knowledge of this countryside. Today, because of such details, much more attention must be paid to the historical narrative of the Fourth Gospel than was necessary or even possible only fifty years ago. These two brief examples, one from the Old Testament and one from the New, illustrate the importance of archaeology for the understanding and interpretation of the biblical text.

All this serves to underline the obvious fact that considerable knowledge of Palestine during the biblical period is of first importance to anyone seriously interested in studying the Bible. The Bible itself is, of course, one of the primary sources of such knowledge. This is a fact surprisingly overlooked by many. At the same time it must be remembered that the Bible is not first of all a history book. There are large gaps in its historical narrative. This is not due to any flaw on the part of the writers of the Bible. Rather it is because their concern was not only chronology or cultural history. Even if they had wanted to they could not tell us everything we want to know. Apart from the sheer impossibility of completely chronicling any given period, they did not see their primary task as one of helping later generations recapture the spirit of their times. This is our task. As contemporary as the biblical message may remain for all generations, we are sure to misunderstand Isaiah, for example, if we interpret him merely or mainly in twentieth-century terms. We must undertake the difficult task of seeing what he said to his contemporaries in their own times if we are properly to understand what he can say to us in our situation.

This is where archaeology is playing such an important role. It is slowly, bit by bit, telling us more about many of the things reported in the biblical narrative. Furthermore, it is actually writing history previously only guessed at if not completely unknown. The vitality of ancient times is beginning to unfold for us. It is becoming more and more difficult to view the participants in the divine drama as wooden characters, as actors in a sort of original passion play. Increasingly they are being seen against the background of their own times. The fabric of their history is recognizable to us—not merely in a narrower scholarly sense, but in the recognition that in spite of the vast differences between their society and ours the warp and woof of life has scarcely changed. As the previously unreal character of these men and women gives way to an appreciation of them as people not unlike ourselves, their struggle between faith and unfaith and the spiritual power which many of them found becomes our struggle and our possibility.

With this in view we are now prepared to return to an earlier observation. *Biblical archaeology* includes much more than *Palestinian biblical archaeology*. The latter is defined by area and by time. The former is defined in terms of influences upon biblical man and his thinking. Clearly the two go hand in hand and cannot be separated. Yet it is important to keep the distinction in mind. The central drama of the sacred story, both in Old Testament and New, is concentrated in a small area. Yet the Bible grows out of the totality of ancient Middle Eastern life. Mesopotamia, the home of Hebrew origins, and Egypt, the house of bondage, form a larger part of this wider setting. At the same time pre-Israelite Canaan, the land into which the Hebrews came, can hardly be overlooked if the greater part of the biblical narrative is to come alive for us. These three areas, Mesopotamia, Egypt, and Canaan, provided the major influences upon the beliefs and practices of biblical man. That this is so may perhaps be seen in an illustration from American history. When is the beginning of the American story and what are the influences that have combined to make America what it is? Is it 1776 and the Declaration of Independence, or should we look to 1781 and the victory over the British at Yorktown as the beginning? Perhaps the correct date is 1789 and the adoption of the Constitution. Possibly one needs to move in the opposite direction and speak of the first permanent English settlement: the Jamestown Colony of 1607. But the adventurous men of that settlement surely had English backgrounds with English ideas, laws, and forms of religion. And was not this law Roman and this religion Middle Eastern in origin? Moreover, in the centuries since the small band under John Smith moved slowly up the river they called "James" in honor of their king, countless men, traditions, and ideas have come to the North American shores. The "Melting Pot of Nations" owes something to almost every culture in every corner of the globe. On a smaller scale so also did the culture and people of biblical Palestine, an ancient melting pot standing at the crossroads of the great civilizations of its day.

The epic of man is a continuously flowing stream. Within it new directions and new departures can be seen. Sometimes these seem so utterly new and significant that they are said to be unique. Yet uniqueness itself is a part of the continuous stream. When the Hebrews spoke of their novel belief in the creator God they did so by retelling stories familiar to them from Mesopotamia. These stories were adapted and their meaning often changed. These people used old and well-known thought forms to express their new faith. The same thing is to be found in the language of the Early Church. A completely new thing had happened in their midst, they said. God had become man. Still when they began to talk further about this unique and enormously significant event, they found themselves talking about "Messiah," "prophet," "priest," and "king." These were all time-honored Hebrew ways of thinking. Later, as the new faith spread down Roman highways and into Greek

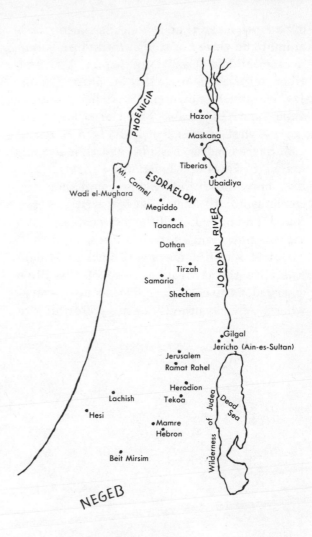

minds, the missionaries again found themselves using old categories of thought. Soon they were adopting even the philosophical arguments of the academies to meet their growing need for ways of thinking and of expressing themselves.

This process was not only true of the more verbal and mental expressions of faith, but also had to do with the customs of worship. The midwinter festival had a long career as a pagan celebration before the Christians took it over, adapted it, and made it into *Christmas*, the Feast of the Nativity of Christ. Similarly, Passover is far older than its Hebrew form. Other acts of worship and religious practices followed this same path

1838

41

of adoption and adaption. Sacrifice, both animal and cereal, was ancient and universal in the Middle East long before the first Hebrew priest approached an altar. Prophecy was well known much earlier than its appearance in Israel. The Christians were not the first to speak of a dying and rising god. Sacred places, seasons, and time are not unique to Jews or Christians. Prayers, fasting, holy men, and divine commands are common to all men. Sacred writings are found among many differing peoples from various times and scattered places.

Out of a rich panorama of ancient Middle East life the central message of the Bible emerged as a beacon calling to men everywhere. God, says the Bible, has suffering love toward all men. As the lives and faith of millions down the years testify, this message can be understood and appropriated without any detailed knowledge of the Ancient East. At the same time, for the person who wishes to know how this message came to be, what was the context of its development, and the more precise meaning of those who proclaimed it, a close acquaintance with the life and times of ancient Palestine and its neighbors is not a luxury, but a necessity. And here also, as the lives and faith of many will testify, such an effort has its rewards in terms of deepening faith and expanding horizons. In this quest for a better understanding of the Bible and its message archaeology has become an invaluable tool.

II: CANAAN IN ITS OWN RIGHT

4. CANAANITE LIFE RECOVERED

Canaan, according to the general use of the term in the Old Testament (e.g., Genesis 12:5; 50:13; Numbers 13:2, 17; 33:51), refers to all the country west of the Jordan River including Phoenicia. The people who live on this land are called Canaanites (Genesis 34:30; Numbers 21:3; Deuteronomy 11:30; Joshua 7:9). In this usage the Hebrews were apparently following the borders of the Egyptian province of Canaan. At other places, however, Canaan seems to designate a smaller area consisting mainly of the coastal plain and parts of the Jordan Valley, for the Canaanites are said not to be in the hill country which is inhabited by Amorites (Numbers 13:29; 14:25; Joshua 11:3). In an even more limited sense Canaan is later taken to be only Phoenicia on the south Syrian coast (e.g., Isaiah 23:1-12).[1]

All three uses of the term are correct. A rapid look at the history of Canaan will show us why this is so. One of the major dis-

coveries of archaeological activity in Palestine, Syria, and Egypt is an awareness of various migrations of people which swept over the area in ancient times. Generally these did not affect Egypt so much as the others since the intruders came from the northern steppes and eastern deserts. Among these migrators were a people known to us as Canaanites. They seem to have come from the north although there is a tradition which is gaining some acceptance among scholars that they came from the region of the Persian Gulf. Prior to 3200 B.C. they settled along the eastern Mediterranean coast. Essentially agriculturalists as over against shepherds, they sought out arable land rather than grazing areas. Sedentary instead of nomadic, they gathered into cities surrounded by farms. For the most part this caused them to avoid the hill country and to find their way into the more easily tilled valleys and plains. Eventually, however, their language, religion, and culture spread all over southern Syria and Palestine. For this reason the area came to be known as "Canaan," and it is this region which is usually meant today when the term is used.

Beginning late in the thirteenth century,

[1] Once, in Genesis 50:10-11, the term refers to a portion of Transjordan. This use seems curiously contradicted by the statements in the following verses.

B.C. and continuing through the twelfth century, the territory of the Canaanites was greatly reduced. Hebrews broke into Palestine from the east and spread rapidly into the hills and gradually onto the plains. The Sea Peoples, known in southwestern Palestine as "Philistines," occupied most of the coast of Palestine and possibly even some areas north of Phoenicia. Arameans, sweeping over eastern and northern Syria, effectively isolated the Canaanites in the great sea ports of southern Syria such as Tyre, Sidon, Byblos, and Ugarit. Excavations have shown that these cities, some built upon islands and others upon peninsulas and around bays, were fortified against the land and not against the sea. In these merchant-sailor cities Canaanite culture reached its zenith. Elsewhere this widespread culture tended to be mixed with other elements. But here along the south Syrian coast the most unalloyed form of Canaanite life existed. At about the same time these ports were flourishing, the Hebrew monarchies rose to the pinnacle of their power.

Thus the Canaanites lived in Palestine for over two thousand years before the coming of the Hebrews. Their influence upon the lives of the people of the land was very great indeed and did not disappear with the influx of new groups. Canaanite culture has come to be regarded as the indigenous culture of Palestine. The purpose of this chapter is to come to an appreciation of this culture which confronted the Hebrews when they entered Palestine in the thirteenth century B.C. Furthermore, we will see how the Hebrews sought to deal with it and what effect this may have had upon Israelite religion.

None of this would be possible without the results of the archaeological activity of the past thirty or forty years. Only during these relatively few years have we recovered enough material to know something of what it was like to live as an ancient Canaanite. Until the nineteenth century A.D. almost nothing was known about this sort of thing. By the early 1840s investigation of surface ruins had begun to bear fruit. Many sites mentioned in the Bible had been tentatively identified. It has also become clear that some traditional locations of biblical places were incorrect. While many sites were being more correctly established, there was little recovery of the culture of Canaan and still less awareness of the antiquity and pervasiveness of Canaanite life. Biblical sites and not life in ancient Palestine seemed to be the primary interest. There were excavations at Taanach, Jericho, Shechem, Gezer, and Megiddo in the 1890s and shortly after the turn of the century. In 1907 Father L. H. Vincent of the *École Biblique* in Jerusalem published a remarkable survey of ancient sites. Yet only after the First World War did the real dimensions of Canaanite culture begin to come to light. In 1920 the British established the Palestine Department of Antiquities and reversed the old Turkish policy which had made it so very difficult to excavate in the country. With generous British encouragement digs flourished. The American School of Oriental Research, although founded in 1900, had until the postwar period restricted its activity to minor excavations. Now it began a series of co-operative digs that placed it in the forefront of Palestinian archaeology, a position in which it has rendered distinguished international service ever since. At Shechem, Lachish, Beth-shan, Megiddo, Jericho, Bethel, Ai, Tell Beit Mirsim (possibly biblical Debir or Kirjath-Sepher), and other places evidence of a highly developed civilization began to appear. After the Second World War work was resumed at some of these and at other sites, such as Hazor, Tell el-Farah (possibly biblical Tirzah), Taanach, Beth-Yerah, Dothan, Tell Deir-'Alla, and Nahariyha. These and other excavations produced ample materials from which a picture of the sophisticated culture of Bronze Age

(Canaanite) Palestine could be constructed.

In addition to these Palestinian excavations, archaeological efforts in Egypt and Syria added written documents to the growing evidence. From Egypt came the *Execration Texts,* so called because they sought to cast out the pharaoh's enemies by means of magical powers. These show us something of nineteenth- and eighteenth-century B.C. Canaanites under Egyptian domination. They name localities such as Askalon, Jerusalem, Akko, and Jaffa. They also mention the chieftains of these places. These leaders have various theophoric names (names compounded with the names and titles of gods). From these comes the oldest written evidence of a Canaanite pantheon. The Execration Texts also reveal something of the political and social organization of nineteenth-century B.C. Palestine. Localities have more than one chieftain, a fairly certain indication of tribal structure. Some scholars think that the situation described in these texts is reflected in Genesis 26 where Abraham and Isaac are potential rivals of Abimelech, the chieftain of Gerar.

In the 1930s at Tell Hariri (ancient Mari) in northern Mesopotamia, André Parrot, a French scholar, discovered a palace containing over twenty thousand cuneiform tablets. From these eighteenth- and seventeenth-century B.C. *Mari Letters* we have learned, among other things, that Canaanite Palestine and Syria were in the cultural orbit of Mesopotamia. The laws and religious epics of the northerners were finding their way into the south. This may help to explain the close similarity between the laws of Leviticus, for example, and those of the Code of Hammurabi. It may also indicate why many of the early stories in Genesis have Mesopotamian parallels.

In addition these letters show a continuing influx of peoples into Palestine. Among these peoples were most probably the Hebrew patriarchs, although it is not possible to establish this with certainty.

Again our attention turns southward where the *Amarna Letters,* discovered in Egypt in 1888, show us the unsettled conditions in Palestine during the fifteenth century B.C. In a time of lessening Egyptian authority over the area, the Canaanite princes fell once more to fighting one another as well as trying to hold off the various raiding and invading groups which plagued Palestine continually throughout its ancient history.

By far the most important of all the written documents which throw light upon Canaanite life are the *Ras Shamra Texts.* More will be said of these finds later (see pp. 73-79). Excavators at Ras Shamra, ancient Ugarit, found a vast library of fourteenth-century B.C. Canaanite writings. In perhaps as many as eight languages these clay tablets contain a wide spectrum of the literature of the people who dwelled in Canaan just prior to the incursion of the Hebrews. Many of these writings had to do with religion, and from these contemporary documents we have gained extensive knowledge of the religious beliefs and practices of the Canaanites.

There are other writings which tell us of the Canaanites. But many of these, such as the annals of Tyre (as reported by the first-century A.D. Jewish historian Josephus) and the *History* of Philo of Byblos, are late and of relatively minor importance. The Bible, however, continues to be a major source of our knowledge of Canaanite life. It would be foolish to discount this vast and largely contemporary source of information. Yet we must read the biblical accounts of the Canaanites for what they are: polemical treatments which view the religion and life of Canaan as abominations before the Lord. Prophets, priests, and poets in Israel looked upon the Canaanites with indignation and stigmatized the culture of the Promised

Land. With its pantheon of fertility gods and goddesses, Canaanite religion appeared to the moralistic Hebrews emerging from the desert as an evil which was to be opposed and destroyed. Whatever the truth of the Hebrew picture of the Canaanites, and whatever the superiority of the Hebrew morality and religious insights, we would certainly be wrong and would run the further danger of misreading the Old Testament, if we did not attempt to see Canaan in its own right. This we can now do thanks to archaeology.

The Early Bronze Age

The work of the last generation of archaeologists has established that Canaanite culture in Palestine was predominant from *ca.* 3200 B.C., the beginning of the Bronze Age, until *ca.* 1100 B.C., after the beginning of the Iron Age. This Canaanite period, longer than the period from the birth of Christ until today, is known as the Bronze Age. It is so called beçause this was the time when man first began to use metal implements in addition to his stone ones. The metal which was used was copper and bronze. Of the first part of the Bronze Age (the Early Bronze Age, *ca.* 3200 B.C.-2300 B.C.) we know a good deal less than we would like to know. Archaeologists are just now beginning to uncover sufficient material remains to gain confident knowledge of what life was like in the hills and valleys of the Holy Land in those days. It is not yet possible to write a history of Palestine for this period. We do not, for example, have enough information to say in detail what the political organization was like. Nor can we be sure of Canaan's relations with Egypt and Mesopotamia. Also lacking is geographically broad-based evidence for the social and religious life of the people. Nonetheless, even with the incomplete state of our knowledge and the many problems associated with this period of Palestinian life, history written from the earth has made some conclusions possible. And every new excavation containing Bronze Age remains has tended to confirm and expand these.

First, "Bronze Age" is merely a term of convenience used to describe a significant change in the living patterns of man. The distinction between this period and the preceding one is not always easily drawn. Nor does it occur in every place at precisely the same time. Even the distinction of metal over against stone is not entirely accurate since man was beginning to manufacture metal implements in the late Stone Age. From the latest stage of development at Teleilat Ghassul, for example, have come at least two metal axes, the blade of a third, and several other fragments of metal tools. Ghassul, comprising three low hills close to one another on the plain just northeast of the Dead Sea, was a major center of Late Stone Age culture in Palestine. Analysis has shown that the metal used there contained seven percent tin. This perhaps indicates that in the fourth millennium B.C. there was already the attempt to harden copper into bronze.

Still, it is true that increasingly during the Bronze Age man began consciously and consistently to use hardened metals in addition to stone to plow his fields, to fight his battles, and even for his own personal hygiene and beautification. Yet in Palestine at any rate, the distinguishing characteristic of the Early Bronze Age was the appearance of a new culture marked by several new crafts. The red-and-grey burnished pottery of the northern Stone Age Palestinian villages suddenly began to mingle with a more beautiful, sensitively delicate type of pottery made possible by an advanced craftsmanship and a new way of firing clay. A new style of architecture appeared. Brick, not stone, houses were built close together and were surrounded by massive defensive walls. The use of brick, even in the hill country where an abundance of stone was readily available, suggests that newcomers brought with them a settled tradition of construction. This fact taken together with the unity of pottery style with southern Syria and the apparent slow penetration of this pottery into southern Palestine indicates that this culture came from the north. But one should not look too far north. Excavated sites in northern Syria and in Mesopotamia have not produced close parallels to the pottery and the architecture which suddenly make their appearance in Palestine near the end of the fourth millennium before Christ.

Second, this culture was not an outgrowth of the Ghassulian culture of the Dead Sea and Beer-sheba regions. Nor did it develop from the red-and-grey burnished pottery culture farther north. It was due to the influx of a new people. The Ghassulian culture disappeared apparently without influence upon succeeding generations. The red-and-grey burnished pottery people seem to have existed peacefully alongside the newcomers until they were absorbed into the superior culture which had entered their land.

The name we have given to these newcomers to Palestine is *Canaanites*. They are the founders of this Bronze Age culture.

Like other groups which were to come after them they were Semites. That is, their language was basically triconsonantal in form. The term Semite is originally a language designation. But words tend to be plastic, picking up new meanings and losing older ones. Semite, in its stricter meaning having to do with neither race nor religon, has come to have reference to both. Thus Semite legitimately has ethnic and religious connotations today as well as its more precise use in historical linguistics.

Unlike the other groups which were to follow them, these early peoples who founded the Bronze Age brought with them a developed culture, a high order of craftsmanship, and a knowledge of an agriculturally based urban society. Probably their most unique feature was the large fortified city. The visitor to Late Stone Age Palestine could have traveled from village to village and in the process would have encountered an essentially tribal society. In general the settlements were small, sometimes occupied by no more than one large family. In spite of the fact that many of the men were farmers, they maintained a relatively high degree of mobility. As one result their houses were often little more than huts or pit dwellings.

Contrast this with the sight which greeted the traveler in Early Bronze Age Palestine. As he made his way across the plains and down the valleys he would frequently see towering walls crowning the brow of a hill. Behind the massive walls generally tiny houses huddled together along small paved streets echoing to busy commercial traffic. At Hazor, Megiddo, Taanach, and Dothan in the north; at Ai, Jericho, and Ophel (Jerusalem), in the midlands; and at Lachish, Mirsim, Hesi, and possibly Hebron in the south, he would find such urban centers. Each would have its own dominion of agricultural lands surrounding it and providing for it.

These cities were for the most part built of brick. The huge walls were occasionally reinforced by a framework of tie beams such as have been found in the Early Bronze Age walls of Jericho. The recent excavator of Jericho, Miss Kathleen Kenyon, speculates that the timbers reinforcing this seventeen-feet thick wall were not so much for defense against human enemies as they were an anti-earthquake measure. The Jordan rift is an earthquake fault not unlike that known on the west coast of the continental United States and Alaska. Serious quakes occur in Palestine about four times a century, and archaeologists have found abundant evidence of damage due to earth slippage. Quite close to Jericho, at Qumran, the steps leading down into the largest of the baptismal pools are split down the middle with one part fourteen inches lower than the other. It is easily possible that some of the seventeen rebuilds of the Early Bronze walls at Jericho were made necessary by earthquakes. The timbers may indeed have been to localize the damage along the walls.

As a defensive measure the timbers would hardly have been successful. Fire was a major weapon of attack. Again at Jericho, against the outer face of the southern wall, an ash layer three feet thick was found. This seems to have been the result of an enemy's deliberate firing of an enormous pile of brushwood. So hot was the fire that it burned the brick red throughout the entire seventeen-feet thickness. This process was no doubt aided by the internal network of timbers. While such a fire would have strengthened the wall by hardening it, the result for the houses built against the interior of the wall would have been nothing short of disastrous. A great conflagration could thus be set inside the city where the houses of the period contained much timber and probably had reed-covered roofs. Fire, once kindled, easily and quickly leapt from house to house.

As they became more expert in working the native Palestinian stone, so easily availble everywhere except in the Jordan Valley, the Canaanites gradually replaced their brick defenses with this material. Stone was not

The southern walls of Early Bronze Taanach as they appear today at the end of three seasons of digging (above), and as they were shown in the architect's drawing after the first season in 1963 (below).

Joint Expedition to Tell Taanach

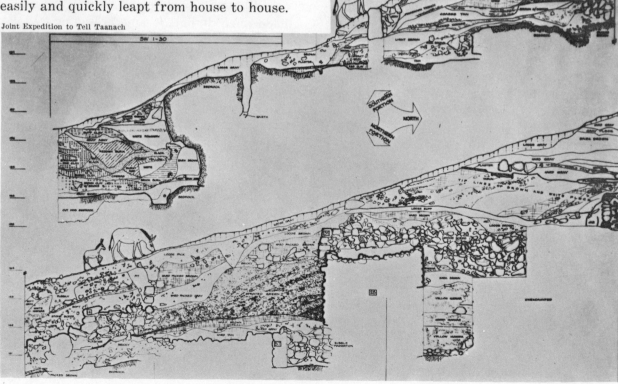

liable to either water or fire, the two enemies of brick. This process of the substitution of stone for brick is visible in the excavations of Ai and Tell el-Farah. At Taanach, farther north on the Plain of Esdraelon, enormous stone walls sometimes thirty feet thick were set on bedrock. These walls show signs of at least three major rebuilds perhaps indicating that in the continuous ancient arms race between battering ram and wall the citizens of Taanach were not always successful.

In times of peace, life in these cities was well regulated and somewhat uncomplicated by today's standards. Early in the morning the city would come to life. The gates would swing open and the farmers, refreshed from a night of rest safely behind their stout city walls, would go into the fields where they would toil until dusk. The potter's wheel would begin to spin. Broken pottery had to be replaced and so did those jars which had been lost down wells and cisterns. Perhaps, too, a few pots might even be made for trade with other cities. In some homes and shops hand looms would be weaving material from goat hair which for centuries has provided the middle easterner with clothing and shelter. Fragments of ancient materials have been found at Jericho and at Bab edh-Dhra'. That from Jericho contained eleven threads of warp and twelve threads of woof to the square centimeter. This would yield a fairly strong cloth not unlike that used by the Bedouin today. Merchants, desperately trying to avoid the children dashing about, drove the burdened donkeys through the narrow streets. Their destination was the marketplace, focal point of city life then as now. Here wheat, barley, and lentils, the main crops of Palestinian soil, were being bartered. From the ruins of Lachish and Jericho we know that beans and peas were also grown. Perhaps they were also available farther north. Olives and almonds, already ancient favorites in the Early Bronze Age, were in abundance. But much interest was

Paul Lapp

A disarticulated burial at Bab edh-Dhra' showing the pottery and other artifacts placed in the tomb for use in the next world.

being shown in fresh and dried grapes, new delicacies just being introduced into the land. Barley beer, so long a standard beverage, stood in large jars side by side with jars containing the new grape wine.

Men in fringed, knee-length loincloths tied at the waist by a belt hurried to and fro. Many women, however, tarried first here and then there as they admired the shell earrings or the amulets and pendants of worked stone or bone. Sometimes blue faïence beads were to be seen, and more rarely adornments made of gold were displayed. Doubtless many women inwardly sighed as they thought how wonderful it would be to decorate their long tunics or head bands with some of this jewelry. But reality would return soon enough, and the women would go back to their homes to perform their household duties. There was grain to be ground by hand in stone bowls, fires to be tended, the children to be fed.

The houses to which these women returned were normally of one room, usually rectangular in shape, with floors of beaten earth. An oven, often an inverted large jar with one side broken out, was in the corner of the room or sometimes in a small courtyard. Occasionally a hearth would be paved with stone. In rare cases the hearth was covered with limestone paste which had been baked hard by the heat. Usually large jars buried in the ground served as storage for grain, oil, and water. At Jericho and Beth-shan, however, silos with walls of brick were found associated with individual dwellings. At Ai and Tell el-Farah the same thing was found except the lining was limestone instead of brick.

So far no walls of sufficient height have been found to determine what kind or even whether windows were present in these Early Bronze dwellings. Abundant evidence from many places is available, however, to show that much wood was used in the construction of houses. The deforestation of Palestine, going on during this time, had not yet progressed to the point of prohibiting the large-scale use of wood for buildings. Unfortunately, no roofing has yet been discovered in excavation. Yet it is certain that beams supported a roof which most archaeologists think was flat and probably covered with reeds. At Jericho, to cite only one example, many houses were found with burnt timbers from the roof lying on the floor. As the rooms became wider, wooden post supports were used to compensate for the apparent unavailability of longer timbers. One room discovered at Beth-shan has six such supports set in two rows. The usual construction procedure was to set these wooden supports on paving slabs. Numerous examples of this have been found at Ai and at Tell el-Farah.

There is some suggestion of town planning. At Megiddo where a haphazard town had grown up there was in the middle of the Early Bronze Age a major attempt to terrace the slopes of the hill and to lay out an elaborate new city complete with monumental public buildings. At Tell el-Farah houses were separated by straight, paved streets six and a half feet wide. A street of similar width ran around the inside of the city wall unlike Ai and Jericho where houses were built right against the defenses. As the cities became more crowded, living space be-

came more precious. Occasionally, as in the fifteenth rebuild of the wall at Jericho, the city took in more land by moving the wall outward. But this was more often than not impossible because of the curve and slope of the hill. The only choices were to build on open areas and to build upward. It is not always easy now to distinguish an open courtyard from one that was roofed over and used as a dwelling. And while there is clear evidence of two-story houses in later periods, as in the twelfth-century B.C. remains at Taanach, definitive evidence from the Early Bronze Age is lacking. It is nonetheless to be inferred from the thickness of certain walls, such as at Ai, or some other abnormal features, such as were found at Jericho, that there were some two-story houses in the Early Bronze Age cities.

The religious life of these early Canaanites remains mostly a mystery to us. This is due in part to the relatively small amount of excavated material with which we have to reconstruct their religion. Only three undeniably religious structures from this period have so far been fully excavated and reported. In light of a mistaken general tendency to read the documented faith of a later period back into their time, it is best, as always, to confine ourselves strictly to the specific evidence bearing on our particular issue.

Between 1933 and 1935 at Ai, Madame Marquet-Krause uncovered a sanctuary built against the inside of the city wall. This structure, rebuilt at least twice, is by far the most important Early Bronze religious building yet identified. One of the more interesting features of this sanctuary is its division into three parts, each of which seems to have borne the same function as the three parts of Solomon's Temple constructed ten miles to the south approximately fifteen hundred years later.

The outer and larger (thirty feet three inches by twenty-one feet five inches) por-

The Early Bronze sanctuary at Ai as it appears today. It is built against the ancient city wall.

tion of this sanctuary was for all those wishing to take part in the ritual sacrifices at a given time. In the middle of this area two rectangular incense burners were found. Near these the excavators found a roughly squared tree trunk. Some have suggested this is an *asherah,* a sacred pole so well known to the biblical critics of later Canaanite religion. But this understanding of the function of this particular tree trunk probably owes a great deal to what we know from later times. In all likelihood it was merely a supporting timber for the roof. If this tree trunk had no cultic purpose, the benches found on two sides of the room certainly did. Here the worshipers probably laid their offerings where they would stay until either the worshiper himself or a priest—it is not known which—would remove them to a recess in the corner where they would be ritually prepared for the altar.

A door led from this outer area into a somewhat smaller room which was raised one step. Here was found another bench or dais on which thirteen shallow cups were sitting.

These may have been used to hold liquid offerings such as oil, or they may simply have functioned as lamps to light an otherwise dim place. Along the walls were several irregular recesses which seem to have been for the refuse from offerings and sacrifices.

To the left of the door of the second room is a small raised chamber containing an altar six feet one inch long and two feet six inches high. It is so placed that it could not be seen except by entrance into this Holy of Holies. In the plastered stone wall above the altar was a niche of flat stones painted red. Very likely this was for depositing offerings. On the altar were found fine alabaster and stone bowls thought by excavators to have been manufactured in Egypt in the First or Second Dynasty (*ca.* 3000-2700 B.C.). Many animals' bones were found in the sanctuary along with an elaborate ivory handle of a knife, incense burners, and magnificent plates and cups of Egyptian design. These latter are characteristic of the Fourth Egyptian Dynasty (*ca.* 2650-2500 B.C.) and date the Canaanite sanctuary at Ai. If this dating is correct, it means this place of worship is contemporary with the three pyramids of Gizeh which were themselves the zenith and everlasting monument of Egypt's first period of material and artistic glory.

The Ai sanctuary ceased to be used when the city was destroyed at the end of the Early Bronze Age. When the site was reoccupied some centuries later, worship presumably took place at other locations within the rebuilt walls.

A second Early Bronze sanctuary has recently been uncovered among the ruins of Tell el-Farah. Unlike Ai this holy place contains only two chambers. Missing is the larger outer court. There is, in fact, no evidence of its ever having been a part of the construction. The sanctuary was composed of a cult chamber containing an altar and a bench which may have been an offering table serving the same function as the benches in the outer chamber at Ai. But that is speculation. The sanctuary at Farah is not the same as that at Ai. The Holy of Holies, for example, was entered through a narrow door and contained not an altar, but benches along the sides. As at Ai, however, the walls and floor of this Holy of Holies had been carefully and completely plastered.

If the shrine at Ai is the most important of the Early Bronze holy places yet discovered, the one at Megiddo certainly evokes the most biblical associations. Among the ruins of the "town-planned" Early Bronze

The high place at Megiddo. The most perfectly preserved structure of its kind yet discovered.

city is a conical stone structure which survives to a height of five feet. It measures thirty-five feet eight inches by thirty-one feet on the top. It can be ascended by a flight of seven steps which appears to be complete. This leads to the assumption that the present height is probably the original height or very close to it. This altar, or "high place," together with the walls that enclose it in a narrow rectangle constitutes a sanctuary. Numerous animal bones and broken vases leave no doubt as to its function. This is the oldest example of a "high place" which persisted as a part of Canaanite worship far into the Hebrew period.

At Jericho is an Early Bronze room which has affinities with the sanctuaries at both Ai and Tell el-Farah. It contains a bench and a dais, and its walls and floors have been carefully plastered. Moreover, it has unusually thick walls to separate it from neighboring structures. Nonetheless, for all its similarities to other sanctuaries described, we would be unwise at this time to include it as evidence of Early Bronze Age worship in Palestine.

The evidence for the religious life of the early Canaanite is thus skimpy. Still some observations are possible. If these cannot be definitive they are nevertheless suggestive. First, there is as yet no example either of divine symbol or image for this period. As we shall see, both symbol and image were in abundant and consistent use among the Canaanites when they were encountered by the Hebrews. Second, proof of animal sacrifice is undeniable. But we do not know if this type of sacrifice was performed by the worshiper or by a priest. Third, there seems not to have been any human sacrifice, at least not at the known altars. Whether or not live humans, possibly children, were placed as sacrifices in the foundation stones of city walls we do not yet know. This practice, perhaps occasional among later Canaanites, was widely condemned by the religious leaders of the Hebrews. Fourth, major cultic areas have been uncovered in at least three of the Early Bronze cities. In the opinion of many archaeologists, the distinguished Dominican Roland de Vaux among them, every city of this period had one or more temples. It would be most surprising if excavations in the years to come failed to uncover more sanctuaries.

A Nomadic Flood

Sometime around 2300 B.C., Early Bronze Age culture came to an end in Palestine. It was destroyed by a combination of nomadic warriors and shepherds who infiltrated from the north or northeast. The recent expeditions at Bab edh-Dhra' indicate that some of these newcomers were mingling with the Early Bronze inhabitants as early as the twenty-fourth century B.C. Whether this was the case in other cities we do not know. At any rate, in the next one hundred years increasing numbers of these new, essentially nonurban people had succeeded in completely overthrowing the cities of Palestine and in destroying its flourishing urban life. The land entered its "dark ages," the Intermediate Bronze period, when technical, social, and political progress came to an end and past gains disappeared under the incoming tide of less sophisticated culture.

At every excavated Early Bronze site archaeologists have found unmistakable evidence of these newcomers. In some cases, such as Tell en-Nasbeh, Ai, and Tell el-Farah, the towns were abandoned altogether. At others, notably Jericho, Tell el-'Ajjul, and Tell Beit Mirsim, the remains of nomadic camps were found on top of the rubble of stilled towns. In the hills surrounding these once-proud places it was clear shepherds had grazed their flocks in disregard of the fields now fallow and soon to be wilderness again. After some time when these people did build dwellings more permanent than their goat hair tents, they were rude, of irregular

shape, and usually of soft brick. At Jericho, and perhaps other places as well, they built a shrine. Most likely it was a nomadic sanctuary much like that one from a later period now under examination at Deir 'alla farther north in the Jordan Valley. It was an open shrine without defensive walls. Its holiness was its security. After the seasonal migration the tribe would return to this spot to offer sacrifices and to renew its spiritual strength. At Jericho the walls of the shrine had been dedicated by means of child sacrifice. The bones of the victim were found still buried in the foundation.

Technically backward, these people did seem to possess skill in pottery manufacture and in tomb construction. The consistent and widespread presence of a vastly different type of pottery and of new forms of burials have convinced scholars that the destruction of the Early Bronze Age cities was the work of newcomers to the land, and not an uprising of people of the countryside against urbanites. The pottery not only had new shapes, but was thin to the point of being brittle, poorly fired, and devoid of the red slip and burnish of earlier times.

Burials were in tombs of various types (Miss Kenyon has identified five and possibly seven types at Jericho), but were mostly multiple burials as over against the single tomb interments common among the earlier and later peoples of Palestine. A number of disarticulated burials have been found, not only at Jericho, but at Bab edh-Dhra', Tell el-'Ajjul, and elsewhere. They may be an indication of nomadic practice of transporting the bodies of their dead back to a tribal burial ground after the seasonal migration. This may be what is reflected in Jacob's charge to his sons regarding his burial (Genesis 49:28-33).

Many scholars have long considered Abraham and the other Hebrew patriarchs to be a part of this pastoral invasion of Palestine at the end of the second millennium. Some have identified them with the Amorites. There is no doubt that during this time there was great movement of peoples and a general unrest in the Middle East. Egypt, invaded by "sand dwellers," had entered the First Intermediate, that period of rapid decline from the pinnacle of power and glory of the Old Kingdom. Egypt's main interest was defense of its northeastern border. The civilizations of Mesopotamia and Syria were likewise in decline and on the defensive. There was a consistent pastoral attack upon urban life. It is not impossible that the Hebrew patriarchs were a part of this movement. Yet at the moment evidence against this possibility is stronger than that favoring it. No conclusive findings have linked the newcomers into Palestine with the life of upper or lower Mesopotamia. Yet it was here, at Haran and Ur, that the Bible locates the origins of Abraham. Furthermore, the flourishing town life reflected in the patriarchal stories is difficult to correlate with the emerging archaeological evidence for the end of the Early Bronze Age. We must look to a slightly later period for that context in which the Chosen People first appear.

So the Early Bronze Age in Palestine came to an end. In a drama which was to be repeated with variations twelve centuries later when the Philistines and Hebrews came, the cities which had warred so often against one another were in the end unable to unite against a common foe. They all disappeared, swiftly and most likely brutally. Yet the very suddenness of their destruction may indicate they were merely islands in a larger sea and not the dominant factor that we usually take them to be. The invaders who destroyed these cities and the culture they represented plunged the area into a dark age lasting four hundred years. When further Semitic incursions caused the land and its culture to revive in the Middle Bronze Age, the stage was set for the appearance of the patriarchs of those Chosen Ones who were to be "a light to the

The recovery of urban life in Canaan brought with it a high degree of artisanship as indicated in the sixteenth-century pitcher from Megiddo (above), and the sickles and knives of the period (opposite above). The newly excavated toggle pin (opposite below) held the flowing outer garment at the left shoulder.

nations" and from whom would come "The Prince of Peace."

5. UNITY OF CULTURE— DIVERSITY OF PEOPLES

By the middle of the nineteenth century B.C., Palestine had begun to recover from the disaster which had overtaken it some four centuries before. Here and there cities were beginning to flourish once more, and the arts and crafts were coming to life. In the Negeb Desert villages serving the Egyptian trade appeared. No longer a political and economic backwater, the land of the Canaanites was rapidly assuming those roles for which it became famous in history. As

the trade routes were reestablished, it became a land bridge between continents and middle man in ever-increasing international commerce.

As in an earlier time, a change in the way of life in Canaan was due to the incursion of new groups of people. The now ancient but seemingly endless drama was played once more as men with their women, children, and flocks moved slowly but relentlessly over the hills and valleys of Palestine. From Syria they came, bringing with them a new culture based upon technical advancement and the idea of an agriculturally based urban society. So far as archaeology has been able to determine, this was an incursion, an infiltration, not an invasion. The new forms of pottery and other artifacts which distinguish these people are found side by side with those of the pastoral folk who roamed the land. Some scholars say this points to a peaceful settlement. However, this is slim evidence indeed upon which to base the suggestion that the coming of this new people was a peaceful one. We must remember that the culture which they found in Palestine was a semi-

nomadic pastoral one of a people living on sparsely settled land. Evidence for the character of a destruction of this kind of society would not be the type that even the most trained archaeologist would read with assurance. There were no city walls whose remains could show signs of fierce combat, no burned timbers nor quantities of pottery smashed by collapsing stone. There are few surrounding contexts by which one can establish the date of skulls crushed by axes or of skeletons pierced by spears such as is possible when these things are found within datable structures.

All that we can say with confidence at this time is that the society which characterized the late Early Bronze period in Palestine was replaced by a new culture which had no apparent continuous development from its predecessor. The cultural change introduced by these newcomers is evidenced by a complete break in type of artifacts, by different burial habits, and by the reappearance of cities.

Pottery, the archaeologists' chronometer and general guide to culture, serves here as a faithful indicator to what was going on in history. The monotony of the earlier forms is replaced by a considerable variety recognizable by their design and the craft techniques used in their making. In place of generally dull, rough pots the founders of the Middle Bronze Age in Palestine had vessels made entirely on a fast wheel and burnished to such a high degree that the red finish on their clay suggests copper.

In weaponry and other artifacts the superiority of the later technology is also obvious. Fenestrated axes were replaced by those with socketed blades. Long, thin daggers gave way to a much shorter, but greatly strengthened blade which was triangular in appearance. Metal was rapidly replacing stone weapons, and there is the suggestion, not yet completely verified, that bronze, a stronger metal, was being used in place of copper. Functional jewelry, such as toggle pins which fastened cloaks on the shoulder, became more graceful but no less sturdy.

Burial habits among the newcomers were similar to those of the urban peoples whom the pastoral semi-nomads had overthrown. In place of the multiple burials of the semi-nomads, single burials with complete skeletons were the common practice. Even the positioning of the bodies in the grave, supine rather than crouched, was different in this later time.

There is the further evidence of the re-emergence of cities. Not surprisingly there are no large amounts of materials available from the first part of the Middle Bronze Age. Yet we know that at least two sites, Megiddo and Tell Beit Mirsim, had rapidly developing towns. At the latter the houses were built closely together and apparently without much thought to overall development. Soon, however, the inhabitants were able to build a defensive wall. Of comparatively small stones laid in rough courses and broken by square towers, this wall is reminiscent of those of Early Bronze Age cities. It was, in fact, a type of fortification common in Palestine until the coming of the Hyksos and the chariot.

At Jericho, Tell el-'Ajjul, and Ras el-'Ain, considerable burial evidence has been found to indicate that the new urban-minded peoples were returning to the old city sites during this time. But, possibly apart from Jericho, no clear proof can be shown to indicate that these places were flourishing towns like Megiddo and Tell Beit Mirsim. But cities were not long in coming, here and elsewhere. Within a very short time almost all the Early Bronze Age sites had been resettled, and once more there were stout walls, paved streets, and well-built houses. For some reason, however, the central hill country did not see this revitalization. A 1965-1966 American survey of the environs of Shechem concluded that the lack of archaeological evidence for the period under discussion was "striking." Shechem seems to have been "a virtually isolated impregnable city with hardly any surrounding villages" during this period.[1] The ruins of Ai and Shiloh also show no evidence of occupation until later. But these were exceptions. North, south, east, and west the cities sprang up once more. And around them the fields were cultivated and in bloom. In addition to the sites mentioned, fortified cities from this time have been excavated at Lachish, Hazor, Tell el-Farah, Beth-shemesh, Nahariyah, and half a dozen or more other locations. They are all dated from about the eighteenth century B.C. Archaeology may thus have reconstructed the historical situation reflected in the Egyptian Execration Texts (see p. 45) which indicate an increasing number of city-states and a parallel decrease in the tribal structure of Palestinian society.

At Jericho Miss Kenyon, with her characteristic good fortune, uncovered tombs from the sixteenth century. These contained wooden household furniture intact! The recovery of ancient wooden objects is extremely rare and even more so in the Middle East. But there they were—boxes inlaid with bone, tables, stools, and even a well-preserved bed. From them it is possible to gain a fairly good idea of how houses were furnished then, of ancient craftmanship, and of what these people thought about life after death. Several stools were recovered, one large enough to seat two persons. The design and workmanship of this larger stool were typical of the others. It had molded feet and legs that swelled to an inside curve. The top was woven with cords some of which survive. In overall effect it is reminiscent of Egyptian furniture of the period and shows the strong influence of Egypt on certain aspects of Palestinian culture. Only one bed was found.

[1] R. J. Bull and E. F. Campbell, "The Sixth Campaign at Balatah (Shechem)," *Bulletin of the American Schools of Oriental Research*, no. 190 (April 1968): 40.

Upon it the remains of the owner were still lying. It has two long sides and four crossbars. Beneath the skeleton were a few remnants of the stringing which ran transversely. Although most of this had disappeared, it was evident where the pieces had been looped over the sides. The owner's right hand rested upon a magnificent wooden table, over five feet long. Of one piece, thicker at the center than at the edges, this table was once loaded with food. Its convex upper surface is thought by the excavator to be due to warping in decay. But it is characteristic of each table found and may have been a part of the original design. This particular table and others have been found flat on the ground. Sockets on the bottom (two on one end and one in the middle of the other end) indicate that there were legs. But whether they were removed by the undertakers for practical purposes in the small tombs, or whether there is some more profound significance, is unknown.

Next to the table was a wicker basket containing toilet articles such as combs. Another basket was found across the tomb along with plates and goblets and jars once containing drink. In this tomb and in others also there were fragments of wooden boxes decorated with bone inlay. These apparently contained toilet articles similar to those deposited in the wicker basket. Beads, scarabs, and other jewelry were found scattered in the debris. Perhaps these were once in the boxes. From another tomb came a wicker basket containing a somewhat strange fibrous object which Miss Kenyon has identified as a wig.

The design of the various items of wood is pleasing and the craftsmanship well executed. Joints were carefully fitted together by tenon and mortice. There was no indication of any metal used in construction. Wooden pegs, standard in furniture-making until a few hundred years ago, held the pieces together. Chisels, drills, small axes, ripping saws, and some sort of a lathe were employed by the ancient carpenters of Jericho. The skill of these men was remarkable and is nowhere more striking than in the workmanship of the wooden combs whose tiny teeth presumably were cut with a bronze saw.

A few fragments of cloth were recovered. These were in association with the skeletons and doubtless are remains of burial clothing. But not enough survived to indicate the type of garments then in use. A number of bodies, however, had a toggle pin lying at the left shoulder indicating the securing of clothing at that point. At the head of almost every skeleton was a comb which had once been in position in the hair. An exception to this was the head of a youth; fragments beneath it indicated that he was buried wearing a round skull cap.

The contents of the Middle Bronze tombs at Jericho present a picture of living conditions at the time as being, in Miss Kenyon's words, "simple comfort but by no means luxury." [2] The bed and some of the other larger pieces were evidently associated with the burials of some important and probably rich persons. It is assumed, therefore, that such items were not commonplace and that most of the inhabitants of the town slept and ate on rush matting of the type recovered from the tombs.

Clearly the ancient Jerichoeans held well-formed views of another life. They made elaborate preparations and provided the dead with food, drink, and many household and personal items that were thought to be needed. This, of course, was characteristic of the ancient Egyptians. Still the tombs of Jericho show a significant difference. In Egypt great care was taken to prepare the body for entombment. Mummification, a lengthy, expensive, difficult process not entirely reproducible even today, was developed to insure the preservation of the body for

[2] Kathleen Kenyon, *Digging Up Jericho* (New York: Frederick A. Praeger, 1957), p. 252.

the next life. Moreover, representations of various gods were placed in tombs to ward off any evil threatening the deceased. At Jericho some care was taken to prepare the body. But this seems not to have extended beyond the more superficial matters of clothing and hair. Further, far from reverencing the body, the undertakers were more than a little careless in placing it in the burial chamber. And finally, apart from decoration on scarab rings, no statues or other representations of deities have been found among the dead at Jericho.

Instead of to Egypt some scholars looked northward to Syria for some clue to the origins of this new urban civilization of Middle and Late Bronze Age Palestine. Specifically, these men have looked to Byblos, a city on the Syrian coast whose name derives from the same source as our word "Bible," meaning "book." Whatever the strength of Byblos' claim as the originator of this culture, there is no question that it did arise somewhere in Syria and spread over the whole of that region and Palestine. From Ugarit (modern Ras Shamra) in the north to Tell el-'Ajjul in the south archaeologists have found conclusive evidence of a cultural unity. At site after site technical developments succeed one another in the same order and at about the same time. Pottery forms and styles show similar and continuous development everywhere. Craftsmen perfected works of art not only of copper and bronze, but also of lead and gold. Truly great cities were built and provided with fortifications which, considering the times, were a tribute to the people's engineering genius. Within these defenses modest houses of serfs surrounded more pretentious dwellings of the rich, suggesting something of the feudal character of the society.

This grand unity of culture produced the Golden Age of Canaan and maintained itself until *ca.* 1200 B.C., when it was shattered by the invasion of the "Sea Peoples" from the east and by the Hebrews who drove in from the southwestern deserts. The effect of these various invasions was to reduce the effectiveness of Canaanite control to a few major ports on the Syrian coast. This is the situation of the Canaanites during the time of the Hebrew monarchies when we get our clearest biblical picture of them. But long before this they had become a seafaring commercial people. As early as the seventeenth century B.C. Canaanite ships plied the Mediterranean and the Aegean laden with wood and textiles which were their principal exports. The wood was the famous "Cedars of Lebanon." The textiles were even more famous in their time and were desired partly for their quality but mostly for their color. Our English expressions "born to the purple" and "of the purple royal" owe their origin to the distinctive and expensive purple materials made and sold by the Canaanites to royalty and other wealthy persons. Indeed, it has been maintained that even the name *Canaanite* refers to this most celebrated of ancient industries. The name of the dye was *kinahhu.* This was made from shell fish native to the shores north of Mount Carmel. These shores were called *kinahna,* "the land of the purple." [3] The Greeks applied their word for purple, *phoinix,* to the land and to its inhabitants. From the Greek we have derived the English *Phoenician.* Hence the Phoenicians and the Canaanites were the same people.

[3] This popular and widely held view of the origin of the term *Canaanite* is not without opposition. Father de Vaux maintains that the ancestry of the work *kinahhu* is inexplicable. Perhaps it originally referred to the "west country," or what we might loosely call "the land of the setting sun." At any rate, according to de Vaux the use of the term to designate the color of the dye was derived from the name of the land and not the reverse. To this view, then *kinahhu* was so called because of the place of its origin just as the bayonet is named for Bayonne, France, the place of its first modern manufacture. For more on this view, see R. de Vaux, "Le Pays de Canaan," *Journal of the American Oriental Society,* 88, no. 1 (January-March 1968) : 23-29.

These folk who in later days had influence as far away as Carthage, their main colony in western North Africa (modern Tunisia), imported into Syria-Palestine the wares of Mediterranean and Aegean countries as well as those of Egypt and Mesopotamia. This extensive trade accounts for the diffusion of Mycenaean ceramics throughout the area particularly in the Late Bronze Age (*ca.* 1500-1200 B.C.). In addition to many excavated examples of the graceful pottery of the Greeks and Cretans, numerous less well-done copies have been found. Apparently the genuine article was both expensive and in demand. This created a market for imitations, and many potters lent their hands to this lucrative undertaking.

Doubtless the highest manifestation of this culture and the most important contribution of the Canaanites to civilization was the development of the alphabet. At Byblos the Canaanites evolved a syllabic script from the Egyptian hieroglyphic, or picture-writing. By the fourteenth century B.C., Canaanite poets were composing epic verses in an alphabetic cuneiform, as the materials at Ugarit show. They were also well on their way to developing a linear alphabet, a process completed by Ionian Greeks. This became the direct basis of our alphabet.

At this time there was in Syria-Palestine an increasingly sophisticated cultural unity over the whole area. This amazing unity is more remarkable when one considers that it was accomplished in spite of a wide diversity of peoples who dwelled in the land. In particular Palestine was a "melting pot." We have already noted the mammoth incursions at the end of the third millennium. These produced what has come to be considered the indigenous population and gave to it a basically Semitic character that has not changed in five thousand years. Throughout the centuries most of the larger infiltrations and invasions have tended to reinforce this Semitic stock. Yet there were numbers of non-Semites in the land. After 1600 B.C. and on into the Late Bronze Age this number increased considerably. In the Bible and other ancient texts we read about Canaanites, Amorites, Hittites, Perizzites, Hivites, Jebusites, Horites, Hurrians, and Girgasites. Joshua 9:1 mentions six of them as being "beyond the Jordan in the hill country and in the lowland all along the coast of the Great Sea toward Lebanon."

The Canaanites were the native population. They were, as we have seen, north Semitic in origin. The Amorites were also Semitic, northeastern in origin. They came from the north and out of the deserts approximately a thousand years after the coming of the Canaanites and considerably fortified the Semitic stock of the country. Generally interchangeable groups, they are nonetheless almost consistently distinguished in the Bible. This distinction may point to a different orientation on the part of the two. One, the

Canaan

Canaanite, may have been basically urban-agricultural, while the other, the Amorite, was more pastoral in outlook. Be that as it may, they constituted the majority of the population.

The Hittites were non-Semitic. They were certainly from the Indo-Aryan, Caucasian Hittite Kingdom of Asia Minor. During the Late Bronze Age this kingdom dominated the north, and early in the fourteenth century overthrew the kingdom of Mitanni. It was perhaps from this latter that three of the other groups came. These would have been the Horites, the Hurrians, and the Hivites. *Hor* in Hebrew means *cave*. *Hurru* in Egyptian means the same thing. Apparently the Horites and the Hurrians were the same people known by two names indicating their habit of dwelling in caves. The Hivites may have been a part of the same general grouping. When the Hebrews came to Canaan in the thirteenth century, Hivites occupied four city-states west of Jerusalem. When they heard of the destruction of Jericho and of Ai, they tricked Joshua into an alliance and thus escaped the fate of the more easterly cities (Joshua 9).

If our knowledge of some of the groups just mentioned is tentative, what we know of the others is practically nonexistent. Indeed, there are many scholars who say that, in fact, we know nothing about the origin and ethnic makeup of the Perizzites, Girgasites, and Jebusites. Yet some take this very lack of knowledge as suggesting a non-Semitic origin for these groups. This may well be so. Others, however, single out the Jebusites as being Canaanites who lived at Jebus (Jerusalem).

For all the tentative state of our knowledge and in spite of the confusion of scholarly argument over these various peoples, it is possible to isolate several stable factors. First, there was a Semitic population with significant non-Semitic elements. Second, considerable fluidity of movement was present during the entire Middle and Late Bronze Ages. Groups, even ethnic groups, seem to have been able to enter the land with relative ease. This is perhaps a reflection of the political situation at which we shall glance presently. Third, Canaanite, which may once have had primarily an ethnic connotation, came to designate a culture embracing a variety of ethnic stocks. Still it was more a matter of groups coming into the culture and adapting themselves to it than it was of an amalgamation of cultures. Fourth, when the Hebrews entered Canaan they were, as Semites, ethnically related to the majority of the population. Perhaps Amorites themselves, they nonetheless found it impossible on religious grounds to adapt to the flexible culture as had both Semite and non-Semite before them.

III: POLITICS, PATRIARCHS, AND RELIGION

6. EGYPTIANS, PATRIARCHS, AND HYKSOS

Readers of the Old Testament are familiar with the name of Nebuchadnezzer, and with those of Shalmaneser, Sargon, Sennacherib, and other kings of the north whose imperial ambitions and endless quarrels with Egypt were a constant threat to the security and well-being of the people of Palestine. These readers will also know some of the Egyptian pharaohs such as Ramses II, that splendid monarch of the Exodus, and Neco II before whom good King Josiah fell at the Battle of Megiddo in 609 B.C. (II Kings 23:29 ff.; II Chronicles 35:20-24). Even a casual acquaintance with the story told in Scripture indicates that ancient Egypt considered Syria and Palestine to be within her sphere of influence. This claim was often and bloodily contended by the Mesopotamian powers, whether Assyria, Babylon, or some other. Nonetheless, at virtually no time from the wakening of Egyptian power during the third and fourth dynasties (ca. 2500 B.C.) until the coming of the Romans (69 B.C.) did Egypt fail to have an interest in the lands beyond her northeastern border. This does not mean, of course, that the Egyptians were able or even wished to exercise an iron-clad control over the area all the time. Her grip on the country fluctuated with her strength and with her needs.

During the thousand years before the establishment of the Hebrew Kingdom (in itself possible only because of relative and temporary Egyptian weakness) Egyptian control over Palestine can roughly be divided into three periods. In the first, which is the time of the early patriarchs (ca. 2000-ca. 1750 B.C.), the Canaanite city-states seemed to have been fairly free of Egyptian interference so long as they paid their tribute to the pharaohs. In the second, which may have been the time of the journey into Egypt of Jacob and his sons (Genesis 45:16–47:12), Egypt itself was under the domination of foreign rulers, the Hyksos. These were Semitic warriors who established themselves on the throne of the pharaohs and also held Palestine in their power. The third period was for Israel a time of sorrow. When the Egyptians threw off the foreign yoke they not surprisingly turned on those within their land who had been identified with the oppressors. Israel was in bondage. But God through his servant Moses led them from slavery to freedom and from sorrow to joy (Exodus 1:8–15:21).

In the first period, from around 2000 B.C. until about 1750 B.C., as an urban-agricultural civilization was reestablishing itself in Palestine, Egyptian power was also recovering and making itself felt beyond the borders of the Land of the Nile. Archaeological evidence found at Lachish and at Megiddo suggests that some contact with Egypt may have been as early as the reign of the founder of the glorious Twelfth Dynasty, Amenemhet I (1991-1961 B.C.). There is no question that by the time of Amenemhet III (1840-1792 B.C.) the city-states of Palestine were at least nominally his vassals. When they failed in their expected duties this ruler sent his army as far north as Shechem to guarantee the unhindered passage of Egyptian commerce over the trade routes. Byblos, a thriving Syrian Canaanite port, was at this time more or less an Egyptian colony whose princes were apparently supported with generous gifts from the pharaoh. For their part these men wrote in Egyptian and acknowledged themselves to be vassals.

This meager evidence combined with Egyptian objects found elsewhere such as Gezer in Palestine and Ugarit in Syria suggests that the main concern of the Egyptians was trade. The kings and princes of the city-states seemed to have exercised effective control over their localities and even carried on intermittent warfare against other city-states whose interests clashed with theirs. Thus politically Palestine appears to have been composed of a number of independent city-states all or almost all of which were in loose vassalage to Egypt. That these cities had a large measure of freedom of action is shown by the Execration Texts. These nineteenth-century documents listing many vassal cities in Syria and Palestine indicate that the pharaoh, fearful of his subjects, had resorted to magic in order to seek to control his enemies, both actual and potential. There is abundant archaeological evidence, however, to suggest that these Canaanite subjects were more interested in warring upon one another than in conspiring against the pharaoh. This was a constant factor in the history of the Canaanites. Always at one another's throats and unable to unite in the face of a common foe, they were in the end spectators while two groups of foreigners, the Philistines and the Israelites, fought for control of the land.

The whole of Palestine at this time was, however, under the control neither of the Egyptians nor of the local Canaanite kings and princes. It has already been noted that the highlands and particularly the central hill country did not share in the revival of urban-agricultural life in the Middle and Late Bronze Ages. These were the grazing areas and attracted the infiltrating clans of semi-nomads whose sheep and goats found adequate natural pasturage among the innumerable rocks and stones so characteristic of this portion of Palestine. Many others coming into the land were caravaneers plying their trade as far as Egypt. All were clans, most likely Arameans (Amorites) from the far north, from Mesopotamia, and the deserts. Among them were the patriarchs of Israel.

The Patriarchs of Israel

It is not easy to speak with authority about the patriarchal origins of Israel. First, the primary source of our knowledge, Genesis, is a theological writing concerned to show the marvelous workings of God in calling and establishing his People. It is not and never should be taken to be a book whose main interest is an account of history. Moreover, much of this narrative in the form in which we have it is very late. Some of it may come from postexilic times. That is, it may be as recent as the fifth century B.C.

Second, Abraham, Isaac, and Jacob seem to have been part of a general nomadic movement which extended over several centuries. This memory is preserved at various places in the Hebrew tradition. For example, the Deuteronomic "creed" begins, "a wandering Aramean was my father" (Deuteronomy 26:5). During the Exile, Ezekiel reminds the Hebrews that "your father was an Amorite, and your mother a Hittite" (Ezekiel 16:3). The Hebrew patriarchs were, in short, a wandering part of the shifting and mixing of peoples at the end of the Early Bronze Age and beginning of the Middle Bronze Age. It is not possible even to establish the centuries in which they lived. From the point of view of world history they were insignificant nomads in occasional contact with the great empires of their day. The biblical narrative agrees at every point that they came from northern Mesopotamia, in the region of Haran, and that they traversed the land as far south as Egypt. But no specific historical information is given. Even the pharaohs are not mentioned by name (Genesis 12:15-20). The details of the beginning of the history of Israel remain in the shadows.

Yet not all is historically so negative as it may seem. While archaeology is incapable of demonstrating that the patriarchal narratives took place exactly as the Bible presents them, it has shown that these stories reflect the general historical situation of the Middle Bronze Age. This is considerable gain. Some years ago many scholars were saying that the stories about the patriarchs were more or less epic-poetic fabrications of a later time written to convey religious truths. There can be no question that these accounts are epic poetry and that they did have a religious-theological function in the life of Israel. They spoke and speak of the way God fulfills his promises in his own way and in his own good time. But just because

these are religious epics it does not necessarily follow that the events spoken of were therefore made up by men of a later time. On the contrary, archaeology has now shown that the names, incidents, and general life reflected in the stories about Abraham, Isaac, and Jacob fit into the period 2000-1750 B.C. This historical coincidence is no doubt due to the faithful preservation of ancient tradition by both word of mouth and by writing.

The names of the Fathers of Israel were apparently fairly common. The name *Abraham* is mentioned in seventeenth-century B.C. Babylonian texts and also in the Execration Texts. Serug, a name associated with Abraham's brother and with one of his ancestors, was also the name of a village west of Haran. Nahor, the name of Abraham's grandfather, appears in the Mari Texts as the designation of a town in the same vicinity. It is known that in the eighteenth century B.C. it was inhabited by Amorites. Later Assyrian materials mention Terah (compare the name of Abraham's father), in a similar way. Such names as Jacob, Benjamin, and Ishmael were known to the writers of eighteenth-century B.C. Mari. The names Zebulon and Issachar are mentioned in the Execration Texts. Jacob, seemingly a very popular name, is found in compounds (Jacob-el, etc.) not only at Mari, but is used of a Hyksos chieftain, and also to designate a Palestinian in a fifteenth-century B.C. list of Pharaoh Thutmoses III.

It would be wrong, however, to suppose that these or any other known extra-biblical uses of these names allude to biblical persons. We have no direct reference outside the Bible to any biblical figure before the monarchy. The abundance of these names merely points to the probability of the historical character of the nomenclature of the Genesis accounts. Further, the frequency with which these names designate towns and villages suggests that clans and not merely chieftains may be indicated by the use of a given name. If this suggestion is correct, it may help explain among other things how Abraham was able quickly to rally a large body (318) of "trained men" to make war upon the kings of the east (Genesis 14:13-16). In his recent book, *Yahweh and the Gods of Canaan*,[1] W. F. Albright suggests another and equally plausible possibility for Abraham's military strength. In his view Abraham was a wealthy caravan leader plying the donkey trails between Canaan and Egypt. Such a person, and *only* such a person in Albright's view, would be likely to have 318 armed retainers. Such possibilities are enhanced by Nelson Glueck's surveys of the Negeb and his discovery of a number of previously unknown caravan way stations.

Similarly, a number of once puzzling incidents associated with the patriarchs are also shown by archaeological discoveries to have been commonplace in the early second millennium. We have already seen that Abraham's haggling with Ephron concerning the purchase of the Cave of Machpelah was in accordance with common ancient practice. Apparently Abraham wished to purchase only the cave itself in which to bury his wife, Sarah. Yet governed by Hittite practice he had to buy not only the cave but the land and the arbors associated with it. This assumption of feudal obligation described in Genesis 23:1-20 is exactly in accord with recovered Hittite documents from Boghazköy in which such details are stressed.

We also noted at the same time that Abraham's fear of Eliezer and his terrible treatment of Hagar and Ishmael are illuminated by the Nuzi Texts. Again, it is these later texts which make clear the earlier legal basis of the agreement between Jacob and Laban (Genesis 29:1–31:55). The adoption of Jacob into the family with the express condition that he not take a wife other than the daughters of Laban, the bitterness of Leah and Rachel toward their father, and Rachel's

[1] (London: Athlone Press, 1968).

theft of the household gods to insure legal title to the inheritance, all have parallels from Nuzi.

These examples from Boghazköy and Nuzi along with others which could be cited from Mari, the Cappadocian Texts, the Alalakh Tablets, and similar recently discovered materials leave no doubt that the patriarchs belonged to the Middle Bronze Age. They also make it certain that, while the Hebrew narratives telling about these Fathers are late and are theological histories, they nonetheless faithfully represent the period about which they are written. Finally, the consistency of the detail of the legal matters in Genesis suggests strongly that the legal practices of the patriarchs approximate much more closely those of their contemporaries than they do those of later Israelite times. One simply cannot look to patriarchal usage as the standard for later Hebrew law.

In their manner of living also, the patriarchs were doubtless similar to their contemporaries. The Bible presents a picture of semi-nomads, living in tents, seasonally traversing Palestine in search of pasture for their flocks. Occasionally they went as far south as the attractive grazing lands of the Nile Delta in Egypt, and they even may have returned to Mesopotamia now and then. According to Scripture, when in Palestine they restricted themselves to the highlands, a procedure which archaeology has shown would keep them from contact with the cities. Lot was perhaps the only one interested in agriculture and in the life of the cities, a matter which proved to be a source of considerable troubles (Genesis 13:1-13; 18:16-38).

The daily routine of semi-nomads has hardly changed since the day of Abraham. It is a hard life, stark, simple, Spartan. Strong, black, goat hair tents, sometimes single, often in clusters, form the focus of living. Here the shepherd returns when possible to be greeted by his wife and children. Their possessions are few because their wants are restricted to basic necessities and by the need for mobility. In winter they gather with other members of their clan around a shrine in the Jordan Valley, the Negeb, or some similarly warm place. The spring sees them once more on the move as they disperse in search of the sparse grass and flowers which are life to their sheep and goats. Although domesticated camels may have been known in the Middle East as early as the First Egyptian Dynasty (ca. 3000 B.C.), their mention in the Bible in connection with the Fathers of Israel seems to have been an anachronism reflecting general life in later times. Donkeys, not camels, would likely have been their beasts of burden. While camels were not unknown in patriarchal times as Middle Bronze Mesopotamia lexical lists show, they were not widely domesticated. Indeed, while ancient records from the Middle East mention numerous large donkey caravans from early times (a table from Mari makes reference to 3,000 donkeys in one train), it is not until near the end of the Bronze Age, around the thirteenth century B.C., that camel caravans came generally into use in the area.

The religious lives of the patriarchs are a considerable puzzle. The Bible makes it clear that Moses is the founder of Hebrew religion. The religion of the Israelites was, in their own eyes, a continuous development from that of Moses. Yet the Israelite God is often referred to as "the God of Abraham, Isaac, and Jacob." Further complicating the matter is the spiritual experience of Abraham. No doubt there were economic and social reasons for his leaving his own country and launching out into the unknown. But his decision was also an act of faith, for it was based on a boundless confidence in a divine promise. The book of Genesis is the story of the working out of this promise. Indeed, one could go so far as to suggest that the entire Bible shows God at work to fulfill his promise that through Abraham and his seed the whole world should be blessed (Genesis 12:1-3).

Thus we have the religion of Israel said to begin with Moses and yet to be prior to him. Many solutions have been offered which seek to show the intimate relation of Patriarchal religion with Mosaic religion and with that of the later Israelites. Yet no solution seeking to make detailed comparisons can succeed. It is a simple matter of having too little information. In fact we know very little about Moses' religious practices. Even less is known about the patriarchs in this regard. This book seeks to indicate what archaeology can tell us about the Bible and about biblical man. One can excavate evidences and consequences of various beliefs, but one cannot excavate a belief itself. The light that archaeology can throw upon patriarchal religion is slight, but when taken with other evidence outside the archaeological scope, it can be helpful.

Indications are that the religion of the patriarchs corresponded more closely with what we know of northwest Semitic religion than it did with the Semitic Canaanite fertility cults. That is, the existence of a personal bond between the patriarch as the head of a clan and his God is typical of purely Amorite religion. This God was identified with a particular clan and would be known by the name of the head of that clan. "The God of Abraham" may be an example of this. Another may be the binding of the agreement between Jacob and Laban. Laban invoked "the God of Abraham and the God of Nahor" (Abraham's brother) in addition to "the God of their father" (Terah), while Jacob "swore by the Fear of his father Isaac" (Genesis 31:53). Analogous examples are found in the Cappadocian Texts and other materials from the same period. Similarly the idea of "cutting a covenant" (RSV "make a covenant") between a clan as represented by its patriarch and its God is referred to both in Genesis (15:17-18, and others) and in texts from the Middle Bronze Age such as the Syrian Qatna documents.

These covenants were sealed by sacrifices which were cut in two to allow the parties of agreement to pass between. Sacrifice was not limited to these occasions however. Indeed animal sacrifice seems to have been an important part of patriarchal religion just as it was generally among the ancient Semites. Each of the sanctuaries associated with the Hebrew patriarchs (Shechem, Bethel, Beersheba) was consecrated by a sacrifice offered to the ancestral divinity of the clan. On such occasions the head of the clan, in the absence of any organized priesthood, would perform the very simple rites.

Thus in religion as in law, the patriarchs of Israel showed undeniable links with their Mesopotamian Amorite origins. When the Hebrews began to settle on the land and turned their hands to agricultural concerns, many fell prey to some of the less worthy features of Canaanite religion. In the end the quality in Hebrew religion that rejected human sacrifice, cult prostitution, and similar practices was the strength of its spiritual dedication to a covenant between God and his people. The later struggles between Hebrews and Canaanites were partly a conflict between the desert and the sown. The difficulty was to adapt the values of the former to the circumstances of the latter. It was not easy. It was not done overnight; nor, indeed, was it ever fully accomplished. But that which made the religion of Israel live and go beyond every boundary set upon it by man was its profound consciousness of a bond of solidarity between the man of faith and his God. If one wishes to find the patriarchal contribution to Hebrew religion, this is a fruitful direction in which to look. Little will be gained by comparing cultic details which in any case were probably not greatly varied among their contemporaries.

To some, these conclusions concerning the patriarchs, their mode of living, and their religion may seem overly cautious. Yet they are as far as one can go considering the present state of our knowledge. In almost every regard the Fathers of Israel appear to have been like their contemporaries. Still, like their descendants, the patriarchs were apparently religiously distinguishable from the Canaanites. It was this distinction which was emphasized by the writers of the Bible as they set down the epics of Israel and reminded the people of God of their goodly heritage. To be a "Son of Abraham," as John the Baptist indicated (Matthew 3:7-10; Luke 3:7-9), was to be a man of faith believing the promises of God and aware of the signs of their fulfillment.

The Hyksos

The second of the three periods into which the Middle and late Bronze Ages have been divided is dominated by the presence of the Hyksos both in Palestine and in Egypt. Until recently these people were something of a mystery. The history of the Egyptian Manetho (ca. 280 B.C.) noted that the Hyksos, whom he called "shepherd kings," ruled Egypt during the Fifteenth and Sixteenth Dynasties. They are not mentioned by name in the Bible and almost nothing else was known about them until archaeologists began to recover the Middle Bronze Age. It now appears that they were a warrior aristocracy who dominated not only Egypt but also Syria-Palestine for about two hundred years from ca. 1780-1550 B.C. Their use of bronze weapons and especially their introduction of the horse-drawn military chariot gave them superiority throughout the region and made them its masters.

Little is known of the actual Hyksos conquest, but there is now evidence of their presence and of their relation to the existing cultures they ruled. The major architectural contribution of these hard-riding warriors was a new type of fortification, probably perfected as a defense against improvements in the battering ram. These large Hyksos walls stressed depth as over against the largely single-wall defenses of earlier times. Plaster faced beaten earth ramparts with sloping revetments serving as foundations for the city walls found all the way from northern Mesopotamia (at Carchemish for instance) to the Nile Delta (at Tell el-Yahudiyeh) are indications of the engineering skill of the Hyksos. In Palestine such walls have been found at Jericho, Lachish, Tell el-'Ajjul, Tell Beit Mirsim, Megiddo, Hazor, and other places. At Jericho the sytem was sixty-six feet wide and at least forty-six feet in height above ground level.

City life prospered considerably under this alien rule. Some places not previously rebuilt were fortified. This was the case, for example, at Tell el-'Ajjul. Other well-established cities took advantage of the rebuilding of their walls to expand. Hazor, the largest known site in Palestine, increased its size seven times to enclose twenty-six and a half acres within massive fortifications. Yet apart from military innovations there was apparently no infusion of new techniques or new ideas. The existing culture continued without a break. All recovered material evidence bears witness to this continuity. Pottery forms, architecture, burial customs, and the like in Palestine are clearly Canaanite, not Hyksos. The same is true in Syria and in Egypt: the native culture remains. Clearly the Hyksos were merely a ruling aristocracy, governing the population but not significantly changing its way of life. It would seem that the Hyksos, a Semitic group with a non-Semitic minority, were not only tolerant, but sought to accommodate themselves to the cultures they found. Once in power these conquerors, like many before and after them, sought to maintain a quiet *status quo*. This meant in part a dampening of communications with the result that trade slowed to a trickle. Palestine prospered, but provincially. Cities grew, but haphazardly. Men lived quietly and for the most part well, but simply. This picture of the Hyksos rule is not altogether unattractive, yet it suggests that Palestine became once again a backwater. This was its fate whenever trade slackened.

A number of temples and sanctuaries from this period have been recovered. One of the most interesting of these is that at Nahariyah excavated in 1954 and 1955 by Israeli archaeologists. Working in a building discovered seven years earlier, these scholars found it to be a temple built about 1750 B.C. and considerably enlarged approximately a hundred years later. The first temple was an almost square single room. Just outside was a circular construction of stones which was shown by related objects found there to be a "high place," a place of sacrifice.

When the later temple was built it incorporated the earlier structure into its three rooms, one a large hall, the others smaller adjoining rooms which were evidently living quarters for the priests. The large hall was for ritual purposes. But the focus of worship was in the courtyard where a considerably larger "high place" was located. Near this stood an altar associated with a stone box. It has been conjectured that worshipers entering this sacred area would come to the small altar, deposit gifts (perhaps metal figurines such as those found nearby) in the box and proceed to the "high place" for the climax of their ceremony. Here the sacrificial animal was slaughtered by a priest and then divided among the priesthood and the worshipers (similar practices were followed by the Israelites; see, for example, Leviticus 7: 6-7; Numbers 18:9-10).

The "high place" is still covered with oily matter suggesting that libations, the pouring out of holy oil, were a part of the presentation of the sacrifice. Offering vessels containing seven cups have been found here and were probably the instruments used for libations. The significance of the number seven is not known, but it has had religious importance, not only for the Canaanites, but also for the biblical Hebrews and for Jews throughout the centuries.

Many extremely important artifacts have been recovered from the Nahariyah temple. Votive vessels and incense burners were in profusion as were figurines of monkeys, doves, and cattle. These and the semiprecious beads and fine jewelry found there were probably gifts used in the fertility rites celebrated at this site. There can be no question that this was a holy place of the Canaanite fertility cults. Silver and bronze images of female deities were discovered. The naked bodies with prominent breasts, navels, and knees, the high crown and pointed horns on the heads of these figures indicate that Asherah was worshiped here. Asherah, well known to us from the Bible and from the Ugaritic Texts, was a fertility goddess, chief deity of Tyre and Sidon not far from Nahariyah.

There were, however, various representations of Asherah at Nahariyah. Yet they are variations only, not basic differences. They may point to dissimilarities of belief owing to a more or less polyglot population. Or they may indicate nothing more than differing craftsmanship. At any rate, we have here a distinctively Canaanite shrine with clearly recognizable affinities both with worship as described in the Ugaritic Texts (where the ritual number seven is stressed and sacrifices and offerings in silver are required) and in the Bible (see for example the condemnation of the "high places" in Amos 7:9 and II Kings 23:8).

Similar shrines with "high places" have been found at Megiddo and at Byblos. These taken together with the Nahariyah and Shechem excavations tend to show that in matters of religion as in other aspects of culture the Hyksos did not disturb native elements and practices. The cults and shrines so roundly and consistently condemned by the priests and prophets of Israel were well and firmly established in the land long before the coming of the Hebrews from Egypt. There is reason to suspect, however, that these cults were known to and rejected by the Hebrew patriarchs. These men were pastoralists and caravaneers who would have had little interest in an agricultural religion which sought to guarantee the fertility of the land and an abundant harvest.

The Hyksos may have had other biblical connections. In one of the most intriguing narratives in the entire Bible we are told how Joseph was sold into slavery by his jealous brothers, how he rose from prison to become the pharaoh's first minister, and eventually brought his aging father and forgiven brothers to dwell in the lush fields of Goshen (Genesis 39:1–47:12). When in the vast sweep of the Bronze Age are such things most likely to have happened? Would it not have been at a time when Semites ruled in Egypt? These "foreign rulers" (and this is a better understanding of *Hyksos* than is Manetho's "shepherd kings") would have been more susceptible to the rise to power of another Semitic foreigner than would have been the somewhat prideful Egyptians. The latter, after all, referred to nomadic Semites by the disrespectful epithet "sand dwellers."

This is, of course, a speculation based upon probabilities. Yet it is wholly plausible and fits with the dating of the patriarchs, on the one hand, and that of the Exodus, on the other hand. If it is correct, then the "king who knew not Joseph" (Exodus 1:8), that is, did not recognize the place of honor of Joseph's people, was Ahmose (*ca.* 1570-1546 B.C.). Ahmose was the founder of the New Kingdom, and the Egyptian principally responsible for the expulsion of the Hyksos. The collapse of alien rule would mean dark days for those, both Egyptian and foreign, who had been closely associated with the hated invaders. If this conjecture is right the Hebrews, as friends and favorites of the

Hyksos, would suffer cruel taskmasters and hard times. In this way, perhaps, the Hebrews entered a "house of bondage."

In bloody battles Ahmose, having mastered the art of the chariot, drove the Hyksos out of Egypt, across the sands, northward through Palestine and Syria, and right out of history. Egypt meanwhile reasserting its imperial power in Asia came to the second and greatest pinnacle of its glory. The New Kingdom in all its splendor arose along the Nile. Almost all the mammoth and beautiful Egyptian monuments and temples scattered today in museums around the world and in the sands by the Nile are products of this time of greatness. Few empires in history have been as resplendent or as secure. At Abu Simbel, Assuan, Thebes, Memphis, and on down the great river workmen labored and craftsmen composed in wood and stone to celebrate the glory of Egypt and the immortality of the pharaoh.

In the northeastern Delta, press labor gangs, among them Hebrews, worked under miserable conditions to build treasure cities and a northern capital from which Egypt could govern an expanding empire. Sethos I (*ca.* 1309-1290 B.C.) and Ramses II (*ca.* 1290-1224 B.C.), the magnificent pharaohs of the Nineteenth Dynasty, were particularly interested in this work. Avaris, the former Hyksos capital, was chosen as the location of the northern capital and summer palace. Modestly Ramses renamed it for himself.[2] This city and neighboring Pithom (Tell er-Retabeh) near Lake Timsah became symbols of imperial wealth, power, and cruelty. At least they exemplified cruelty to the Hebrews whose traditions (Exodus 1:11-12) say that it was precisely these places (excavated by Flinders Petrie in 1935-1936) which were built at the cost of affliction and heavy burden. Here the Hebrews made brick, felt

the whips of taskmasters, schemed to survive, and bided their time.

7. CANAAN ON THE EVE OF THE HEBREW SETTLEMENT

While the Hebrews languished, Egypt solidified its position in Syria and Palestine. For almost four hundred years, from the emergence of the glorious Eighteenth Dynasty (*ca.* 1570 B.C.) to the disastrous decline of the once-mighty Nineteenth Dynasty (*ca.* 1200 B.C.), Egyptians were virtually unchallenged as they organized their imperial territories, collected taxes and bribes, and grew more powerful as a nation and richer as individuals. Archaeological excavations at various Syrian and Palestinian sites have not surprisingly revealed a greatly increased number of Egyptian artifacts. At the same time they have shown that the native Canaanite culture continued an undisturbed development. Indeed, it not only continued without major outside cultural interference, but reached its zenith particularly in the Phoenician ports of the Syrian coast.

This was due in part to Egyptian colonial policy. Whenever possible they did not disturb local institutions. No attempt was made to "egyptianize" the area. On the contrary, the Egyptians wisely understood as did the Romans after them that the more "native" a locality remained the less likely it was to cause trouble. As a result only two major administrative centers were established, one at Gaza in the south and the other at Joppa on the north-central coast. Military posts were restricted to the more strategic locations, such as Beth-shan where excavators have uncovered an Egyptian fortress whose use spanned almost all this period. Local princes, addressed as "king" by their Canaanite subjects, were allowed not only to remain in power but to retain their feudal rights including that to war upon one another which they frequently did.

[2] In the eleventh century B.C. its name was changed to Tanis. It is known to Numbers 13:22 as Zoan.

All this and a good deal more we know through the chance find at Tell el-Amarna of over 350 letters from the Royal Egyptian Archives. Archaeology must for the most part be content to tell a kind of faceless story. Cultural and technical history are its usual domain. But the recovery of ancient documents adds interest, details, sometimes names and dates, always flesh to the bare bones of history written by spade and trowel. Never was this more true than in the contribution of the Amarna Letters. The darkness of an almost entire era was swept away by their contents. Fourteenth-century B.C. Palestine has come alive before our very eyes. It

Below is one of the Amarna Letters.

Cairo Museum

Amenophis IV, his queen Nefertiti, and their children in a family grouping. This kind of informality is rarely associated with the pharaoh in ancient Egyptian art.

breathes of intrigue, charge, countercharge, and of splendor and squalor.

A large number of tablets were found in 1887 at Amarna (ancient Akhet-aton), Egypt. They were discovered by a peasant woman and recovered by other people of the village who sold them piece by piece. Bought by many private collectors and museums, they made their way to various parts of the world, the largest collection ending up in the Berlin Museum. In addition to over 350 tablets in the original find, some nineteen more have been unearthed at Amarna by professional archaeologists.

When scholars were finally able to read all these letters they were astonished to learn that they were from the royal archives of Amenophis III (ca. 1406-1390 B.C.) and his more famous son, Amenophis IV (ca. 1370-1353 B.C.). One letter may have been addressed to Tutankhamen, the youth who succeeded Smenkhkare (Amenophis' son-in-law) on the throne. Amenophis IV is better known as Akhet-aton. He worshiped the solar disk as the only true god and was perhaps the first monotheist. In the fifth year of his reign this religious monarch moved his capital from Thebes to Amarna in order to escape the power of the priests of the old state religion. There he ruled and worshiped in peace with his queen, Nefertiti, whose painted limestone bust recovered from the ruins of their ancient capital remains one of the artistic wonders of the world. In the fourth year of the reign of Tutankhamen, the generals and the priests, rightly sensing that Akhet-aton's overwhelming concern for religion had proved a disaster for Egypt's empire, forced the boy-king and his court to Thebes where they could exercise control. But for some reason not all archives were removed from Amarna.

One hundred and fifty of these letters were written to or from Palestine. These and similar documents found in Palestine at Tell el-Hesi, Gezer, Jericho, Shechem, Taanach, Megiddo, and Hazor show us the political and social conditions of the day. It was an ethnically mixed society, as we have seen from other sources, and had a severe stratification with a few rich and many poor. This stratification is confirmed by excavations in Palestine where some large, well-built patrician houses were found among the

The famous Gezer high place (below) consists of *massebot* unique for their size. This shrine is very different from the equally well-known Megiddo high place (see p. 52).

many hovels of the poor. From indications in the Amarna Letters it would seem that the non-Semitic "foreign" elements, such as the Hurrians, were generally better off than the Canaanites whose names are for the most part conspicuously missing from the royal correspondence. Interest in the Canaanite masses is restricted mainly to their ready availability as *corvée*, press labor gangs.

The feudal character of the society is underlined by the almost constant state of warfare which seemed to have been carried on by one prince against another. It was important for each of these warring princes—all subjects of the pharaoh—to keep his relations with Egypt proper and unquestioned. It was also helpful if one could impugn the loyalty of one's enemies. The Amarna Letters are full of such attempts. The bulk of the correspondence is given over to accusations of disloyalty to the pharaoh on the one hand, and professions of fealty on the other. These confessions of allegiance are often so groveling that one suspects some charges of political infidelity to have been true. The complexity and absurdity of this situation in which rulers were both independent and bound is shown time and time again. For example, in at least one letter, that from Tell el-Hesi, it is an Egyptian officer who accuses

the prince of Lachish of being traitorous. Yet so involved were the intrigues of the times that it seems this officer himself stood charged with the same offense!

At least three other important matters consistently appear in this correspondence. The first is the heavy financial burdens under which the population struggled. Taxes were high and ever present. Requirements for press labor gangs were insistent and heartbreaking for men and families. In addition to these continuous demands it was frequently necessary to supply food, clothing, and shelter for Egyptian soldiers moving back and forth between Egypt and Syria.

These various demands were difficult enough in themselves for the princes and the people to meet. Yet to them were added the "requirements" of some of the Egyptian commissioners, particularly the military officers. Milkilu of Gezer writes that Iankhuamu, a commissioner, has demanded two or three thousand shekels from him. To guarantee payment Iankhuamu has taken Milkilu's wife and children as hostage. Also from Gezer but somewhat later, a certain Ba'lushipti complains that a minor Egyptian official at Joppa, Pe'eya, has used a press labor gang from Gezer for his personal projects. Not only so, but now he refuses to allow the men to return home unless he is paid one hundred shekels per man. Ba'lushipti points out to the pharaoh that even bandits in the hills required only thirty shekels as ransom for a man.

The second matter of concern to the princes was the behavior of the Egyptian garrisons. Generally these were composed of Egyptian soldiers and Nubian archers (African Negroes known to the Bible as "Cushites") in fairly equal numbers. Although the Syrian and Palestinian princes repeatedly requested the presence of troops as protection against the marauders (Hapiru), they made it clear that these soldiers needed to be kept under strict control. Probably as a result of official corruption the garrisons were not always given their rations and their pay. In such circumstances they resorted to robbery, terrorism, and other such acts against the local population. Even the princes themselves were not always safe. 'Abdi-Kheba of Jerusalem, while asking for more soldiers, notes that on one occasion plundering Nubians broke into his palace and almost killed him.

The reason for desiring the often troublesome troops was the large and rapidly increasing numbers of Hapiru in the area. The Hapiru are the third consistent concern in the Amarna correspondence.

Some time ago it was fashionable to equate these people with the biblical Hebrews and to see in the Amarna Letters evidence of the Hebrew invasion of Canaan. This equation is no longer possible. First, other archaeological evidence shows it is still at least a century too early for the Hebrew incursion. Second, while the question of the Hapiru is still complex, archaeologically recovered documents now indicate that they were an ethnically mixed group, speaking several different languages, but bound together by their occupation: brigandage. While there may have been Hebrews among them, they were not the Hebrews nor were they even nomads. Their name Hapiru may originally have meant "tramp," "dusty one," or perhaps "wanderer," but it came to designate a "robber," a "bandit." These were stateless persons, a fourth class in a highly stratified society. They lived by stealing, smuggling, and increasingly by raiding and destroying settled areas. Eventually they became a threat even to the cities. Over and over again in the Amarna Letters princes accuse one another of being allied with these outlaws. Indeed, in some cases the very word "Hapiru" seems used as a term of abuse.

Hapiru were not confined to Syria and Palestine nor did they appear only in the fifteenth and fourteenth centuries. The eighteenth-century Mari Letters mention them. They are also known from sixteenth-century Hittite documents to have been as far north as Asia Minor. But thanks to the Amarna materials we get our best glimpse of them in Palestine. One specific example will have to suffice. Labaya ("the lion man"), unlike most Hapiru, is mentioned by name. Apparently this chieftain, operating from Shechem, had gained virtual control over much of central Palestine during the first part of the reign of Amenophis IV. So strong was he that some princes had in fact allied themselves with him for their own safety, not to mention whatever profit it might bring to them. Shuwardata of the southern highlands writes to the pharaoh: "The chief of the Hapiru has taken arms against the lands which the god of my king, my lord, gave me, but your servant has struck him down. Also let the king, my lord, know that all my brothers have abandoned me and that it is I and 'Abdi-Kheba (of Jerusalem) who fight the chief of the Hapiru. Zurata, chief of Accho, and Endaruta, chief of Achshaph, agreed to come to my aid in return for fifty chariots —they cheated me!—and now they are fighting against me." The land in question was that held or threatened by "the lion man." Indeed, not much later another letter names Labaya by name and indicates that the traitor Zurata is indeed his ally. Clearly Shuwardata's claim to have "struck down" Labaya was a bit premature.

From Amarna come intimate views of various aspects of life in Palestine toward the end of the Eighteenth Dynasty. Egypt's Asiatic empire was deteriorating. This process of decay, already well established by the end of the reign of Amenophis III, increased rapidly as Akhen-aton turned his eyes toward the heavens and left the earth and its kingdoms to sort themselves out. The major victim of all this was the Eighteenth Dynasty itself. Haremhab, a general supported by the powerful priests, seized the

throne (reigned *ca.* 1340-1309 B.C.) and by wisdom, energy, and sheer force sought to reverse Egypt's sinking fortunes. Although he was not able to pass the crown to a son, he did succeed in his major purpose. The downward trend was halted. Sethos I (*ca.* 1309-1290 B.C.), the founder of the Nineteenth Dynasty, and his illustrious son Ramses II (*ca.* 1290-1224 B.C.) sat upon the most glorious throne the ancient world ever saw. We should remind ourselves that this was the time of Hebrew bondage, and that Ramses II was probably the pharaoh of the Exodus.

The Amarna period was then but a brief pause in the New Kingdom, Egypt's most splendid moment in history. Yet the conditions revealed by this correspondence resulted only partly from Egypt's momentary decline. The structure itself, unlike Roman provincial administration, did not have built-in safeguards to prevent demoralization of the conquered peoples and deterioration of political control. Heavy taxation coupled with rampant extortion and bribery, constant warfare among the princes, and marauding brigands hardly made for stable conditions or good morale among the general populace. It is little wonder that after almost four centuries of Egyptian rule the peoples of Palestine were both unwilling and unable to resist various invaders who fell upon them from almost every direction.

Ugarit and Its Religious Drama

Farther north Canaanite cities along the Syrian coast were plagued with many of the same difficulties that beset Palestinian cities. We have previously noted that these cities were fortified against the land and that at certain periods their princes practically besieged the pharaoh with requests for infantry and chariots. Yet in many ways these places were very different from the urban centers in Palestine. While most city sites were chosen because of their proximity to fertile soil and pasture, the coastal settlements were founded chiefly for commercial ends. Their life was the sea. As early as the seventeenth century B.C. they were equally at home on the Mediterranean and the Aegean. By the time the Israelties came into contact with these people, the word *Canaanite* had become synonymous with "merchant."

Unlike the Palestinian princes, the king-priests of Phoenicia did not war upon one another. There was rivalry, intense and deadly serious rivalry, particularly between Tyre and Sidon. But diplomacy was the watchword. There is no recorded attempt at aggrandizement by means of intercity warfare. So long as the seas were open, life was fairly secure. When the somewhat small cities became crowded there was no aggressive movement inland. Colonies were founded and commercial links spread and strengthened. Moreover, it was in the interest of other powers to see that these Syrian channels of trade were kept relatively unclogged. Only once, during the general upheavals of the late thirteenth and twelfth centuries, did Phoenician commercial traffic cease.

Trade, stability, and peace brought with them the development of the artistic skills. For the first time in many centuries there were goldsmiths whose craftsmanship rivaled that of ancient Ur. Carved Syrian ivories were renowned throughout the Mediterranean basin. Their embroideries were the accepted standard of excellence. Architects perfected basic designs which became normative over much of the region. When the Temple of the Hebrew God was erected in Jerusalem, Solomon employed Phoenician Canaanites who designed and built what was basically a Phoenician type of sanctuary. The same was true of King Omri of Israel; when he sought the finest workmanship available he too turned northward. The ruins of his city and royal palace at Samaria show unmistakable Phoenician craftsmanship including some of the finest carved ivories yet unearthed.

In these mercantile cities at the heart of Canaanite culture, writing developed and literature flourished. In one of these cities, Ugarit (modern Ras Shamra), was discovered in April of 1928 one of the most important archaeological finds yet known for the light it sheds upon the Old Testament. As a farmer tilled his field the plough struck what proved to be an ancient tomb. Upon finding that local villagers had come across other objects from time to time, French scholars from Beirut and Paris determined to undertake a full-scale inquiry. Early in April 1929, excavations began. Almost· at once pottery, statuettes, and other artifacts came to light. More tombs were discovered. On May 20 the first group of tablets with alphabetic cuneiform writing appeared. Unearthing written documents is a matter of considerable pleasure to an archaeologist, and May 20, 1929 must have seemed a particularly profitable day to those men as they retired for the night. Little did they know what future days would bring. For ten years they continued to recover administrative, literary, and ritual texts! In addition to royal archives found in the palace of Ugarit, the excavators were fortunate enough to come down upon an ancient library containing hundreds of tablets in addition to a scribal school.

Among these writings were the sort of things one might expect to find in a commercial, cosmopolitan city. There is an abundance of business letters and records, many of them dealing with the purchase and shipment of the renowned purple of the area. Private letters, military dispatches, lists of offerings made at the temples, and even a veterinary prescription for curing horses were discovered. The so-called "foreign office" of the palace yielded voluminous diplomatic correspondence still in the neat geographical order by means of which it had originally been organized. Shortly after excavations began in 1950, a tablet (also found in the palace) indicated that while the shrewd inhabitants of Ugarit may have had their feet firmly planted on the earth, their eyes were also upon the heavens. An omen text notes the movement of the stars and shows these people to have been keen observers of the astral bodies.

More important for our purposes, however, are those writings from the temple scribal school and those having to do with civil administration. The school served to teach writing and as a center for copying and preserving the ancient and sacred texts. The cuneiform "ABC" tablet found here contains the oldest known listing of the letters of the alphabet in order. This thirty-letter alphabet corresponds closely to the Hebrew alphabet and, when taken in conjunction with other discoveries at Ugarit, may yet furnish the clue to a relation between Hebrew and Indo-Aryan languages. The religious epics, of which more will be said shortly, yield significant information regarding the Canaanite religion encountered by the biblical Hebrews.

The administrative texts likewise illumine biblical practices. From them we learn that, while the tribal basis of the social order was still discernible administratively, the population was divided along territorial and class lines. This is reminiscent of a tactic employed by Solomon in his successful attempt to reduce the power of the tribal leaders in Israel (I Kings 4:7-19). It has been further suggested that Solomon's use of forced labor (I Kings 5:13; 9:15; 11:28; and others) was likewise a reflection of a Ugaritic practice of allowing taxes to be paid in labor as well as in silver or produce.

The religious writings from Ugarit are major Canaanite literary works. The epics found at Ugarit had been edited and reworked for at least four centuries prior to the destruction of the city in the late 1200s B.C. How much older the oral tradition underlying them may be we cannot say on the basis of currently available materials. But analogies from other literatures of the ancient Middle East suggest that the tradition embodied in these epics is very old indeed. It is the view of many that this tradition with local and national variations was common to the entire ancient East and is even a possible ancestor of much of Greek mythology.

The basic story of this tradition concerns the struggle of the forces of life with those of death. To men of that day so completely dependent upon flocks and fields, this involved not merely the personal bodily functions but other processes of nature as well. The prompt and not too violent presence of the autumn rain at the beginning of the growing season, and the beneficial downpour of the spring (the "early and late rains" of the Bible, see Deuteronomy 11:14; James 5:7; and others) were literally a matter of life-and-death. The same was true of the continued fertility of the flocks. Last but by no means least, barrenness in a wife was a disaster against which special arrangements had to be made (see, for comparison, Genesis 6:1-18:15; 21:1-7). The various forces having to do with the continuance of life in flocks, fields, and family and with those things that threatened existence, were personified as gods and goddesses. Through religious ritual and epics accompanying it the worshiper reenacted and participated in the struggles of the gods, for these were in fact his own struggles for life.

From the white hills surrounding the harbor at Ugarit we have learned in detail about the influential Canaanite version of this old, old story. The chief actor in the Canaanite drama is Baal, "the Lord." Baal, familiar to even the casual reader of the Old Testament, was apparently neither High God nor Creator. This position and function belonged to El, king of the gods. Yet El, in the Ugarit epics at least, is a static figure offering advice and consent and receiving respect from the other gods. He is otherwise uninvolved, above the struggles. Baal, on the other hand, is a dynamic force representing the orderly progression of the seasonal cycles of nature.

Two major themes concerning Baal are developed in the Ugaritic materials. One is his struggles against "Sea the Prince and River the Ruler," and the other is his battle with Mot. Sea (also known as the Dragon, Yam) and River are unruly and uncontrollable waters which bring chaos in their wake. With insolence and arrogance the renegade waters defy the assembly of the gods, but none will answer their challenge. In sober silence the assembly cowers before these forces of destruction. Then Baal, the god of the clouds who dwells upon the sacred mountain of the north, comes forth as the champion who will join combat with Sea and River.

> Wherefore, O gods on your princely thrones,
> (says Baal)
> have you bowed your heads upon your knees?
> Do I see gods being cowed with terror
> before the messengers of Sir Sea,
> the delegation of the Ruler of the Streams?
> O gods on your princely thrones,
> raise your heads from your knees,
> Verily, I will cow those messengers of Sir
> Sea,
> that delegation of the Ruler of the
> Streams! [1]

Koshar, the divine craftsman, presenting Baal with magic weapons for the ensuing combat, salutes him in language reminiscent of the Psalms (see, for example, Psalms 92:9; 146:10):

> Then up spake the Skilful and Percipient
> One
> "Have I not told thee, O Prince Baal,
> Have I not repeated, O thou who mountest
> the clouds?
> Behold, thine enemy, O Baal,
> Behold, thine enemy thou shalt smite:
> Behold, thou shalt subdue thine adversaries.

[1] Theodore H. Gaster, trans., *Thespis* (Garden City, N. Y.: Doubleday & Co., 1961), p. 157.

> Thou shalt take thine eternal kingdom,
> Thy sovereignty everlasting." [2]

After a furious fight, Sea and his allied forces are subdued by Baal who is proclaimed Lord by his vanquished foes. The aftermath of victory is not sweet, however. Baal unfortunately finds himself an object of jealously particularly on the part of some of the goddesses. Certain that a place heralding his powers and befitting his status will bring him the respect he has earned, Baal sets about to secure El's blessing upon his plans to build such a place. Asherah, mistress of the gods, implores El on Baal's behalf. Content that he himself will not have to do the manual labor, El consents to the building of the palace. Designed and constructed by the divine craftsman, the palace of gold and silver containing the finest cedars of Lebanon is ready for Baal who inaugurates it by serving a banquet for the other gods. All now seem orderly and secure. In the midst of his banquet Baal makes a tour to enlarge and consolidate his kingdom and to assure adequate and controlled rainfall for its prosperity. "The windows of heaven," under the watchful eye of this conquering hero, will open beneficently at his command. The gods praise their victorious champion as order triumphs over chaos.

In this happy moment a new and more sinister danger presents itself. The unruly waters have been contained, but what of the other side of the matter? Drought, an ever-possible calamity, lurks with the coming of each new season. In his moment of glory Baal speaks of his desire to overcome Mot, the god of drought, sterility, and death:

> I shall indeed send a guide for the god
> Mot,
> A herald for the Hero, beloved of El
> To call Mot to his grave.
> To conceal that "darling" in his tomb.

[2] John Gray, trans., *The Legacy of Canaan* (New York: Humanities Press, 1967), p. 26.

I alone am he who will reign over the
   gods,
Yea, be leader of the gods and men,
Even marshall the multitudes of earth.[3]

Vineyard and Field, present signs of the power of Baal, are sent to Mot, but with the caution that they take care not to fall prey to him. It is their task to banish Mot to the underworld, the abode of the dead. There and there alone he may be powerful. Cunningly Mot, barred from the banquet at Baal's palace, invites Baal to his table in the underworld. In his invitation Mot complains of his unending thirst occasioned by the summer drought which is his dominion while at the same time speaking of the bounty of Baal:

One lip to earth, one lip to heaven,
And the tongue to the stars
That Baal may go into his inside,
Yea go down into his mouth,
As the choicest of olive oil which the
   earth produces
Even as the fruit of the trees.[4]

These are subtle words indicating that at the height of Baal's power (the time of the maturing of the fruit) the death of Baal is already in sight. This message is not lost upon Baal who instantly sees his dilemma. As the champion of the gods he cannot refuse the invitation. Yet if he goes he passes into the power of drought and death. In terror he tries to appease Mot and get out of the invitation. Mot replies mockingly reminding Baal of his claims to power. Again Baal tries vainly to bribe and appease Mot. Realizing that he already has Baal in his power, Mot presses his invitation with increasing boldness and arrogance. Leaving his powers of fertility with a bull and equipped with his full insignia of office, Baal descends to the underworld. The seasons change as the fer-

tile green fields give way to the burnt brown of summer. Baal is buried as the gods mourn.

Now the third act of the drama opens. Baal, in the snares of Mot, no longer brings the rains and fertility. Is Mot to conquer all? In the presence of El the goddesses bitterly accuse one another of jealous motives in refusing to support Baal. At last El appoints Ashtar to occupy the empty throne. Unfortunately for all, this ruler is not able to exercise the needed power. Anath, Baal's lover, sister, and virgin consort, takes matters into her own hands. She determines to find Baal, rescue him from the power of Mot, and restore him to his rightful sovereignty. At length Anath encounters Mot and pleads for the return and restoration of her beloved:

As the heart of the cow after her calf
As the heart of the ewe after her lamb,
So the heart of Anath yearns after Baal.
She seizes Mot by the hem of his clothing,
She restrains him by the border of his
   mantle;
She raises her voice and cries:
"Thou Mot give me my brother."[5]

Mot, in the fullness of his glory and strength, refuses. Eventually Anath withdraws. After several months she again seeks out the vicious Mot. But this time she has come neither with meek supplication nor with stern demand. Anath savagely attacks Mot, flaying at him with her sword until ripped apart he is scattered. The power of drought is broken, but not entirely defeated.

Now comes the final act of drama. In a dream El sees the return of fertility as "the heavens rain down fatness, and the streams flow with honey." He realizes that Baal is not dead. Summoning the sun-goddess who surveys the earth every day he instructs her to search for Baal so that the dry springs may bubble again and the land may be cul-

[3] *The Legacy of Canaan*, p. 54.
[4] *Ibid.*, p. 58.

[5] *Ibid.*, p. 67.

tivated. Meanwhile, Baal is restored. He gives battle to Mot and to various other enemies. It is a furious engagement with first one and then the other seeming to have the upper hand. The sun-goddess coming upon the commotion intervenes. She threatens to make El remove from Mot even his dominion over the underworld if he persists in his challenge to Baal. Terror-stricken at the thought of El's siding with Baal, Mot allows fertility and life to return to the land as he retires from battle. Baal rewards the sun-goddess by permitting her to drink his refreshing rains as together they bring peace and abundance.

Baal, regnant once more, gives an immense banquet. Not only his friends, but many of his former enemies are guests at the meal whose size and lavishness startle even the gods. Anath seizes the opportunity. She closes the palace gates and falls murderously upon her brother's foes. Reveling in slaughter she wades in blood. Baal, however, is in a mood for generosity and orders his sister to cease her vengeance. It is a time for peace, not struggle. Cleansing herself in the blood and gore of the fallen, and in "the dew of heaven, the oil of earth, and in the shower which the clouds rain down," Anath returns to the banquet table as fertility, peace, and joy are found again in the land.

The order of events in this Canaanite seasonal, fertility drama is not entirely certain and the story has been greatly simplified here. But the main thrust is clear enough. We should remind ourselves that this was not merely a story passed on from generation to generation for entertainment or literary purposes. It is the essence of religious drama and was connected with the sacred ritual of the agricultural year. Its tensions reflect the emotions and hopes of the Syrian-Palestinian peasant as he anxiously watched the skies for evidences of the autumn ("early") rains. Without these rains there could be no cultivation; drought and death were then clear prospects. The spring ("late") rains, too, were likewise a time of crisis. If they were not on time the searing winds of the desert would sweep through the grain fields with disastrous results. The ritual epic of Baal's struggle with Sea and River was probably associated with the New Year Festival which came at the beginning of the autumn agricultural festival. It expresses both the hope and the confidence that in Baal's triumph order would be maintained and the frequently heavy rains would not result in serious damage through soil erosion. The epics depicting Baal in his struggles with Mot are likewise connected with the seasonal ritual and were perhaps celebrated just prior to the harvest. Be that as it may, they were solemnly and sacredly acted out at some point late in the growing season to insure the fertility of the worshiper and of his flocks and crops. The prominent role of Anath, the virgin mistress of Baal, is typical of the widespread fertility cults of the ancient Middle East. She and others like her are known to the Bible where again she represents the fierce, constant struggle of fertility with sterility.

In the Bible "struggle" normally has a different connotation, a moral thrust. To "fight the good fight" is to contend for righteousness; it is to insure justice, to protect the widow and the orphan, and to be upright in one's dealings with one's neighbors. It has often and widely been said that the religion represented by the Ugaritic materials lacked such emphases, and was immoral or at best amoral. It is true that the Baal epics have little speculative or moral concern. They are intensely functional in that they involve the worshiper intimately with the powers and processes of nature. Yet it would be wrong to say that they represent the totality of Canaanite thought. In other epics found at Ugarit, particularly those dealing with the legendary kings, Dan'el and Keret, there are passages reflecting a Canaanite concern for morals, and the royal archives at Ugarit show how the city's rulers were charged with judicial responsibility. Furthermore, a citizen was expected to uphold justice. It is only when the horizon of morality is reduced to sexuality that one fails to appreciate Canaanite ethics. A single example of Ugaritic concern with justice will suffice here and will remind us of similar words in the Old Testament. It was said of Dan'el that

He rises to sit at the entrance of the gate
in the place of the notables who are in the
   public place;
He decides the case of the widow;
He judges the suit of the orphan.[6]

Moreover, while no legal code even remotely resembling the Code of Hammurabi or any of the great biblical codes has yet come to light at Ugarit, there are a number of legal texts. These, dealing with such matters as marriage contracts, deeds of sale and adoption, trusteeships, and slavery, seem to refer to an objective legal tradition. Such a tradition, if it did exist, has yet to be established. What is clear is the feudal nature of the society to which these laws applied. The king also seems to have been able to issue absolute royal decrees.

Furthermore, the thought of the Canaanites was but a local variation of a more general pattern of the ancient Middle Eastern manner of dealing with reality. The epics telling of Baal's conflict with forces of chaos strongly resemble in outline and various details the *Enuma elish* epic so fundamental to Mesopotamian thought. *Enuma elish*, in a late Babylonian version in which we have it, speaks of the warfare of Marduk (Order) with Tiamat (Chaos of the Unruly Waters). It includes scenes of a cowered divine assembly, a bloody goddess, and other scenes and figures similar to the Baal epics from Ugarit. It is to be noted, however, that along with *Enuma elish* the Babylonians had the Code of

Hammurabi whose spirit and even specific laws are thought by many to have influenced the law codes of the Old Testament.

Still Canaanite religion seems to have laid greater stress upon fertility than any other of its time and area. This may be partly explained by the acute tension of peasants entirely dependent upon capricious rains. In fertile Mesopotamia nourished by two mighty rivers, and in Egypt fertilized by the regular and dependable overflow of the Nile, the situation was somewhat different. Fertility of the soil and adequacy of water could more or less be taken for granted. This was more true in Egypt than in Mesopotamia, but in either case the land was qualitatively vastly superior to Syria-Palestine.

Worship of Baal in Palestine

It was in Syria-Palestine that the worship of Baal with its accompanying fertility cult flourished. This type of religion was apparently coextensive with the Canaanite culture described earlier. Evidence of its widespread and persistent existence is abundant and comes from a variety of sources. The most common proof of its presence is the numerous statues and figurines of the Canaanite gods and goddesses. These have been unearthed in abundance at almost every Syrian and Palestinian site with Late Bronze Age ruins. Many are also found in Palestinian

Two fertility plaques from the Iron Age (Israelite) strata at Ai. This type of plaque is commonly found in Late Bronze strata and not unusual in Iron Age materials.

[6] *Ibid.*, p. 107.

Iron Age remains indicating that this worship continued well into the Israelite period.

Such representations of gods and goddesses are by no means as massive as their Egyptian and Mesopotamian counterparts. They are, in fact, quite small and can usually be held with ease in one hand. Generally of two types, they show either Baal himself or a goddess, possibly Asherah. One of the finest figures of Baal comes from Ugarit itself. A limestone stele depicts him standing with a mace in his right hand as his left hand strikes downward with a spear. The end of the spear appears to have flames coming from it. Undoubtedly this is Baal in his most characteristic role as the winter rain god, or "the thunderer who mounts the clouds." Equally fine statues of Baal have been found in Palestine at Lachish and at Megiddo. The latter is a gold-covered, seated god wearing the conical hat typical of Baal. Often the hat has horns symbolizing the association of the bull as cultic animal of worship.

Fertility goddesses are represented by a vast number of figurines most of which were apparently for household use. In this regard they may have been similar to the teraphim of the Old Testament. Many functions have been suggested for these small clay figures usually found on plaques. It has been said that some may have been magical charms to aid women in childbirth. This is quite possible. It has also been said that they were merely children's playthings. This is hardly credible. One would not likely give a figure of a nude woman with exaggerated sexual organs to a child as a toy. Probably all or almost all these figurines and plaques were images of the mother goddess, a personification of the mysterious forces of fertility upon which human existence depended.

It is not usual to find images associated with Canaanite shrines, although the Baal statues from Ugarit and Megiddo were found in temple settings. Tanaach, too, may provide an exception. Eighty-three figurines

Louvre

A limestone stele from Ugarit showing "Baal of the lightning."

were found at this site in the 1963 and 1966 excavations. Over half of these were the ordinary nude female with hands supporting the breasts. But one of the figurine objects was extremely rare. It was a mold for casting statues.[7] Some seven inches tall the goddess from this mold, naked and apparently pregnant, is holding a round object over her left

[7] A similar mold has been uncovered at Nahariyah. Excavators of that site claim it was used to cast statuettes of the goddess to whom the temple must have been dedicated.

A fertility figurine made from a mold found at Taanach. The room in which the mold was found was Iron Age, but the excavators think that the mold is older than the surroundings in which it was found.

breast. Mesopotamian parallels suggest this object is a tambourine which may indicate something of the musical cultic practices associated with this goddess. At Megiddo, well within sight of Tanaach, a figurine has been found which evidently came from this very mold. This discovery was made in a cultic area at Megiddo. Likely this type of figurine, unlike the more ordinary plaque type, was associated with shrines. The excavators of Tanaach speculate that it was produced in the cultic area there. But what was its function? Was it required for worship? Was it to be carried home for further veneration in the same manner as souvenir crosses were done in the Middle Ages of the Christian Era? Was it an idol become amulet? We do not know. Yet for our immediate purpose it provides another and very interesting piece of evidence for the solid presence of fertility cults in Canaanite Palestine.

Further kinds of evidence can be summarized briefly. Numerous *massebot* (sacred pillars of stone) have been found in Palestinian Canaanite shrines. These and the *asherim* so hated by writers of the Old Testament were religious objects, but apparently not images. Their presence may explain the relative lack of images in the places of worship. Perhaps they were sufficient to remind the people of the presence and active powers of the deities. In passing mention should be made of the extraordinary *massebot* found in the shrine at Hazor. This discovery is similar to and rivals the *massebot* of the Temple of Dagon (also dedicated to Baal) at Ugarit. At Hazor the thirteenth-century B.C. *massebot* shrine was found more or less intact. It contains rows of small basalt stelae with rounded tops. The central one bears a bas-relief of two hands stretched upward in adoration of an emblem of the sun-god. Hard by these stones is a basalt statue of a seated male figure, perhaps a god. At some point the head of this statue was broken off, perhaps deliberately, and thrown on the floor.

Nearby a storeroom was found containing a number of sacred stones similar to those in the shrine, some of which are unfinished. This sanctuary is unique in Palestine, and Y. Yadin, its excavator, has speculated that it is perhaps the only one known in the Holy Land which represents the *massebot* mentioned in the Old Testament.

In addition to images, sacred pillars, and poles there are a number of Palestinian place-names which were compounded of the name of Anath, the most active goddess of the fertility cult. Perhaps Beth Anath (Joshua 19:38), Beth Anoth (Joshua 15:29), and even Anathoth the home of Jeremiah (Jeremiah 1:1) were cultic centers dedicated to this goddess.

Considerable other materials including inscribed plaques attest to the presence and deep attachment of the Baal cult in Palestine. These could be mentioned. But the point has been made. In addition, more will be said about Canaanite religion in Chapter Nine where we shall see it in conflict with Hebrew religion. For that reason I have not mentioned here the voluminous witness of the Old Testament to the tenacity of fertility cults in Canaanite and Israelite Palestine.

A relatively rare statue of Baal from Ugarit (above) shows him with his typical gold conical hat and his hand upraised to throw a lightning bolt. The purpose of the hinged left arm on the statue is unknown.

IV: CANAANITES AND HEBREWS

8. HEBREWS, PHILISTINES, AND THE SETTLEMENT IN CANAAN

The Exodus is the fountainhead and touchstone of Israel's faith. As the Hebrews looked back upon the darkness of their Egyptian bondage they remembered the cruelty of their taskmasters and the groanings of their brothers. They recalled, too, the rising splendor of the cities on which they labored: glory bespeaking the might of Egypt, while they were but shepherds with neither power nor advocate. Yet the Lord God sent them a deliverer. Moses spoke. They obeyed. The waters loomed before them, parted, and closed again as the pharaoh's soldiers screamed in terror and gasped for breath. The voices of the Hebrew women bore a different sound:

> I will sing to the Lord, for he has
>   triumphed gloriously;
> the horse and his rider he has
>   thrown into the sea.
> The Lord is my strength and my song,
>   and he has become my salvation;

> this is my God, and I will praise him,
>   my father's God, and I will exalt him.
> The Lord is a man of war;
>   the Lord is his name.

> Pharaoh's chariots and his host he
>   cast into the sea;
> and his picked officers are sunk in
>   the Red Sea.
> The floods cover them;
>   they went down into the depths
>   like a stone.
> Thy right hand, O Lord, glorious
>   in power,
>   thy right hand, O Lord, shatters
>   the enemy.
>
> Exodus 15:1-6

The glorious victory of the Lord who has brought life and hope out of the jaws of despair and death—this is what the Hebrews understood the Exodus to be, and this is what they recited over and over again in their memories and their worship. "A wandering Aramean was my father," said the Hebrew as he approached the altar with the first fruits of his land laid across his hands, "and he went down into Egypt and sojourned there, few in numbers; and there he became a nation, great, mighty, and populous. And the Egyptians treated us harshly. . . . Then we cried to the Lord the God of our fathers, and the Lord heard our voice. . . ." (Deuteronomy 26:5-7). Remember, says the preface to the Ten Commandments, "I am the Lord your God, who brought you out of the land of Egypt, out of the house of bondage" (Exodus 20:2; Deuteronomy 5:6). Even today the Exodus theme remains at the heart of Jewish and Christian thought and ritual. The central festival of Judaism is the Passover, for which the Haggadah begins: "Why is this night different from all other nights?" The answer of the father opens: "Slaves were we to pharaoh in Egypt. . . ." In the Christian sacraments of baptism and the Supper there are also overtones of the Exodus theme. In passing through the waters and into newness of life the Christians, like the Hebrews of old, confess that God has acted to redeem the hopeless and to bring life out of death. In these and other ways Exodus memories have served as constant reminders to God's people that the meaning of their community and the basis of their responsibility lie in the fact that they have been redeemed from slavery.

This most glorious moment in the Old Testament, this Exodus with such influence over the whole of Hebrew and Christian history and thought, is unfortunately lacking in extra-biblical confirmation. Yet there is no reason to doubt the substantial historical kernel of the biblical tradition in spite of its having undergone considerable theological elaboration. A people would hardly invent an account of their slavery. Nor should we expect any non-Hebrew contemporary documents to have referred to such an event. It was of little or no importance to anyone else.

We do not even know when the Exodus took place. There are two main theories concerning its date. One places it during the reign of Thutmoses III (*ca.* 1490—1435 B.C.) or perhaps that of Amenophis III (*ca.* 1406—1370 B.C.). This view identifies the Hebrews under Joshua with the Hapiru mentioned in the Amarna Letters. We have already noted several reasons to doubt whether this is a correct identification (see p. 72). Further arguments to support this earlier date also have weaknesses. Recent excavations at Jericho, for example, have shown that severe erosion has removed almost all the fourteenth century and later remains from the site. This means that Garstang's earlier contention of archaeological evidence of possible destruction by Joshua was incorrect. Indeed, what he understood as Late Bronze Age walls have now been shown to be from the Early Bronze period. Jericho, as the ruins now exist, is of importance for its illumination of Canaanite urban life during patriarchal days and earlier. This does not mean that we need to take the path of skepticism as regards the destruction of Jericho so vividly described in the book of Joshua (Joshua 6). It merely signifies that if there was ever any archaeological witness to this portion of the conquest narrative, it no longer can be recovered.

This narrows support for the earlier dating of the Exodus down to the complex matter of the statement in I Kings 6:1 which says it was 480 years from the Exodus to the fourth year of the reign of Solomon. If Solomon came to the throne about 960 B.C., as is generally agreed, this would place the Exodus in the middle of the fifteenth century. Those who contend against this dating note that forty is widely acknowledged to be used in the Bible as a round number indicating a generation. On this reckoning 480 years is a round number for twelve generations. But a generation is more nearly twenty-five years than forty. Thus if the Bible means to note the passing of twelve generations, then I Kings would place the Exodus in the middle of the thirteenth, not the fifteenth, century. This is a clever suggestion and deserves consideration. Yet it cannot be applied with equal neatness to the figure in Exodus 12:40. This says Israel's sojourn in Egypt lasted 430 years. To be sure this refers to the other end of the matter—to the time when the Hebrews entered Egypt and not when they left. But is this number to be taken literally while that of I Kings is seen as symbolic? Perhaps the answer lies in Genesis 15:13 which indicates that the sojourn was 400 years. If taken as the symbolic number, this would indicate ten generations.

However it is viewed, biblical chronology at this point is extremely difficult. Yet if the 480 years of I Kings 6:1 are taken literally, other problems arise. It then becomes necessary to disregard both the biblical assertion that the Hebrews labored at Pithom and Ramses (Exodus 1:11), and mounting archaeological evidence that points to a date in the thirteenth century. Pithom and Ramses (Tanis, Avaris, Zoan) declined after the expulsion of Hyksos from Egypt. They were rebuilt by Ramses II (ca. 1290—1224 B.C.) when he sought a summer capital and a convenient place from which to govern his Asiatic empire. This has been confirmed by contemporary Egyptian materials and by excavations at these sites. Not only does the book of Exodus speak of the Hebrews laboring to rebuild these cities, but a later Israelite tradition also connects the Exodus with this site (Psalm 78:12, 43). Finally, during the reign of Haremhab (ca. 1340—1310 B.C.) Tanis celebrated its four-hundredth anniversary. Later, when Ramses renamed the city after himself he erected a stele there referring to that anniversary. Numbers 13:22 says that Hebron is seven years older than Tanis. It is hard to resist the assumption that the Hebrews knew of Ramses' stele. In short, there is considerable material in the Bible to connect the darkest days of the bondage—the forced labor—with the building projects of Ramses II in the "land of Goshen," the eastern Delta.

Further evidence also points to the thirteenth century as the more likely time of the Exodus. Numbers 20:14-21 and 21:10-20 tell of the Hebrews' detour around Edom and Moab and of the journey through the breathtaking gorge of the Arnon River to avoid giving offense to the kings of these nations. Is this tradition to be taken historically, or is it to be accounted for in some other manner? If it is seen to be based upon historical memory, then the Transjordanian surface explorations of Nelson Glueck and B. Rothenberg are to be taken into consideration. These two scholars working independently and a number of years apart have shown that the southern and eastern borderlands of Palestine did not have a settled population until near the end of the Late Bronze Age. In short, Edom and Moab did not exist before the thirteenth century B.C.

In 1906 Sir Flinders Petrie found a ten-feet-high by five-feet-wide granite stele from the reign of Amenophis III (ca. 1406—1370 B.C.). The importance of this find, however, lay in the hymns of victory inscribed on its reverse side. These are from the fifth year of the reign of Merneptah (ca. 1220 B.C.) and recorded the successes of Ramses II's son at the expense of his foes. The last stanza of this lyrical poetry exalts over the destruction of enemies in Canaan:

The princes lie prostrate, saying "Salaam!"
    Not one lifts his head among the Nine
    Bows.
Destruction for Tehenu! Hatti is pacified;
    Canaan is plundered with every evil;
Ashkelon is taken; Gezer is captured;
    Yanoam is made non-existent;
Israel lies desolate; its seed is no more;
    Hurru has become a widow for To-meri;
All the lands in their entirety are at peace,
    Everyone who was a nomad has been curbed
    by King Merneptah.

This is the earliest known written reference to Israel and requires Hebrew presence in Canaan no later than 1220 B.C. It

85

refers to Israel as a people and not a nation. This agrees with other evidence concerning the incursion into Canaan of the Hebrews who were a part of the Exodus from Egypt.

Other archaeological discoveries indicating a thirteenth-century dating for the Exodus have to do with the violent destruction of a number of Canaanite cities at this time, for example, Bethel, Lachish, Hazor. Many assume that this was due to a massive incursion into the land, and that it was accompanied by a general lowering of the cultural level in Canaan. Yet the mere destruction of cities is not sufficient grounds upon which to posit the presence of a new group of people. Nor in the almost total absence of new artifact forms is a cultural decline necessarily to be explained by alien incursions.

All the problems have not been solved, and many complexities remain and are likely to do so. Nonetheless, the weight of evidence indicates that the Exodus took place during the early or mid-thirteenth century B.C. The pharaoh of the Exodus was likely Ramses II whose regal mummified corpse keeps its own secrets in the Cairo Museum where it can still be seen today. If this dating is correct the Hebrews left Egypt at the height of the New Kingdom and entered Canaan just as the ancient East plunged into the convulsions that ushered the Late Bronze Age to a close. This time of mass movements of peoples, disappearance of empires, violent unrest, and general chaos has left scanty records. All the greater is the pity for the student of the Bible. This was the time of Moses and the founding of what we know as biblical religion. It was, moreover, the time of the conquest of Canaan, an event of decisive importance not only for the culture of the Hebrews, but also for their religion.

In Palestine the major victims of the unrest were the Canaanites who, over a period of some 2000 years, had inhabited the land and developed there one of the finest civilizations of the ancient world. Their fatal flaw, at the end as always, was an inability to unite and thus to present a common front to various intruders and invaders. In the fourteenth century, though sorely troubled, they were still masters in their own house. Scarcely two centuries later their effective sphere of political and military influence had been reduced to a small area of the Syrian coast dominated by the ports of Tyre, Sidon, Arvad, Berytus, and Byblos. Nonetheless, Canaanite culture and religion were firmly planted in the soil of Palestine and did not suffer the same rapid decline.

Not surprisingly, the cause of this end of Canaanite power in Palestine was the coming of new peoples. To be sure, numerous groups had come on countless occasions before. But the incursions of the thirteenth century were different from earlier ones. For these latter-day invaders, the Hebrews and the Philistines, however deeply affected by the superior culture they found in the land, were intent upon having political control for themselves. By the eleventh century B.C. the hapless Canaanites were more or less spectators as these two new groups fought for supremacy. The Hebrews, as everyone knows, were the eventual victors.

Yet for a very long time, perhaps a century and a half, the Philistines had almost everything their own way. How these people actually came to settle in southwestern Palestine (mainly in and around the area known today as "Gaza") is not entirely clear. They were certainly a part of the "Sea Peoples" who, being driven from their homes in the islands and Asia Minor by the Dorians, attacked others in their search for new homes. They struck inland in Asia Minor making a complete end to the Hittite rule there. The coasts of Syria and Palestine felt their ferocity. Ugarit, that magnificent citadel of trade and learning, was among the victims. Finally they battered upon the gates of Egypt.

The distinctive headdress of these prisoners identifies them as Sea Peoples who failing to invade Egypt withdrew northeast into Gaza and settled there. This scene is from Medinet Habu, the tomb of Ramses III.

The Twentieth Dynasty in the persons of Set-nakht and his son, Ramses III, had just brought to an end thirty-five years of internal confusion in Egypt. An attempt was being made to reassert and strengthen Egyptian influence in Palestine and perhaps even farther north. The fortress at Beth-shan was rebuilt and its temple rededicated, as archaeological work on that site has shown. At Ashkelon, too, was found evidence of expanding Egyptian power under Ramses III. An inscribed box bearing that pharaoh's name tends also to suggest that a temple to the Egyptian god Ptah existed at Ashkelon at this time. Perhaps this is the same temple referred to by a collection of ivories from Megiddo which mention a singer of the god Ptah from Ashkelon.

At this moment of growing strength the Egyptians found the "Sea Peoples" upon them. The course of the various engagements is not clear. Apparently in the fifth year of Ramses III's reign (*ca.* 1170 B.C.) there was a land battle perhaps as far north as Phoenicia. This was followed some time later by an attempted invasion of Egypt itself by land and sea. Without decisive injury to either force this attempt failed. Then, in the eighth year of Ramses' rule, another and greater endeavor was made to settle in the Land of the Nile. At Medinet Habu, Ramses III's magnificent temple at the southern end of the Theban necropolis, the smashing victory of the Egyptians is recorded in vivid reliefs accompanied by triumphal if somewhat stereotyped hymns.

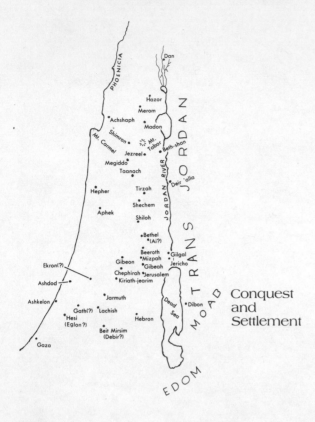

Conquest
and
Settlement

Whatever the arrangements after the battles along the Nile, it is clear that the Philistines occupied the Canaanite cities and territories in southwestern Palestine and exerted independent political control over them. Gaza and Ashkelon, important Egyptian centers, and Ashdod, known from Ugarit writings to have long been an exporter of fabrics, wool, and fish, became seats of Philistine kings. The other strongholds with their own kings were Gath and Ekron. The location of these two cities is not certain. Ekron, however, was probably Khirbet el-Muqenna. This site both corresponds to the biblical description of the ancient city (Joshua 15:11) and has yielded substantial archaeological materials from the Philistine era. Indeed the fortified city was founded in the Iron Age, and excavators speculate that it was originally a Philistine city. The surprising thing about this city is its size. With forty acres within its walls, it was one of the largest cities of Palestine. Twice the size of Megiddo, it was two and a half times the size of Lachish.

Gath has not yet been discovered. Several locations have been suggested, but each in turn has been shown by excavations to be something else. The sequel to the story of David's victory over Goliath says that Gath was near Ekron (I Samuel 17:52). This clue combined with archaeological evidence has led some to identify Gath with Tell es-Safi, a large site abounding in Philistine pottery. Sitting at the western end of the Valley of Elah, Tell es-Safi is admirably located to control one of the important passes leading into the hill country and Jerusalem. If this is indeed ancient Gath, it together with nearby Ekron would have given the Philistines considerable control over movement in this area. Excavations undertaken at Tell el-Hesi in 1970 have so far failed to indicate whether this fortified acropolis was also a Philistine site, or was a stronghold against further Philistine incursions.

Egypt had expended the final ounce of its strength in this one last, desperate, and successful defense of its land. As the "Sea Peoples" withdrew northeastward into Palestine, the pharaoh was unable to prevent their settling on the fertile lands between the hills and the sea in the area of Gaza. Some scholars have suggested, probably correctly, that Ramses made the best of a difficult situation and entered into a shrewd deal with the temporarily weakened enemy. Unable to prevent their settling in his provincial administrative capital and the lands surrounding it, he became their allies and they became his buffer to prevent further threat to the always vulnerable northeastern border of Egypt. Discovery of older Philistine graves at Bethshan indicates that prior to his conflicts with them the pharaoh probably hired Philistines as mercenaries. If this assumption is correct, Ramses would have known of both their military ability and their loyalty.

Philistine strategy was to exercise effective control over movement in southwestern Palestine. An alliance of the kings of the five major cities wove their armies into a well-coordinated, highly trained, and superbly led military force. In addition the equipment of a Philistine soldier was superior to any other of his day. This equipment is listed in detail in I Samuel 17:4-7 where the frightful battle appearance of Goliath is described. Not the least of Goliath's terrors was his iron spearpoint. Apparently the Philistines had and were able to maintain a monopoly on iron right down to the dawn of the Hebrew monarchy (I Samuel 13:19-22). Iron weapons, vastly superior to the bronze swords and spears of their foes, were a Philistine hallmark. It is even possible that iron-making was introduced into Palestine by these transplanted men of Asia Minor. Be that as it may, iron played a large role in the foundation of Philistine strategy which was military preparedness.

Disciplined and with no internecine warfare to sap their strength, the Philistines dwelt securely on the southern coast of Palestine. Their distinctive pottery indicates their settlements reached at least as far north as Aphek (I Samuel 4:1; 20:1) and perhaps even into the Plain of Esdraelon. Yet on the whole these people once settled were relatively pacific and showed a remarkable lack of interest in territorial aggrandizement. With garrisons at Bethlehem and a few other places in the highlands, they were not so much concerned with occupation as to make sure occupation did not become necessary. It was not until the second half of the eleventh century B.C. that the Philistines struck into the hill country with force. These blows were not aimed at the native Canaanites, but at a new people whose infiltration in the land had brought them such numbers that they now sought control. Such a threat could hardly be ignored. The stories about Samson (Judges 13–16) show the beginnings of this clash between the Philistines and the Israelites, who were to emerge from this confrontation and bloodshed as master of the land.

Hebrew Settlement in Palestine

Few matters in biblical history are as complex and as difficult of solution as the nature and extent of the Hebrew settlement in Canaan. The perplexities are for the most part due to the character of the available evidence and to the mainly pastoral concerns of the Hebrews who were either already in the land or who came pouring in as Egyptian control in Canaan weakened and faded. Biblical traditions of the conquest are at variance, perhaps superficially, perhaps in substance. Moreover, much of the archaeological material which may have bearing upon the issue is ambiguous at best. Nonetheless, if we are modest and do not expect exact chronology or detailed information at every point, it is possible to gain at least an impression of the impact of the Hebrews upon Canaan in the early days of the Iron Age (ca. 1250—1050 B.C.).

According to the book of Joshua, after the death of Moses "all Israel," now under the command of Joshua, miraculously crossed the Jordan (Joshua 3), was dedicated at the shrine at Gilgal (Joshua 4–5), and in a "holy war" defeated the Canaanites and divided the land among the various tribes. In the course of this war not only were Jericho and Ai reduced to rubble, but a coalition of five southern Canaanite kings fell before the invincible Israelites who thus came to rule in the south (Joshua 6–8, 10). Turning north, Joshua and his forces engaged and decisively defeated another Canaanite coalition under the leadership of Jabin, king of Hazor (Joshua 11, 12). Joshua, now an old man, divided the allotments among the various conquering tribes. Finally, having welcomed the the return of the Transjordanian Hebrew tribes (Joshua 13–21, 22), the hero of the conquest charged the elders of Israel to be faithful to the law of Moses, made a covenant with various groups gathered at Shechem, and died (Joshua 23, 24). Thus the conquest of the Promised Land was the result of a three-stage continuous campaign under a single leader. It was successful and total.

The book of Judges, however, leaves no doubt that the process was neither so simple as Joshua suggests nor did it come to pass in a brief period of time. Indeed, Judges indicated that it was many generations before the land was securely in Israel's hands. Joshua conveys the studied impression of one war with regional campaigns. Judges, on the other hand, points to a twofold sort of conquest. In addition to various sieges and occasional pitched battles under several different leaders, there was a lengthy process of infiltration with settlement in the hill country where Canaanites were sparse. The careful reader of Joshua will note that the book contains a number of passages which support the picture of the conquest as given in Judges. The most notable examples are in chap. 17. At one point a list of *unconquered* Canaanite cities is given (vss. 11-12). These are the cities of the great northern plain and show that the Hebrews had failed to win supremacy in that region. This is confirmed later in the chapter by Joshua's attempt to deal with the complaint of the Joseph tribe. When they say that their allotment in the hill country of Ephraim is not enough, Joshua tells them to clear away the forests in other areas. But hills and forests will not satisfy this tribe which has cast covetous eyes upon the rich fields below. "The hill country is not enough for us," say the men of Joseph, "yet all the Canaanites who dwell in the plain have chariots of iron, both those in Beth-shan and its villages and those in the Valley of Jezreel" (vs. 16). This revealing verse leaves no doubt that the general

impression of the conquest given by the book of Joshua is not an accurate record of actual events, nor perhaps was it intended to be.

The book of Joshua is part of the Deuteronomic history of Israel, and as such its main concerns are theological rather than historical. Its statement about the conquest is in the nature of a religious affirmation. In the end "all Israel" did indeed dwell in the land in accordance with the promises of God. To illustrate this truth, the Deuteronomic authors of Joshua make the initial successes of the House of Joseph a symbol of the total and final occupation. In the process of the development of this tradition, stories and events originally associated with other leaders were accredited to Joshua. This tended to unify but also to distort the historical picture of the settlement in Canaan.

In fact the violent and bloody incursions into the hill country from the east were probably the work of certain tribes within the larger House of Joseph. Included in this larger unit were Ephraim and Manasseh and perhaps Benjamin also. All these may well have been the second generation of the escapees from Egypt, although serious doubt must be raised about Manasseh in this connection. It is difficult, of course, to establish exactly which groups participated in the Exodus. Perhaps the Judah tribe that invaded Canaan from the southern desert and reaped the fruits of many of the victories of Joseph had likewise been in Egypt. Some have said that Reuben, closely connected with Judah and Benjamin, was in Egypt and perhaps Gad was also. Yet Gad's association with Asher as one of the Leah tribes almost certainly indicates its presence in Canaan prior to the Exodus. This is one of the first things that should be remembered about the Hebrew settlement in Canaan: Many of the tribes moved around its borders and in the relatively uninhabited highlands and never entered Egypt at all. Some of these people may have been among the Palestinian Hapiru of the Amarna Letters. They and some of their allies probably occupied Shechem and the surrounding area which may explain why this important yet unconquered center played so large a role in Hebrew history at this time. This was the region settled by Manasseh and serves as an example of one of the three modes of the Hebrew settlement.

The first mode has to with non-exodus Hebrews who had been in Canaan for many generations. Genesis 34 is clear evidence of such groups. Moreover, the Bible records no conquest by Manasseh. At first sight this may seem surprising since Shechem, the chief city of the Manasseh region, emerges as the focus of the tribal covenant (Joshua 24). Yet this situation is instructive. The fortress temple of Baal-berith ("Lord of the Covenant") at Shechem continued in use at least until the city was destroyed by its former king, Abimelech, about 1100 B.C. (Judges 9:45). While the exact identity of Baal-berith is a matter of controversy, there is no doubt that this shrine along with that of Shiloh farther south served the Hebrews as important religious centers prior to the establishment of the monarchy (Joshua 18:1). From the Amarna Letters we know that Shechem entered into agreements with the Hapiru and like other Canaanite cities generally sought to use these semi-nomads to its advantage. It seems quite likely that Manasseh, too, had friendly arrangements with Shechem and probably other Canaanite cities in the region (Numbers 26:31 ff. mentions Tirzah; Joshua 17:2 names Hepher). Until the balance of power was upset by the coming of others of the House of Joseph in the mid or late thirteenth century B.C., the Hebrews continued to live amicably in the forests and grazing areas near the urban centers.

A second mode of settlement is represented by the experience of Ephraim. They inhabited the southern and higher part of the northern hill country of what was later Israel. In this region the Canaanites, who were mostly farmers and city folk, found little to interest them. Therefore it was relatively unpopulated by the indigenous people and rapidly became a strong and uniform center of Hebrew life. The isolated Canaanite towns in Ephraim's territory were apparently destroyed soon after the coming of the Hebrews who built rude dwellings upon the ruins.

Benjamin serves not only as an example of the third mode of the settlement, but also provides a model for the kind of conquest reported by the book of Joshua. This bellicose tribe invaded a small but densely populated area north and east of Jerusalem. In addition to the Canaanites a four-city non-Semitic (Hivite) confederation (Gibeon, Chephirah, Beeroth, and Kiriath-jearim) opposed the ambitions of Benjamin. A covenant placing these cities in a servile relationship to the Hebrews alarmed the king of Jerusalem who forged an alliance to punish Gibeon and to oppose the increasing danger to the area. The ensuing battle is described in Joshua 10, when the sun stood still as the Hebrews soundly defeated the alliance and then moved to demolish its cities among which were Hebron, Eglon, Jarmuth, and Lachish.

Thus the conquest was sparked by a warlike invasion of the central highlands leaving in its wake a series of smoldering ruins where once-proud Canaanite cities had stood. But this was not the whole story. Other Hebrews, almost all of whom had neither been in Egypt nor taken part in the Exodus, took the occasion to move in from border areas where they had grazed their flocks for generations. Still others who had dwelt in the land perhaps since patriarchal days looked anew at their relations with their Canaanite neighbors. As time went by, the old, old story repeated itself in Canaan. Incoming peoples, mostly pastoral, brought increasing pressure to bear upon the cities many of which they eventually destroyed. At every place human suffering was immeasurable as always where the baser instincts are organized and directed against one's fellowman. In some places destruction meant liquidation of the local population (Joshua 6:21, as one example). Nevertheless, for all the privations and humiliations visited upon them, the Canaanites managed to survive in Palestine, and their culture and religion nourished on the soil proved to be more effective weapons against the Hebrews than did chariots, walls, or swords.

Archaeology has played a helpful but ambiguous role in pointing to a solution of the problem of the settlement. Much interest has naturally centered upon Jericho. Its spectacular position in the conquest narrative (Joshua 5:13–6:27) is matched by its prominence in the history of archaeological excavation in Palestine. The conspicuous mound near the Jordan was examined from 1907 to 1909 by Ernst Sellin and Carl Watzinger, pioneer German archaeologists. John Garstang, head of the British School of Archaeology in Jerusalem, dug at the site for seven years beginning in 1929. It was mainly Garstang's work that seemed to correlate findings at Jericho with the account in Joshua. The last Canaanite wall had indeed been burned and destroyed. Yet even in the mid-1930s scholars did not agree on the date of these walls. Garstang himself said they were thrown down in the early fourteenth century B.C., a date which would favor identification of the invading Hebrews with the Hapiru of the Amarna Letters. Father Vincent of the French School of Archaeology (the famed *École Biblique* in Jerusalem) favored a date nearer the end of the reign of Ramses II, perhaps *ca.* 1230 B.C. W. F. Albright held an intermediate position of about 1300 B.C. Garstang's view, however, predominated. This was particularly the case among those anxious to find tangible evidence of events described in the Bible. Even today many of such persuasion have failed or refused to take account of K.

Kenyon's recent excavations at Jericho. Using her more highly developed stratigraphic method, Miss Kenyon, a successor to Garstang at the British School, has shown conclusively that his walls belong to a considerably older time than he thought. They are, in fact, Early Bronze! Even the Middle Bronze Age wall has almost entirely vanished. "It is a sad fact," says Kenyon, "that of the town walls of the Late Bronze Age, within which period the attack of the Israelites must fall by any dating, not a trace remains. . . . The excavation of Jericho, therefore, has thrown no light on the walls of Jericho of which the destruction is so vividly described in the Book of Joshua." [1]

What happened to the Late Bronze wall? Was there ever such a wall or did the inhabitants of that period reuse the Middle Bronze wall of which so little now remains? We shall perhaps never know. The mound is located at one of the lowest spots on earth, only a few miles north of the Dead Sea. Intense summer heat turns the clay soil to dust which the heavy winter rains carry off into the surrounding oasis. In short, erosion has damaged ancient Jericho to such an extent that much of its later history can no longer be read in the earth. The skimpiness of the remaining Middle Bronze Age town combined with two other pieces of evidence has convinced some scholars that Jericho was little more than an insignificant and perhaps undefended village when the Hebrews came upon it. The other pieces of evidence are a Late Bronze (fourteenth-century) juglet found on the mound and a considerable amount of Iron Age pottery. The juglet is the only piece of Late Bronze pottery found in location on the mound, while the later pottery points to a possible Hebrew resettlement on the site.

Scholars who hold that Jericho was undefended at the time of the Hebrew invasion account for the biblical story by saying that

[1] Kathleen Kenyon, *Digging Up Jericho*, pp. 261-62.

it was an earlier victory by someone else. It became attached to the Hebrew tradition and was used to glorify the hero, Joshua, at a time when Israel's central shrine was Gilgal, quite near the huge ruins of Jericho. This may well be. But if we are not allowed to outrun the evidence in one direction, we must forbid its being done on the other extreme. So far as the archaeological evidence is concerned we simply cannot confirm or deny the biblical account of the capture and sack of Jericho. If the evidence were ever there, nature has conspired to make it no longer available to us.

After the destruction of Jericho, according to the book of Joshua, the Hebrews under Joshua moved west and slightly north and attacked Ai. Initially repulsed because of the sin of Achan, Joshua's forces carried the second assault with the consequent burning of the city and brutal elimination of its inhabitants (Joshua 7–8). There is almost universal agreement among archaeologists and cartographers that Ai is to be located at et-Tell, near Deir Debwan, a small village about nine miles northeast of Jerusalem. What have excavations at this site revealed? In 1933-1935, Judith Marquet-Krause proved that there was indeed an important Canaanite town here. But it had been destroyed before the end of the third millennium, perhaps in the pastoral migrations that brought to an end the first great flowering of Canaanite urban life. There was, so far as Madame Marquet-Krause could determine, no further occupation of the site until a small Israelite village located there, perhaps ca. 1200 B.C. In the mid-1960s an American expedition returned to Ai for several seasons of digging. The Iron Age village, although apparently restricted to the southeastern portion of the mound, is considerably larger than the French scholars realized. It seems also to have had terraced farming not unlike that in the area today. Still there is nothing yet unearthed that substantially contradicts the conclusions of the earlier excavators. The massive defense system discovered in 1966 is probably Early Bronze; certainly not Late Bronze. Joseph Callaway, leader of the recent work, has suggested the interesting possibility that Joshua was post-1200, and that the Iron Age ruins of the site may yet prove to be the Ai of the book of Joshua.

A Late Bronze destruction level has unquestionably been found at Bethel which lies very close to Ai. Expeditions in 1934 and 1954 have confirmed that this site was destroyed in the thirteenth century, abandoned for a short time, and reoccupied by a people with a somewhat lower standard of architecture and craftsmanship. W. F. Albright, one of the 1934 excavators, identified a new type of jar rim in the rebuild. This "collared rim" as he called it, was thought to be distinctively Israelite. Its discovery at other sites, mostly in central Palestine and at certain twelfth-century B.C. mountain settlements, has been taken as clear proof of the arrival of a new people, the obvious candidate being the Hebrews.

It was, again according to the book of Joshua (chap. 9), the destruction of Ai that caused the Gibeonites to trick Joshua into an alliance. This in turn roused a group of Canaanite kings to concerted action against the Hebrews. But was it not the destruction of Bethel rather than Ai that set off this chain of events proving so disastrous to the coalition of Canaanite kings? Many scholars now tend to think so. The name "Ai" is, after all, Hebrew for "ruin," a name by which the Arabs still call the site (et-Tell in Arabic, meaning "the ruin"). Perhaps the size of the mound at et-Tell was a matter of interest to the Hebrews, and the local stories of its destruction gradually became incorporated into the oral traditions of the Hebrew victory at Bethel. This possibility is often cited by those who contend for a similar explanation of the story of the sack of Jericho where the evidence, however, is hardly strong.

Archaeologists have found other destroyed sites farther south which may have been the result of the campaign following the Hebrew success at Gibeon (Joshua 10). The narrative specifically mentions Debir, Lachish, and Eglon as the principal cities overcome by "all Israel" during this foray in force into the southern part of the country. Excavations leave little doubt that these cities were destroyed during the thirteenth century B.C., probably during the latter half of the 1200s. Tell Beit Mirsim, identified as Debir (although some still suggest it may be Kirjath Sepher), was victim of an extremely violent fire. While the responsibility probably belongs to the Hebrews, it is not impossible that Merneptah's forces, who campaigned in the area at roughly the same time, could have caused the conflagration. The same is true of Lachish (Tell ed-Duweir) which suffered a similar fate at approximately the same date. Working at this site from 1932 to 1938, J. L. Starkey uncovered Egyptian tax lists on inscribed jug fragments. They note "the fourth year" of an unnamed pharaoh. From the datable context in which these burned pieces were found, the pharaoh referred to is doubtless Merneptah. This destruction then would have been no earlier than *ca.* 1200 B.C. and surely not much later. The presence of Egyptian artifacts does not, of course, guarantee that non-Egyptians destroyed the city.

Tell el-Hesi (identified by Albright as Eglon) was ravaged by flames at about the same time as Debir and Lachish. Like nearby Lachish, Hesi lay unoccupied after this for approximately two centuries. It was then inhabited by Hebrews. During the era of the Hebrew monarchies it attained some significance but not so much as the bastion of Lachish. Lachish, as a key to the defense of Jerusalem, suffered siege and capture by both the Assyrians, as the Bible tells us (II Kings 18:13 ff.), and by the Babylonians, as we know from archaeology.

Again, it is possible that the conquerers of Hesi were not Israelite. The Egyptians, as has been said, were seeking to reassert their failing authority in the area. Moreover, the "Sea Peoples" ravaging the coasts may have struck here as well as elsewhere. There are non-Hebrew possibilities for these various destructions. Nothing at any of these sites immediately or conclusively identifies the attackers. Still less is there any proof of the presence of a new group of people. According to Professor Albright, a new settlement occurred at Debir in a relatively short time. This new village was marked by an "extraordinary simplicity and lack of cultural sophistication." [2] But this could be as true of a people seeking to recover from the ravages of war as of less cultured newcomers. At Hesi and at Lachish the identifiable Hebrew settlements are two hundred years later than the massive thirteenth-century destructions. They are thus hardly helpful in identifying those who made war at these places.

In the north we have a similar situation. There were probably numerous unrecorded confrontations of various sorts and sizes between Hebrews and Canaanites. Two major conflicts, however, are mentioned in some detail in the Bible. One pitted Deborah and her Hebrew guerrillas from the hills against Sisera and his chariots of iron which were masters of the plains. To cast lightly armed men into battle against the heaviest armor of the day must have seemed madness to many. Yet through a series of unusual events, each of which seemed miraculous to the Hebrews, the chariots were driven from the field in defeat become rout. Were the victors able to follow up their success by attacking the cities from which the Canaanite men and chariots had come? The account in Judges mentions only Taanach and Megiddo but

[2] W. F. Albright, *The Archaeology of Palestine* (Harmondsworth: Penguin Books, rev. ed., 1956), p. 119.

does not indicate that they were either besieged or captured. Taanach was apparently the rallying point for Sisera's army before the battle and together with Megiddo guarded the passes by Mount Carmel. These two large cities atop prominent hills would have been within sight of the combatants as they struggled, bled, and died in the mud at the foot of Mount Tabor. Both are named in Joshua 12:21 in the list of Canaanite cities taken by the Hebrews. Beyond this the tradition is strangely silent about their fate. Excavators at Taanach in 1966 found evidence of a late twelfth-century B.C. destruction layer which would place it about the same time as Deborah's victory. But not much can be made of this since as yet not even the extent of this layer is known. Was it a localized fire near the walls, or was it a more general conflagration? Moreover, it should be remembered that at nearby Megiddo archaeologists do not credit the destruction of the city in the mid-eleventh century to the Hebrews.

Thus neither Bible nor spade tells very much about the consequences of Deborah's success as regards the Canaanite cities of the great northern plain. With reference to the second major battle of the north, on the other hand, Scripture and archaeology combine to indicate that victory in the field was followed by the storming, destruction, and appropriation of the enemy cities. At the Waters of Merom near Hazor the Canaanites seem to have made their last concerted effort to defend the north.

Apart from Garstang's brief dig at Hazor in 1928, little archaeological work had been done in the area until recently. Now there has been not only a major excavation at Hazor, but a considerably less-publicized but equally important archaeological survey in the northern hills by the Israeli scholar, Yohanan Aharoni. Aharoni examined fifty ancient sites and conducted two small excavations. He concluded that a large Canaanite population worked the fertile soil of the northern plateau from a chain of important urban centers. Just south of the plateau, where the mountains reach heights up to 3,962 feet, there is no indication of Canaanite life. Rather, many Iron Age settlements were found in close proximity. These small villages, usually fortified, were seldom more than a mile apart. And in the remains of these places was found a considerable quantity of what Aharoni calls "special pottery." This pottery is, in fact, quite similar to Albright's "collared rim" from Tell Beit Mirsim (Debir). But it is not the same, says Aharoni who assumes it came from farther north. This means, in his view, that the original Hebrew settlers in the north had no connection with the warlike tribes of the south until long after the northern mountains had been settled.

The battle of the Waters of Merom seems to have been an attempt by the King of Hazor and his allies to prevent the increasing numbers of Hebrews from gradually encroaching upon the Canaanite lands in the area. It may also have been an action designed to destroy Hebrew strength in the north before larger numbers of southerners made them capable of overwhelming the Canaanites. Whatever the motivation, the action certainly came too late.

Two items will serve to show these northern cities under pressure. One is a letter of an Egyptian merchant who describes the terrors of journeying from city to city. The narrow passes in the mountains are full of robbers, he says, adding that the trip is hardly worth the risk. From time to time throughout the centuries highwaymen and others have often made the major arteries of commerce unsafe. As Egyptian rule collapsed at the end of the Nineteenth Dynasty and the hills and forests of Palestine became increasingly inhabited by those who took every opportunity to seize the wealth and goods of the cities, the conditions described by the frightened Egyptians would tend more and more to isolate one city from another. Indeed, many have suggested that it was precisely such conditions which brought about the decline of the Canaanite cities just prior to their destruction by the Hebrews.

The second item is indication from the Hazor excavations (begun 1955) that a sharp decline in the city's fortune did, in fact, take place just prior to its final destruction. Although it was once the largest city in size yet known in Palestine (approximately 200 acres), in its last stages its fortified area had shrunk to not more than fifteen acres comprising the highest point on the mound. The enormous lower city which dated from early Hyksos days was abandoned, its temples plundered, its houses pulled down. This dramatic reversal in the fortunes of a once-proud and powerful city was likely due to rapid Hebrew settlement in the area surrounding Hazor. Perhaps the victory of Deborah farther south had removed a defensive shield from more northern regions. At any rate, the King of Hazor with his rather wide-ranging allies from Madon, Shimron, and Achshaph made a vain attempt to stem the tide and reclaim sovereignty for the Canaanites. According to the book of Joshua, following the battle at the Waters of Merom the Hebrews pursued the King of Hazor, captured his stronghold, killed him with his subjects, and burned the city to the ground (Joshua 11:10-11).

Archaeology tends to confirm this account of the destruction of Hazor. The latest Canaanite city crowded on the height was utterly destroyed and burned. In its stead rose a village of rude dwellings, the "special pottery" of which identifies its inhabitants with the people of the small fortified places in the mountains round about. It seems fairly clear that the Hebrews, having overthrown a symbol of Canaanite power, sought to settle the strategic point themselves. The attempt was apparently unsuccessful for reasons which

must remain conjectural. The site was abandoned. With the exception of a few random buildings it was left in ruins until rebuilt and fortified by Solomon. Only once more does it appear in Scripture. II King 15:29 lists it among the prizes of Tiglath-pileser during his campaign against Pekah of Israel (733-732 B.C.).

What then can be concluded about the Hebrew settlement in Canaan? First, the biblical text is both selective and highly idealized in terms of theological preconceptions. It neither attempts nor desires to give a complete and historically accurate account of the events which lead to the Hebrews' dwelling in the Promised Land. That they dwell in the land in consequence of the fulfillment of God's word is the important and unmistakable point. Moreover, one should not think that the traditions and literature of the Hebrews are entirely immune from many of the processes of elaboration and self-glorification that are to be seen at work in the accounts other peoples give of themselves and their history. To say that the Bible is holy and inspired does not require that it be seen as a detailed chronicle of events.

This does not mean, of course, that there is no history in the Bible. The conquest narratives are a case in point. Although they are theologically idealized, they are nonetheless clearly founded upon actual experiences from the lives of the Hebrew people. There is a growing body of archaeological evidence to support this. While it must remain silent about the Hebrew destruction of Jericho and Ai, it can point to Bethel. The struggle at Gibeon between the Hebrews and the Canaanite confederation must rest for support upon the record in Joshua 10. Yet archaeology can show that in the immediate area, at Gibeah (Tell el-Ful) and at Mizpah (Tell en-Nasbeh) settlements were founded in the thirteenth or twelfth centuries B.C. whose remains point to Hebrew origins. Were such settlements one of the consequences of the battle? Certainly the stated consequence of the battle—the destruction of the southern cities of Debir, Lachish, and Eglon—finds exceptional support from excavations. And in the north, Aharoni's work in identifying a large number of Iron Age settlements coupled with the evidence from Hazor lends both background and detailed support to the narrative in Joshua 11. The mosaic slowly emerging from these varied archaeological endeavors forms a picture in essential accord with the impression of the settlement as given in the book of Judges. It was a long process encompassing both peaceful settlement and warfare. Apparently the bellicose incursion into the central highlands from the east sent a shock throughout the land and disrupted the balance of power. In time it brought those Hebrews who had long been in the land in alliance with the newer arrivals and finally into conflict first with the Canaanites and later with the Philistines.

For all the foregoing in which we see a relatively harmonious wedding of biblical narrative and archaeological finding, a certain caution must be exercised. The Hebrews, both those long in Canaan and the invaders from the desert, were, after all, mainly pastoralists. This means that their material remains are not such that the archaeologist is likely to recover them. Even if they were found, it is by no means certain that they could be correctly interpreted. Apart from Aharoni's evidence of settlements in the north, almost all materials come from urban areas. It is precisely these areas which the main body of Hebrews avoided from patriarchal days until almost the establishment of the monarchy. No doubt some ventured into the cities, but for the moment at least it is not possible to distinguish their material remains from those of the Canaanite population. Moreover, the likelihood is that they were materially assimilated to the dominant and more highly developed culture. History suggests that such has almost always been the case with minorities moving from a less-developed to a more sophisticated environment. When this happens they are placed beyond the archaeologist's reach.

As we have seen in previous chapters, the evidence of new people has been a change in the material culture. Radically different burial practices and a break in pottery development are almost sure clues. So one can identify Philistine presence not only in the southwest but in other parts of Palestine as well. Their pottery rapidly adapted itself to Canaanite modes. Yet it bears the unmistakable stamp of a Mycenaean heritage both in design and decoration. Moreover, their distinctive practice of burial in anthropoid coffins sets them apart from all other people who inhabited Palestine. No such clear-cut evidence can be cited for the coming and geographical extension of the Hebrews. So far no distinguishing Hebrew burial practices have been established. And Albright's "collared rim" pots have recently been found in Canaanite contexts. It can be argued that Hebrews used them there. But that cannot be established and archaeologically speaking this type of pot has lost its distinct diagnostic value. This throws heavy responsibility upon Aharoni's "special pottery" which may well prove to be the material point of recognition needed for distinctive early Hebrew culture. Yet Aharoni himself has suggested that such pottery is probably only to be identified with certain northern Hebrew groups. Future excavations will no doubt cast more light upon this potentially decisive matter.

Why must one be so cautious in evaluating archaeological materials? It is because one must neither outrun the evidence nor rule out any feasible explanation. While the archaeologist may be a man of faith, his work *as an archaeologist* can never be principally informed by religious motivations. At the same time, as one who is dedicated to an unbiased evaluation of all the evidence, he may not overlook the witness of the Bible, one of the major sources of our knowledge of the ancient Middle East. The biblical traditions note that important ethnic changes took place in Palestine in the Late Bronze and Early Iron Ages. Apart from this we would probably not guess that this was so; at least the material remains so far excavated are not sufficient to establish it.

So the archaeologist and the student of the Bible have the same two major sources of information available: history as reconstructed from the earth and the biblical record. If the archaeologist is by training and of professional necessity more cautious in conclusions, it is nonetheless to be acknowledged that at certain points there is a strong if often incomplete agreement between the two major sources. The Hebrew settlement in Canaan is one of those points.

Finally, according to the Bible the most distinguishing characteristic of the Hebrews was their religion. This religion forbade the making of images and until relatively late had no uniquely identifiable shrines. It thus remains for the most part an archaeologically irretrievable attribute. Available evidence tends to indicate that the Hebrews had little or no unique material culture to distinguish them from the Canaanites. Yet as we shall see shortly, their religion, although profoundly affected by Canaanite life, prevented the total absorption of the Hebrews into the more sophisticated culture and in the end produced a distinguishable and distinguished Hebrew culture.

9. CANAANITE RELIGION AND HEBREW FAITH

So far we have seen Canaanite life primarily from a Canaanite point of view. This has been made possible mainly by archaeological discoveries since World War I. A major source has been the finds at Ugarit, of course. But other excavations producing varied materials have played their part in bringing to life the complex but unified culture that dominated the eastern Mediterranean coast for a thousand years. For the student of the Bible as for the historian this gain has been immense. No longer is the canvas upon which so much of the biblical narrative is painted a shadowy background. Canaan stands in its own right and speaks for itself.

Now, however, the angle of vision changes. As control of the country gradually passes to another people, we look at Canaanite life through new and different eyes. How did the Canaanites appear to these people? The literature we have from the newcomers, the Hebrews, is their religious writings. In these, our Old Testament, there is a vivid picture of intense and sustained conflict with "the abomination of the Canaanites," a religion which in concept and detail filled many Hebrews with horror and indignation.

It was not that certain of the Hebrews were being unreasonably intolerant. At issue was a fundamental threat to their conception of reality and thus to the entire structure of values and way of life they had known. At whatever time the pastoral Hebrews moved from the deserts into Canaan, they found themselves in a radically altered situation. Even if different groups settled in the hills for varying periods of time and there continued their pastoral habits, as no doubt they did, envy of the plains and gradual infiltration into an agricultural existence threw them into conflict with their new neighbors. We ought not to think, however, that difficulties arose merely between individual Canaanites and Israelites. Many, probably most, of the newcomers accommodated themselves one way or another to the expectations and needs of their new home. In the over two hundred years in which they passed from a nomadic to an agricultural way of life, the Hebrews saw their religious concepts and practices undergo severe stress and change. The real conflict was a conceptual one, vitally influencing one's life. The religion of Canaan, as we have seen, was a fertility cult whose emphases upon vegetation and fecundity were appropriate for agriculturalists. A religion of the desert, such as that of the Hebrews, was uniquely unsuited to the demands of the new situation. The problem, then, was one of adapting nomadic values to an agrarian society.

The process of necessary adaptation took place in the context of what has been called "a triangular conflict." [1] Economic and social factors were as basic to the struggle as were the religious values from which they were often indistinguishable. The ownership of private property, for example, was opposed by a nomadically oriented sense of clan heritage where any generation's holding was viewed as a trust. A corollary to this was the whole system of finance. Could a man borrow capital funds? If so, from whom, at what interest, and with what final risks? These were not the sort of issues that had previously arisen among a people of wandering existence. In these and other ways the entire fabric of nomadic Hebrew society was menaced and faced disintegration. In the end the key to the matter proved to be the distinction between Canaanite and Hebrew conceptions of deity. Compromising, adapting, and surrendering at innumerable points, the Hebrews found at last that their basic conception of God was fundamentally incompatible with that of Canaan. The one was of a dying and rising God, rooted in the soil, identified with the processes of nature, and capable of being represented by the work of the hands of man. The other conceived of a God beyond nature, identified neither with the caprices of nature nor with the reproductive potentialities of man and animal. He is the invisible deity for a "people" with whom he is in covenant relation. He is, in the Hebrew view,

[1] J. M. P. Smith, *The Moral Life of the Hebrews* (Chicago: University of Chicago Press, 1928), *passim*.

known in obedience to divine will.

What is being described, of course, is the end of the process. Although the distinctions were always present, the lines were often and sometimes permanently blurred. Israelite religious life was deeply influenced by the native religion of Canaan. The prose and poetry of the religious literature of the Hebrews—our Old Testament—contains numerous examples showing such influences. Repetitive style in Hebrew poetry (Exodus 15:11 is but one of many examples) owes a great deal to the repetitive parallelism of Canaanite poetry. Much of the religious symbolism of Canaan was taken over wholesale by the Hebrews. Psalm 18, for example, casts the Hebrew God in the role of Baal, while the mythical struggle with the primeval waters is reflected in several passages, among them Psalm 29 and Habakkuk 3. Isaiah 14:12 calls to mind the battles for supremacy among the gods and the casting out of him who would sit in the place of the Most High.

But it is perhaps in Israel's religious festivals that Canaanite influence is most evident. The religious calendar in Exodus 34: 18-24 as well as the Book of the Covenant mentions (in Exodus 23:14-17) three annual feasts at which all Israelite males are to present themselves for worship at a sanctuary. The Feast of Unleavened Bread took place in the spring. The Feast of Weeks was seven weeks later and coincided with the wheat harvest. At the end of the agricultural year, the Feast of Ingathering celebrated the bounty and safe recovery of the crops. Other Israelite festivals, such as Passover and Sheepshearing, may well speak of the pastoral origins of these people. But the Canaanite influence is abundantly clear in a series of major religious occasions attuned to the growing season. It is instructive, moreover, to compare the description of a festal celebration at the temple of Baal-Berith at Shechem (Judges 9:27) with the "feast of the Lord" held at Shiloh (Judges 21:19-21). At Shechem the vintage festival, perhaps purely Canaanite, perhaps in process of becoming Hebrew, celebrates the maturing of grapes. At Shiloh it has clearly become a feast in honor of the Hebrew God and is being celebrated by Israelites.

Archaeological work in Palestine indicates that if there were ever a distinctive early Hebrew material culture it assimilated so rapidly to Canaanite ways as to be almost entirely unrecognizable today. There is no reason to doubt that the same process went on apace in religious matters also. Numerous passages in the Bible, some of which have been cited, indicate that it not only occurred to a large extent, but that it continued right through until postexilic times. This conflict between basic conceptions of reality was, therefore, neither simple nor was it over in a few weeks or months. Even the Temple in Jerusalem, a potentially powerful barrier to non-Israelitic ways, was not immune to the baser sorts of Canaanite religious practices. Manasseh, King of Judah (686-642 B.C.), established a fertility cult within the holy precincts, dedicated it to "the hosts of heaven," and surrounded it with images, male prostitutes, and women who wove lewd hangings for the shrines of Asherah (II Kings 21:1-9; 23:6-7; II Chronicles 33:1- 20). It was ten years after he began his reign that the young reformer, Josiah, was able temporarily to purge the Temple of this sort of thing (II Kings 22:3; II Chronicles 34:3 says it was twelve years). Yet as Ezekiel 8–10 and the ministry of Jeremiah indicate, there was a strong reaction to the efforts and momentary successes of Josiah.

Nonetheless, for all the considerable assimilation and outright substitution which did take place, there were powerful forces at work which prevented total absorption. These forces, both ideas and men, held their ground tenaciously in the face of continuous pressure. Time after time priests and prophets in Israel lashed out at this or that as being unworthy of the Chosen People and in violation of the nature of the God of Holiness. And nothing was a greater threat to Hebrew faith and received more condemnation than cult prostitution which was most entrenched at local sanctuaries where Canaanite influence was greatest.

Fertility, as we have learned from Ugaritic materials, was the province of Baal, the storm-god, who showers life upon vegetation and man. That this god was honored in Israel is beyond doubt. As only one example, Gideon's father, who bore a perfectly good Hebrew name (Joash, "God has given") set up a shrine to this Canaanite god complete with a cult object representing the erotic nature of the worship that took place there. This shrine Gideon ("Jerub-*baal*"!) destroyed in obedience to a divine command (Judges 6:25-32). Archaeology, too, has confirmed the presence of the worship of Baal in Palestine. But somewhat surprisingly the recovered number of images of Baal have been few. This is in contrast to the numerous representations of fertility goddesses which have been unearthed.

Later Canaanite worship seems to have had considerable difficulty in distinguishing the various fertility goddesses from one another—unless our information is inadequate. In the Ugaritic texts Asherah is the great mother-goddess, the female counterpart of El. Astarte, a goddess of war and fertility, sister and wife to Baal, appears rarely in these epics and generally is upstaged by Anath. Anath, the more warlike sister and wife of Baal, plays a large part in the drama including a somewhat confused role as the one who slays Mot. Already at Ugarit, Astarte and Anath are overlapping in their functions. Some centuries later in provincial Palestine the distinction between these various figures ceases to be clear. By the twelfth century B.C. the Egyptians found it almost impossible to distinguish Asherah, Astarte, and Anath. Moreover, Anath, so prominent in the Ugaritic epics, vanishes almost entirely in the Old Testament, being mentioned only in connection with the enigmatic Shamgar (Judges 3:31; 5:6). Anathoth (the plural of Anath) is mentioned twenty times, eighteen of which refer to a priestly town in Benjamin and the other two to relatively insignificant individuals.

Like Anath, Ashtar is normally referred to in the plural, not to indicate more than one but to denote majesty. Judges 2 says that when Joshua dismissed Israel to take possession of the land of Canaan, the first generation served the Hebrew God. But the second generation "forsook the Lord, and served the Baals and the Ashtaroth" (Judges 2:13). Could there be a better example of the difference between the desert and the sown, between the first wave of immigrants and their children? After the disaster on Mount Gilboa, Saul's decapitated body was hung upon the wall of Beth-shan and "they [the Philistines] put his armor in the temple of Ashtaroth" (I Samuel 31:10). Not merely second-generation immigrants and Philistines did homage to this Canaanite divinity. "For Solomon went after [i.e., worshiped] Ashtoreth the goddess of the Sidonians" (I Kings 11:5). *Ashtoreth,* by the way, is a vocalization of *Ashtaroth* with the vowels of *bosheth,* a Hebrew word meaning "shame." In this case it shows what later editors thought of this particular activity of King Solomon.

Asherah, seemingly interchangeable with Ashtaroth in the Hebrew Scriptures, is by far the most widely known fertility goddess in the Old Testament. She is mentioned over forty times. A cult symbol, also called an *asherah,* signified her presence at the sanctuary or shrine. Generally this symbol is thought to have been a stripped tree, a pillar, or a pole as a phallic symbol. These would be the *asherah* and *asherim* (the word is here in the masculine plural), often called "groves" in the King James Version.

This identification of the asherah and asherim as phallic symbols, although widely held, is by no means certain. These cult objects are nowhere described in detail in the Old Testament. Since they are said to be "planted" (Deuteronomy 16:21), "cut down" (Exodus 34:13 and others), and "burned" (Deuteronomy 12:3 and others), they were doubtless of wood. Wood, unfortunately, does not survive well in Middle Eastern ruins, and it is rare indeed when wooden objects are recovered in Palestinian excavations. So we have neither description nor archaeological evidence for this object.[2] It could have been the phallic pole of popular identification. Yet it could equally have been an image of the goddess or some other symbol. Whatever it was, there is no question that to the Hebrew religionists it was an abomination before the Lord and a threat to their faith.

Of the many passages dealing with the worship of Asherah the one in the covenant renewal ceremony in Exodus is perhaps the most instructive. It shows both the context of such worship and its end result.

Take heed to yourself, lest you make a covenant with the inhabitants of the land whither you go, lest it become a snare in the midst of you. You shall tear down their altars, and break their pillars, and cut down their Asherim (for you shall worship no other god, for the Lord, whose name is Jealous, is a jealous God), lest you make a covenant with the inhabitants of the land, and when they play the harlot after their gods and sacrifice to their gods and one invites you, you eat of his sacrifice, and you take of their daughters for your sons, and their daughters play the harlot after their gods and make your sons play the harlot after their gods.

Exodus 34:12-16

---

[2] The so-called *asherah* from the Ai sanctuary was likely a roof support. At best it is only the most meager circumstantial evidence that identifies it as a cult object.

So tenacious were *asherim* that even so late as the third Christian century coins minted at Byblos showed Phoenician temples with sacred pillars occupying the central place in the sanctuary. And so prevalent and seemingly indestructible was the institution of sacred prostitution that some of the strongest words in the Old Testament are reserved for those who even seek to entice another "to serve other gods." Such people are to be put to death (Deuteronomy 13:6). These harsh words were aimed at those who frequented the sanctuaries of the fertility cults where male and female prostitutes plied their trade. These were the "holy ones," the *qadesh* and the *qedeshah* (from the Hebrew root meaning "holy"; the same root which today gives us "kosher"). *Zonah* (female) and *kelev* (male, also "dog"), in contrast, were ordinary streetwalkers. Apparently at one time among the Israelites a distinction was made between religious prostitution, which was socially acceptable, and the more ordinary type, which was not. At least this seems to be one of the points of the story of Judah and Tamar (Genesis 38). This story reflects Canaanite practice among Hebrews. Hosea, however, does not make the Canaanite distinction (Hosea 4:14), and the Deuteronomic legislation (Deuteronomy 23:17-18) bans all forms of prostitution as "an abomination to the Lord your God."

The moral code of the nomadic ideal was certainly a good deal more strict than that of an urban-agrarian society. Without it the clan could hardly survive. It was true in the desert then; it is true in the desert now. Yet the ancient Hebrews were scarcely the moralists we make them out to be. Women had not attained the status that safeguarded the purity of the home. That came later. The major objection of certain Israelites to erotic worship of the Canaanite type was theological. Participation in the fertility rites with its excessive use of wine, its frenzy, and its eroticism was an attempt to place oneself in a certain relation to nature and to seek to attain its blessings. That the Israelites should have desired these blessings and thus adopted Canaanite ways is not strange. It would have been surprising had they not. If the Israelite learned from his neighbor and accepted his apparently successful agricultural methods, why should he have rejected the fertility rites? There was as yet nothing in his own religion that served the same purpose. And besides, many saw no reason not to serve Baal and Asherah so long as they also continued to worship the Hebrew God. The fundamental contradiction involved was not always and everywhere immediately apparent. But it was clear enough to many who understood the essential connection between the fertility rites and the dying and rising god of vegetation and nature. Such worship was opposed by Hebrew religionists who understood that the divine will of the Lord God of Israel is known, not in the processes of nature, but through his word spoken in history. His blessings are found in obedience.

Some of the plaques bearing representations of the nude mother-goddess show her with a snake draped over her shoulders or occasionally wound about her body. A striking example of this comes from Hazor. This is a silver plated Bronze standard bearing a representation of a goddess holding snakes. The serpent and the bull have long been used symbolically in the Middle East to indicate potency. In Canaan both were associated with homage paid to Baal. Of the serpent very little is said in the Old Testament, with two striking exceptions. In the Garden of Eden story the instrument of the fall of man from paradise is a serpent, the most subtle of the wild creatures (Genesis 3:1-19). What is the meaning of this choice of symbol in light of its Canaanite and general Middle Eastern background? The rabbis of the Talmudic period (*ca.* A.D. 500), at least, understood the serpent to represent lust and the chasm by which it divides man against man.

Similar questions have arisen in understanding the use of a bronze serpent by Moses (Numbers 21:4-9). There can be little doubt that it functioned for the afflicted Hebrews in much the same way that it did for the Canaanites. It signified life in the face of ever-present death.[3] This same idea seems to underlie the use of the Moses story by the author of the Fourth Gospel when describing the new life which Jesus Christ has brought into the world (John 3:14-15). But what of the bronze serpent of Moses? How was it understood by ancient Hebrews? The account in Numbers is too brief for us to draw conclusions. But II Kings 18:4 reveals a good deal more:

He [Hezekiah] removed the high places, and broke the pillars, and cut down the Asherah. And he broke in pieces the bronze serpent that Moses had made, for until those days the people of Israel had burned incense to it; it was called Nehushtan.

The context makes it clear that Nehushtan, the snake-god sacred to the worshipers of Baal, was a part of a Hebrew fertility cult during Hezekiah's time (715-687 B.C.). Further, the chief symbol of this god is understood by adherents and kings alike to be nothing less than the bronze serpent made by Moses. Moses, who gave Israel the divine law, can also give an image encouraging the worship of other gods! This is the way the people obviously thought. Here is syncretism which in the minds of many Israelites carried the sanction of the foremost of their ancestors. There is a possible indication, by the way, that Hezekiah was not so successful in eradicating the worship of Nehushtan as II Kings 18 might suggest. King Jehoiakim's mother was named Nehushta (II Kings 24:8). Jehoiakim was one of the last kings of

[3] It should also be noted that Aaron's rod turned into a serpent and worked miracles (Exodus 7:8-13).

A Canaanite goddess with a snake, a symbol of fertility, around her neck.

Judah (609-598 B.C.). Nehushta may mean "as strong as bronze," or even "magnificence." Some scholars, however, see a connection with the name of the snake-god. This is not an altogether impossible suggestion.

Sacred bulls were at least as common in ancient Israel as were serpent images. The bull has, like the serpent, been a symbol of fertility known to us from Mesopotamia and Egypt as well as Canaan. It was in Canaan, however, that adoration of symbolic bulls—again a part of Baal worship—was most widespread. From Hazor, to take only one example, come fragments of a god in the form of a bull. In the Ugaritic texts Baal took the form of a bull, and his actions with a heifer are graphically described. Just before entering the dominion of Mot, Baal left his reproductive powers with a bull. Hosea, whose prophetic imagery daringly used Canaanite sexual language in an attempt to turn it against non-Israelitic worship, rails against the bull image at Bethel (Hosea 4:11-17; 8:5; 10:11; 13:22). This prophet looks longingly back to the days of pristine worship in the desert wanderings—and conveniently forgets about Aaron's "golden calf" (Exodus 32:1-35). Here is the gold image of a bull, declared to be the Hebrew God. The description of the worship accompanying it is precisely what we know went on in the shrines of Baal. Offerings came first, followed by eating and drinking, and then "play." The feast continued with a steady crescendo of wild abandon until restraint and self-control were no longer to be found in the ecstacy.

When Solomon built his Temple, the Sea of Bronze was supported by twelve bulls. But perhaps the most enigmatic presence of sacred bull images in Israel came at the time of the division of the kingdom (*ca.* 922 B.C.). As David had wisely seen, where a person's religious loyalty lies there his political allegiance is likely to be also. Now Jeroboam, King of North Israel, was faced with undoing the work of David and of winning his subjects' devotion to new shrines rather than to Jerusalem, which was in South Israel, now called Judah.

And Jeroboam said in his heart "Now the kingdom will turn back to the house of David; if this people go up to offer sacrifices in the house of the Lord at Jerusalem, then the heart of this people will turn again to their lord, to Rehoboam king of Judah, and they will kill me and return to Rehoboam king of Judah." So the king took counsel, and made two calves of gold. And he said to the people, "You have gone up to Jeru-

salem long enough. Behold your god, O Israel, who brought you up out of the land of Egypt." And he set one in Bethel, and the other he put in Dan.

I Kings 12:26-29[4]

What did these royal bulls symbolize? Were they, as probably was true of Aaron's work, to be representations of the Hebrew God himself? Most scholars tend to think not. Although popular religion in ancient Israel may have made them little more than idols, there was a tradition in the ancient Middle East which saw the bull as the steed for the gods. At Arslan-Tash in northern Syria archaeologists have found a large stele (perhaps a sacred stone) bearing the image of Hadad (in Canaan "Baal") standing on a bull. Thus it seems that whatever the actual result of the presence of the golden bulls at Dan and Bethel (and it was not good, see I Kings 12:30–14:20), the official intent was to provide a common type of shrine. But it was to be one with the invisible God absent from the back of his mount. Nonetheless, there was an Asherah at Bethel, at least (II Kings 23:15). But we cannot tell if it was a part of Jeroboam's original design.

Surely the most degrading of all the religious practices encountered by the Hebrews in Canaan was human sacrifice. This particularly horrible form of worship seems first to have appeared in Israel during the reign of Ahab (869-850 B.C.) and is generally considered to be a part of the alien worship encouraged by his Sidonian wife, Jezebel. While it became firmly established in the two Hebrew kingdoms, often enjoying royal patronage, it is by no means certain that Phoenicia was its origin. In the extensive Ugaritic materials so far discovered there is no mention of human sacrifice; nor is there any other archaeological evidence establishing its presence in Phoenicia, nor for that matter is it in-

[4] Note the translation, "Behold your god," rather than the less preferred, "Behold your gods," of the RSV which follows the KJV.

contestably established to have been normal practice in Canaan.

At least one form of human sacrifice was a part of Carthaginian life, however, and Carthage (founded *ca.* 850 B.C.) was a Tyrian colony (the Sidonians had had a trading station in the area since the sixteenth century B.C.). On the surface the religion of Carthage was similar to what we have seen in Canaan. Its chief deities were Baal and Astarte. However, its Baal was identified as Baal-Ammon or Moloch. Does this point to Ammon in Transjordan as the source of human sacrifice by fire in Carthage, Canaan, and Israel? Moloch (from the Semitic root meaning "king") was an Ammonite god and can be identified with the biblical Molech (I Kings 11:7 and many others). That he can also be identified as the biblical Milcom for whom Solomon built a temple (I Kings 11:1-8; II Kings 23:13) is probable, but not certain. At any rate, we know that Jerusalem having become an international city, and North Israel a mecca for all kinds of influences, attracted foreign gods and their customs. Isaiah (2:6-22) and Jeremiah (7:18; 44:19) complain about this, while Zephaniah (1:4-6) gives the impression of Jerusalem as a city literally overrun with idolatrous priests serving Baal, Milcom, and a host of other divinities.

Human sacrifice by fire in Israelite Canaan was condemned by Hebrew religionists as a practice foreign to the nature of the Hebrew God. Yet it was clearly participated in by Hebrews. Ahaz, king of Judah (735-715 B.C.) "walked in the way of the kings of Israel. He even burned his own son as an offering . . ." (II Kings 16:3; II Chronicles 28:3). Manasseh, who in the eyes of the biblical writers was the worst of a bad lot of kings, did likewise. "And he built altars for all the hosts of heaven in the two courts of the house of the Lord. And he burned his son as an offering . . ." (II Kings 21:5-6; II Chronicles 33:6). Moreover, Manasseh, like

Solomon before him (I Kings 11:7), built a shrine to Moloch. Manasseh's shrine, in the Valley of Hinnom just outside the walls of Jerusalem to the southwest, must have served its purpose only too well, for it became particularly reprehensible to those who loved the God of Israel and contended for the purity of the worship of the God of Israel. Josiah, the reformer who came to the throne two years after Manasseh's death, made this sanctuary a prime target of his work. "And he defiled Topheth [from the Aramaic meaning "fireplace"; note again the conflation with *bosheth*] which is in the valley of the sons of Hinnom, that no one might burn his son or his daughter as an offering to Molech" (II Kings 23:10).

A number of biblical passages indicate that the consecration of the firstborn of man and beast was a religious obligation. Whether this originally implied sacrifice is not clear but is hinted at by such commands as that in Numbers 18:15. Here the firstborn of man is to be "redeemed" at the price of five shekels of silver paid at the sanctuary. This is difficult to interpret. But the words of the prophets leave no doubt about their views. Ezekiel speaks of child sacrifice with prophetic irony (Ezekiel 20:25-26). Jeremiah looks back upon the Topheth of Manasseh as one of the greatest evils of Judah (Jeremiah 7:30-34), while Micah speaks of true Israelite worship:

"With what shall I come before the
　　Lord,
　　and bow myself before God on
　　　high?
Shall I come before him with burnt
　　offerings,
　　with calves a year old?
Will the Lord be pleased with thousands
　　of rams,
　　with ten thousands of rivers of oil?
Shall I give my first-born for my
　　transgression,
　　the fruit of my body for the sin of
　　my soul?"

He has showed you, O man, what is
    good;
  and what does the Lord require
    of you
  but to do justice, and to love
    kindness,
    and to walk humbly with your
    God?

Micah 6:6-8

This prophetic moral indignation in the face of Molech worship is reflected in the Deuteronomic, Priestly legislation:

"When the Lord your God cuts off before you the nations whom you go in to dispossess, and you dispossess them and dwell in their land, take heed that you be not ensnared to follow them, after they have been destroyed before you, and that you do not inquire about their gods, saying, 'How did these nations serve their gods?—that I also may do likewise.' You shall not do so to the Lord your God; for every abominable thing which the Lord hates they have done for their gods; for they even burn their sons and their daughters in the fire to their gods."

Deuteronomy 12:29-31

In a similar vein Deuteronomy 18:9-14 lists those who are to be outcasts from the nation Israel. The first named is "any one who burns his son or daughter as an offering." Leviticus 18:21 simply forbids the giving of children to Molech. But Leviticus 20:2-5, a part of the same Priestly legislation from the postexilic period, decrees the sternest punishment for the worshipers of this god:

Say to the people of Israel, Any man of the people of Israel, or of the strangers that sojourn in Israel, who gives any of his children to Molech shall be put to death; the people of the land shall stone him with stones. I myself will set my face against that man, and will cut him off from among his people, because he has given one of his children to Molech, defiling my sanctuary and profaning my holy name. And if the people of the land do at all hide their eyes from that man, when he gives one of his children to Molech,

and do not put him to death, then I will set my face against that man and against his family, and will cut them off from among their people, him and all who follow him in playing the harlot after Molech.

Human sacrifice by fire is not the only form known to the Old Testament. There was also the foundation sacrifice. Here a living child was placed as an offering in the foundation of a structure. Apparently when Ahab ordered the reconstruction of Jericho, Hiel of Bethel, the architect and builder, sealed his oldest son, Ahiram, into the foundation. His youngest son, Segub, was a similar offering for the sanctity of the gates (I Kings 16:34). This is particularly interesting in light of the curse laid upon Jericho by Joshua:

Joshua laid an oath upon them at that time, saying, "Cursed before the Lord be the man that rises up and rebuilds this city, Jericho.
    At the cost of his first-born shall
      he lay its foundation,
  and at the cost of his youngest son
      shall he set up its gates.

Joshua 6:26

Judges 11:29-40 records a clear example of human sacrifice on the part of a Hebrew. Jephthah, battling the Ammonites, vows to the Lord that if victory is his "whoever comes forth from the doors of my house to meet me, . . . shall be the Lord's, and I will offer him up as a burnt offering" (vs. 31). In the too-familiar story it is his daughter, his beloved only child, who greets the conquering hero upon his return home to Mizpah. After granting her two months of grace, Jephthah sacrificed her according to his vow.

A final example is given of human sacrifice. This one is Moabite and is associated with the god Chemosh, Moabite equivalent of Moloch. Again, it is an unusual occasion. When a coalition of Israel, Judah, and Edom attacked Moab sometime in the late 840's B.C., Mesha, King of Moab, found himself in an almost impossible situation. Having in armor every able-bodied man regardless of age, he found himself unable to break the siege clamped upon his city. Desperately he tried to win a victory over any single part of the forces opposing him. He mustered 700 swordsmen against the Edomites, but like the Israelites the Edomites inflicted fearful slaughter upon the men of Mesha. With hope gone, the king mounted the ramparts of the city with his son, the crown prince. There in sight of the Israelite troops, he burned the designated king as an offering (II Kings 3:4-27). The enemy fled in terror and Mesha was able to pursue them with great profit to himself and to his kingdom.

The famous Moabite Stone (see p. 155, n. 5), discovered in 1868 at Dibon in Moab, is dedicated to Chemosh and gives Mesha's account of this war. He notes that eventually he overcame the Israelites (he omits to say how) and captured four of their cities in Transjordan "devoting the spoil to Chemosh, and the women and girls to Ashtar."

Canaanite religion confronted Hebrew faith with two other major challenges. These —wine and economics—have already been mentioned briefly. Wine is, of course, the product of settled society and a symbol of an agricultural way of life. The Old Testament has strongly conflicting ideas regarding wine. This is reflective of deep-seated divisions within Israel regarding the desert and the sown. On the one hand, many of the early stories of the Bible show the nomadic abhorrence of settled civilization. Tilling the soil is the result of disobedience and is the mark of a divine curse (Genesis 3:17-19). The prototype of all murderers is a farmer (Genesis 4:1-16). It is this murderer's descendents who forge tools making possible the building of cities (Genesis 4:17-22). And so on through these stories runs a thinly disguised hostility toward the sown, a hostility

climaxing in the story of Noah, who planted a vineyard (Genesis 9:20-27). Quite naturally, from this point of view at any rate, this leads to drunkenness. The result is a curse placed upon Canaan. This clever story revealing unmistakably the struggle between Canaanite religion and Hebrew faith condemns Canaan not merely for its excessive use of wine but also for its sexual perversions. Canaan has looked upon the naked drunkenness of Noah. Here two themes, two basic objections to the settled society of the Promised Land, are skillfully woven into one short, vivid, and devastating narrative.

On the other hand, there is the certain expectation that every Hebrew will enjoy the fruits of his tribal inheritance; that each man will have his land, his vines, and his shade trees. There is, in short, an anticipation of and a rejoicing in the agricultural life that contrasts sharply with what we have just seen. In Jacob's blessings on his sons, Judah "washes his garments in wine and his vesture in the blood of grapes; his eyes shall be red with wine, and his teeth white with milk" (Genesis 49:11-12). Joseph's orchards are to be so abundant that "his branches run over the wall" (vs 22). Similar words and an equal joy in the fruits of the field are found in the blessings Moses bestows on the various Israelite tribes. Joseph is to have "the choicest fruits of the sun, and the rich yield of the months, . . . the finest produce of the ancient mountains, and the abundance of the everlasting hills, . . . the best gifts of the earth and its fulness, . . ." (Deuteronomy 33:14-16). "So Israel dwelt in safety," begins the benediction of these blessings, "the fountain of Jacob alone, in a land of grain and wine; yea, his heavens drop down dew" (vs. 28).

So the conflict was set in Israel. Hostility and rejection on the one side, joyful acceptance on the other with every shade of attitude in between. Among those who totally rejected the new way of life were the

Nazirites and the Rechabites. The former were individuals who took a vow not to touch wine, to avoid contact with dead bodies, and to refrain from cutting their hair. Judges 13:2-7 represents Samson and his mother as ideal Nazirites. As such Samson is able to perform mighty deeds. Samuel was dedicated as a Nazirite by his mother (I Samuel 1:11). There is no doubt that such vows carried prestige in ancient Israel. Amos, for example, regards Nazirites so highly as to rank them with prophets (Amos 2:11-12).

The Nazirite vow retained its place in Israel well into New Testament times. The apostle Paul bound himself by such an oath (Acts 18:18; 21:23-24). This particular vow was a temporary one. Whether it was temporary or permanent in Old Testament times is not clear. Be that as it may, the Nazirite laws in Numbers 6 make it clear that the vow carried strict requirements, requirements reflecting a nomadic ideal and a certain hostility to the sown and settled life.

In contrast to the Nazirites, the Rechabites were a group for whom religion and the economic organization of society were one. To preserve the old order of the one, they rejected the new order of the other. And reject it they did with a vengeance. They planted no vineyards, touched no wine, built no houses. The desert was their home and tents their shelter. First appearing during the conflict between Elijah, Elisha, and Jezebel, they came out of the desert to join Jehu in his bloody business of destroying the worshipers of Baal (II Kings 10:15-18). Two hundred and fifty years later Jeremiah praises these pure sons of the desert for their unswerving faithfulness to their principles and their loyalty to the Hebrew God (Jeremiah 35).

Nazirites and Rechabites were, of course, extremists. At the other end of the spectrum stood those who had become completely absorbed into the manner of Canaan. Somewhere in between were the prophets who looked nostalgically back to nomadic days, and who looked fearfully around them at the bitter fruits of reality. Reflecting one of the social ills of their day, they point to the increasing problem of alcoholism in ancient Israel. "Wine and strong drink take away the mind," says Hosea (4:11). The fat women of Samaria are like the waddling cows of Bashan and stir from their luxury only to shout to their husbands for another drink (Amos 4:1). Even the House of God is defiled by drunken debauchery (Amos 2:8). Two of Isaiah's seven woes upon Israel have to do with the advanced stages of alcoholism (Isaiah 5:8-23; 10:1-4). *Delirium tremens* was not unknown (Proverbs 24:29-35).

Wine was, therefore, not merely a symbol of the settled life. It was also "a mocker . . . , a brawler" and led many in Israel astray. Those who accepted it strove mightily to warn their fellow Israelites against its excesses. Those, such as the Rechabites, who rejected it and the way of life it stood for, saw also the potential gravity in accepting the Canaanite view of economics. To adopt the agricultural life was almost perforce to change the entire economic structure of Israelite society. This was, in fact, what happened, although it took generations and was ideally never fully accomplished.

The Hebrew economic ideal of clan ownership ran afoul of the Canaanite laissez-faire view. In contrast to the Hebrew who saw himself as custodian of whatever he had, the Canaanite advocated the unhindered buying and selling of land and human beings. The collision between these two positions is readily apparent in Ahab's attempt to buy Naboth's vineyard (I Kings 21:1-16). "The Lord forbid," said Naboth invoking the strongest oath a Hebrew could take, "that I should give you the inheritance of my fathers" (vs. 3). Vexed and stung by the sharp reminder that this was considered by its owner as inalienable property, Ahab returned to his palace. It seems not to have occurred to him to seek to circumvent the principle involved. Such things came easily to the mind of Jezebel, however. She, learned in Phoenician-Canaanite ways, taught her husband how to deal with recalcitrant subjects, whether Hebrew or otherwise. The hapless Ahab took possession of the dead Naboth's former holding (vs. 16).

Naboth had sought to apply egalitarian, clan ideals of the desert to a very different situation. He was not the last to try this. Although the Hebrews gave in en masse to Canaanite economics, they never ceased trying to ameliorate its worst features. Slavery, for debt or otherwise, was mitigated by the idea of the sabbatical year. In this arrangement a slave could be held for only six years. The seventh he must be freed, for all must remember that they were once slaves to pharaoh (Exodus 21:2). Likewise, in the seventh year crops must not be reaped nor vineyards and orchards harvested, so that the poor animals might eat (Exodus 23:10-11). Also in the seventh year all debts must be remitted (Deuteronomy 15:1-18). It is true that these regulations applied only to Hebrews as did the instruction not to charge interest on money lent (Deuteronomy 23:19; Exodus 22:25). There was no compulsion to free non-Israelite slaves, or to refrain from pressing suit against outsiders in your debt. All the same, within the attempt to maintain a clan identity and unity there is the seed of humaneness which has often borne remarkable fruit both in Judaism and in Christianity.

The Holiness Code, Leviticus 25 in particular, seems to be a summary and elaboration of the Hebrew economic ideal adjusted to its new context. So far had Canaanite ways conquered the Hebrews that the issue was now one of seeking to remove the causes of increasing poverty. The regulations regarding the sabbatical year, loans, and reaping were repeated and expanded. To these this idealized code added a new institution.

On the tenth day of the seventh month of seven weeks of years (i.e., the forty-ninth year) the trumpet shall sound, and it shall be announced that the fiftieth year is to be a Jubilee Year. In this holy year all property shall revert to its original ownership, for no land can be sold in perpetuity. All land is God's who has given it to whom he desires.

This attempt to redistribute wealth on a regular cycle was, of course, never implemented. Not only was it founded on a view of a completely static economy, but even its idealistic framers foresaw many difficulties. Purchase of property would in reality be rent calculated on the basis of the nearness of the Jubilee Year. The next of kin was under obligation to come to the aid of one losing or in danger of losing an estate. Special arrangements were necessary for the cities and for the Levites who, having no allotment among the tribes, have a special claim on urban property. And so on, and so on. What we have here is both a recognition of the failure to retain the ideals of Israel and an attempt to hold on to them. Even if the letter of the law failed, as it did, the spirit survived.

What then shall we say to summarize the struggle between Canaanite religion and Hebrew faith? It was a lengthy process involving men of high and low estate. Most intense during the period of the Judges, it had not abated in New Testament times. All Hebrew life and thought was touched, changed, modified. Two areas in particular were profoundly affected. These were cultic practice and economics. The Hebrews had more success in adapting the former than they did the latter. Even so a Hebrew of Patriarchal days suddenly finding himself in a monarchical sanctuary would scarely have recognized it. With the exception of human sacrifice, which was never a part of Hebrew faith, the sacrificial system was practically indistinguishable from its Canaanite counterpart. Even the place of sacrifice was more likely than not a Canaanite shrine. In these the worship of Baal and Asherah probably flourished alongside that of the Hebrew God. The great altars, "the high places," are seen in the books of Samuel and Kings as merely pagan. Amos (7:9), Hosea (10:8), and Jeremiah (7:31; 19:5) inveigh against them. Yet they were not always condemned in Israel. Saul was able to find Samuel because the latter had come to Ramah, his home, to preside at the sacrifices "on the high place" (I Samuel 9:11-14). "Solomon loved the Lord, walking in the statutes of David his father; only, he sacrificed and burnt incense at the high places. And the king went to Gibeon to sacrifice there, for that was the great high place; Solomon used to offer a thousand burnt offerings upon that altar" (I Kings 3:3-4).

The often-cited denunciations of these great altars including the ferocity of the prophetic attack are but an indication of their prevalent usage by Israelites. Hezekiah sought to destroy them ((II Kings 18:4), his son Manasseh rebuilt them apparently under royal patronage (II Kings 21:3). As a part of the reaction against Manasseh's excesses Josiah defiled the high places of Judah (II Kings 23:8) and sought to implement the Deuteronomic legislation. This dealt with the high places and other such matters by the stern expedient of abolishing all sanctuaries apart from the one and central shrine in Jerusalem (Deuteronomy 12: 1-14; 15:19-18:22). The hoary Canaanite shrines identified with Hebrew priests, prophets, and Kings—Shechem, Bethel, Mamre, Beer-sheba, Gilgal, Shiloh, Mizpah, Gibeon, and all the rest—were shut, defiled, cursed.

But what of the shrine at Jerusalem? Would a patriarchal Hebrew have acknowledged this house as the house of his God? It was a Canaanite temple with Egyptian features. Bearing similarities to an older three-division temple at Hazor and a con-

temporary shrine at Tell Arad (perhaps itself Hebrew, see p. 142), it was perhaps little more than a version of the Temple of Melkart, the Baal of Tyre. The skilled workmen who executed the design, cut its woods, and carved its stones were Phoenician. Two great pillars before its doors had their counterpart in a number of known examples of Canaanite sanctuaries. The gold-covered cherubim covering the width of the walls and reaching halfway to the ceiling behind the Ark of the Covenant were more likely to call to mind the mammoth sphinxes of the north than the simplicity of the Tabernacle of the Wilderness.

Yet the most foreign of all the influences in Israel were neither altars nor shrines. Kingship was about as un-Israelite an institution as one could imagine. The demand of the people for a king was, in the words of I Samuel, a desire to be "like all nations" (8:5, 20). This was, from the religious point of view, precisely what Israel was not. Even the request for a king was blasphemy in Israel and signified a rejection of God as king over Israel (I Samuel 8:7). Many, however, felt that political and military necessities weighed heavier than religious considerations and that somehow the latter could be reconciled with the former. This reconciliation is, in fact, perhaps the greatest achievement of David and is why he is regarded as the ideal king to whom all others are (unfavorably) compared. Yet in Israel the king never occupied the supreme and unchallenged position enjoyed by monarchs in many of the surrounding nations. Anointed of God, separated to holy station, he was never deified. Powerful, often capricious and cunning, he was liable to prophetic denunciation. It was no easy thing to be king anywhere, still less in Israel where the institution itself was basically incompatible with the religion which created, sustained, and preserved the people. At length "like all nations" the petty Israelite monarchies disappeared, and with them perished the political office of king in Israel. But the people persevered, survived, and looked forward to the coming of another king, a new anointed one, a Messiah.

To gauge with precision the measure of Hebrew assimilation to Canaanite religion is extremely difficult. The sacred texts of Israel have been written and edited in such a way that it is not possible to know a great deal about Hebrew religion prior to the settlement in Canaan. Needless to say, many details subsequent to that watershed experience are hardly clear either. At most what can be done is to indicate the enormity of the adopting, adapting, borrowing, and general assimilation. This we have done with the suspicion that it has been vastly understated.

On the other hand, this matter can be over-emphasized as is often the case today. There were conceptions and ideas in Israel which drew limits around Hebrew faith. These were seen, held, and voiced by strong personalities who said to Canaanite religion, "This far and no further." Fundamental to any distinctive Israelite view was its conception of God. This God would find no place in the Ugaritic pantheon. Monotheism is not entirely the reason for this, since it is by no means established how early we can attribute monotheistic belief to the Hebrews. Monotheism aside, the God of Israel was neither naturalistic nor cyclical. He simply was not to be identified with the processes of nature. It is true that this God came to be seen as the giver of the rains which produce the grain, the wine, and the oil (Deuteronomy 11:14 and others). It is also true that many of the titles of Baal such as "he who mounts the clouds" (Isaiah 19:1 and others) were associated with the Hebrew God. Yet at no point is there a hint of a female consort [5]

[5] Jewish literature from Elephantine, an island in the Nile at Assuan, does mention a female consort of God, the goddess Anath-yahu. But this is a

or of a dead god being rescued from the powers of death and sterility. The dominant view of the Hebrew was not one of endless recurrence of the same fundamental pattern. On the contrary, it saw purposeful history moving relentlessly toward its divinely appointed ends. The mysteries of divine will were known, therefore, in God's saving acts in history. As a part of blessings poured out upon all creation God may give the rains. But his character is revealed in the Exodus. He may cause both man and beast to be fruitful and multiply. But his true presence is known in his relationship with his people. In the worship of this kind of God there is no reason or place for eroticism or for any of the myriad magical rites of fecundity known among the Canaanites. Consequently sacred prostitutes,[6] witchcraft, and all other mechanical means to secure holiness and blessings are declared to be foreign to Israel and an abomination before her God.

It is not always easy even after thousands of years of Judaism and Christianity to conceive of an invisible, yet ever-present and all-powerful divinity. It was at least as difficult for the ancient Hebrews. So far as we know none of their neighbors held such a view. More normally there was a pantheon of deities, personifications of natural forces and processes, and represented by images of every sort and size, carefully or crudely made of wood, clay, gold, or what have you. There were no images of the God of Israel. He was "seen" in the desires of the heart, in the volition of the will, and in obedience to the divine word spoken in history.

singular instance and comes from a highly syncretistic and heterodox community in the postexilic period.

[6] It is interesting in this connection to note that women were not allowed to exercise the sacred offices of priest, prophet, and king. Athaliah, Queen of Judah from 842 to 837 B.C. is an exception. But this daughter of Ahab and Jezebel murderously seized the throne. Further, she was considered a usurper and was put to death by Jehoiada the priest as soon as Jehoash, the sole survivor of her crimes, was old enough to ascend (II Kings 11).

111

When the end product is seen first, the process that underlies it is either forgotten or compressed. Moreover, it seems the more ancient the history, the greater the danger of its compression. Israel's religion did not, like Athena, spring full-blown from the head of Zeus. Its ultimate origin and the stages of its development are not so obvious as they were once thought to be. Still it is undeniable that Hebrew faith passed through the refiner's fire until it understood, however imperfectly, what its irreducible minimum was, in short, a crucible from which emerged some of mankind's most sublime sureties.

V: THE GLORY OF ISRAEL

10. SAUL

Within a few years, no more than one generation and perhaps even less time,[1] the scattered, historically diverse and loosely related Hebrews of the hill country of Canaan were transformed into a united people. Out of the events of the latter part of the eleventh century B.C. emerged an Israelitic monarchy at one point exercising sovereignty on both sides of the Jordan from the Euphrates in the north to the Brook of Egypt in the south. The relative military and political superiority enjoyed by Israel in the brief moment of its glory is indicated by the vastness of this area, which included such historic and persistent enemies as the Kingdoms of Edom, Moab, Ammon, Damascus, and the alliance or perhaps vassalage of the Kingdom of Hamath.

This spectacular achievement, involving an almost complete reversal of roles for the Hebrews, is generally credited to David. It was he who smote Israel's enemies, extended the boundaries of the infant kingdom to imperial proportions, and established a dynasty that continued virtually uninterrupted for approximately four hundred and fourteen years.[2] So commanding is the figure of Jesse's son in the biblical narrative that the achievements of Saul pale into insignificance and the splendor of Solomon seems but a footnote. Yet the reasons for David's ascendency in biblical and later traditions are more theological than historical. Without the substantial accomplishments of the ill-starred Saul, there could have been no David. Without the political acumen of a Solomon, the United Monarchy would have ended long before it did, and the history of Israel, not to mention the fate of the throne, would have been vastly different.

Saul is the man who set the stage for Israel's golden age. He forged an alliance out of the divergent, often mutually hostile Hebrew tribes. Yet he is given little credit. Indeed in the Bible he is a tragic figure

---

[1] The chronological reference in I Samuel 13:1 is obscured by lack of an adequate text. The length of Saul's reign is not known. It may have been twelve or even twenty-two years from his anointing at Gilgal to his death on Gilboa.

[2] The current British dynasty, by comparison, has occupied the throne for two hundred and fifty-seven years.

worthy of a Sophocles or a Shakespeare. Few things were more undeserved by him than his progressive disappearance from the sacred record. Almost all the stories about Saul in I Samuel are in reality stories about David whose steady rise to the throne is always in view.

Chronicles' prosaic account of his reign adds only the story of his death, while the outlines of the history of Israel in Psalm 78 and in the apocryphal Ecclesiasticus 44 omit him entirely. Likewise, the New Testament contains no reference to this first king. The religious perspective of the Scriptures understands Saul as the anointed one who slipped from the Lord's hand. "So Saul died for his unfaithfulness," says the summary judgment of I Chronicles 10:13-14, "he was unfaithful to the Lord in that he did not keep the command of the Lord, and also consulted a medium, seeking guidance, and did not seek guidance from the Lord. Therefore the Lord slew him, and turned the kingdom over to David the son of Jesse."

There can be little doubt that the poorly defined extent of Saul's sovereignty ran afoul of the authority and power of the major religious leaders in Israel. The opposition of Samuel and his quarrels with Saul whom he himself had anointed to be prince over Israel (I Samuel 10:1-8) are sufficient evidence that the inevitable clash between the old order and the new did, in fact, take place. Moreover, few will question that Saul's religion, like that of many, perhaps most, Hebrews of his day, was a combination of Canaanite and Israelite elements. At least one of his children, Eshbaal, who succeeded to his father's throne (II Samuel 2:8), had a theophoric name honoring Baal. *Eshbaal* (I Chronicles 9:39) means "man of Baal" or perhaps "Baal exists." The editors of Samuel, following generally accepted later practice in the Hebrew Scriptures, substituted *bosheth* ("shame") for the name of the alien god. Thus in I Samuel 2:8 and

elsewhere in the following account this son of Saul who warred with David for a united throne (II Samuel 2:12–4:12) is known as Ishbosheth ("man of shame").[3]

Saul's turning to necromancy the night before the battle on Mount Gilboa (I Samuel 28:3-25), taken to be a sign of his religious apostasy by the biblical writers and occasionally by modern scholars, is more likely the result of his deranged mind combined with his fear at the recognition of impending military disaster. This disaster which ended Saul's reign and appeared to give the Philistines undisputed sway over the country is the event by which many historians evaluate this man. Martin Noth goes so far as to say that the final outcome of Saul's short reign was as hopeless as it could possibly be. Such judgments are unduly harsh. They do not take account of the anti-Saul sentiment of the writers. Moreover, they fail to keep in view the Hebrew situation in Canaan after Saul as compared with what obtained before. Prior to his ascension the Hebrew tribes were at best loosely related to one another through a religious loyalty to the shrine at Shiloh. Apparently each tribe undertook to maintain this shrine for a given month each year, supplying not merely funds but religious personnel as well. This pattern of quasi-political unity, well known to us from ancient Greece, is called an *amphictyony*, literally, "a gathering about a shrine." In their Greek form the amphictyonic leagues involved stronger political and military obligations than did their Hebrew counterpart. Only when immediate self-interest was directly threatened did one Israelite group join with another for concerted action. This is the pattern seen throughout the period of the

---

[3] There was also a Mephibosheth, the sixth son of Saul, the second son by Rizpah (II Samuel 21:8). This form of the name, meaning "he who scatters shame," was originally Meribaal, "loved by Baal." He is not to be confused with the Mephibosheth of II Samuel 21:7; I Chronicles 9:40. This latter was Jonathan's son who was befriended by David.

Judges. In Deborah's victory over Sisera in the northern plain, the tribes of Zebulun and Naphtali were principally engaged (Judges 4:10; 5:18). There was also aid from Issachar, Machir, Ephraim, and Benjamin (Judges 5:14-17). Other tribes either removed from the area of immediate conflict (such as Judah, Dan, and Reuben) or at peace with their Canaanite neighbors (such as Asher) were not involved. Likewise, the struggles of Samson with the Philistines (Judges 13:21–16:31) were local concerns reflecting at one point the frustrations and eventual failure of the tribe of Dan to settle the northern Shephelah. These two examples, one of a battle and the other of the adventures of a folk hero, are typical of the Hebrews' relations with the Canaanites and Philistines prior to Saul. Such actions produced some limited successes, but at no time was there a viable unity enabling the Hebrews to act in force out of a common interest. Saul was able to bring the people together and to weld them, however tentatively, into a political and military whole. This was one of his two major accomplishments. The other was the establishment of the institution of monarchy in Israel.

The series of events which brought Saul to power is not altogether clear. A handsome, strapping son of a wealthy family of Gibeah of Benjamin, he grew up in the central highlands, long a center of Israelite life. As a result of a battle at Eben-ezer sometime around the middle of the eleventh century B.C., the area had come under increasing Philistine pressure. The battle ended with a decisive Philistine victory over the Israelite tribal league. Shiloh, center of the tribal league, twelve miles south of Shechem and about the same distance north of Gibeah, was destroyed. Excavations at the site have revealed no trace of the Israelite sanctuary, but have shown that the site was occupied (by Hebrews) and destroyed in the first centuries of the Iron Age (ca. 1200-1000 B.C.).

The paucity of information recovered by archaeologists tends to underline passages such as Jeremiah 7:8-15; 26:4-9, where the absolute desolation of Shiloh is cited as an example of God's wrath upon the wickedness of the people. What, if any, historical reflection there is in the Jeremiah references is unclear. It is probable that in Jeremiah's day the solitude of the once-important site was viewed as a silent witness to the judgment of God.

With the symbol of Israelite unity in shambles, the Philistines moved to insure tranquillity. They established garrisons at new places in the highlands. Gibeath-elohim, the location of a "highplace" served by Samuel, became the seat of a Philistine governor. This place was scarcely more than three miles from Gibeah. In addition to the presence of soldiers, the Philistines exacted levies and laid prohibitions upon the Hebrews. The most serious of these was the prohibition on smiths. Fearing that the Hebrews would make iron swords and thus redress the arms imbalance, the conquerors required that all farm implements be brought to Philistine smiths for sharpening. If the writer of I Samuel 13:19-22 has not greatly exaggerated the situation, charges for such services were very high. Control, however, does not appear to have been such that these and similar matters were closely watched. Even in Saul's time some of the Hebrew warriors had equipment equal to the best in the Philistine armory. Some scholars, noting the iron plowshare found among the ruins of Saul's fortress at Gibeah, cite this as evidence that Saul had broken the Philistine iron monopoly in Canaan. This monopoly probably was broken on a large scale during his reign. Yet one plowshare is hardly decisive proof. Besides, this implement, the oldest datable iron object yet found in the highlands, could easily have been Philistine. Hebrew armament is a much better criterion for the coming of the Iron Age among the Israelites.

I Samuel contains two stories of the anointing of Saul. In one he set out to find his father's lost asses. Searching the hills northeast of Gibeah he finally came in desperation to seek out a holy man who would hopefully be able to tell him where the beasts were. The man was Samuel, who in obedience to revelations from the Lord anointed the young Benjaminite to be prince over Israel and so presented him to the people (I Samuel 9:3–10:27). The other story indicates that Saul was proclaimed king at the ancient shrine of Gilgal after his successful campaign to deliver Jabesh-Gilead from a siege by the Ammonites (I Samuel 11:1–12:25).

Scholars have differing views about these two accounts and their relation, if any, to one another. Nearly all agree that they are both compounded of early and late sources for the Samuel narrative and reflect both pro- and anti-monarchy arguments. This may partly explain the somewhat ambiguous role Samuel plays in each. But scholars are by no means agreed on other matters. Were there two anointings, one private and the other public? Or was there in fact only one anointing with considerable confusion in the tradition concerning its nature? We do not know for sure.

At any rate, Saul's first military action was not in Canaan against the Philistines, but in Transjordan against the Ammonites. Nahash of Ammon had laid siege to Jabesh-Gilead and had offered impossible terms for sparing the city (I Samuel 11:2). The besieged inhabitants, some of whom had affinities with the Benjaminites (Judges 21:8), stalled for time while they sought for aid. Saul, then at Gibeah, angered and uttering threats against any Israelite who refused to join him, gathered a sizable force and moved swiftly northward to Bezek. From this base halfway between Tirzah and Beth-shan in the hills of Ephraim, he struck across the Jordan surprising and decisively defeating the Ammonites around Jabesh-Gilead (I Samuel 11:1-11). From this victory the conquering hero proceeded southward to Gilgal near Jericho where he was "made king before the Lord" (I Samuel 11:12-15).

Why would the Philistines, wary of allowing the Hebrews to arm, allow Saul to raise an army and to conduct military action? It has been suggested that Saul moved too swiftly for effective Philistine action. Others have said he acted in secret until he had accomplished his objective in Transjordan. Still others think he may have been a trusted Philistine vassal similar to David at a later time. Perhaps none of these is true, and he was encouraged by the Philistines who hoped the Hebrews would turn their interest and growing energies toward the east leaving western Palestine alone.

Whatever the Philistine attitude, a Hebrew attack on Geba and its subsequent capture by Jonathan, Saul's oldest son, set the sword between Israelite and Philistine (I Samuel 13:3-4).

The die was cast. The struggle for supremacy which had been so long building in Canaan was joined. Hoping to crush the growing strength of Saul before it was consolidated, the Philistines moved in force into the central highlands. Driving the Hebrews from Michmash they struck at Israelite camps and villages north, east, and west. Again it was the daring Jonathan who supplied the impetus which allowed his father to drive the Philistines from Michmash and from the highlands. Thereafter Saul maintained a relatively free hand in controlling the Hebrew tribes on both sides of the Jordan. Of course, he fought continuously with the non-Hebrew peoples of the Transjordan and with the Philistines in the west along the borders of the Shephelah. Apart from the sparse information of I Samuel 15:4-9, we have few details about his Transjordanian wars. But from the Philistine wars comes one of the most widely known stories in history. In the Valley of Elah near

Azekah on the border between the kingdom of Saul and the territory of Gath, Philistine and Israelite armies faced one another. From the Philistine ranks stood forth Goliath the champion, a huge man who taunted the Hebrews to send forth a man for single combat. How amused must have been this disdainful warrior when he saw a stripling unarmed lad coming out to accept his challenge. But boasts and taunts turned to death as David's slingstone buried deep into the forehead of Goliath (I Samuel 17:19-54).[4]

Struggles along the borders were a fact of life for the first Hebrew monarch. Yet from non-Hebrew enclaves at Jebus (Jerusalem) and around Beth-shan, he ruled, apparently tranquilly, a kingdom from Mount Hermon in the north to the northern Negeb in the south. On the west the foothills of the mountains were his limits, while in the east he held much of the Transjordanian heights. But territorial boundaries can often be misleading. While it is possible to draw lines on a map to show the extent of Saul's kingdom, such will not tell very much about the situation in the country. In fact, the Hebrews continued to dwell mainly in the hills while the large Canaanite population predominated in the cities and lowlands. Philistine power, checked in the central highlands, continued a relatively free sway in the great valleys. It was in trying to end this dominion that Saul lost his life.

Benjamin, that fierce tribe of highland warriors, became the center of Saul's kingdom. At Gibeah of Benjamin, his home, Saul built his palace fortress and established his administrative center. Gibeah, thereafter known as "Gibeah of Saul," is today called Tell el-Ful ("hill of beans"). This pleasing hill, 2754 feet above sea level, is about three

miles north of the walls of Old Jerusalem. Today it is in danger of becoming a part of the suburbs of the expanding city. Here King Hussein of Jordan began constructing a palace in 1965-1966. In 1843 the site was identified as Gibeah of Saul. Twenty-five years later Lieutenant Charles Warren, on behalf of the Palestine Exploration Fund, conducted one of the first archaeological excavations in Palestine, partly exposing a fortress on the summit of Tell el-Ful. But Warren, contrary to his usual careful practice in Jerusalem, published no report of his findings north of the city. It remained for Professor Albright, digging in 1922-1923 and again in 1933, to confirm the correctness of earlier identification. Paul Lapp, whose Jerusalem home was beside the hill, excavated there in the early summer of 1964. He wanted to explore the site once more before modern royal buildings rendered the ancient royal site inaccessible to the archaeologist's spade.

Albright noted minor occupation of the

---

[4] This version of the story is from a later source and may have identified David with the exploits of another. At least this is suggested by II Samuel 21:19 where a man named Elhanan, from Bethlehem, is named as the slayer of Goliath.

site in the Middle Bronze Age. But it was not until the early Iron Age, perhaps in the last quarter of the thirteenth century B.C., that substantial occupation occurred. This "pre-fortress" period was the first of five periods of occupation described by Albright on the basis of his excavations. The hill was apparently in use until the time of Titus. Josephus says this general spent the night there in A.D. 70 before reaching doomed Jerusalem the next day. After the Roman juggernaut had passed through, the occupational history of Gibeah was at an end.

Pottery in the pre-fortress levels suggested Hebrew settlement between approximately 1300 B.C. and 1100 B.C. A large layer of ash found by the excavators indicates that a general conflagration apparently ended this period. This may be mute evidence of the grim events described in Judges 19–20.

The most important discovery at Tell el-Ful was the remains of a fortress. Rebuilt a number of times, this structure's oldest

A corner of Saul's palace-fortress at Gibeah. The rude construction perhaps is one indication of the lack of opulence at the court of the first king of Israel.

American Schools of Oriental Research

level consists of the foundations and lower walls in the southwest corner. These horizontally laid rough-dressed stones formed a wall up to four feet thick. Adjoining this wall was a larger tower, fifty-eight feet by thirty-seven feet. Its walls were up to six and a half feet thick. Albright concluded that the fortress walls were of the casemate type, that is, a double wall divided into interior sections by cross walls. Such fortifications, perhaps known in Palestine earlier, were reintroduced by the Philistines and were widely used by the Israelites, particularly during the United Monarchy.

On the basis of the existing ruins, especially the tower, and taking into consideration the contour of the mound, Albright projected the minimum size of the structure (apart from the corner towers) to be 169 feet by 114 feet. This hypothetical reconstruction was challenged by Father de Vaux to whom such a fortress could not have been built on the summit of Tell el-Ful. He suggested that a tower only, not a fortress, had been the distinguishing structure of the early Iron Age town. De Vaux's position caused some of the excavators, although not Albright himself, to say that, far from reducing the hypothetical dimensions of this perhaps first Israelite palace, they should be enlarged northward. This is, in fact, one of the modifications Lapp's later findings made in Albright's conclusions.

This first fortress seems to have been destroyed in the late eleventh century. It has been suggested that this destruction, if indeed that is what it was, resulted from Saul's victory over the Philistines (reading "Gibeah" for "Geba" in I Samuel 13:3, 16). Thus the second fortress, of less massive masonry, was the palace of Saul. Here David played the lyre before his king—and dodged a few spears (I Samuel 18:10-11). After a short occupancy this building was abandoned, apparently at Saul's death. Not until the late eighth century B.C., almost 300 years later, was it again a place of importance.

Lapp's 1964 excavations tended to highlight the general excellence of Albright's earlier work. Few modifications were required in the general conclusions of the previous excavations, yet a couple of these bearing upon the time of Saul are of importance. North of the southwest wall tower, the later excavators were fortunate enough to find a fragment of the west wall of Saul's fortress almost ten feet long. This helps to vindicate Albright's views against those of de Vaux, but also requires him to abandon his position that this structure had casemate walls. The more recently discovered section, clearly belonging to the same construction as the rest, is a single wall up to four feet thick. Moreover, Lapp has challenged the view that Saul destroyed an earlier Philistine fort and rebuilt it. On the contrary, he asserts that there is no evidence of Philistine occupation on the site. The so-called rebuilding of the earlier fortress will, if this conclusion is correct, have to be explained in another way. Albright had also failed to find distinctive Philistine pottery. But some scholars holding to the view that Saul had captured the hill from the Philistines suggested that by the late eleventh century B.C. the Philistines had become so at home in Canaan, they had ceased to manufacture distinctive pottery. Some arguments supporting this position make a distinction between pottery manufactured around 1050 B.C. and that fashioned approximately twenty-five years later. Lapp, who was rightly leery of such precise pottery chronology, was probably correct in rejecting views which owe much to this kind of dating.

Whatever the exact dimensions of his palace fortress and however Saul came into its possession, it was by contemporary royal standards a poor show. At best a small, austere building occupying a two-acre hilltop, it was, like Saul himself, a symbol of transition. Hardly impressive in light of the royal Hebrew magnificence which in less than

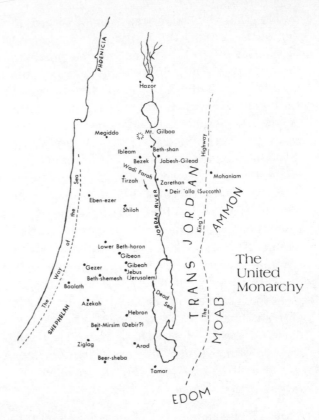

The United Monarchy

a century would dominate Solomon's capital only three miles away, it was nonetheless, like Saul himself, monumental in the promise it embodied. For here was proof of the unity of Israel, a unity considerably more solid than that of Shiloh which was so ineffective in crisis. Here was a king, however much he resembled the judges, those warrior-chieftains of older days. Here was a monarchy, however fledgling. Moreover, the kingdom of Saul was not so primitive as many scholars suggest. The historic differences between north and south were handled well enough, better, it seems, than either David or Solomon was able to do. The north and Transjordan were divided into five administrative districts.[5] Judah, which favored David over Eshbaal after Saul's death, seems to have been firmly in the grasp of Saul. Even David, made outlaw by Saul's jealousy, could not find safety among his

[5] Benjamin, Ephraim, Jezreel, Asher, and Gilead.

native Judahites and was finally forced to flee to the land of the Philistines (I Samuel 27:1, and others). As Saul moved north to prevent the Philistines from cutting his kingdom in half and also to try to wrest Beth-shan from their hands, he could rejoice in his considerable accomplishments. He had made the beginnings of a nation. Not many could have done any better, and probably few could have done as well.

He fell with three of his sons on Mount Gilboa, and the Philistines hanged the slain royal bodies on the wall of Beth-shan (I Samuel 31:1-10). Saul and Jonathan, "swifter than eagles . . . stronger than lions," were dead. In time the biblical writers would first strip them of their honor and later omit them entirely from the recitation of the mighty deeds of Israel. But perhaps the career and accomplishments of Saul were more accurately reflected in the behavior of the men of Jabesh-gilead who had not forgotten:

When the inhabitants of Jabesh-Gilead heard what the Philistines had done to Saul, all the valiant men arose, and went all night, and took the body of Saul and the bodies of his sons from the wall of Bethshan; and they came to Jabesh and burnt them there. And they took their bones and buried them under the tamarisk tree in Jabesh, and fasted seven days.

I Samuel 31:11-13

11. DAVID

It is difficult to gain an accurate picture of David and of his kingdom. "The throne of David" is a phrase full of meaning for Christians and Jews. The Messiah, the Anointed of the Most High, would come from the house and lineage of David, and would rule a blessed kingdom whose saints would be sons of David. Already by the time of Jeremiah the idea of the throne and kingship of David was being transformed from a temporal, earthly quality to a more abstract definition in such terms as "justice" and

"righteousness" (Jeremiah 22:2-4). The true successor to David would heed the plight of the alien, the fatherless, the widow. He would, in short, be an ideal ruler in an ideal kingdom.

Jeremiah's oracle concerning the royal house of Judah, to cite only one example, shows us a stage in the process of the transformation of David from a person into a religious symbol. By the time of the writing of I Chronicles the process is complete. A comparison of II Samuel 9–22 (the so-called "court history") with I Chronicles 11–29 indicates that David, a tremendously complicated personality capable of opposite extremes of emotion and action, had become a more or less one-dimensional individual. He is in I Chronicles the spotless holy king, the chosen of God, a commanding figure of uncompromised religious purity. There is no mention of Bathsheba, still less a whisper of the premeditated murder of Uriah. David's utter failure as a father in his own house is glossed over and the shameful treatment of the loyal Joab a thing forgotten. Where Saul had failed, David made a workable marriage between religion and the state. While Solomon introduced foreign gods into Jerusalem and built temples in their honor, David was faithful only to the God of the Hebrews. The religious writers of Israel did not forget these things when they made their evaluations of their kings.

David, of course, stands deservedly astride the biblical tradition like a giant colossus. This position was gained not merely for his religious politics and personal piety, but also because he brought Israel to its hour of economic, military, and political glory.

David's great friend, Jonathan, the crown prince of Israel, fell with his father at Gilboa. Eshbaal, the next son, supported and probably manipulated by Abner, Saul's first cousin and commander of his army, established the throne at Mahanaim, a religious center long associated with Israel's traditions (Genesis 32:1-2). It is not known why Eshbaal chose this location, although it is generally speculated that after the defeat of Israel at Gilboa the Philistines took steps to render Gibeah unsafe for Hebrew leadership. Whatever the reason for the choice, Mahanaim's location in Transjordan almost due east of Shechem offered Eshbaal two immediate advantages. First, it removed him from the sphere of Philistine power. Apparently little interested in expansion west of the Jordan, they never sought conquest across the river to the east. Second, Mahanaim was well situated to maintain effective communication with the Hebrew tribes west of the river. The Wadi Farah, a beautiful and verdant gorge, joins the Jordan Valley with Shechem, long recognized as the crossroads of Palestine. The valley of the Jabbok, near which Mahanaim was located, gives easy access to the Wadi Farah. Eshbaal, then, could hope to recoup his father's losses while holding together the hard-won Hebrew federation. But he had reckoned without David. The five tribal regions of the north (Benjamin, Ephraim, Jezreel, Asher, and Gilead) accepted this new king as their rightful ruler. "But the house of Judah followed David" (II Samuel 2:8-10).

Anointed by Samuel while Saul yet reigned, hounded into the wilderness as an outlaw, David had spared the life of his sovereign once and perhaps twice.[1] When an Amalekite, apparently hoping for a reward, told David of Saul's death and claimed to have had a personal hand in it, the king-to-be had the man put to death. "How is it," David asked, "you were not afraid to put forth your hand to destroy the Lord's anointed?" (II Samuel 1:1-16). While Saul lived David made no attempt to seize the kingdom. Quite apart from David's recognition of Saul as "the Lord's anointed," such an attempt

would doubtless have failed anyway. Religious belief and political realism combined to prevent an ill-timed and likely futile coup.

But plans were being laid and political and personal due bills being collected, so that when the moment was right Jesse's son, the shepherd from Bethlehem, could reach for the throne with reasonable hope of success. After being driven from his native Judah by Saul's relentless efforts to kill him, David allied himself as vassal to Achish, king of Gath. This Philistine overlord welcomed the valiant Hebrew and his fighting band of six hundred retainers into his service and established them at Ziglag. From this base on the fringe of the Negeb, David could serve his new master by keeping the Amalekites and other troublesome peoples in check. This he did with some success (I Samuel 27:8). But his distance south of Gath (approximately twenty-three miles) coupled with the fact that he was raiding still farther south gave him the chance to serve his own interests as well. By lying and by slaughter he concealed from Achish his activities on behalf of the Judahites who were supposed to have been numbered among his victims (I Samuel 27:9-12). "He has made himself utterly abhorred by his people Israel," thought the king of Gath to himself, and all the while David was using his position at Ziglag to ingratiate himself to the elders of Judah. So trusting was Achish when he moved northward with the other Philistines to confront Saul, that he insisted upon David and his men coming to fight at his side. It was the objection of other Philistine commanders that removed David from the embarrassing position of engaging in war against "the Lord's anointed" (I Samuel 29:1-11). It was indeed in this very battle that Saul fell mortally wounded. Had David been involved against Israel on this occasion, his monarchical hopes could have expired with Saul on Mount Gilboa.

While the issue was being joined in the north, David returned to Ziglag to find it

---

[1] The number depends upon whether I Samuel 23:14–24:22 and I Samuel 26:1-25 are seen as two incidents or two reports of the same event.

burned. The Amalekites had struck in his absence. Overwhelming the garrison, they carried off booty and the whole population including two of David's wives. With characteristic decisiveness he overtook the raiders and recovered people and property. It is instructive that even on this occasion David, who had in turn taken Amalekite booty, was careful to send part of it "to his friends, the elders of Judah" (I Samuel 30:1-31).

For over a year David had been in exile. Now the time had come. Saul was dead. A weak successor dominated by an ambitious relative was in an undistinguished city surrounded by a tribe (Gad) of questionable loyalty. David returned to Judah with his family and army of retainers. He went to Hebron, hallowed by the grave of Abraham, and one of the cities whose leaders David had carefully courted (I Samuel 30:31). There the men of Judah came and anointed him king (II Samuel 2:1-4). Whether or not he knew Eshbaal had established court at Mahanaim is questionable. Perhaps David reigned first. At any rate he dropped broad hints that others besides the Judahites might recognize him as king (II Samuel 2:7). Moreover, once having set his hand to the plow he did not look back.

Hebron, where Abraham died, David reigned, and Absalom revolted, is one of the biblically most important and archaeologically most disappointing sites in Palestine. Located about nineteen miles south of Jerusalem in a generously watered valley high (3040 feet above sea level) on the mountainous spine of Palestine, it has been almost continuously occupied since its founding in the middle of the fourteenth century B.C. The ancient city lay on the western side of the valley, but after the Crusades shifted somewhat to the east. Today it centers upon the massive Haram el-Khalil, "the sacred precinct of the friend." This is the great mosque built over the traditional tomb of Abraham, "the friend of God." Since 1948 a large num-

Middle Bronze Age walls at Hebron. Excavations in 1966, hampered by modern buildings and arbors, failed to unearth any significant materials from the Israelite period, and hence, nothing connected with David.

ber of Arab refugees has swelled the population of this sacred city and has caused modern dwellings, some substantial, some otherwise, to spread across the valley. For the archaeologist this means that much important land is temporarily or permanently beyond exploration.

Apart from the Haram el-Khalil there is little of archaeological importance to be seen today in Hebron. The western slope of the valley has yielded some Late Bronze Age pottery and parts of an ancient wall not yet sufficiently identified. In the summer of 1966 the American Expedition to Hebron carried on extensive excavations under frustrating circumstances. More Bronze Age walls were uncovered and also what may prove to be important structures with considerable pottery for dating purposes. But the presence of dwellings and of mature orchards severely hampered work. What has been unearthed is tempting but inconclusive. In any event, nothing of Davidic Hebron has been found. One might hazard a guess, however, that in spite of its importance and hallowed connections the first royal city of David was a small, rude place. Because of its sufficient water and the fertility of the surrounding area (this may have been "the land of milk and honey," see Numbers 13:23) it was probably relatively prosperous for its time. Yet with the possible exception of the Haram (whose walls and present scale are Herodian), it has had little to distinguish it through the years. Surely it was no different in that respect in David's day. We can hardly expect that he glorified a city while all his efforts were focused on winning and securing a kingdom. He did little to enhance the beauty of Jerusalem in more favorable circumstances. Hebron, too much overlooked by historians, theologians, and archaeologists, was an important way station for David, but only a way station.

Secure in Hebron, and with the Philistines regarding him as a faithful vassal, David moved against Eshbaal. Perhaps it would be more accurate to say that the inevitable struggle for the kingdom of Saul began in earnest. It began with an incident not altogether clear but with far-reaching implications for some time to come. Eight miles north and slightly west of Jerusalem, at Gibeon, the forces of David and those of Eshbaal met for the first time, perhaps by design, perhaps by accident. There had not as yet been any blood shed by supporters of the rivals for the throne. When they initially confronted one another, it was agreed that the main groups would sit on either side of the great pool of Gibeon while twelve young men of Benjamin engaged twelve of David's young retainers. Whether or not this was to be mortal combat we do not know. But what happened is clear enough. The men fell

to killing one another and almost at once both armies were engaged in a full-scale military engagement probably resembling a riot. David's forces prevailed and pursued Abner and his men as they fled. Somewhat dismayed by the whole affair, Abner, regrouping his scattered men, implored Joab to recall his forces before the two sides devoured each other. Joab agreed (II Samuel 2:12-32). But Abner had already killed Joab's brother, Asahel. Twice Abner had warned the relentlessly pursuing Asahel to turn back. The second time he warned him saying, "Turn aside from following me; why should I smite you to the ground? How then could I lift up my face to your brother Joab?" (II Samuel 2:22). If this was known to Joab he paid no heed to his rival's efforts to spare his brother. From that day there was a blood feud between him and Abner, a feud which ended with Abner's death at Joab's treacherous hands (II Samuel 3:26-30).

In the past few years our knowledge of the setting of some of these events has been greatly enhanced by archaeology. Digging at el-Jib for five seasons between 1956 and 1962, scholars not only established beyond reasonable doubt that the site was Gibeon, but they excavated a great pool. This enormous cylinder is thirty-seven feet in diameter and eighty-two feet deep. Its perpendicular sides contain a spiral stairway of seventy-nine steps. A tunnel cut 167 feet through solid rock brought water from this pool inside the city in times of siege. J. B. Pritchard, director of the work, cautiously dated the original construction of the reservoir and its tunnel "within the twelfth and the eleventh centuries." This, then, is almost certainly the place of that first and disastrous meeting between the militant supporters of David and those of Eshbaal. Incidentally, during Jeremiah's time the pool at Gibeon seems also to have been the location of the battle between the men of Ishmael, murderer of Gedaliah, and those of Johanan who avenged the murder and then fled to Egypt taking Jeremiah with him (Jeremiah 41:1-18).

The fight at Gibeon was but a preview of things to come. As the war dragged on, Eshbaal's strength grew weaker while David's power increased. Then Abner, who was of the royal family, made a move toward the throne, and an angry scene ensued between him and Eshbaal (II Samuel 3:6-11). As a result Abner conspired with the elders of Israel to make David king in the north as well as in the south (II Samuel 3:12-19). He then came to Hebron to make necessary arrangements with David (3:20-21), only to fall victim to Joab's hatred (3:26-27). This murder at a moment of delicate negotiations and in Hebron where Abner had doubtless come under promise of safe conduct seriously compromised David's chances of being crowned in the north. To counter this danger David, who was innocent of the deed, made a public show of his grief and was among other things the chief mourner at Abner's funeral (II Samuel 3:28-39).

Some in Israel saw in the death of Abner the inevitability of David on the throne of Saul. The only remaining question for those of this view was how to switch sides as facilely as possible and with as much profit as they could. Accordingly, two captains of Saul's commandos, Rechab and his brother Baanah, foully murdered Eshbaal in his bed and brought his head to David at Hebron. They expected to be greatly honored as a result of David's gratitude. Instead they were put to death and their bodies disgraced (II Samuel 4:1-3, 5-12). Apart from punishing those who apparently played a role in the revolt of the northern tribes under Sheba (II Samuel 21:7-9) David never wavered in his public respect for Saul and his descendants. But even the deaths of Saul's descendants on that later occasion were given a bizarre twist by David (21:10-14). Still David went to great lengths to protect respect for the office he hoped to make secure.

With Eshbaal and Abner dead there was no serious rival to David. The elders of Israel came to Hebron and David reigned "over all Israel and over Judah" (II Samuel 5:1-5). This curious phrase shows the deep divisions inherited by David. But he moved swiftly to solidify his newly won dominion. The first requirement was a new capital. Unsure of the loyalty of the north, he could hardly strengthen the professed good faith of the elders of Israel by continuing to rule from Hebron in the heart of Judah. Yet the north offered no suitable alternative. Whatever else Gibeah had against it, that city was after all Saul's home. And Gilgal, an ancient shrine, was unsuited not only because of its connections with Saul but also because of its lack of adequate natural defenses. Shechem and several other possible capitals had the same drawback as Hebron: they were too far from the other half of the kingdom. David had played upon the natural divisions between north and south in order to gain his throne. It was a stratagem full of terrible prospects for the future of the kingdom as events were to prove. Immediately it confronted him with the need to heal the breach he had exploited. Proper choice of a capital was therefore not merely important, but crucial. And the perfect location was there.

Jerusalem had been a Jebusite fortress for centuries. Early Hebrew attempts to capture it had failed (Joshua 15:63). Even during the reign of Saul it sat unchallenged only three miles from the Israelite capital. On the border between the northern and southern Hebrew tribes and without historical connections with either element, it could not but attract David's attention and envy. Moreover, it was a formidable stronghold in the high mountains (2500 feet above sea level) and would provide the warrior king a defense he was almost sure to need. So David and his private retainers moved against the Jebusites.

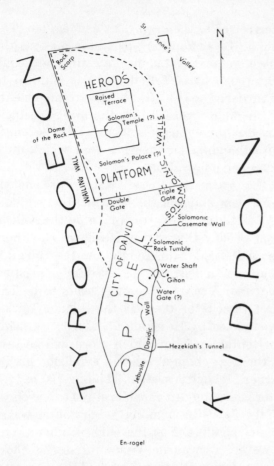

Jerusalem, the Holy City, is also a bloody symbol of hatred, narrowness, bigotry, provincialism, and a host of other evils which every religion that has fought to possess it has claimed to have disowned. It has been fought over too often by too many people with too much loss of life. An imposing citadel in a highly defensible location, it has seldom been taken cheaply. The Jebusite city confronting David was no exception. It occupied 10.87 acres of Ophel, that wedge-shaped ridge just south of the Temple platform of today's Old City. On the west Ophel is bordered by the Tyropoeon Valley, long since filled in, but in David's day a formidable depression. To the east across the narrow ridge (one hundred to one hundred and fifty yards wide) is the Kidron Valley whose western slopes, at places with a surface angle of forty-five degrees or more, further enhanced

the feeling of security of the inhabitants. With the battering ram instead of the bomb as the main means of destroying the walls, they could afford to hurl their taunts at David. Indeed, at first sight it would have appeared that "the blind and the lame" could provide adequate defense in such a natural stronghold (see II Samuel 5:6-8). Only on the north where there is a more or less gentle slope did nature fail to provide. Yet it can be surmised that the Jebusites had strong fortifications here. At least David seems to have made no attempt to take the city from this direction. The British School of Archaeology, excavating Ophel from 1961 to 1967, established the line of the Jebusite north wall with some certainty and even suggested that it was a heavy wall over twenty-six feet thick. But they failed to uncover a portion of the wall itself. This is hardly surprising. Ophel suffered major damage when Titus destroyed the city in A.D. 70. With even more disastrous consequences for archaeology, it served Hadrian's builders as a rock quarry when they built the Roman city of Aelia Capitolina in A.D. 135.

II Samuel 5:8 says that David found the weakness of the defense of Jerusalem to be its water shaft. By this means the Hebrews led by Joab (I Chronicles 11:6) entered the town, smote the Jebusites, and established David in his royal city that was thereafter to be a symbol of faith to millions down through the years. The brief accounts of Samuel and Chronicles make it sound very easy. Archaeology, however, has unearthed the Jebusite water system and has shown the difficulties facing Joab and his companions who scrambled into a hostile city.

An adequate water supply in time of danger was a major problem facing ancient engineers as they planned and executed plans for fortifying their cities. Few were fortunate enough to have natural wells or springs on the hill tops which were otherwise pre-

The Pool of Siloam today, showing the mosque built atop the entrance to the tunnel. Construction at the site, ancient and modern, has removed much of the evidence the archaeologist needs to reconstruct the occupational history of the Pool.

ferred defensive sites. In Palestine, at least, cisterns were widely employed to correct this lack. But beside being dependent upon the fickle rains, these basins were lined with porous mud plaster until the Late Bronze-Early Iron period when impermeable lime material came into general use. Cisterns were, therefore, unsatisfactory, and other means were sought. Many of the cities had springs at or near the bottom of the hill, below the city wall which usually sat upon the brow of the ridge. The problem was to bring the water within the walls without reducing the defensive posture of the city. The answer which archaeology has made familiar to us from a number of sites[2] was a water shaft penetrating the rock beneath the wall. This would either cause the water to flow into the city, as in the case of Hezekiah's later tunnel at Jerusalem, or allow the inhabitants to visit the water source without exposing

[2] In addition to those at Jerusalem, rock-cut water tunnels have been excavated at Gezer, Gibeon, Ibleam, and Megiddo.

themselves to the enemy, as at Megiddo. The Middle Bronze system at Gezer may be the oldest yet excavated in Palestine, although that found at et-Tell in 1969 is claimed to be earlier. The twelfth-century arrangements at Megiddo are certainly the most spectacular. But the Jebusite system at Jerusalem is an astounding engineering feat which must command admiration.

The major source of water for ancient Jerusalem and the factor which determined its exact location was a spring on the Kidron slope. Today this spring is known as Gihon, its Old Testament name, or the Virgin's Fountain, a designation used by Christian pilgrims. A maze of tunnels leads to it. The most famous of these is the Siloam Tunnel constructed by Hezekiah about 700 B.C. This horizontal shaft, of which more will be said in the next chapter, was an extension of the earlier Jebusite system. The walls of the later city extended considerably beyond those of the Jebusites making a horizontal water tunnel possible. For the earlier inhabitants, however, it was necessary to dig a short horizontal shaft and connect into it by means of an almost vertical drop. Warren, working under the original impetus of the Palestine Exploration Fund, first excavated these shafts in 1867/68. But it was not until 1911, when the Siloam Tunnel was being cleared by a British expedition, that Father H. Vincent of the Ecole Biblique took the opportunity to trace out the various passageways and to suggest possible datings of the constructions.

The first attempt by the Jebusites to reach the spring from the summit was an abortive vertical shaft abandoned when the lower strata of hard rock proved to be impenetrable. Another attempt following a circuitous route sometimes sloping, sometimes horizontal, threaded its way through softer rock until it was able to plunge over thirty-five feet vertically into a horizontal shaft tapping the Spring Gihon.

It was difficult to reconcile the position of the upper end of this tunnel, thought by Vincent to be Jebusite, with the so-called "Tower of David" identified by R. A. S. Macalister in his excavations from 1923 to 1926. If Macalister were correct the opening would have been over ninety feet outside the walls. This would hardly have satisfied the defensive needs of the city or have allowed access to attackers as indicated in II Samuel and I Chronicles. For this reason Miss Kenyon began her work in 1961 by digging at the foot of the tower. Soon she established that Macalister was incorrect. Under what he thought was the base of the tower, Miss Kenyon found seventh-century B.C. houses. The tower was, in fact, a later structure belonging to the Maccabean defenses of the city. The Jebusite wall was discovered somewhat farther along the slope, well beyond the opening to the tunnel. Moreover, even though the remaining pottery data were scanty, they were sufficient to date the remarkable water system to the later stages of Jebusite occupation.

Either the Jebusites blocked and sought to conceal the opening leading into their stronghold, or they thought the difficulty of scaling the vertical shaft was enough to dissuade or foil any enemy. Perhaps they rested secure in a combination of the two. But either or both failed to prevent Joab's entry by this route. His penetration of the defenses perhaps at the same moment David was assaulting the walls was successful in delivering the city into the hands of his king.

The recent work of the British School has tended to confirm the statements in II Samuel 5:9 and I Chronicles 11:8 which suggest David made extensive repairs to Jebusite construction but did not expand the city. Perhaps David did considerable damage in his assault. Or perhaps the Jebusites had allowed their city to fall into a state of disrepair. Excavations in 1962 showed that the Jebusite town wall continued in use during David's time, intact until the beginning of the seventh century B.C. when it was replaced by another wall at a different angle to the hill. Furthermore, Miss Kenyon surmised that an excavated tower in the western Jebusite wall is possibly the northern tower of the Water Gate of ancient Jerusalem. If this educated guess is correct, this would have been Solomon's path into the city after he was anointed by Nathan and Zadok at Gihon (I Kings 1:32-40).

Too late the Philistines became aware of David's power and of his even greater potential for the future. Hoping to repeat their former victories over the Hebrews, they moved into the highlands with the obvious intention of breaking David in his newly won stronghold. If the story of David's "three mighty men" (II Samuel 23:13-17; I Chronicles 11:15-19) comes from this period, as some scholars think, the Philistines would have occupied Bethlehem only six miles south of Jerusalem. But their attempts to move against Jerusalem itself were repulsed in the Valley of Rephaim southwest of the city (II Samuel 5:17-21; I Chronicles 14:8-12). A second time the Philistines gathered in the same valley and menaced the new king. A second time David scattered them and caused them to flee as far as Gezer (II Samuel 5:22-25; I Chronicles 14:13-17). These engagements did not entirely end Israel's troubles with the Philistines, but they put an effective brake on Philistine hopes of dominating Canaan.

At this juncture, with Jerusalem secured and the Philistines on the defensive, David struck another masterful blow in his efforts to forge a united people. Amid scenes of wild excitement the Ark of the Covenant, that old symbol of the presence of God among his people, was brought to the new capital. David himself leaped and danced, apparently naked, before the Ark. He then caused it to be placed in a tent prepared for it. Here, at what was to be the religious center of Israel,

David offered sacrifices, blessed the people, and distributed gifts among them (II Samuel 6:1-19; I Chronicles 15:1–16:43).

Of all the moves of the wily David this one, compounded of his deep religious faith and his political wisdom, was the shrewdest. At one fell swoop he made Jerusalem the holiest site in Israel and sought to weave Hebrew tribal loyalties into the fabric of his kingdom. Where Saul failed in matters of religion and the state, David succeeded, perhaps all too well, at least as far as the development of the religion was concerned. Politically the system did not fare so well.

When David came to the throne, he ruled over "all Israel" and Judah. To overcome this division between the five tribal districts of Saul and Judah, he tried to revive an older tribal structure which had apparently obtained during the early days of the settlement in Canaan. This system, involving twelve units[3] instead of six, offered him the opportunity to circumvent the rivalry between the two tribal alliances which had grown out of the earlier arrangements. Jerusalem was to be the center of the new state. Not only was the shrine there, but David made Abiathar, the legitimate high priest of the Shiloh line, a court official and head of the Jerusalem cult. The difference between this and the older situation was, of course, a strong monarchy in place of the ineffective priestly leadership which Shiloh had offered.

This was a new order in Israel. At the same time it shows how religious and traditional David was. To give effective organization to his administration he looked to the religious traditions of Israel for his model. In doing so he produced an astounding success and a miserable failure. When he brought religion and politics successfully together, he indelibly stamped a divine nationalism upon the religion of Israel. In time

the lines between the Kingdom of Israel and the Kingdom of God became blurred. The two were on occasion seen to be coextensive. Some of the worst excesses of this kind of thinking appear in certain intertestamental writings where a militant nationalism has alloyed and degraded the basic themes of covenant and judgment (see, for example, I Enoch 89–90). Perhaps some of the finer expressions are to be found in the writings of II Isaiah (Isaiah 40–55) and in Paul's conception of a "new Israel" as the kingdom of the saints of God. But for better or for worse, David gave a definite change to Hebrew religion by infusing it with nationalism, and Judaism and Christianity have wrestled with the positive and negative aspects of the issue throughout their respective histories.

This change in the direction of religious development was the spectacular achievement of David and is more than any other factor the reason why he is remembered and venerated. His failure was administrative. The older tribal structure was not viable. The ease with which Absalom used it to undermine his father's authority (II Samuel 15:1–18:33) shows that a government could not at length rely on a system where so much depended upon one man while at the same time considerable actual or potential power was in the hands of the tribal elders. Moreover, the rallying cry of Sheba in his revolt against David [4] indicates how unsuccessful David was in his attempt to turn time back. In spite of all his efforts, "all Israel," Saul's old five-tribe league, was ready to align itself against Judah. With some defection on the part of Benjamin, this was in fact exactly what happened after the death of Solomon. Not even extreme measures succeeded. David was always king of Israel *and* Judah; the division was constantly recognized. His son Solomon, who at once saw the weakness of

[3] This does not include the Levites who were settled in special cities, mostly Canaanite ones incorporated into Israel.

[4] "We have no portion in David, and we have no inheritance in the son of Jesse; every man to his tents, O Israel!" (II Samuel 20:1). See also I Kings 12:16.

this political structure, reorganized the kingdom into administrative districts having little to do with tribal boundaries (I Kings 4:7-19). David's reinstated twelve-tribe system continued in the organization of the Jerusalem temple, but in terms of its political effect it had never really succeeded.

Yet in the moments of his early successes and for some time to come, whatever doubts there were about David were erased by his defeat of the Philistines and by his own genuine concern for the faith of his fathers. He had not only lifted the threat that hung heavy over the land, but had reduced these descendants of the Sea Peoples to such a state that they never again were a major factor in military or political affairs. And Jerusalem, "the royal city of King David," was also the place of the presence of God.

With the nation rallied behind him, David turned upon Israel's ancient foes. One by one the Ammonites, the Edomites, the Moabites, and the various peoples of the southern desert fell before the warrior, and their lands were added to his dominions. Least surprising was his assimilation of the Canaanite cities of the plains, so long a barrier to Hebrew hegemony. Most surprising he defeated the Arameans in northern Transjordan and Syria, annexed Damascus, and held sway as far north as the Euphrates. The Phoenician cities dominated by Tyre and its King Hiram, who had already had dealings with David (II Samuel 5:11; I Chronicles 14:1), remained at peace. They turned their eyes westward and entered their greatest period of maritime activity. At the same time the influence of Phoenician culture upon Canaan, now Israel, did not cease. Archaeology is only beginning to show the strength of this influence. What little progress there was under David in the refinement of the plastic arts is more and more being shown to have been inspired by the highly developed if somewhat eclectic Phoenician civilization of the time.

With this vast extension of territory came enormous economic advantages. In addition to slaves and booty, the normal reward of victory in that day, there were the two great trade routes, *The Way of the Sea* in the east and *The King's Highway* on the Transjordanian heights. David fully controlled both, and their value to his treasury can hardly be exaggerated. They were to be the foundation of the splendor of Solomon. Moreover, David's eager conquest of Edom (II Samuel 8:14; I Chronicles 18:11-13; I Kings 11:15-16) may have in part been due to the large amounts of copper and iron in the southern part of that land. Solomon is usually credited with developing this resource, and both the Bible and popular lore maintain a certain interest in "King Solomon's mines." But there is a Muslim tradition which speaks of David in the role usually assigned to Solomon. Professor Glueck's researches in the area of Elath at Tell el-Kheleifeh and in the Arabah have indicated that the ancient mining and smelting operations, traces of which have been found in this region, were worked during the early Hebrew monarchy. Pottery chronology can be no more precise than that. There is no doubt that Solomon profited by mining and refining activity here. Still the possibility that he may have inherited this too from his father is a suggestive one.

David may also have begun the fortification of the country, a task which occupied a good deal of Solomon's interest when he became sovereign. But here the evidence is very slim indeed. Under David Israel was internally basically much as it had been. His policy of incorporating non-Hebrew elements into the kingdom meant that there were few if any population dislocations within the original borders of the country. Canaanites doubtless continued for some time to predominate in many cities, while the kingdom as a whole remained principally an agricultural and pastoral state. Perhaps this partly explains why archaeology has produced almost no structures which with confidence can be attributed to David. The particular problems of Ophel have been noted. Yet there are two sites which may suggest that the extensive fortification of the country by Solomon was actually begun by David. At Beth-Shemesh and at Tell Beit Mirsim (Debir), casemate walls dated to the early tenth century B.C. have been unearthed. These, it is widely held, were of Davidic construction. Against the idea that this was part of an actual or projected general fortification of the kingdom, it should be noted that both sites are on the Philistine frontier. They may therefore represent little more than David's attempts to guard against Philistine resurgence.[5]

The last years of David's long reign saw the beginning of inevitable change in Israel. Ready availability of slaves and vast amounts of money from new sources were certain to make a difference in the standard of living, to take only two examples. While the zenith of this development was not reached until Solomon exploited the resources provided by his father, there can be little doubt that during David's lifetime there was an increased perfection in the style and execution of various artifacts. This rise in technical perfection is noticeable in many archaeological excavations with tenth-century B.C. Hebrew remains.

The country prospered, and David grew old and sat upon the throne of Israel. Like Caesar Augustus he lived too long, and his latter days were full of sadness occasioned by his children. David's earlier failures as a father in his own house came upon the old man with a vengeance. Relative weakness in Mesopotamia and in Egypt combined with the subjugation of ancient foes to allow Israel freedom from foreign wars in the latter

[5] It has been suggested that a portion of the casemate wall at Megiddo is Davidic in origin. If so, evidence of his fortifications would not be restricted to the southwest and the main Philistine frontier.

part of David's reign. Internally, however, the kingdom was shaken by intrigue and open revolt in which the royal princes played no small part. Yet in the end David lived to see a strong son secure on the throne with him as coregent. The shepherd from Bethlehem had reunited a kingdom, secured it, expanded it, endowed it, and safely passed it on to able hands. "Then David slept with his fathers, and was buried in the city of David. . . . So the kingdom was established in the hand of Solomon" (I Kings 2:10, 46b).

12. SOLOMON

Solomon's magnificence, heralded in his own day, has subsequently become fabled. A master builder the like of whom was not seen again in the land until Herod, he not only glorified Jerusalem but erected massive structures throughout the land. Trade routes by land and by sea enriched his treasury and introduced luxury items on a wide scale. This grand monarch, cosmopolitan, eclectic, urbane, brought Israel to the pinnacle of its glory as an international power, an economic force, and perhaps also in self-indulgence. Like Louis XIV, Solomon basked in splendor unprecedented in his nation. But as was the case with this later French counterpart, the costs were enormous. Solomon's varied and vast sources of income could not keep pace with his expenditures. His administrative structure emphasized tribal antagonisms exploited by his father. His religious practices and views caused him to be remembered as the one who sacrificed at the "high places" and who introduced a host of foreign gods into Jerusalem. At his death internal discord combined with the resurgent strength of ancient external foes to bring down his throne and return his dominions to their former condition as a variety of petty states.

Solomon's claim to the throne was tenuous. First, there was no dynastic principle in Israel at that time. Saul's son had not succeeded in claiming his father's throne. Sec-

THE GLORY OF ISRAEL

ond, Solomon was not the oldest living son of David, still less was he the crown prince. Of the six sons born of David's wives in Hebron (II Samuel 3:2; I Chronicles 3:1-4), at least the first and third, Amnon and Absalom, were dead. The fate of Chileab ("Daniel" in I Chronicles 3:1), the second born, is not known. Solomon, the second son of David and Bathsheba, ranked well down the list of the sons born in Jerusalem (II Samuel 5:13-14; I Chronicles 3:5-9; 14:3-8). With title to the throne clouded both by lack of tradition and by the absence of a crown prince, a fratricidal struggle—at the very least—was in prospect when the time came for the aging David to "sleep with his fathers." No one was more keenly aware of this than David himself who had already witnessed the murderous hatred the royal princes bore one another.

As David tottered toward death, his oldest living son, Adonijah, prepared to inherit the throne. Gathering about him a lordly retinue including some of his father's oldest followers and most faithful men, this heir presumptive went just south of the city, to En-rogel, where he more or less held court (I Kings 1:5-10). But David, under the urging of Nathan and Bathsheba, strangely allied, moved to forestall a power struggle after his death. He named Solomon as coregent and caused him to be anointed as king.[1] By so doing he perhaps delayed the eventual break-up of the kingdom. He also prevented, for the moment, further fratricidal struggle within the royal family. But upon David's death Solomon, motivated by his mother Bathsheba, killed his half-brother Adonijah. So a third of the Davidic princes royal fell in the family struggles. With him fell many of those who had been faithful to David, including Joab, ever loyal, deserving of more attention than he usually receives from his-

[1] This was a singular example in Israel. Jotham reigned as coregent with his father Azariah (the "Uzziah" of Isaiah). But Jotham was not anointed until after his father's death.

torians and students of the Bible.

Established in unquestioned power, Solomon set about to solidify the kingdom and to exploit its resources. Whether the considerable shrinkage of Israelite territory and sphere of influence which occurred at this time was a deliberate part of Solomon's policy is a matter of debate. Some scholars say that the new monarch recognized that the dominion of his father was too large to be managed efficiently. Therefore he gave up certain lands and sought to place the rest in a more viable economic context. There may well be some truth in this view. At least it does not appear that Solomon fought very hard, if at all, to retain the large areas which detached themselves from his rule. In the north the Syrians rose up against Israel and reestablished a king in Damascus (I Kings 11:23-25). This had the dual effect of removing a sizable land area from Israelite control and of reducing and perhaps ending the sphere of influence David had enjoyed as far north as the Euphrates. There is a hint in II Chronicles 2:8 that Solomon tried to retain a measure of this influence by fortifying Tadmor (Palmyra) on the trade route northeast of Damascus. How successful this attempt was we do not know. But Damascus harassed the Israel of Solomon and proved over the years of the Divided Monarchy to be a force to be reckoned with in any Israelite plans.

There was also at some point a revolt in Edom (I Kings 11:14-22). This uprising, backed by Egypt, succeeded in taking from Solomon's rule almost the entire territory south-southeast of the Dead Sea with the exception of the valuable mines on the shores of the Gulf of Aqabah. However, the evidence of massive fortifications unearthed at Tell el-Kheleifeh suggests the precarious status of Solomon's authority over the territory surrounding his mines.

A passing remark in I Kings 9:16 and a story told in I Kings 11:26-40 indicate that

Solomon's troubles with the Egyptians were hardly confined to Edom. The passing remark notes that Pharoah seized Gezer, burned it, and then gave the ruined site to Solomon when the Israelite king married an Egyptian princess. Does this chance statement not indicate a campaign in Philistia with the likely result of the re-establishment of Egyptian influence over the area after a hiatus of some two hundred years? At any rate, as the Bible says and excavations at the site show, Gezer was rebuilt by Solomon as one of the three strongest fortified cities in his kingdom. The threat from the southwest was sufficiently clear to command expenditure of large amounts of money and effort to construct a frontier bastion of considerable proportions.

Jeroboam, who became king of north Israel at Solomon's death, is the central figure of the story in I Kings 11. A person of outstanding engineering ability, he was a valued and honored member of Solomon's service. But when singled out by certain religionists of the north ("all Israel"), perhaps those of the line of priests who had served at Shiloh, he had to flee the country. These priests, opposed to the religious practices of Solomon, saw in Jeroboam a man who would remove the northern tribes from the influences of Judah. Thus this young man represented both a religious and political threat. As such he must be dealt with in the same manner as Adonijah, Joab, and others. But he escaped, found refuge and encouragement at the court of Egypt, and waited until the time was ripe to return and detach the northern tribes from the Throne of David. He had to wait until the death of Solomon, as did the Egyptians themselves who then invaded Israel destroying and exacting tribute.

The kingdom of Solomon was diminished in size when compared with the territory ruled by David. But it was watchfully secure and remained so as long as Solomon lived.

In spite of or perhaps because of a loss of land, the Israelite holdings remained an empire of considerable strength, size, and potential wealth. Command of *The Way of the Sea* and of *The King's Highway* was in Israelite hands, as was the opportunity of exacting fares from the Arabian camel caravans which had been plying the desert routes since the twelfth century B.C. To this extremely lucrative business Solomon added a merchant fleet based at Ezion-geber at the head of the Gulf of Aqabah (I Kings 9:26-28; II Chronicles 8:17-18). The ships, furnished by Hiram, king of Tyre, were the same kind that had been carrying Mediterranean commerce for several centuries. These were the "ships of Tarshish" capable of long voyages. They were called *tarshish* ("ore" or "refinery") because they connected the mines of Sardinia and Spain with Phoenicia. From Ezion-geber such vessels sailed on three-year trips (probably one full year and parts of two others) to Ophir, modern Somaliland on Africa's east coast. On their return to Israel these ships were loaded with gold, silver, jewels, sandlewood, ivory, apes, and baboons (I Kings 10:11-12, 22; II Chronicles 9:10-11, 21). Even though this maritime venture was undertaken in cooperation with Hiram and with Phoenician ships, not all the sailors must have been Phoenician. Asher, Nephtali, and Dan, the far northern Hebrew tribes, had long been in contact with Canaanite maritime commerce. Indeed, as early as the last part of the twelfth century B.C., Danites had a reputation as sailors and Asher was associated with the sea (Judges 5:17).

So by land and sea the commercial interests of Solomon spread. In addition to grain, oil, wine, copper, iron, the items mentioned above and others as well, he is said to have dealt in armaments. I Kings 10:29 notes the prices he paid for chariots and horses and indicates that he resold many of these to "the kings of the Hittites and the kings of Syria." Moreover he is reported to have

The stable area at Megiddo as it appeared while under excavation by the Chicago expedition in the 1930s (above). Below is an artist's conception of what the area looked like at the time of the Israelite kingdom. The original excavators identified these structures with Solomon, but later work has suggested that they are from the time of King Ahab.

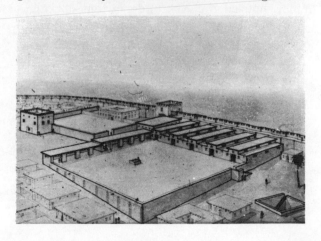

maintained a vast mobile army in Jerusalem and at various "chariot cities" (I Kings 9: 19; 10:26). These cities were thought to be both military bases and commercial centers. The large stable complex at Megiddo, apparently misidentified as Solomonic in the 1925-1939 excavations, has often been cited as evidence of just such a dual-purpose site. Further work at Megiddo in 1960, however, indicates that the stables once capable of accommodating from 450 to 480 horses as well as a sizable number of chariots is post-Solomon, probably from the time of Ahab. Megiddo is, it should be noted, not specifically listed among Solomon's chariot cities. Moreover, an inscription of Shalmaneser III indicates that at the battle of Qarqar (853 B.C.) Ahab of

133

Israel was able to field two thousand war chariots. Even though the southern fort at Megiddo with its small number of accompanying stables (spaces for 150 horses) was probably built by Solomon, the site can no longer be given as evidence of his trade in armaments. At least one scholar, John Gray of Aberdeen, has gone so far as to say that Solomon never engaged in such traffic. In his view I Kings 10:29 has been mistranslated. It does not indicate that Solomon *exported* horses and chariots, but that the Hittite and Syrian rulers got their mobile arms *"by the agency* of Solomon's dealers." This was presumably a way of defraying expenses and also of guaranteeing safe passage from Asia Minor where the best horses were to be found. Gray further notes the Greek text of I Kings which merely says that the other monarchs got their horses and chariots from the same places and at the same prices as Solomon.[2] Since neither Megiddo nor any similar place can be cited against Gray's argument, it stands at the moment as one which must be given serious consideration. Still there are few if any who will question the essential correctness of the figures given in I Kings 10:26. If Solomon did not actually traffic in arms, he nonetheless secured a mobile force amounting to some 1400 chariots and 12,000 horsemen. This military force alone represents an enormous drain on the nation's income and suggests that crippling expenditures for weapons are no modern invention.

But the monarch's expenditures were by no means limited to the military. He may have "made silver as common in Jerusalem as stone" (I Kings 10:27; II Chronicles 9:27), but in the grand manner of his personal life he displayed a passion for gold, literally surrounding himself with it to whatever extent possible (I Kings 10:16–21; II Chron-

icles 9:15-20). II Chronicles 8:18 even suggests that the primary purpose of the fleet at Ezion-geber was to bring gold to King Solomon. While the hoarding of gold may from one point of view be correctly considered as an investment, it may also be viewed as requiring a considerable outlay of the products and labor of the country.

Solomon did not surround himself only with gold. His harem was said to consist of seven hundred wives and three hundred concubines (I Kings 11:3). These women combined with the army of servants, managers, priests, officers, and other bureaucrats who swarmed about the royal presence make it abundantly clear that Solomon's household was equal in oriental splendor to any of its day. But Israel was not Egypt nor Jerusalem Babylon. The resources were not there to sustain this kind of life over a long period. Even in Egypt and in Mesopotamia the court dwelt in magnificence at the expense of the people. Solomon found the same to be necessary in Israel and did not hesitate to lay the heavy hand of despotism upon the people who hailed him as king.

For all this, the focus of Solomon's glory was not his chariots, nor his gold, women, or servants. It was his house and the house he built for the Lord. When he ascended the throne Jerusalem was in almost all essential details the same as it had been under the Jebusites. David had reworked the fortifications, housed the Ark under a tent doubtless in some sort of sacred area, and built a small palace with the help of Hiram, king of Tyre. Otherwise, apart from the purchase of the threshing floor of Araunah where he erected an altar (II Samuel 24:18-25), he seems to have done little if anything to expand or enhance the royal city.

This threshing floor was just north of the city wall, perhaps six hundred yards away, perhaps less. Here on a ridge between two valleys, David intended to build a permanent temple to replace the tent that housed the

[2] John Gray, *Archaeology and the Old Testament World* (London: Thomas Nelson and Sons, 1962), pp. 133-35.

Ark. This was a revolutionary idea with far-ranging implications. The Ark had always been housed in a tabernacle, a portable tent suiting the needs of the nomadic desert Hebrews. But now a portable sanctuary indicating the wandering status of the nomad was to be transformed into a national shrine bespeaking of permanence and a religious claim to the land.

Such was David's dream. But it was not to be, not, at least, in his lifetime. Nathan brought the word of the Lord that David was not to build the holy structure (II Samuel 7:1-29; I Chronicles 17:1-27). The Lord would build a house for David (that is, a dynasty), but a warrior who had shed blood should not build the Lord's house. Solomon, a man of peace, would fulfill his father's hopes. Accordingly David laid aside the glittering materials he had gathered for the Temple and gave to his son and his designated heir detailed instructions for constructing and appointing the shrine. Moreover, before his death he required from the various leaders, officials, and officers of Israel contributions for the projected work (I Chronicles 28:1–29:30).

The Dome of the Rock seen through arches added later. Local lore holds that on the day of judgment scales in these arches will weigh the deeds of men.

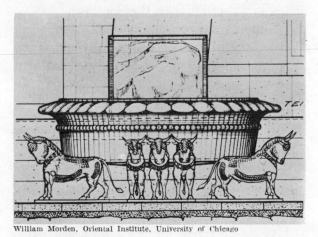

William Morden, Oriental Institute, University of Chicago

An artist's conception of the Great Bronze Sea that stood in the courtyard of Solomon's Temple. Note the bulls, reminiscent of the fertility cult of Canaan, and the Great Sea itself, recalling the Canaanite myths of chaos.

Solomon's Temple

The location of the Temple is beyond question. Since that day sometime around 950 B.C. when Solomon consecrated it, the site has been continuously venerated and almost continuously occupied by a succession of sanctuaries. Solomon's Temple stood until the Babylonian Exile in 586 B.C. Even during the Exile sacrifices continued amid the ruins of the building (Jeremiah 41:5), and those in exile were allowed to make contributions to maintain these. In 516 B.C. the returned exiles finished construction of a second temple, a rude affair hardly rivaling its predecessor or its successor. As with many temporary arrangements, this temple lasted the longest of any Hebrew sanctuary. About 20 B.C. Herod, the master builder of Palestine, began a grandiose scheme to replace the less-worthy structure with one which would be unsurpassed in the world. So massive was his conception that it took eighty-four years of continuous daily work to bring it to completion. Alas, it stood in its pristine beauty for only six years. In A.D. 70 it was burned and utterly destroyed in the final Roman push to secure the city. The enormous platform (some thirty-five and a half acres) which Herod had constructed for his Temple remained virtually undamaged. Hadrian rebuilding the city after the war of A.D. 135, avoided this for some reason, built to the west of it, and banned Jews from his new city, *Aelia Capitolina*. By the fourth century, Christians more or less controlled Jerusalem and its environs, but their interest focused on the Mount of Olives just east of the platform across the Kidron Valley. Jews now returning went to the great rock near the center of the platform and there at the *lapis pertusus* bewailed the barrenness of the site and the loss of its glory.[3] Over the years the open area became a dump crisscrossed by pious feet. In A.D. 638 the Muslim flood engulfed Jerusalem, a city associated by the faithful with Muhammad himself. According to tradition Omar Ibn el-Khattab, the gracious Arab who wrested the city from Christian control, set an example for others by using his own cloak to carry debris from the neglected Temple area. Somewhere within the platform limits, once again a *haram* ("sacred precinct"), he constructed a simple wooden mosque. This was the forerunner of the Dome of the Rock. This octagonal build-

ing was begun in A.D. 685 and completed in 691 by Abdul-Malek Ibn Marwan. It is the earliest example of Arab architecture in existence today.[4] Its graceful combination of lavishness and restraint makes it one of the most beautiful buildings in the world. For almost thirteen centuries it has sheltered the sacred rock and has dominated a *haram*.[5]

If there are no doubts about the general location of Solomon's Temple, there are few certainties regarding its exact position and design. Miss Kenyon's excavations at Ophel confirmed what was known from the Bible: Solomon did extend the city northward. It was also discovered that he enlarged it slightly westward into the central (Tyropoeon) valley. This latter came as something of a surprise since it had not been seriously suggested until the digging in the mid-1960's. On the east side of Ophel it was possible to trace a casemate wall in a northerly direction for some distance. Unfortunately, later construction has destroyed much evidence associated with this wall. At present it is not possible to determine whether it was a city wall or an acropolis enclosure of the type found at the Omride palace at Samaria (see p. 163). More important for our immediate purposes, the point of junction with the southern wall of the Temple platform could not be established. Benjamin Mazar's current excavations at the western and southern walls of the platform have shed no light on this question. We do

---

[3] The antiquity of the Jewish custom of weeping at the Wailing Wall is a matter of debate. It seems not to be so ancient as is often claimed. Wailing at the *lapis pertusus* or opening in the great rock is documented by pilgrims in the earliest days of Christian domination of the city. Later, in the seventh century, Abdul-Malek built over the rock with the intention of creating a pilgrimage shrine at the site of the temples of Solomon and Herod. The traditional association of this rock with Solomon was further noted by Al-Harawi, an Arab historian who visited Jerusalem in A.D. 1173. He recorded that the Crusaders, then holding the city, had placed a picture of Solomon in the cave beneath the rock. The Wailing Wall is in any case a part of Herod's platform and does not come from the time of Solomon.

[4] The Mosque of 'Amr in Fostat was built in Cairo in 642, a year after the Muslim conquest of Egypt. This structure had neither *mihrab* nor inner courtyard until 673. Later its early design was further modified by the addition of a huge pillared hall and open courtyard. It is thus a conglomerate building unlike the Dome in Jerusalem which, apart from the Crusader fence around the rock, is in all essentials unchanged from its original design and construction.

[5] Almost all mosques of the seventh and eighth centuries were fortresses. This is not the case with the Dome of the Rock. Its unique design is due in part to Abdul-Malek's desire to surround the great rock with a sanctuary which would compete with another holy stone, the *Kaaba* in Mecca.

not know the size of the platform on which Solomon placed his Temple.

The idea of a "platform" here is obviously a reading back to Herod. It is possible and even probable that Solomon did not extend a platform over the valleys as did Herod. But there seems little doubt that he found it necessary to carry out extensive leveling operations. I Kings 6–7 suggests as much. Furthermore, Warren's singular survey of the *haram*, conducted in 1867, showed that the configuration of bedrock is considerably different from the ground level which presents itself to today's visitor. The crest of the ridge runs nearly in a straight line from the northwest angle of the sacred enclosure southwest to the present location of the Triple Gate. The sides of the hill are steep, falling away 162 feet at the northeast corner of the *haram*, 163 feet at the southeast corner, and 150 feet at the southwest corner. Warren contended that the Temple site that attracted David and greeted Solomon's engineers was "a series of rocky slopes, the ledges covered here and there with a few feet of red earth." The mention of Araunah's threshing floor strengthens rather than weakens Warren's conclusion. It is well known that a ridge with a flattened top is an ideal place to toss grain into the air so that the winds can carry away the chaff.

I have to submit, then [says Warren], that where the sides are as much as one in two or three, where the ground slopes very nearly in the same degree as does the rock of Gibraltar to the west, it seems incredible that the temple, a building which was so conspicuous, and which was to perform such an important part in the fortifications of the city, should have been placed down in a hole, or even along the sides of the hill, or anywhere except on the ridge, where there is just enough room for it to have stood, for it is somewhat flattened on top.[6]

[6] Capt. Wilson and Capt. Warren, *The Recovery of Jerusalem* (New York: D. Appleton, 1871), pp. 245-46.

Warren's findings indicate, among other things, that the vast number of people involved (I Kings 5:13-18) and the time consumed (I Kings 6:38) in constructing the Temple were necessitated not merely by the extravagance and care that marked the building of the structure itself. The preparation of the site required the attention of many men over a long period of time. Attention is naturally drawn to the finished sanctuary. People observing a building seldom give much thought to the modifications required of and by the location. Still less did the religious writers of the Bible concern themselves with the engineering details of a shrine as important to nation and faith as was the Temple. Nonetheless, while archaeology never has and probably never will be able to recover any remains of Solomon's Temple, it can and has given hints of the enormous difficulties faced by those entrusted with its construction. In short, the location of the Temple quite as much as the actual structure may have been something of a marvel. This is a point almost universally ignored in any discussion of Solomon's building projects.

If Warren was substantially correct about the configuration of the hill in Solomon's day, the Temple probably stood in the vicinity of the sacred rock now covered by the Dome. This location is further favored by the fact that Solomon's Palace was south of the Temple probably in the area now occupied by the vast Al-Aqsa Mosque. Moreover, the sacred rock with its cave very likely has sacred connections predating Araunah. It has in any event survived (not without damage) many major changes on the ridge and is with the rock scarp in the northwest corner of the *haram* the last vestige of the original nature of the hill. Venerated throughout the years it was undoubtedly a part of the sacred complex of Solomon. It may well have been that the Holy of Holies, with its elevated floor, covered a portion of this rock.[7] Assuming that

[7] The rock's size, fifty-eight by forty-four feet,

was so and that the sanctuary was oriented east and west (see below), Solomon's magnificent House of the Lord stood at the site of the present Dome of the Rock and extended slightly to the east.

The considerable uncertainty requiring as it does a generous use of educated guesswork is due to two factors. The first is subsequent building activity on the ridge. This has involved not only the replacing of one sanctuary with another, but an almost total renovation of the very contour of the ground level. Herod's work alone was probably enough to destroy any archaeologically identifiable remains of earlier work. But less than a century later Hadrian filled in much of the Tyropoean Valley with whatever was at hand. Further, his men scavengered and quarried in various parts of the older city and its environs. Between them Herod and Hadrian combined to remove for all time much, if not most, of the materials which could have given an idea of the city prior to the dawn of the Christian Era.

A second factor is the sacredness of the *haram*. Second only to Mecca in Muslim piety, it is one of the most venerated spots on earth. It thus is not and should not be an object of archaeological excavation. One might as well dig in the central aisle of St. Peter's! Warren was able to make soundings just outside the walls and was permitted to explore the numerous caves, water channels, and basins that honeycomb the platform. But his work, some of it conducted surreptitiously, occasioned considerable protest from the religious authorities and was eventually abandoned. Miss Kenyon made soundings outside the southeast corner in 1966. Prior to 1967 only one scholar was allowed to explore beneath the sacred precinct. He was restricted to a specific area of the western

wall (see p. 246). Since the June 1967 War, however, Israeli scholars have carried out extensive work on the southwestern wall of the platform.

The design and appointments of Solomon's Temple are likewise surrounded by uncertainties. Over the years there have been many attempts to reconstruct the Temple in drawings and models. While some of these have much to commend them, most have been flights of fancy. In spite of detailed descriptions in the Bible (I Kings 6–7; Ezekiel 40–41), we do not know what the Temple looked like. Yet a combination of the biblical narrative with archaeological results of recent years produces a slowly clearing picture and some sense of the kind of structure Solomon built and the way it was equipped. While no materials are available from Jerusalem itself, increasing amounts are being discovered elsewhere and can by analogy help fill the gaps in our knowledge.

We know from the Bible that the Temple was entirely Phoenician in design and execution. Hiram I, king of Tyre (*ca.* 969-936 B.C.), is known to Phoenician records as a master builder and as one who constructed several temples in Tyre. To this man, a friend of David's, Solomon turned for help. Archaeological evidence is almost unanimous in suggesting that the Hebrews never attained the skill of craftsmanship characteristic of their Phoenician neighbors. It was only natural that Solomon, like David before him (II Samuel 5:11), should turn to Hiram for architects and skilled laborers.

According to the biblical descriptions, the Temple was a rectangle some ninety feet long and thirty feet wide (interior measurement). Its height was about forty-five feet. Three stories of small rooms supported the exterior walls and helped to bear the weight of the roof which was exceptionally large for its day. The entire structure may have stood on a nine-foot-high raised terrace similar to the slightly higher one that elevates the

precludes the idea that the Holy of Holies embraced the whole of it. The Holy of Holies was thirty feet square. Some have said that the bronze altar of Solomon stood on top of the rock.

American Schools of Oriental Research

Solomon's Temple. An artist's conception based upon the researches of W. F. Albright and G. E. Wright. According to this view Solomon's Temple did not differ greatly from contemporary Phoenician sanctuaries.

Dome of the Rock above the level of Herod's platform. The worshiper entering the building, most likely from the east (I Kings 7:21; II Chronicles 3:17; Ezekiel 8:16; 11:1; 43:1-4; 44:1-3), would find himself in the first of three rooms. This entrance porch, or vestibule, sheltered huge doors that opened to reveal the nave. Measuring sixty by thirty by forty-five feet, this nave was the largest room in the Temple. It was lighted by perhaps eight to ten recessed windows high up on the walls. Beyond the nave and up a short flight of steps was the Holy of Holies, a thirty-foot square. The cube of the innermost sanctuary was effected by raising the level of the floor and lowering the ceiling.

The whole building was constructed of stone carefully cut at the quarry so that the sound of hammers would not be heard at the holy site (I Kings 6:7). Yet the worshiper would see no stone on the interior. The floors were of cypress. Olivewood seems to have been preferred for certain significantly religious items such as the lintels, doors, and doorposts of the Holy of Holies and for the

cherubim that stood guard over the Ark. But in greatest abundance was cedar of Lebanon which covered the walls mingling its pleasant aroma with more pungent odors arising from burning incense. Everywhere there was gold. The cherubim, palm trees, open flowers, pomegranates, and other decorations carved on the walls and doors were inlaid with the precious metal. In the Holy of Holies the cherubic statues were overlaid with gold, as was the holiest altar in the nave. Moreover, barring access to the inmost sanctuary were chains of gold.

Further to enhance the beauty of the building Solomon summoned from Tyre another Hiram[8] who was a master metallurgist (I Kings 7:13-15). This man, son of a Hebrew mother and a Tyrian father, brought with him a number of skilled workmen who among other things cast the mammoth pillars that stood before the main door, the massive molten sea, the bronze altar, and various

[8] He is not to be confused with the king of the same name. II Chronicles 2:13 calls him Huram-abi as distinct from the king who is called Huram.

other religious artifacts such as lampstands, lavers, pots, shovels, basins, and snuffers (I Kings 7:15-50; II Chronicles 3:15-22). It is possible to speculate that the metal used by Hiram came from Solomon's mines near the Gulf of Aqabah and that it may have been smeltered at Tell el-Kheleifeh. Wherever the material came from, it was cast north of Jerusalem and east of the Jordan between Succoth and Zarethan (I Kings 7:46; II Chronicles 4:17). Here the consistency of the clay soil is well suited to such operations. Moreover, excavations at Deir 'alla, which many identify as Succoth, have shown the soil at that particular site to have a high metallic content. This has suggested to some that the entire process took place in this area without any reference to mining and smeltering farther south. But this cannot be established one way or the other until extensive archaeological work has been done at ancient copper-producing sites in the nearby hills.

Among the more interesting items adorning the sacred area in front of the Temple were the twin pillars, the molten sea, and the altar of bronze. Massive in conception and doubtless awe-inspiring in actuality, they have long been objects of controversy. According to I Kings 7:15-17, the pillars plus the capitals decorating their tops were approximately thirty-seven feet high.[9] With a circumference of over eighteen feet, they were hollow with sides three inches thick. What was the purpose of such columns? Some have suggested that "in the vestibule" in I Kings 7:19 is to be taken literally and that they stood within the porch and supported the roof. Examples of this can be seen in the excavations at Tell Tainat and Tell Arad. This is not likely, however, to have been their function. It is also unlikely that they were lampstands, although flames burn-

ing at great height may have had a symbolic meaning which now escapes us. Among the many functions that have been suggested, the one noting that they were free-standing columns designating a royal chapel has much to commend it. Considerable evidence from various historical periods points to this use of dual columns, free-standing and otherwise, throughout the lands of the eastern Mediterranean. Royal temples attached to palaces have been excavated in Mesopotamia at Nineveh and at Khorsabad and in Syria at Tell Tainat, to note only a few examples. At Khorsabad the Nabu temple of Sargon II had two pillars flanking the main entrance. Likewise, in Egypt obelisks found always in pairs recited the accomplishments of the ruler and signified the royal connection of the sanctuary before which they stood. The same was apparently true at Tyre according to the Greek historian Herodotus. Moreover, at Tell el-Farah, Father de Vaux has unearthed a temple model having the same feature. The names Jachin and Boaz given to the columns in front of Solomon's building may, in fact, have been the first words of royal inscriptions. A similar pattern may be seen in the names of the books of the Hebrew Bible which are the first words in the text. Professor R. B. Y. Scott thinks that the writings on Jachin began, "God will establish thy throne forever," or something similar, while those on Boaz may have begun, "In the strength of God shall the king rejoice." [10]

The Molten Sea was a huge bronze bowl some fifteen feet in diameter and seven to ten feet high. This object, perhaps weighing as much as thirty tons and holding ten thousand or more gallons of water, rested on the backs of twelve bronze oxen arranged in threes so as to face the four major points of the compass. II Chronicles 4:6 says the

---

[9] II Chronicles 3:15 says they were more than sixty feet high. This figure is surely an exaggeration, as columns of that height would tower over the forty-five-foot high structure producing an odd effect indeed.

[10] R. B. Y. Scott, "The Pillars Jachin and Boaz," *Journal of Biblical Literature*, 58 (1939): 143*H*. See also W. F. Albright, *Archaeology and the Religion of Israel* (Baltimore: The Johns Hopkins Press, 1956), p. 139.

Sea was used by the priests to wash in. One should not immediately conjure up a mental picture of men actually in the bowl. Rather, some sort of arrangement such as is found at the great mosques would have allowed the priests ritual ablutions. No matter what use, if any, the Hebrews actually made of this Sea, the dual connection of its design with Canaanite religion can hardly be overlooked. Its very name, "The Molten Sea," preserves the ancient Canaanite concept of chaos in conflict with divinity. The twelve oxen were fertility symbols par excellence and had been for centuries in the ancient Middle East (see pp. 103 ff.).

The altar of bronze, mentioned in II Chronicles 4:1 and in Ezekiel 43:13-17 but omitted from the descriptions in I Kings, was about thirty feet square at its base. Its sacrificial area was approximately fifteen feet above the surrounding ground level. Ezekiel indicates that this was an affair terraced perhaps after the Babylonian fashion. Steps leading to the top were oriented toward the rising sun. Many uncertainties surround this structure. It is sometimes assumed to have been a massive, free-standing mound of metal. But was it bronze cast or overlay? The biblical descriptions of the destruction of the Temple by Nebuchadrezzar (II Kings 25:8-17; Jeremiah 52:12-23) specifically mention the breaking-up of the pillars and the "Sea" but omit reference to the altar.[11] Surely such a mountain would have been a rare prize. Quite likely it was a large stone altar overlaid (decorated?) with bronze. It may even have been the altar built by David (II Samuel 24:25), although there is no evidence for this.

The furnishings that stood inside the Temple were few. So far as we know the vestibule was empty. The nave was flanked by ten golden lampstands, five on either side. In front of the steps at the far end was an incense altar perhaps similar in design to the famous one from Megiddo, perhaps somewhat larger. In any event it was of cedar overlaid (inlaid?) with gold. Somewhere in the room was the table of the Bread of the Presence, again decorated with gold.[12] Opening the doors leading into the Holy of Holies one could see the Ark of the Covenant, a box-shaped object with poles on each side. Looming out of the darkness, for there was only the light from the open door, were the two glistening cherubim, their enormous wings touching the walls and towering over the sacred Ark.

The multitude of implements used in the Temple services were kept in the treasury, a portion of the rooms flanking the sanctuary. Among these varied objects were many made by Hiram and his artisans (I Kings 7:48-50; II Chronicles 4:19-22), some dedicated and laid aside by David (I Kings 7:51; II Chronicles 5:1), and those that had been used in the Tabernacle (I Kings 8:43; II Chronicles 5:5).

After seven years the House of the Lord was finished, and in its inmost recesses lay the holy Ark, the Presence of God. Solomon said,

"The Lord has set the sun in the heavens,
but has said that he would dwell in thick darkness.
I have built thee an exalted house, a place for thee to dwell in for ever."

I Kings 8:12

This brief description of Solomon's Temple and its furnishings is based on the not unambiguous descriptions in I Kings, II Chronicles, and Ezekiel. No direct archaeological evidence is available from Jerusalem for reasons which have already been noted. Moreover, early Iron Age sites elsewhere

[11] The mention of the bronze bulls in Jeremiah 52:20 seems in error. Ahaz had earlier given them to Assyria as tribute (II Kings 16:17-18).

[12] II Chronicles 4:8 mentions ten tables in the nave. I Kings knows nothing of these.

have produced meager results in this regard. The paucity of contemporary evidence from other places is perhaps due to several factors. First, the major period of temple construction was probably, as archaeology is increasingly indicating, the Middle and Late Bronze Ages which saw a rebirth and revitalization of city life in Syria-Palestine. Second, relatively little excavation has been done at Phoenician sites. More work there may well clarify a number of matters concerning the Phoenician-style Temple erected by Solomon. Third, it would appear that the Hebrews, not particularly skilled in design or the construction arts, built few major sanctuaries apart from Shiloh and Jerusalem.[13] Indeed, they had no need to do so. Excavations at Bethshan, for example, suggest that the third temple there was used by Israelites. Whether they actually rebuilt it or, as is more likely, used an existing Canaanite structure, their worship did not markedly differ from what had gone on before. In short, existing temples and shrines were well suited to Israelite ways.

There were uniquely Hebrew sanctuaries however. At Tell Arad an Israelite temple has been found, the only one yet discovered (see p. 110). Its plan is strikingly similar to that reported of Solomon's Temple. From a courtyard one enters the building from the east and passes through a porch, a nave, and into the Holy of Holies. It seems also to have been partly surrounded on the outside by construction which may have been something like the three-storied rooms in the Jerusalem Temple. The Arad sanctuary, which in its first phase was built when Solomon reigned, was much smaller than the royal Temple. It was about fifty feet long and fifteen feet wide. Its height

is not known. The Holy of Holies was a square of approximately seven and a half feet. Was it once a cube? We cannot say. It is interesting, however, to notice two other features of this sanctuary which resembled the Jerusalem Temple. There were apparently two pillars associated with the entrance. This immediately suggests Jachin and Boaz. But at Arad the pillar bases (the actual pillars were not recovered) are inside the porch next to the door to the nave. It is likely, then, that their function was to support the roof. If so, they differed from Solomon's enormous bronze pillars which served a different purpose. There was also an altar for burnt offerings in the courtyard. Again, this feature resembled the arrangements at Jerusalem. At Arad the altar was fairly large, some twelve and a half feet square and seven and a half feet tall. Its top is a large slab of flint surrounded by plastered gutters. The unhewn stone construction calls to mind Exodus 20:25 and Deuteronomy 27:6 which forbade using hewn stone for altars lest the hammer striking the rock profane it. Notice should also be taken of Exodus 27:1 where the dimensions of the altar described are precisely the same as those of the altar at Tell Arad. Are these indications of an independent Israelite sanctuary tradition which combined with features of a more universal ancient Middle Eastern style? We do not yet know; too little has so far been recovered by archaeology.

In face of considerable difficulties, however, results of archaeological excavations to date can be combined with the biblical narratives to produce a much clearer picture of some of the details of the first Israelite temple in Jerusalem. Its floor plan and general design were certainly not uniquely Hebrew. History written from the earth does not testify to any single temple design in Palestine and its neighboring lands, although a large room similar to Solomon's nave does appear as a popular feature. And at least five sites in Palestine and two in Syria have yielded

[13] This refers to the time from the settlement of the land to the end of the United Monarchy. It does not include the Divided Monarchy and the building of royal sanctuaries at Dan and Bethel by Jeroboam I. It also assumes there was some sort of sanctuary at Shiloh.

sanctuaries having a three-part division. Those at et-Tell, Hazor, Beth-shan, and Lachish in Palestine and at Alalakh in Syria are older than the Jerusalem Temple, while the one at Tell Tainat in Syria was built some two hundred years later. The Arad sanctuary is contemporary. All have a vestibule, nave, and inner sanctuary.[14] At Hazor, Beth-shan, Tell Tainat, and Tell Arad the three rooms are in a straight line as in Jerusalem. All except Arad are Canaanite or Phoenician structures.

Moreover, the construction methods employed on several of these (Hazor, Beth-shan, Arad, Tainat) show marked similarity to the "three courses of hewn stone round about, and a course of cedar beams" mentioned in I Kings 7:12. Some excavated buildings at Ugarit also display the same thing.

The descriptions of the decorations enhancing the beauty of the Temple are similarly made more vivid by archaeological finds. At various sites in Syria, and at Megiddo and Samaria in Palestine, Phoenician ivory carvings have been found which have undoubted affinities with the gold inlay used abundantly by Solomon. The Samaria ivories in particular are significant since they were likely done by Phoenician craftsmen for an Israelite king within a century of the building of the Temple in Jerusalem. They show a mastery of intricate detail and of pleasing proportion. From many places, including those mentioned, come carved pomegranates, flowers, palm trees, cherubim, and the like. We are no longer in doubt about what the decoration of the Temple actually looked like. Moreover, it is now clear that the cherubim in the Holy of Holies were winged sphinxes probably of a type long common in the ancient Middle East. They were often associated with sanctuaries and were

variously understood as advisors to the gods, intercessors on behalf of the worshipers, steeds for the gods, or as the animals which drew the divine chariot. The latter two functions of the cherubim are known to the Old Testament (see II Samuel 22:11; Psalm 18:11; Ezekiel 1, 10). A fine example of a Canaanite cherub has been found at Megiddo.

From Megiddo also comes a tall lampstand with triangular supporting legs. The Garber-Howland model of the Temple of Solomon on display at Agnes Scott College in Atlanta, Georgia copies this late bronze Megiddo artifact in its reconstruction of the furnishings of the nave. Many think that the Megiddo lampstand is likely similar to the ten golden "candlesticks." Decorated column bases from Tell Tainat, pilaster capitals from Ramat Rahel and Samaria, and items from elsewhere show design, workmanship, and construction techniques analogous to the finest Solomon could employ. In like manner lavers, pots, shovels, basins, and other sacerdotal equipment have been unearthed in Cyprus and in Palestine at Hazor and Lachish. Archaeology is truly combining with the biblical narrative to give a clearer picture of the kind of structure Solomon built for the Lord and the way it was decorated and furnished.

The Temple was but one part of a larger complex of royal buildings. Adjacent to the sanctuary on the south was Solomon's Palace which required thirteen years to finish. A series of perhaps as many as five major buildings, the king's house was, like the Temple, wholly Phoenician in concept and execution. The House of the Forest of Lebanon, so named because of its forty-five pillars of cedar (I Kings 7:3), was the largest single room in the Palace. It measured approximately one hundred and fifty feet long, seventy-five feet wide, and forty-five feet high. Here Solomon kept his three hundred shields of beaten gold (I Kings 10:16-17). When these were taken away as booty by Shishak,

[14] Some scholars question this arrangement at Lachish saying that the sanctuary there does not have a threefold division in the same sense as the others.

Rehoboam replaced them with shields of bronze, but it is not clear if these of less-precious metal were kept in the House of the Forest (I Kings 14:25-28; to what does "guardroom" refer?). Isaiah 22:8 in a warning concerning the destruction of Jerusalem notes that "the weapons of the House of the forest" were no substitute for trust in God. This hall may have served as an armory for the king. Through the centuries such use was common in large halls of great houses royal or otherwise. A visitor to many of the castles and mansions of Britain, for instance to Glamis or Longleat, or even to the reconstructed Governor's Palace in Williamsburg, Virginia, will be shown entranceways or large halls in which weapons are stored.

The Hall of Pillars (not to be confused with the House of the Forest) was about forty-five feet long, seventy-five feet wide, and forty-five feet high. Its dimensions may indicate that it was an adjunct to the House of the Forest, but we are not told. The Bible merely says that "there was a porch in front with pillars, and a canopy before them" (I Kings 7:6).

The Hall of the Throne, also known as the Hall of Judgment because it was here that Solomon adjudicated, housed the splendid throne itself. Of ivory inlaid with gold, it stood with a calf's head behind it and carved lions on each side. It was raised six steps above the level of the floor. At either end of each step were carved lions. It is little wonder that the emperor of Ethiopia, who claims to be descended from Solomon and the Queen of Sheba, refers to himself as "The Lion of Judah." Is this perhaps a title which matched the magnificence of the man himself. "The like of it was never made in any kingdom" (I Kings 10:20).

These three chambers, the House of the Forest, the Hall of Pillars, and the Hall of the Throne, together with the great court constituted the public rooms of the Palace. They were made of costly stone, carefully hewn and laid out (I Kings 7:12). The interior walls were paneled with cedar, and we may assume that the decorations were not unlike those of the Temple.

The private apartments of Solomon were of the same workmanship. Unfortunately we are told almost nothing about this area of the Palace, an area which surely was vast indeed, housing not only the lavish monarch but his seven hundred wives and three hundred concubines as well. For some reason the Bible is practically silent about the royal living quarters. But it carefully points out that Solomon built a similar house "for Pharaoh's daughter whom he had taken in marriage" (I Kings 7:8b.; see also 3:1; 9:24, and II Chronicles 8:11). There is little question that she was treated with a dignity not officially accorded to any other Solomonic wife. Egyptian power was resurgent. It had reasserted itself in Philistia. If Solomon had been powerful enough to claim one of Pharaoh's daughters and a dowry, he was wise enough to make sure the union provided no cause for hostility.

The Fortification of Israel

After twenty years of construction, the threshing floor of Araunah had become the site of some of the finest and most lavish examples of ancient craftsmen's arts. But Solomon's building activities in Jerusalem were not confined to the Temple and the Palace. The expanded areas of the city needed walls, and in addition the *millo* was rebuilt (I Kings 9:15, 24; 11:27). No one knows what the *millo* was. The word indicates that it was some sort of "filling," and many theories have been advanced to explain its location, form, and use. That it continued to need repair and was vital to the defense of the city is indicated not only by Davidic and Solomonic concern with it, but also by the fact that Hezekiah paid particular attention to it as he set about to strengthen the city against the onslaught of Sennacherib and his Assyrians (II Chronicles 32:5). Still it remains a mystery to us.

Miss Kenyon's excavations on Ophel have revealed houses just north of David's town limits. While it is clear that there was nothing here before these buildings, it cannot be established that they come from the time of Solomon. The closest archaeology can date them is to the tenth and ninth centuries B.C. They may be Solomonic, but they may also have been built during the early years of the divided monarchy. Miss Kenyon has speculated that the earth fill extending the city to the west is Solomonic, but she is quick to point out that pottery evidence may also allow for a slightly later period. Potentially more significant may be a tumble of hewn stones found near the projected line of David's northern wall. Among them were parts of a pilaster capital. Both the stones and the capital are exactly the same as have been found at Samaria, the northern Israelite royal city built by Phoenician workmen around 885 B.C. According to Miss Kenyon this "may be the one architectural relic of Solomon's Jerusalem so far found."

On a hill just east of the city and south of the Mount of Olives, Solomon built shrines and temples to honor the gods of his foreign wives (I Kings 11:1-8). This hill, called today as for centuries the "hill of shame," has yielded no archaeological evidence of these sanctuaries. What other building activities Solomon undertook in Jerusalem we do not know. It may be surmised that apart from other official buildings—is Miss Kenyon's "tumble of dressed stone" evidence of one of these?—many new dwellings, shops, and other such structures appeared. Jerusalem was a growing center of population and a city of considerable wealth. Even if we allow for exaggeration in the statements that silver was as common as stone (I Kings 10:7) and that the king had tableware of gold because it was nothing

to have silver (I Kings 10:21), considerable prosperity had obviously come to Israel's royal city. Prosperous urban centers attract people in any age. Furthermore, as we shall see, archaeology now tends to suggest that at least part of Jerusalem's wealth was at the expense of the relative prosperity of the other parts of the country. If this proves to be the case—further excavations are necessary to establish it with certainty—it will strengthen the view that Jerusalem's opulence was a strong attraction.

Without question Jerusalem was the focus of Solomon's building activities. But these were not restricted to the royal city. I Kings 9:15 reports that he built at Hazor, Megiddo, Gezer, Lower Beth-horon, Baalath, and Tamar in addition to "store cities . . . cities for his chariots . . . cities for his horsemen." In recent years and even continuing now, archaeological expeditions to the first three cities mentioned have produced striking evidence of the massive work undertaken by Solomon's builders. These cities, each in a strategic location, were fortified in keeping with Solomon's mistaken (as it turned out) policy of maintaining peace through armaments. At all three sites excavators have uncovered very large city gates. These magnificent gateways have six inner chambers, three on either side, and twin towers flanking the passageway. Along with their associated casemate walls they made an imposing defensive position. There is no doubt that they are part of the Solomonic fortifications of Israel. Stratigraphy and pottery testify to the dating, and evidence from all three sites is in agreement. Moreover, the gates seem to have been constructed on a common plan, a plan which may be reflected in Ezekiel's vision of the Jerusalem temple gate (Ezekiel 40:5-16). It is possible that Ezekiel was familiar with one or more of the gateways now laid bare by archaeologists. Evidence found in 1968 at Gezer indicates that the structure there was in use until the first century B.C. and had twelve different street levels associated with it. At Megiddo the Solomonic gate was rebuilt in the late eighth or early seventh century B.C. These gates were formidable structures and were in use a long time, well into Ezekiel's day. This does not mean, of course, that Solomon's fortifications were impenetrable. On the contrary, each site excavated tells its silent story of the fall of the city soon after Solomon's death, probably as a result of the military activity of Pharaoh Shishak.

Gezer is still in process of being dug, and it may be some years before the dimensions of the Solomonic city are known. But Hazor and Megiddo were evidently strongholds rather than large walled cities. At Hazor the casemate wall seems to have surrounded only the highest part of the hill, while at Megiddo, where there had possibly been a large Israelite settlement since the early days of David, the wall enclosed a somewhat larger area. Associated with the Megiddo of Solomon's time was a small fort dominating the approach to the city from the north. This fort was built on the very edge of the mound. It is not clear whether it stood apart from the city wall or was a strong point in that wall.

Not all of Solomon's construction works are mentioned in the Bible. Thanks to the work of archaeologists in the past thirty-five years, we now know that the southern desert, the Negeb, was a focus of much of Solomon's interest. Most knowledge of this area comes from the continuing work of Nelson Glueck, the prominent American archaeologist, whose adventurous surveys of sand and hill furnished the impetus and groundwork for much later work. In recent years his findings have combined with those of certain Israeli scholars, particularly Y. Aharoni and B. Rothenberg, to show that there was in the desert to the south a series of Solomonic fortifications similar to but hardly so elaborate as Hazor, Megiddo, and Gezer. In the winter of 1956/57, Rothenberg's survey of a part of this region and certain parts of the Sinai Peninsula established to his satisfaction the existence of the remains of a number of small fortresses from the time of Solomon. He noted seven in the region of Kadesh-barnea alone. But the only major excavated sites so far are those at Tell el-Kheleifeh, dug by Nelson Glueck from 1938 to 1940, and Tell Arad, dug by Aharoni from 1964 to the present.

Tell el-Kheleifeh is now generally regarded as biblical Ezion-geber, the home of Solomon's merchant fleet (I Kings 9:26). It is on the shores of the Gulf of Aqabah halfway between the modern cities of Elath and Aqabah. There two casemate fortresses have been found, one built approximately on top of the other. The earlier construction served David's son while the other is from the time of the Divided Monarchy. Associated with Solomon's fortress were a number of very poorly devised dwellings which have led many scholars to suggest they were quarters for housing slaves.[15] Within the walls the most important structure appears to have been a storehouse which may have been used for grain. This building Glueck once identified somewhat dramatically as a Solomonic refinery which made use of the prevailing winds of the Wadi Arabah. He among others now points to more recent archaeological evidence against such an understanding and to equally strong evidence which has emerged to make the new interpretation (storehouse) more probable.

However, this is doubtless the region of Solomon's mining operations, one of the major sources of the wealth of his king-

[15] The site is somewhat desolate, without adequate supplies of food and water. Many have thought that only slaves would have worked under the doubtless difficult conditions. The fact that until the fourth century A.D. Romans condemned Christians and criminals to penal service in this region may also have contributed to the interpretation of these structures as slave quarters.

dom.[16] Some smelting at least was done at Tell el-Kheleifeh, and it certainly served as a commercial house for shipping metal by land and sea. But for the most part ore was mined and smelted at numerous other places in various parts of the Arabah, particularly in the region of Timnah about twenty miles north of the port. Ezion-geber's main role seems to have been as military and administrative center as well as trading port and focal point for the overland caravan routes to Arabia. It was, in short, an important center although hardly a major city during the tenth century B.C.

Tell Arad stands on the edge of the Negeb about sixteen miles south of Hebron and about nineteen miles east of Beer-sheba. It is thus on the other end of the desert from Tell el-Kheleifeh. Until Aharoni's excavations brought its later history to light, it was known chiefly through its premonarchical biblical connections (Numbers 21:1-3; Joshua 12:14; Judges 1:16). Archaeological work at Arad and surveys of other parts of the Negeb indicate that the entire region apart from a small coastal area under nominal Egyptian control was relatively uninhabited from approximately 1600 B.C. until the time of the Israelite monarchy. The establishment of the monarchy seems to have resulted in a concentrated development of the region. A large number of new settlements were founded in the tenth century B.C. and later. Within a fifteen-mile radius of Beer-sheba alone some fifty sites have been located. But this area is more fertile than the hostile desert farther south. The dense concentration of settlements is therefore not typical. Most identified villages were gathered around a fortress, which was sometimes a rectangle as large as 100 feet by 150 feet with imposing towers. A number of smaller square forts of approximately fifty feet have been found. These had no towers. In addition to these two fairly standard types, some large oval or irregular shaped fortresses have been discovered. Almost all forts found have some form of casemate wall. This by itself is probably enough to indicate that they are either from the time of David and Solomon or from the eighth and seventh centuries. For reasons which will be noted later (see p. 180) casemate walls went out of style for about two centuries. The similarity of design and construction of the various forts together with the sudden interest in settling and defending the area in the tenth century B.C. can be taken as indicating the direction of a central authority. Almost certainly that central authority was Solomon and his ministers.

It would appear that a careful survey was made of the southern part of Solomon's kingdom and fortified settlements placed at strategic locations. Some of these, perhaps those having irregular walls, were at the site of existing villages. Others were built on virgin soil as seems to have been the case at Tell el-Kheleifeh. Tell Arad on the edge of the desert was a strategic location, as is attested by the construction and destruction of no less than six fortresses there during the 400 years of the Israelite monarchy. Solomon fortified the site, and succeeding kings thought it of sufficient importance to rebuild each time it was destroyed by invaders. Moreover, the Romans with their unerring eye for vital positions constructed a fort at Arad in the first century after Christ.

When Solomon built there, it was for all intents and purposes a virgin site. Aharoni's work has shown that older construction was in ruins as early as 2700 B.C. and remained so until the tenth century. At that time the dimensions of the earlier city were ignored (if they were known at all), and a small settlement was concentrated on an isolated

---

[16] Excavations at Deir 'alla in the northern Jordan Valley and surface explorations of the surrounding area indicate an extensive metal industry there during the time of the Hebrew Monarchy. But this matter remains to be investigated thoroughly.

hilltop. Here exceptionally strong fortifications enclosed a square of approximately 125 feet. The stones for the walls were not rough boulders from the surrounding land, but carefully hewn, square blocks well placed in a casemate arrangement. In addition to the type and arrangement of the stones, a wealth of pottery has been found at the site. Succeeding walls were built one on top of the other. These later walls were also found with considerable pottery and in some cases even written materials associated with them. This all combines to make dating virtually certain.

It would seem reasonable to assume that not all of Solomon's construction outside Jerusalem was for the purposes of fortifying the country. At least some of the forts had farming connected with them. Rock-cut cisterns and crude irrigation canals show the difficulties and perhaps also the determination of those who worked the land. At Gezer, one of the more important of Solomon's undertakings, a four-and-one-half-inch limestone plaque containing a rhythmic enumeration of the agricultural seasons was found in 1908. It is written in good biblical Hebrew and is thought by many to be a schoolboy's exercise dating from the time of Solomon.

> His two months are (olive) harvest,
> His two months are planting (grain),
> His two months are late planting;
> His month is hoeing up of flax,
> His month is harvest of barley,
> His month is harvest and *feasting*;
> His two months are vine-tending,
> His month is summer fruit.[17]

Grain, wine ("vine-tending"), and olives, the principle products of ancient agriculture in Palestine (Deuteronomy 7:13; Nehemiah 5:11; Hosea 2:8) are alluded to. This chance text is clear indication of a variegated agricultural year. Farming is the backbone of any nation, and its immediacy to any settled undertaking was of paramount im-

[17] *Ancient Near Eastern Texts*, ed. J. B. Pritchard (Princeton: Princeton University Press, 1955), p. 320.

portance in days before the development of mass rapid transport. The farmer in Israelite times lived in a village somewhat after the modern German and French manner, rather than in the open country as is typical of most American farmers. Primitive implements and poor land kept the size of farms small and within easy walking distance of the village which afforded not only companions, but a measure of protection. Then as now these settlements were on hilltops, and it was not uncommon to have a fortification wall of some sort.

There is indication that Solomon was engaged in expanding agriculture in his kingdom. At Ramat Matred, about ten miles north and slightly east of Kadesh-barnea, Israeli archaeologists have found an Israelite agricultural settlement dated to Solomon's reign. Ramet Matred is deep in the desert. It is not impossible that some of Solmon's southern forts too were designed as centers for developing new agricultural areas. The Negeb ("dry land") is a desert; yet it contains semi-arid areas such as the Beer-sheba region. Some parts of it are well suited for barley crops. As early as 2900 B.C. Tell Arad, which had neither spring nor well near by, possessed large granaries. These indicate the importance of agriculture to the economy of the city. Modern Israeli farmers reap a good harvest from the area once every three or four years. Whether conditions in ancient days provided better crops more frequently is a matter of conjecture.

The Price of Glory

Every aspect of Israelite life was affected by Solomon's consolidation and exploitation of David's empire. Excavations at Beth-shemesh, Tell Beit Mirsim (Debir), and Tell el-Farah (Tirzah), assumed to be more or less typical of provincial Israelite towns of that time, indicate the now familiar casemate walls enclosing what seems to be a new type of house. It contained four rooms. Two walls divided it longitudinally yielding three rooms of about the same size. Across one end of the house was a larger room running the entire width. There is so far no indication of a second story. Dwellings at all three sites show evidence of city planning and are often found back to back with the front opening onto parallel streets. This is particularly the case at Tell el-Farah.

There is thus indication of a generally higher standard of living than at least the Hebrews had hitherto known. But there is no sign of a high order of economic prosperity or of a highly refined culture as was to be seen in Jerusalem. Moreover, at Tell Beit Mirsim (Debir) a number of plaque figurines have been found in the town levels dated to the United Monarchy. Most scholars understand these to be fertility figures of the kind well known in Late Bronze Age Canaanite culture. They are thus usually taken to indicate the continuing influence of fertility rites. W. F. Albright, the excavator of the site, holds another view however. He notes that these figures differ from earlier ones in that they represent pregnant women. To his mind these plaques were not associated with religious rites, but were an aid to women in childbirth. Albright may well be correct. Archaeology does tend to suggest the disappearance of plaque figurines from Israelite levels so far excavated. Yet there is no indication in the Bible or elsewhere that Solomon made any attempt to stamp out such Canaanite practices or that his own personal religion was free from "foreign" elements. On the contrary, the overwhelming evidence is that in religion as in other matters he was eclectic and cosmpolitan.

"Cosmopolitan" may in fact be just the word to describe Solomon's empire. It was, however briefly, the leading nation of its time, and winds of thought and style blew through it. For example, wisdom writings, a type of literature common throughout the ancient east, may have found a friendly reception from the king and among the more urbane class in Solomon's Israel. This may be the source of a tradition ascribing to Solomon authorship of a part of the Wisdom Literature of the Bible (Proverbs). Be that as it may, from the east, north, west, and south did come traders, diplomats, and adventurers. Jerusalem in its Solomonic splendor was, like Athens of a later day, a hub of international civilization. Unlike Athens some of whose visible ancient splendor remains, Jerusalem's began to diminish even before Solomon's death. He had purchased his glory at too high a price, a price which cannot be calculated merely in shekels and talents. The internal unity which he and his father had sought to forge was irreparably shattered by his religious and economic policies.

He successfully made his royal Temple into a national shrine. In his day it was a powerful symbol of unity and subsequently became a devotional focus far beyond even David's wildest dreams. Yet Solomon diluted the effectiveness of this force not only by erecting shrines to the gods of his foreign wives (I Kings 11:1-8), but also by his own personal participation in worship alien to the religion of his father, David (I Kings 3:3-4). By his own example he encouraged the people to see the Temple, however magnificent, as only one aspect of their national religious loyalty. His royal patronage of alien cults set a policy followed by succeeding northern and southern kings, earned him the condemnation of the biblical writers (I Kings 11:9-13), and furnished a rallying point for the disaffected who opposed him. This was the reason cited by the prophet Ahijah when he designated Jeroboam to be king in Solomon's place and to reign over the ten tribes of the north (I Kings 11:26-40).

His economic policies proved even more disastrous. In spite of an enormous income (I Kings 10:14) he found his revenue from trade, tribute, and taxation insufficient to support his grand manner of life and his grandiose schemes. New administrative districts were formed, partly perhaps to break up old tribal loyalties and to reduce the power of the elders, but certainly in part to make taxation more efficient (I Kings 4:7-19). Monies from his monopoly of the two greatest overland trade routes were augmented by an apparently successful merchant fleet. Tribute poured in from the various parts of the empire. Yet it was never enough. More resources needed to be found.

One additional resource was forced labor. From the figures given in the Bible it appears that much of Solomon's building activity was done by men taken from their homes, families, and jobs and pressed into the king's service. II Chronicles 2:17 mentions 153,600 men, while I Kings 5:13-15 notes 180,000 workers and 3000 overseers. II Chronicles clearly intends to convey the impression that no Israelites were among the laborers. A census had identified all the aliens living in the land. They were taken. The historical situation was considerably different from this picture. The Chronicler, like the writer of I Kings 9:22, tried to cover up one of Solomon's graver faults: making slaves out of the Hebrews whom God in the Exodus had redeemed from bondage for all time. There is no doubt that many Israelites were in the forced labor gangs. Not only is the statement in I Kings 5:13-18 explicit on this point, but it was one of the causes of the disruption of the kingdom after Solomon's death (I Kings 12:1-20; note particularly vs. 18).

A second resource was credit: that extended by Hiram, king of Tyre. Solomon paid for the cedar and cypress he got from the forests of Lebanon (I Kings 5:10-11), but his balance of trade with the Phoenician king ran badly against Israel. Indeed, the large imports into Israel apart from what was received from Phoenicia must have severely taxed Solomon's treasury (I Kings

10:22, 26) and probably contributed to an overall poor balance of trade which left Solomon perhaps unwilling, more likely unable, to pay Hiram. In short, he had come near bankruptcy. In order to satisfy the debt, he gave Hiram twenty cities in Galilee near Tyre. It has been popularly said that the world of that time must have been amazed at Solomon's gift to his fellow monarch. It was hardly a "gift," and only Hiram was amazed. The cities were virtually worthless, and when the Tyrian king saw them he realized that his old friend had hoodwinked him (I Kings 9:10-14). All the same, worthless or not, the cities had been reckoned as a part of Israel by David who had captured them (II Samuel 24:6-7). Solomon had thus been forced to cede a part—and an important part—of the Israelite kingdom itself and not merely some remote segment of the empire. II Chronicles 8:1-2 hides this fact by reversing the whole thing saying that Hiram had given the cities to Solomon. It was quite otherwise. From Solomon's time on, even down into New Testament times, the northwestern border of Galilee was the limit of the territory given to Hiram.

Thus even before Solomon's death the price of his glory had begun to be exacted from Israel. When the grand monarch "slept with his fathers, and was buried in the city of David his father" (I Kings 11:42), Rehoboam found his father's legacy a mixed blessing indeed. The northern tribes were in a virtual state of defiance. Its religionists were outraged at Solomon's apostasy, and its workmen furious over the issue of forced labor. In addition it is entirely possible that Solomon had favored Judah over the other tribes in matters of taxation and labor.[18] If this were the case, another grievance

[18] Note the mention of "all Israel" in I Kings 4:7 and 5:13. Is this a technical reference to the northern tribes? Many think so. See also I Samuel 8:10-18 which many scholars take to be an account of Solomon's practices written back into a speech of Samuel by a later writer who opposed the monarchy.

would have been added to an already considerable list. All it would take was a vain, immature young man to galvanize grievance into open rebellion. Rehoboam, Solomon's son and heir, was just the man. So the throne of Solomon fell. Rehoboam reigned over Judah while Jeroboam, now returned from Egypt, sat upon the northern throne. Soon the Egyptians themselves were in the land, laying waste Solomon's magnificent fortresses with their great gates and casemate walls.

The invaders sacked the Temple in Jerusalem and the House of the Forest, the royal Palace, taking away Solomon's 300 golden shields. Rehoboam replaced them with shields of bronze (I Kings 14:25-28; II Chronicles 12:9-11). The contrast is instructive. The glory of Israel had dimmed. The empire of the faithful David and the splendid Solomon was reduced to two petty states, in competition with a dozen others and at the mercy of revived giants in Egypt and Mesopotamia.

VI: A KINGDOM DIVIDED

13. DISRUPTION AND ITS AFTERMATH

Historical distinctions combined with excesses of an autocratic ruler to divide what had been the strongest kingdom of its day. Less than a century after Saul had rallied a united Israel, Rehoboam sat on the throne of the southern kingdom, Judah, while Jeroboam reigned in the north over a nation called Israel. Two generations in common cause had not served to lessen ancient animosities and the petty states faced each other with a bitterness peculiar to civil strife. Henceforth they would join forces only on those rare occasions when mutual self-interest demanded it. For the most part they were actively or passively[1] at war with each other or allying themselves with each other's enemies.

In a curious combination Israel, the northern kingdom, fell heir both to Solomon's cosmopolitan outlook and to some of the more conservative religious ideas from the Hebrew past. Geography, which played a determinative role in the character of each kingdom, decreed that Israel would be in continuous contact with the great and near-great states of the day. The two great trade routes which skirted Judah passed through Israel. The Plain of Esdraelon was a broad avenue along which Phoenician culture flowed into the heart of the country. Moreover, it was the express policy of a number of kings, particularly the Omrides, that capable family which held the northern throne for half a century, to develop an even more cosmopolitan culture and to enlarge an already diverse population base. In pursuing this policy Ahab was caught between Jezebel, his determined Phoenician queen, and Elijah, the tough-minded protagonist of a considerably more conservative Hebrew view. Yet for all the forces and counterforces at work in the land, the way of Israel continued substantially to be the way of Solomon. It was relatively wealthy, urbane, and open to ideas which were non-Hebraic in conception and execution.

---

[1] "Cold War" is a term we would apply today to the relations that normally existed between Judah and Israel.

For this reason it is all the more surprising that many of the concepts underlying some of its basic institutions should have been drawn from the more conservative premonarchical Hebrew tradition. Kingship, for example, was not based upon the dynastic principle as in Judah, but upon the tradition of designation of each individual as was the practice of selecting leadership during the period of the Judges.[2] Jeroboam as a usurper could hardly appeal to the dynastic principle for legitimization of his rule. Thus he and those who followed him denied hereditary right and based their claim to authority on the more freewheeling and less highly structured manner of earlier days. This had dire consequences for Israel. Few sons successfully claimed the thrones of their fathers. Coup d'état, revolt, and regicide were rife.

Judah, on the other hand, isolated, provincial, and fairly secure in the high mountains, had a stable monarchy. Only once in over four centuries was the Davidic line interrupted. On that occasion the chief priest himself led in the restoration of a Davidide to the throne (II Kings 11:1-12:1; II Chronicles 22:10-24:1). This kind of transfer of power did not, of course, entirely free Judah from many of the stresses and strains which tore the fabric of Israel. Yet it did allow the king, firm in his legitimate power, some freedom to pursue a more independent course than would otherwise have been possible. This is one of the factors that produced a number of religious reformers among the kings of Judah. Two, Asa and Jehoshaphat, appeared fairly soon after Solomon and fought against many of his religious innovations. There were no such reformers among

those who reigned in the north where Solomon's pluralistic religious policy found royal favor more or less constantly.[3]

Another factor affecting cultural and religious matters in the south was the geographical situation of the country. Shortly after the death of Solomon, Egypt reasserted its power along the southern part of *The Way of the Sea* and in the Negeb. Judah, with a hostile brother state to the north, found itself cut off in the west and south. To the east lay the less developed and warlike kingdoms of the Transjordan. They exerted little influence upon Judah. Rehoboam's kingdom was thus left virtually to itself. It was, until quite late in its history, bypassed by the major powers. There was small advantage it could offer a conqueror. Moreover, for the most part its rulers wisely played a neutral role in power politics.

As a result of the interplay of these and other factors, Judah remained essentially homogeneous, turned in upon itself, and became more provincial while Israel became more cosmopolitan. In religion there was a similar divergency of paths. After the ninth century Israel, which had heard the voices and felt the effects of Elijah and Elisha, produced only one major native prophet, Hosea. More at home in Israel were Zedekiah and his prophetic band (I Kings 22:11-24) and other "pro-establishment" religionists. Judah, on the other hand, fostered a religious tradition that produced all the other major prophets in addition to preserving, honoring, and transmitting to mankind that vision of faith which today is embodied in the Old Testament. Culturally Judah became a backwater. Religiously it played a historical role which, looking back, we might describe in the words of Isaiah: It was destined to be "a light to the nations."

---

[2] Anointing of the king was important in both nations. But in Judah it was always a descendant of David who was by right to be designated by this holy act. In both kingdoms anointing signified a covenant between God and the king. Judah, however, had a "covenanted dynasty." This is the importance of II Samuel 7 and of God's promise to "build a house" for David.

[3] Jehu's revolt, inspired and supported by the work of Elijah and Elisha, certainly failed to produce the results hoped for by those who wished to purge Israel of foreign religious practices.

These various differences had been held in check and had to an extent even been exploited by Solomon. But when the grand monarch's son tried to ascend a united throne, they emerged with full vengeance. "Rehoboam went to Shechem, for all Israel had come to Shechem to make him king" (I Kings 12:1). Like his grandfather, David, Rehoboam was forced to seek two separate anointings before he could reign over an undivided kingdom. It is indicative of the weakness with which he came to the throne that he journeyed north to Shechem, the major city of the region, in order to be crowned by "all Israel." One would have expected the elders there to come to Jerusalem even if they insisted upon recognition apart from the leaders of Judah. Few things could show more clearly the virility of the ancient divisions and the fruit of Solomon's policies. By the very fact that he journeyed northward the new monarch confessed to all the fragile nature of his position and removed himself from whatever position of strength he might have had in bargaining. Jeroboam, Solomon's enemy who had been harbored by the Egyptians, was present among the northern elders. Yet as the narrative of I Kings 12 (see also II Chronicles 10) makes clear, it was not Jeroboam's agitation but Rehoboam's failure to handle the situation successfully that caused the son of Solomon to leave Shechem uncrowned. When he compounded his strategic errors by tactical mistakes in face-to-face confrontation with the elders of "all Israel," the fate of the United Monarchy was sealed. There were to be two kingdoms more adequately reflecting the tribal structure which was the underlying reality of ancient Hebrew politics.

Following the murder of Adoram, an official in charge of forced labor, Rehoboam fled from Shechem apparently fearing for his own life. Safe once more in Jerusalem he began assembling an army with a view to forcible reunification of the country. The intervention of the prophetic party, whose motives were at best mixed, combined with the inherent weakness of Judah to prevent the outbreak of civil war.

In the north, meanwhile, plans for the establishment of a separate nation proceeded. Jeroboam was crowned king, established his court at Shechem, and immediately confronted the serious problem of how to win the people's religious loyalty away from Jerusalem. So long as their faith centered on David's city and Solomon's Temple, their loyalty was in danger of being captured by Solomon's son. David's accomplishment in binding religion and politics together was a splendid one, powerfully done and lasting in its effects. Jeroboam was now faced with undoing this work. His approach was twofold. First, he deported all those religionists whose loyalty was with the Davidic house. In particular the priests and the Levites who had been settled in the Canaanite cities (Joshua 21; I Chronicles 6:31-81) were made to flee to the south where they demonstrated the wisdom of Jeroboam's action (II Chronicles 11:13-17). Second, two royal sanctuaries were constructed, one in the north at Dan and the other in the south at Bethel.[4] Bethel was the more strategic of the two, lying almost on the main road from the north to Jerusalem. In addition, earlier Israelite practices centered around other shrines, such as Gilgal, were revived. Throughout the length and breadth of the country people were encouraged to worship at the holy places of the northern kingdom. Amos 4:4-5 may preserve a satirized version of an anti-Jerusalemite saying which circulated with official backing in the north:

[4] In 1970 excavators at Dan reported discovery of the Israelite sanctuary. But the disturbed stratigraphy at the site makes precise identification difficult. Further work is needed to clarify the matter. W. F. Albright's excavation at Bethel in 1934 and those of J. L. Kelso in 1954, 1957, and 1960 brought to light the considerable wealth that attended Jeroboam's focus on Bethel. But no trace of the Israelite sanctuary was found.

Come to Bethel (and transgress);
   to Gilgal (and multiply transgression);
bring your sacrifice every morning,
   your tithes every three days;
offer a sacrifice of thanksgiving of
   that which is leavened,
and proclaim freewill offerings,
   publish them;
(for so you love to do), O people of
   Israel!

How successful Jeroboam's religious policy was in reducing the political influence of the Jerusalem Temple cannot be known. It probably succeeded well enough. At any rate, it is clear from I Kings 12 and 13 that it had at least one undesired effect. It caused the alienation of many of Jeroboam's religious supporters in Israel and brought from Judah some of the prophetic party who had argued against civil war in the hope that a division of the kingdom might lead to a revival of the religious purity of David. There was much criticism of the new king's ways and particularly the golden bulls he had established in his royal sanctuaries. Thus the long-term divisive effect of Solomon's religious policies was established in Israel as in Judah.

Yet at the time opposition from the more conservative religious elements must have appeared minor. Matters of great moment were occurring externally and both states were only too soon to feel their full force. Egypt, whose fortunes had languished under the weak Twenty-first Dynasty, now revived with the Lybian, Shishak, on the throne. Once more hungry eyes were cast in the direction of Palestine. Far north, in Mesopotamia, events were transpiring which ultimately would prove even more disastrous for the tiny Hebrew kingdoms than the resurgence of Egyptian power. There the Assyrians were assembling an empire which would eventually swallow Israel and bear heavily upon the fate of Judah.

The demise of Hebrew power had nothing to do, of course, with the reawakening of the giants of the south and north. But it did produce a considerable political realignment along the immediate borders of Palestine. Israel claimed sovereignty over much of the Transjordanian lands that had been in Solomon's empire. Judah's imperial domains were smaller, yet encompassed the Negeb and a portion of Moab. Neither state was able to hold its imperial areas. A part of Edom had already been lost during Solomon's lifetime (I Kings 11:14-22). Moab, judging from the inscription on the famous Mesha Stele,[5] gained independence during this time, was subjugated later by the Omrides of Israel, and subsequently threw off their yoke and established a sizable kingdom east of the Dead Sea. Of Ammon farther north we have almost no information, but it appears this region, too, successfully revolted at this time. The Negeb was lost through Egyptian intervention about which more will be said shortly. Israel and Judah thus found a goodly portion of their actual and potential wealth stripped from them. Moreover, in political matters both would henceforth find it necessary to compete as one among many similar petty states.

The reduced borders of Judah in this period can be seen in a defensive perimeter established by Rehoboam. II Chronicles 11:5-12 lists fifteen fortresses arranged roughly in three lines; one on the west, one south, and the other to the east. Whether these lines were established before or after the invasion of Shishak is a matter of debate, although some evidence suggests that they may have been in consequence of that disaster. There is no question that this defensive stance

[5] The Mesha Stele, also known as "The Moabite Stone," was found in 1868 at Dibon, some twenty miles east of the Dead Sea. The inscription on this four-by-two-feet basalt stone tells of the struggles of King Mesha of Moab with Omri and Ahab of Israel and of his successful war with Jehoram from whom he gained final independence for the area. It recounts the events described in II Kings 3:4-8 from the point of view of the Moabites.

shows Judah huddled in the highlands in a pitifully small area perhaps no more than forty miles from north to south and twenty-five miles from east to west.

Archaeology has so far discovered very little, if anything, concerning these fortresses. Most of the sites in the list have not been dug for one reason or another. Of those which have been excavated only Lachish (Tell ed-Duweir) and perhaps Tell el-Hesi furnish clues. At Lachish fortifications encircling the city have been found. These walls were in use throughout the period of the Divided Monarchy and may originally have been those constructed by Rehoboam's engineers. If so, they show how quickly the casemate wall was abandoned, for the early

Joint Expedition to Tell el-Hesi

The late tenth–early ninth century mudbrick wall at Tell el-Hesi. After the first season of work (1970) excavators were unsure whether it was a Hebrew fortification following the destructive invasion of Shishak, a Philistine defense against Hebrew incursion into the coastal plain, or if its presence is due to some other group with unknown interests.

walls of Lachish were of a glacis type and were built of stone and mud brick. Hesi had a solid mud-brick wall. This may be an indication that Rehoboam's strongholds were constructed after the siege machines of Shishak had made short work of the casemate defenses of Solomon's cities. This vivid and painful demonstration of how offense had outdistanced defense led to a search for a better wall which would withstand improved siege machines. And so goes the arms race ad infinitum.

It may seem strange that Rehoboam did not fortify his northern frontier. This is usually explained by saying he intended to reunify the country and did not want a recognizable border which would *de facto* admit the legitimacy of the northern kingdom. There may well be some truth in this. Yet it should be noted that there is no natural boundary in the area. Other factors were also involved. Primary among these was the disputed status of the tribe of Benjamin. Traditionally a northern tribe and the home of Saul, Benjamin was located at the junction of the two kingdoms and found its loyalty divided. The difficulties involved can be sensed in the fact that both Jerusalem, the capital of Judah, and Bethel, the premier royal sanctuary of Israel, were in Benjamin. The "war between Rehoboam and Jeroboam continually" (I Kings 14:30) was a series of struggles to determine the disposition of this tribe and its important territory. Abijah (915-913 B.C.), Rehoboam's son and successor, took much of the area including Bethel (II Chronicles 13:13-19) in the waning days of Jeroboam. Asa (913-873 B.C.), Abijah's son, lost that and more to a successor of Jeroboam, Baasha (900-877 B.C.). Indeed, Baasha came within six miles of Jerusalem itself. At Ramah, he established himself in strength with the apparent intention of laying siege to Asa (I Kings 15:16-17). In this crisis Asa set the pattern which would be followed by a number of the southern kings;

he sought an alliance against Israel. Sending all the gold and silver left in the Temple and in the Palace to Ben-Hadad in Damascus, he forged a military treaty which brought Syrians in force against Israel. I Kings 15:20 (see also II Chronicles 16:4) does not mention Hazor among the cities captured by Ben-Hadad, but it does note the capture of Ijon, Dan, and Abel-beth-maacah directly north and the area of Chinneroth immediately south. Archaeological discoveries at Hazor now make clear that this city too was overwhelmed as the Syrians swarmed into "all the land of Naphtali." Baasha hastily abandoned his work of fortifying Ramah and hurried north to repulse what was proving to be a large-scale invasion.

So far Asa's plan had succeeded brilliantly, but his kingdom was still not secured against the more powerful Israel. Taking advantage of an opportunity now afforded him and pressing into service every able-bodied person in the area, he dismantled the partially finished Ramah and carried its stones and timbers to two other sites. At Geba of Benjamin and at Mizpah, two strong points dominating the main roads to Jerusalem, he constructed fortresses thus completing the encircling defensive perimeter begun by Rehoboam (I Kings 16:22). Between Mizpah and Bethel three miles away, the boundary of the two kingdoms was now established. When the Omrides came to power a short time later they sought more friendly relations with Judah and made no attempt to alter the frontier. Thereafter it remained unchanged for over a century and a half, and after the fall of Israel in 722 B.C. it became the southern limit of the Assyrian Empire.

Archaeologists working at Tell en-Nasbeh, now widely regarded as the site of Mizpah, have uncovered massive walls which are said to be those built by Asa. Over fifteen feet thick and of rubble stone, these defenses show haste in design and execution. Rectan-gular towers of different sizes were spaced along the wall at irregular intervals. On the east and west a stone-faced glacis in places over twenty-six feet thick at its base further strengthened this fort. This was plastered to make it more difficult to scale. The single gate did not pierce the wall but was formed by overlapping the ends of the wall for a distance of almost forty-eight feet. At the end of the outer wall was a massive tower. Entrance to the town was at the inner end of the passageway between the walls. It was doubly buttressed and protected by chambers which projected from the walls. This arrangement meant that the vulnerable right side of the attackers would be exposed to defenders on the city's inner wall. The stones show none of the beauty and skill of a master mason's craft, and compared with Solomon's work at Megiddo, Hazor, and Gezer the gate is primitive. Yet the strategic and defensible site was well chosen and the construction soundly, if roughly, executed.

Thus about eight miles north of Jerusalem Asa established a boundary dividing Benjamin in half, leaving the sanctuary at Bethel in Israelite hands and a more easily defended Jerusalem as the capital of Judah. After some forty years of war the situation was approximately what it had been at the beginning.

During these forty years, however, events had transpired which had not left other things as they had been. One of the more serious of these events was an Egyptian invasion of Palestine "in the fifth year of King Rehoboam" (I Kings 14:25; see also II Chronicles 12:2-4). Solomon's policy toward Egypt had been one of strength combined with respect. The fact that he took one of the pharaoh's daughters as wife without giving a daughter in return indicates the stronger position of Solomon. Yet he was obliged to give her the highest status in his harem and even to build a separate palace for her. Moreover, the off-hand statement

The walls of Tell en-Nasbeh (left) display a peculiar off-set construction the purpose of which is not entirely known. The stone-faced glacis (above), on the other hand, was once plastered to make it more difficult to scale and almost impossible for effective use of battering rams.

indicating Gezer was her dowry (I Kings 9:16) doubtless reflects renewed Egyptian influence in Philistia. This may be why Solomon never moved to incorporate this area into his Empire. It is also to be noted that Egypt played a role in the successful Edomite revolt against Solomon (I Kings 11:14-22). On that occasion the pharaoh, probably Psusennes II (*ca.* 984-950 B.C.), possibly the same who gave his daughter to be Solomon's queen, seems to have been somewhat reluctant to allow Hadad to return to foment unrest. Shishak, who harbored Jeroboam (I Kings 11:40), had no such hesitations. This strong pharaoh, a Lybian who overthrew the futile Psusennes, was a man of action. During the Twenty-first Dynasty, power had been shared by the merchant princes of Tanis and the military-religious hierarchy associated with the worship of Amon at Thebes. Shishak's seizure of the throne represented a triumph of the commercial interests. Establishing one of his sons as High Priest at Thebes in order to control the often politically troublesome priests he removed the court to Bubastis (Tell Basta), south and slightly west of Tanis. From this position in the Eastern Delta he was well situated to pursue his interests in the northeast, in Palestine and Syria.

His opportunity to move did not come until the disintegration of Solomon's Empire and the division of the Hebrew monarchy. Then he struck. His intention, in keeping with the interests he represented, seems to have been

not so much conquest as acquisition of wealth through booty and especially through securing control over lucrative trade routes. He also meant to see to it that the Israelites who had reaped the benefits of all the major commercial avenues in the area were left in no position to continue such domination. For these reasons he both expelled the Israelites from certain of their imperial territories and laid waste to many of the cities of both Judah and Israel. The Negeb with its port at Ezion-geber and its even more important overland route from Arabia was detached from Judah. *The Way of the Sea* in the west and *The King's Highway* which traced its way along the Transjordanian heights in the east were even more important objectives.

Archaeologists working at Ezion-geber (Tell el-Kheleifeh) think that the Solomonic wall and central storehouse were probably destroyed by Shishak. If so, the Egyptians seem to have made no attempt to revive the place as a port and commercial center, since the next major construction on the site comes from the time of Jehoshaphat (873-849 B.C.). This strengthens the suggestion that Arabian trade was the object of Egyptian activity in the southern desert.

On the external south wall of the great hypostyle hall at Karnak, Shishak recorded his victories in Palestine and Syria. This inscription traces his line of march to Baza where the army, having taken that town, divided in two with one part striking south into the Negeb and the other moving northward. With the ruins of Solomon's once-splendid defenses at Gezer behind it, this northernmost force proceeded by way of the ascent of Beth-horon into the hill country of Judah and menaced Jerusalem. Judging from the Karnak list, all the fortified towns along this route fell to Egyptian arms. Jerusalem alone was spared but only at the cost of much of the gold that had adorned Solomon's capital (I Kings 14:25-26).

Shishak's army now moved northward along the mountain highway in order to reduce his principle target: Israel, which still exercised control over the trade routes.[6] Ancient Shechem felt the Egyptian battering ram once more, and succumbed. By way of the Wadi Farah, Shishak descended eastward into the valley of the Jordan capturing Tirzah along the way. Tirzah had become a royal city under Jeroboam, as had Penuel near Mahanaim in Transjordan. For reasons which we do not know Tirzah had seemed a more appealing capital to Jeroboam than had Shechem. Penuel was perhaps something like a summer palace or even a place of refuge in event of trouble. If this latter were one of its purposes it failed. Penuel, Mahanaim, and other cities of Transjordan fell before the relentless Egyptians as they wrested control of *The King's Highway* from Israelite hands. *The Way of the Sea,* the other principal commercial avenue, passed through the Plain of Esdraelon in Israel. Here the Egyptians now proceeded laying waste the great cities of the Plain, Beth-shan, Shunem, Taanach, and Megiddo among them. At Megiddo excavators have recovered a part of a victory stele erected by Shishak. This suggests among other things that this important site, controlling the trade route as it goes inland around Mount Carmel, remained in Egyptian

[6] Curiously the Bible ignores this attack on Israel. Our information about this part of an extensive Egyptian campaign comes from archaeology.

Gaddis, Luxor, Egypt

On the wall of the temple of Amon at Karnak, Shishak listed the Palestinian and Syrian cities he captured in his military thrust northeastward after the death of Solomon.

hands when the main body of the army finally turned south to Egypt by way of the coast.

Even more graphic evidence of the triumphant march of Shishak's troops has been recovered by archaeologists. In a number of excavation reports, words like "obliteration," "devastation," "violent destruction," and "brutal destruction" are used to describe occupation layers dated to the end of the tenth century. Mention has previously been made of the fate of Solomon's fort at Ezion-geber. Tell Arad in the northern Negeb apparently suffered the same fate as did numerous other smaller fortresses in the area. These are also listed on the walls of the Temple of Karnak. The stones of Gezer, Shechem, and Tirzah bear witness to Egyptian fury, but perhaps the most striking evidence comes from Beth-Shemesh and Tell Beit Mirsim (Debir). At these two towns, surrounded by similar casemate walls probably of Davidic construction, there was such widespread damage that one was uninhabitable and the other rebuilt without reference to the layout of the previous city. Evidence of fire was found at several sites, but nowhere was it so appallingly devastating as at Beth-Shemesh. The city did not rise again for a hundred years or more. Tell Beit Mirsim, on the other hand, was resettled almost at once. This may be because the Egyptians breached the walls but were satisfied with the obliteration of the area inside the defenses. The walls, although pierced, were left virtually intact and were rebuilt to continue in use throughout Israelite times.

Thus archaeologists, by deciphering the inscriptions on the walls of Karnak and by excavations in Palestine, have significantly enlarged our knowledge concerning Shishak's attack on Judah and Israel, an event which receives but scant notice in the biblical record. This invasion was a terrific blow to both kingdoms, catching them at a moment when they were already reeling from internal disaster. The aftermath of the division of the kingdom following Solomon's death was a period of continuing and even increasing instability. Under Asa's long reign (913-873 B.C.) order came once more to Judah. When the Omrides came to the throne of Israel, relative peace and prosperity returned, however briefly, to the torn Hebrew states.

14. THE OMRIDES

It has long been recognized that the biblical writers based their judgments of the kings of Israel and Judah on religious factors: on how faithful a given ruler was to the worship of the Hebrew God. David, whose personal religious practices and royal policies seem to have provided little room for criticism, became the standard by which all others were judged. Indeed, he became idealized as time went by. On the other side, those whose practices and policies had compromised or otherwise threatened the purity of Hebrew worship looked worse than they really were, when later religious evaluations were made. The criterion of judgment plus the effect which the passage of time had on it could not but produce a certain imbalance in the biblical picture of the various kings. The good were not quite so good as they appear, nor the bad so bad. Moreover, the absolute standard used made little room for other factors, such as economic, political, and social ones. This was a major distinction between the prophets and many of the other writers of the Bible who commented on the events of their times and those of earlier days. The prophets saw the intimate relation of religion with other factors. This relation was there whether acknowledged or not. There is no clearer case of this than the Omrides. Their pluralistic religious policy and royal patronage of foreign cults were not merely a continuation of Solomon's view, but a deliberate part of their own political and economic programs. The stratification of society which was a consequence laid the foundation for the later "social prophets," such as Amos and Hosea.

The Omrides were certainly the greatest dynasty of Israel, and Omri himself may have been the greatest of the kings of the north. But the writers of Kings and Chronicles see only Omridian religious policies which come under the harshest condemnation. Although Omri may have "showed might," as I Kings 16:27 notes, the Bible is less interested in his accomplishments than in his marrying his son, Ahab, to a Phoenician princess, Jezebel.[1] This union, which provoked the response of Elijah and others and eventually proved so disastrous to the dynasty and the country, is the focus of the Hebrew religionists. It forms the background for fourteen chapters in I and II Kings. Only six verses (I Kings 16:23-28) are devoted to the reign of Omri (876-869 B.C.) whose accomplishments were so outstanding that

[1] Some scholars think Psalm 45, an ode on the occasion of a royal wedding, is related to the union between Ahab and Jezebel. Verses 10-12 are considered by those who take this view to refer specifically to Jezebel's Tyrian origin and her need to become Hebrew in outlook, something she decidedly did not do.

years later Israel was still called "the land of Omri."

We do not know anything of Omri's background. He appears suddenly in the biblical narrative as commander of an Israelite army besieging Gibbethon, a Philistine city (I Kings 16:15-16). The failure of the Bible to give the name of his father while carefully noting the name of the father of Tibni, Omri's rival, has led many to say he was a foreigner. However, this evidence alone will not support such a conclusion. Contemporary Assyrian records show that the lineage of a commoner who had come to the throne was not given. The silence of I Kings 16:21 may, therefore, indicate nothing more than the fact that Omri was a Hebrew commoner. Foreigner or commoner, he came to the throne by a route well known in the ancient world: he was proclaimed king by the army in the field. Elah, Baasha's son who ruled for only a year (877-876 B.C.), had been murdered while drunk by an officer in the royal chariotry, a certain Zimri. For this deed Zimri's name passed into the vocabulary of ancient Israel with much the same connotation as "Quisling" came to have during and after the Second World War in Europe (see I Kings 9:31). Zimri apparently hoped the army would support his ascension to the throne. Instead, the troops marched north to Tirzah with the name of "King Omri" on their lips. A short siege ensued, and seven days after the death of Elah, Zimri committed suicide by burning the royal palace down upon him (I Kings 16:8-20). Israel had had three kings in one week.

Omri's power was not secured by the death of Zimri. The murder of Elah had sent political shock waves throughout the kingdom. Many rallied around Tibni, a person of family who seems also to have been a military officer. A civil war in the north lasted three to four years. We have no details of this conflict other than its outcome. Tibni was

killed, his movement crushed, Omri held the throne and ruled in Tirzah. Biblical chronology, which is difficult at this point, seems to indicate that he kept this site as his capital for two years. That it had been and probably was then a place of some distinction is inferred from the Song of Solomon 6:4 which speaks of the beloved as "beautiful as Tirzah . . . comely as Jerusalem." In short, the city compared favorably with Solomon's now somewhat despoiled capital. Roland de Vaux's archaeological findings at Tell el-Farah, now generally regarded as Tirzah, show an interesting thing. He and his associates from the *École Biblique* found evidence of destruction dating to the early ninth century B.C. and of construction begun immediately thereafter. Among the new buildings was a large unfinished work. De Vaux understands this to be the royal palace begun by Omri to replace the one burned by Zimri. If this interpretation is correct, it is a remarkable correlation with an incident described in the Bible.

Why was the palace unfinished? Because Omri moved the court from Tirzah to a hilltop about seven miles northwest of Shechem. This was the hill of Shemer, soon to be called Beth-Omri, "House of Omri." It was known subsequently to history, however, as *Samaria,* from the name of the original owner. Samaria thus became the third capital of Israel. When the kingdom divided, Jeroboam's logical choice for his court was Shechem, the most important city of the north and a religious and economic center for a thousand years. Excavations there show that he repaired the ancient walls and probably is the one who constructed a large granary over the site of the famous sanctuary, which may still have been ruins since its destruction by Abimelech a century and a half earlier. Why the capital was shifted from there is not known. Very likely the difficulties of adequate defense outweighed the values of its antiquity and historic importance. Shechem (Tell Balata) lies in a flat area between two towering mountains, Gerizim and Ebal. Its scarred stones tell of many attacks, a number of which were successful.

Tirzah, a former Canaanite royal city (Joshua 12:24), is in the verdurous Wadi Farah approximately six miles north-northeast of Shechem. Larger than Megiddo, twice the size of Jericho, it was strategically located on the main road from Shechem to Bethshan and the Transjordanian region. The selection of this site may have been based purely upon its inherent attractiveness and its ready communications with east and west. Yet it may also indicate something of the preoccupation of the early kings of Israel with the east and northeast, with Transjordan and Syria. Forty years later, as Omri strolled through his unfinished capital, Israelite interests were looking in another direction: to the northwest and to Phoenicia.

Samaria offered Omri a number of advantages. Although it is not the highest hill in the area, it is a prominent mount, standing alone and easily defended. Amos 6:1 speaks of "those who feel secure on the mountain of Samaria." When the final Assyrian assault came in 724 B.C., the city was able to hold out unaided for two years. The valleys surrounding it are so fertile that even today fruits and vegetables from there command higher prices in various markets. Below its western slope runs the major road connecting the south with the Plain of Esdraelon and Phoenicia. Its main disadvantage is its lack of adequate water supply. In the modern Arab village of Sabastiya[2] on the eastern slope, there is a well which was very likely in use in ancient times. It is insufficient to serve as large a city as Samaria. There are springs a mile away, but this was a considerable distance before the Romans came. Ar-

chaeologists have so far not found any trace of a water system such as those at Megiddo, Gezer, or Jerusalem. The Romans, however, brought water to the site from these springs by means of a large aqueduct, parts of which still stand. These things indicate that the problem of water was probably a continuous one for the earlier inhabitants of the city. Cisterns were used at Samaria as elsewhere in Palestine at that time. Those excavated there limited the size of the city's population to about 30,000. This, however, was no small number in that day.

Difficulties associated with the water supply, however vexing, were obviously outweighed by the advantages of the site. Not the least of these was the opportunity Samaria afforded Omri to follow the main outlines of Solomon's policy. Strong internal government symbolized by a unique capital [3] and proper friends abroad were hallmarks of Solomon's power. David's capture of Jerusalem with his private army made it his personal property. Omri was able to purchase the site of his capital from Shemer, and it had the added advantage of being virgin. He was thus able to place his stamp on his city with even more ease than David had been able to do with the former Jebusite stronghold in the south. Also the new location gave easy access to the northwest, to the Phoenicians who were at the height of their power and wealth, and who had shown signs of allying themselves with Damascus, Israel's neighbor and enemy. The shift of the Israelite capital from Tirzah to Samaria was thus a result and a reflection of the policy and intentions of Omri.

Samaria is the only major city founded by the Hebrews. During the Early Bronze Age there were some people living at the site, but their settlement was insignificant and did not influence any of the later building. When

---

[2] The modern name preserves the Herodian designation of the site, *Sebaste* (from the Greek meaning *Caesar*).

[3] A number of rulers in the ancient east built capitals uniquely their own. Among these men were David, Akhenaton, Sargon, and Omri. Solomon placed his unquestioned stamp upon David's city.

Omri and his engineers came, they laid out a royal quarter on the summit and surrounded it by a lower city. The city extended particularly to the east where the hill slopes gradually. On the north, south, and west it falls steeply. The natural plateau which was to form the platform for the royal buildings was enlarged, perhaps in imitation of Solomon's Jerusalem, until it extended approximately 820 feet from north to south and about 525 feet from east to west. Here the palace, courtyards, administrative buildings, gardens, and shrines were built.

Like Solomon half a century or so earlier, Omri sought the aid of Phoenician craftsmanship in building and decorating his royal city. One of the first tasks to be undertaken was the fortification of the summit which doubtless gave to Samaria something of the appearance of a Greek acropolis city. Parts of these Phoenician walls remain and have

The casemate walls at Samaria surrounding the crown of the hill where the royal palace was located. In time of war the chambers could be filled with rubble or dirt depending on the armament of the enemy and the strategy of the defenders.

been laid bare by excavators. They are so meticulously hewn and so carefully laid that they are almost without peer in Palestine.[4] This wall, only a little over six feet thick, seems to have had a dual function. It marked off the limits of the royal area and also served as a terrace foundation to support an extension of the plateau on the summit. Although not primarily defensive, the stones of this wall were so well put together and so perfectly fitted into foundation trenches cut into bedrock that they would not have proved easy to penetrate. Later Ahab surrounded the entire area with a defensive wall, casemate in design and varying from twelve to thirty-two feet in thickness. In places this wall also served to extend the plateau. The difference between magnificent Phoenician work and shoddy Hebrew construction is striking. Even today the visitor does not question the wisdom of the kings in seeking to employ Phoenician skill. At that point in history Hebrew talents did not run in the direction of the plastic arts.

Within these walls lay the palace complex. The royal apartments themselves were two stories high. Not only is there contemporary evidence from elsewhere to suggest this, but II Kings 1:2 relates the tragic incident of how King Ahaziah (850-849 B.C.), son of Ahab and perhaps Jezebel, a year after coming to the throne fell through the protective grillwork "in his upper chamber" and was mortally injured. In the northeast corner of the enclosed courtyard a large artificial pool was found by the Harvard Expedition. It has been speculated that this structure, thirty-three feet long by seventeen feet wide by three feet deep, may be "the pool of Samaria" in which blood was washed from Ahab's chariot after he was felled in the battle of Ramoth-Gilead (I Kings 22:29-38). No recognizable trace has been found of the shrine or shrines which were unquestionably

[4] Some of the masonry at Ramat Rahel and a little at Megiddo compare favorably.

A decorative stone from the entrance to Ramat Rahel is similar to the tops of capitals from Megiddo, Samaria, Hazor, and elsewhere. This style was popular for the entire period of the Hebrew monarchies. In the foreground is a basket for carrying dirt at excavations.

a part of this palace complex. No gate has been found either. Ahab's casemate wall has been traced on the north, south, and west. Later construction has destroyed much of the Israelite work to the east. The gentle slope in this direction and fragments of six proto-Ionic (or proto-Aeolic) pilaster capitals[5] found here suggest that it was on this side that the gate was located in which the prophet Micaiah spoke of doom (I Kings 22:10; II Chronicles 18:9), and where business transactions known to Elisha were carried on (I Kings 7:1).

It is not surprising that many of the Israelite structures at Samaria have disappeared. The site is, on the one hand, an archaeologist's dream. It has been continuously occupied since the days of Omri and has seen at least four periods of considerable magnificence.[6] On the other hand, precisely because so much building has gone on there for so long a time, much of the earlier material has been forever removed. During Herod's reign, to cite only one example, a massive temple dedicated to Augustus Caesar was erected on the summit as a part of the Herodian scheme to adorn his kingdom. What this large undertaking alone destroyed and what today lies beneath its remaining enormous steps we do not know. Nonetheless, in spite of difficulties the three expeditions to Samaria[7] have been able to piece together from their finds and from biblical and Assyrian records a remarkable picture of a magnificent city.

Not the least part of the magnificence of the Omride capital was its ivory decorations. Solomon had chosen gold. Ivory, judging from contemporary evidence, was more the royal style in the Middle East in the mid-ninth century B.C. Ahab, who finished the work envisioned by his father Omri, built an "ivory house" (I Kings 22:39; see also Psalm 45:8; Amos 3:15; 6:4). This was a palace whose walls and furnishings were inlaid with this precious material. Again, it was to Phoenicia that the Hebrew king looked for craftsmanship in design and execution. The Harvard Expedition recovered some five hundred fragments of carved ivory, mostly inlay from furniture and small boxes. This sizable quantity was what was left when the Assyrians looted the palace in 722 B.C. A

---

[5] Similar capitals—a double volute with triangle in the center—have been recovered at Megiddo, Ramat Rahel, and Hazor. It is interesting to note that this design, normally associated with Greek architecture, is found in four Palestinian contexts dating from an earlier time than any yet discovered in Greece.

[6] Israelite, Assyrian, Hellenistic, and Roman.

[7] The Harvard Expedition of 1908 and 1910 directed by G. A. Reisner and C. A. Fisher; a British undertaking from 1931 to 1935 by J. W. Crowfoot; and the work of Paul Lapp and the Jordanian Department of Antiquities which was interrupted by the hostilities of June, 1967.

At Samaria one of the round towers built by Alexander the Great fits into the city wall of Omri and Ahab and welds the whole into the Hellenistic defense of the city.

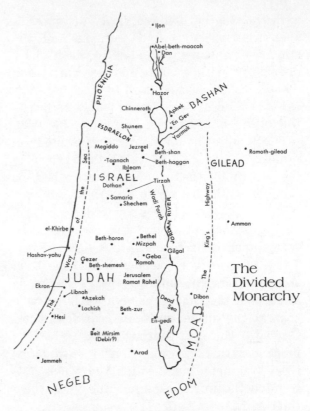

The Divided Monarchy

number of the pieces were inscribed on the back with Phoenician lettering indicating that either craftsmen were brought to Samaria or that the decorations were imported from foreign workshops.

An interesting parallel to the Samaria ivories and their history has been brought to light by the work of A. H. Layard and M. E. L. Mallowan at Nimrud, one of the ancient Assyrian royal capitals.[8] It is known to Genesis 10:11-12 and to antiquity generally as Calah. Working over a century apart, Layard (1846) and Mallowan (1949-1963) recovered enormous amounts of splendidly carved ivories; tens of thousands of fragments and complete pieces. Some of these ivories were contemporary with the Omride dynasty in Israel. In design and execution many are similar to the objects found at Samaria. Of greater interest, Nimrud has

[8] There were four such capitals: Nineveh, Nimrud, Ashur, and Babylon. Not all enjoyed equal favor at the same time.

provided large portions of screens and paneling in such a position that original use can easily be reconstructed. One example will suffice. In the Acropolis Palace at Calah, there was found an auxiliary hall adjoining the throne room. On the floor of the entire length of this hall were extensive traces of intricately carved ivory panels. Closer examination showed that these had been fixed to the wall by means of wooden struts at either end. There was also evidence of the use of some form of adhesive, probably bitumen which was in large amounts on the lower part of the wall. Bitumen, incidentally, was also on the face of a number of ivories. This has led to the suggestion that gold inlay may have been a part of the decoration.

The Acropolis Palace at Calah was destroyed by fire, probably in 612 B.C. when the Babylonians overran the Assyrians. Its struts burned away, the ivory screen fell forward. Almost twenty-six centuries later archaeologists uncovered it, shattered, but with the original pattern easily distinguishable. This splendid find and much of the other materials recovered at Nimrud (Calah) provide us with a contemporary parallel to Ahab's "ivory house," and by analogy indicate the kind of splendor probably known to the rulers of Samaria. Yet this Assyrian capital contained an even more pointed reminder of the kind of thing that provoked the wrath of the prophet Amos when he thought of the luxury of the Hebrew kings. "Woe to those who lie upon beds of ivory," said this man of God, "and stretch themselves upon their couches . . ." (Amos 6:4). Parts of two ivory veneer beds have been recovered at Nimrud. One bears the name of Hazael, the Damascus rival of Israel who came to the throne the same year Jehu overthrew the House of Omri (842 B.C.). Hazael's name occurs again at Nimrud on another ivory fragment, but it is the bed which calls to mind the words of Amos and gives them their point.[9]

The ivories of Nimrud reflect a number of regional and historical styles. Some are from Calah itself, and evidence has been found to sustain the statements of Asshur-nasir-pal and Shalmaneser that they kept elephants in their zoological park there. Other ivories are neo-Hittite in design and come from Hamath. Still others are Phoenician, while some are said to be Egyptian. Three sources were available to the Assyrian rulers. One was to have craftsmen in their local employ. A second was import of objects. The third was booty taken in war. There is considerable evidence of this last. A statue of Shalmaneser

III found in the ruins contains an inscription noting his conquests. Among them is mentioned a vast amount of booty taken from Hazael. This is no doubt a reference to Shalmaneser's campaign of 841 B.C. when he came against Damascus and Samaria. Although taking much booty and laying waste to its gardens and groves, he was unable to take the Syrian capital itself. Tribute from Jehu, of which more will be said shortly, prevented his besieging the Israelite stronghold at Samaria. Within a few years, tribute in the form of ivory furniture was paid to Adad-nirari III by Ben-Hadad II, successor to Hazael. Beds probably came to Nimrud and Arslan Tash at this time. The inscribed bed at Nimrud was found among a large number of other Phoenician and Syrian ivories which are dated to the ninth century, the time of Omri, Ahab, and Hazael. The Assyrian kings claimed enormous amounts of the material from their cowed or beaten foes; from Hamath, Carchemish, Syria, Israel, and even Egypt. Damascus was finally sacked in 732 B.C. and Samaria ten years later. It is not impossible that some of the ivories found at Nimrud could have been booty taken from these campaigns and even include parts of Ahab's "ivory house." Comparison with ivories recovered at Samaria tends to strengthen this suggestion. Yet there can be no proof. It remains merely a tempting possibility.

The accomplishment of building Samaria, spectacular at any time, was not carried out in an atmosphere of peace. The Syrian king in Damascus had succeeded in bringing other smaller Aramean kingdoms under his rule and had replaced Israel as the dominant power in the region. According to I Kings 20:1-34; 22:1-40, and II Chronicles 18:1-34, Ahab fought three major battles against Ben-Hadad I, the man who forged Syrian power and meant to use it. Omri had succeeded in preventing a lasting alliance between Ben-Hadad and the Phoenicians which

---

[9] At Arslan Tash, the ancient Assyrian provincial capital *Hadatu*, a part of an ivory couch was found bearing the words "belonging to our Lord Hazael." Moreover, a number of the late ninth-century ivories from Samaria are similar in design and workmanship to many at Arslan Tash. This has led many, including Albright (*The Archaeology of Palestine*, p. 137), to the view that a number of the Samaria ivories were Damascene in origin. It is generally thought that the materials at Arslan Tash were part of tribute received from Damascus by Adad-nirari III, *ca.* 804 B.C.

would have made matters worse. Secure in their most extensive maritime trade since the Sea Peoples wreaked such havoc upon them in the Late Bronze Age, the Sidonians, Tyrians, and others had no desire to become embroiled in an inland power struggle. The field was left to Damascus and Samaria, and it was Samaria which first felt the hot blast of war. Some archaeologists think that the casemate wall at Samaria was erected by Ahab in the face of the Syrian danger. Perhaps so, but it is clear from the Bible that actual war did not begin until the last five years of Ahab's nineteen-year reign (869-850 B.C.). Ben-Hadad laid siege to the Israelite capital. In spite of great strength the Syrian army was not able to maintain its hold and fled with considerable loss of men and material. But damage was not such as to prevent Ben-Hadad's immediate preparation for further war against Israel. Believing defeat was due to his marching into the mountains, he determined to challenge Ahab's army on the plains where his supposedly superior force might prevail. In the spring of the following year, perhaps 854 B.C., the two armies faced each other in the valley of the Yarmuk River near where it empties into the Jordan just south of the Sea of Galilee. At issue was sovereignty over Gilead and Bashan, the northern portion of Transjordan. Judging from the large number of chariots Ahab was able to put into the field at Qarqar a year later, we may safely assume Ben-Hadad had underestimated the strength of the Israelites on the plains. Once more the Syrians were sent fleeing. They retreated a few miles north to Aphek, footman and king alike. There Ben-Hadad was made prisoner. Taking the defeated king into his chariot, Ahab extracted from him a promise to return land and cities captured from Israel and to grant commercial rights in Damascus itself. These were surprisingly slight demands. Having readily covenanted himself to these lenient terms, Ben-Hadad was re-

leased while Ahab found himself the object of strong criticism. It was even said that his life was forfeit because he had not killed the Syrian king when he had the chance. The criticism stung Ahab (I Kings 20:43), but, looking northward, he realized that survival was more important than revenge. He knew that Israel would soon need all the friends she could get.

A year later Ahab and Ben-Hadad were allied with ten other kings in common cause against the Assyrians. Petty wars had blinded them to the much greater threat which was embodied in the rise of northern power under Asshur-nasir-pal II. By the time his son, Shalmaneser III, came to the throne in 859 B.C., several of the Phoenician cities were already paying tribute to prevent the Assyrians, who were by now firmly established in northern Syria, from coming into their flourishing ports. In 853 B.C. Shalmaneser left his capital at Nineveh, crossed the Euphrates, and captured several cities including Aleppo as he moved toward the Mediterranean at the head of his army. As he turned south along the Orontes River he found himself confronted by a coalition of western kings.

The Battle of Qarqar, which in sheer numbers of men involved was one of the largest ever fought in the ancient Middle East, is not mentioned in the Bible. I Kings 22:1 merely states that Syria and Israel remained at peace with each other during the time. Nothing is said of their monumental struggle with Assyrian arms. No doubt this was recorded in the "Book of the Chronicles of the Kings of Israel," woefully lost. The Assyrians, however, kept careful military records, and thanks to excavations at Nineveh, Nimrud, and elsewhere, many of these are available to us. Among the recovered materials is the Kurkh Stele, now in the British Museum, on which Shalmaneser tells his version of the events of Qarqar. He notes that he had "demolished, destroyed, and burned down

Qarqar," the royal residence of Irhuleni, king of Hamath, when he found himself confronting a very large army. He proceeds to list the forces opposing him. Ahab the Israelite is said to have presented 2000 chariots and 10,000 infantry on the field of battle. This number of chariots is over half the entire mobile force of the coalition. The northern kingdom of Israel had fallen heir to most of Solomon's chariotry, and it may be that even this considerable strength had been enlarged. This may well be one of the inferences to be drawn from the expanded stables at Megiddo. It is also possible that the large number attributed to Ahab included a smaller but significant Judahite corps. It is surprising that Jehoshaphat and Judah are not mentioned by the Assyrians on this occasion. They were certainly allied with Israel a short time later. Moreover, the inferior status of Jehoshaphat to both Ahab and Jehoram (I Kings 22; II Kings 3:7-8) has suggested to some scholars that Judah was vassal to Israel during this time. Perhaps Judah was not represented at Qarqar, but this would certainly be strange in light of the nature and extent of the coalition.

The battle was joined. We have only the Assyrian account of the outcome:

They rose against me [says Shalmaneser in the Assryian Annals] (for a) decisive battle. I fought with them with (the support of) the mighty forces of Ashur, which Ashur, my lord, has given to me, and the strong weapons which Nergal, my leader, has presented to me, (and) I did inflict a defeat upon 'them between the towns Karkara and Gilzau. I slew 14,000 of their soldiers with the sword, descending upon them like Adad [Baal] when he makes a rainstorm pour down. I spread their corpses (everywhere), filling the entire plain with their widely scattered (fleeing) soldiers. During the battle I made their blood flow down the *hur-pa-lu* of the district. The plain was too small to let (all) their . . . souls descend (into the nether world), the vast field gave out (when it came) to bury them. With their . . . corpses I spanned the Orontes before

there was a bridge. Even during the battle I took from them their chariots, their horses broken to the yoke.[10]

In short, Shalmaneser says Shalmaneser won the day inflicting upon the coalition tremendous losses in men and material. This was likely so. But the sword cut both ways. The Assyrian was unable to follow up the victory he claimed to have won, and there can be no doubt that his army was also badly mauled. So everyone won something. Shalmaneser held the field, but the coalition had stopped him—for the moment at any rate.

Israel was considerably weakened by the battle. Its proud chariot corps never recovered. The ensuing wars with Damascus and Moab and the disastrous revolt of Jehu also took a toll. Scarcely forty years after Ahab had mustered his enormous force at Qarqar, there were but ten chariots left for the Israelite king to command (II Kings 13:7). When Sargon took Samaria in 722 B.C., he noted that only fifty chariots were found.

Three years after Shalmaneser had turned homeward to recoup his losses, the members of the coalition fell to warring with one another again. Ramoth-gilead,[11] vital to the control of northern Transjordan and its trade, was still in Syrian hands four years after Ahab's treaty with Ben-Hadad. It was one of the cities that was to have been returned to Israel under conditions of that agreement. Ahab now became impatient and determined to take the city by force. Accompanied by Jehoshaphat, whose interests in southern Transjordan relied in part upon Ahab's success in the north, an Israelite army advanced eastward. Micaiah the prophet warned Ahab of a defeat (I Kings 22:13-23). Indeed, disaster did strike. Ahab, dis-

[10] *Ancient Near Eastern Texts*, p. 279.

[11] On the basis of surface explorations in northern Transjordan twenty-five years ago, Nelson Glueck identified Tell er-Rumeith as ancient Ramoth-gilead. In 1962 Paul Lapp and other scholars of the American School of Oriental Research in Jerusalem made archaeological soundings at the site and tentatively confirmed Glueck's view.

guised and using the well-robed Jehoshaphat as a decoy, was nonetheless struck in the chest by a hostile arrow. In spite of his command to take him from the field, he was propped up in his chariot and kept in the thick of the fighting. About sunset, having bled all day, he died. Israel fled the battle, and the king's chariot was returned to the capital where it was washed by "the pool of Samaria" (see p. 163).

The occasion now presented itself for Moab farther south in Transjordan to throw off the Israelite yoke Omri had reimposed. Shalmaneser's account of the coalition forces at Qarqar had mentioned the independent presence of Ammonite soldiers indicating that the central Transjordanian region, once part of Solomon's empire, had retained its freedom even when Omri came to the throne. Moab, on the other hand, had been giving a considerable part of its wealth to the king at Samaria (II Kings 3:4). When Ahab fell, Mesha of Moab refused further payment. This in the ancient world was a declaration of independence. Jehoram's futile attempt to reassert sovereignty is told from an Israelite point of view in II Kings 3:21-27 and from a Moabite perspective on the Mesha Stele (see p. 155, n. 5). The Israelites conveniently failed to note a further extensive loss of territory including their last remaining portion of *The King's Highway* and the use of Hebrew forced labor by Mesha who fortified his land against further attacks.

Jehoshaphat (873-849 B.C.), the king of Judah who had been present at Ramoth-gilead when Ahab was killed, accompanied Jehoram in this abortive campaign into Moab. With the demise of Egyptian power following the death of Shishak, Judah's interest in the south had revived. Jehoshaphat rebuilt Ezion-geber (Tell el-Kheleifeh) and sought to imitate Solomon's success with a merchant fleet. Archaeologists have identified this reconstruction. It owes little to the former structure. The new mud-brick for-

tifications were of considerable strength: a double wall with a dry moat between. The inner wall was about twenty-six feet high, six feet wide at the top, and thirteen feet thick at its base. It was further strengthened by a glacis. Ten feet from the base of the glacis was the outer wall betraying the same design and construction features as the inner wall, only not quite so massive. A single double-chambered gate penetrated the walls on the south. The necessity of such fortifications indicates the generally hostile region in which it was located. This was Edom, and the Edomites were held in uneasy vassalage to Judah. Hence Jehoshaphat's more than casual interest in Israelite control over Gilead, Bashan, and Moab. With these lost and Ammon independent, only Edom of the Transjordanian states remained in subjection. Jehoshaphat was able to hold firm. But under his son, Jehoram (849-842 B.C.), there was a successful Edomite rebellion (II Kings 8:20-22; II Chronicles 21:8-10). Even though Jehoshaphat rebuilt and held Ezion-geber, his commercial venture there came to naught. For some reason the ships were wrecked while they lay in port (I Kings 22:48; II Chronicles 20:35-37). Ahaziah of Israel desired to join in seeking to rekindle the potential source of wealth, but Jehoshaphat refused, and in the end nothing came of it. Judah thus held Edom, the Arabah, and parts of the Negeb temporarily, but no fleets sailed from Ezion-geber. Jehoshaphat's external ventures were on the whole unspectacular.

At home considerably more success attended him. He reorganized the royal administration following general principles Solomon had used when he divided the northern part of his kingdom into districts (II Chronicles 17:2). He also built forts and storehouses (II Chronicles 17:12). Something less than the reforms they are often made out to be, his religious policies and practices were nonetheless not an occasion for offense.

Jehoshaphat thus drew mild approval from the writer of I Kings 22:41-46.

How different was the case of Ahab, king in the north, object of the fiercest kind of attacks from the religionists in his lifetime and after. Indeed, the internal strife in Israel during his reign proved even more disastrous for the kingdom than reverses on the battlefield and loss of territory. Omridian economic and foreign policies, like those of Solomon, involved foreign wives and cosmopolitan ideas. And like Solomon, Omri and his successors could not pursue their aims without giving offense to the religious and social customs of a lately nomadic people. The daughters of foreign princes, queens in Israel, brought with them not only dowries and the good will of their fathers, but alien social views and compromising religious habits. At the same time it must be said that too much blame has been laid at the door of these women. The Hebrew kings themselves made little attempt to preserve the egalitarian ideals of the old tribal tradition. Instead they threw in their lot with the Phoenicians and sought to emulate and exploit their momentary mercantile supremacy. This involved a number of things including the spreading influence of the Canaanite idea of laissez-faire capitalism which in Israel, at least, produced a widening gap between the various economic and social levels. No better example of royal involvement in this process can be found than the story of Naboth's vineyard (see pp. 108-9 and I Kings 21). This story also shows that the marriage of Ahab to Jezebel brought Phoenician influence to bear upon the highest level of government decision-making. This was particularly unfortunate since this strong-willed woman apparently sought and received royal patronage for the cult of the Tyrian Baal. Elijah and others who shared his religious convictions probably thought that she intended to make this worship into a state cult, and their suspicions may have been well founded. Yet perhaps nothing more was involved than Ahab's wish to broaden the pluralistic base of Israelite society and thus make it more attractive for skilled workmen, particularly Phoenician, to live in Israel.

Whatever the motive for royal patronage of this foreign cult, response from the more conservative religionists of Israel was strong. Reaction was met by repression (I Kings 18:4), but as always this only produced greater strength among the opposition. One man in particular refused to be driven underground. He was the prophet whom Ahab called "the troubler of Israel"—Elijah. A Transjordanian from the desert's edge in Gilead (I Kings 17:1), he was austere in appearance, Spartan in habits, and prepared for a holy war to eradicate from the land the ideas and the people who threatened the purity of the worship of the Hebrew God. No milksop in character, he not only confronted Ahab and Jezebel and condemned them openly to their faces (I Kings 18; 21), but also laid plans for the violent, bloody overthrow of the state (I Kings 19:15-17). Although he did not live to see these plans carried out, his successor, Elisha, enlisted the aid of Jehu and together they exterminated the Omrides. Jezebel correctly understood the nature of Elijah's opposition and from her point of

Herbert G. May

A wall at Samaria, perhaps from the time of Ahab, showing header-and-stretcher construction.

view was justified in seeking to kill him (I Kings 19:1-8). Yet in the complicated web that is a political-religious struggle it was perhaps the very display of Jezebel's power which brought to Elijah's mind the solution of bloody revolution. Force, counterforce, action, reaction, suppression, hatred, extremism, and violence—the complicated morass so well known to the modern world was present in Omride Israel.

But it was not merely state policy, Jezebel, and the Tyrian Baal that produced explosive opposition. In the strange way of things the economic prosperity which came to Israel at this time also prompted unrest. Archaeology has shown that a number of cities in addition to Samaria saw considerable building and an economic upswing. At Megiddo Ahab built extensive stables. These structures covered one-fifth of the site and accommodated about five hundred horses as well as chariots. From these measurements they seem to have been designed by an Egyptian architect. A palace and other public buildings occupied the remainder of the summit. Similarities to building methods at Samaria are everywhere. The city wall of Megiddo in this period was of well-cut large stones carefully laid in a header-and-stretcher pattern; that is, some stones laid across the thickness of the wall while others were laid lengthwise. The Solomonic casemate wall which had suffered from Shishak's conquest of the city was not utilized, with the exception of the gate which was modified. Pottery from this level, wheel burnished and with a light wash, is the same as that from Omride Samaria and leaves no doubt as to the builders of this new and splendid Megiddo.

At Hazor, administrative center for Galilee, archaeologists have also unearthed remains of extensive construction on the part of the house of Omri. The city had shown marked decline since the days of its Solomonic greatness. At one point it had been burned and presented itself in the early ninth century B.C. as merely a shell of what it had once been. The citadel of Hazor was fortified by Ahab and crowned with a massive complex consisting of a palace, administrative buildings, and workshops. The largest structure was a storehouse whose roof was supported by two rows of pillars. Here and in the chambers of Solomon's casemate wall were stored grain and other goods taken in payment of taxes. An earthquake did extensive damage to this city. It may have been in the reign of Jeroboam II (876-746 B.C.) and be the one referred to in Amos 1:1 and Zechariah 14:5.[12] But we cannot be sure of this. At any rate, the basic city survived and continued in use for a few more years, until the coming of Tiglath-pileser III ended its career as an Israelite city.

Tirzah (Tell el-Farah), too, was apparently an administrative center and regained some of its former beauty. Abandoned briefly when the court moved, it was the object of intensive construction only a few years later. Again, the pottery from there when compared with that of Samaria, Megiddo, and Hazor leaves no doubt as to its builders. Near the city gate was a large two-story building with paved court and a room full of broken jars. This was a public building, likely the governor's house and administrative center. The jars bespeak of taxation. At Tirzah was found unmistakable evidence of overt social stratification of the type which filled Amos and Hosea with indignation. There were two residential quarters separated from each other by a long straight wall. On the one side were relatively large, attractive houses with pleasing courtyards. Their walls were of well-trimmed stone laid two abreast and bonded at the corners. Careful planning had produced a regular, uncluttered effect. On the other side of the wall

[12] In his excavations at Dothan some forty-six miles south of Hazor, Joseph Free thinks he has found evidence of the same earthquake.

small, roughly built dwellings huddled together almost higgledy-piggledy.

Unfortunately almost all our other archaeological evidence of towns in this period comes from Judah. Houses in Mizpah (Tell en-Nasbeh), to cite one example, show a simple plan not differing much from earlier days. The center of the mound is denuded. Furthermore, no shops have been uncovered. Still, we can assume that barter continued in and around the city gate as in past times. No articles of furniture have survived, but a number of scholars think a likely parallel is the simple furnishings of the peasants of intervening and contemporary times. This includes goat-hair carpets, couches by day, beds by night. Woven leather or straw mats served as tables. Pots for water, wine, oil, grain, and other items were standard as were the stone pestle and mortar used by women to grind grain. Beds of ivory, grillwork in upper chambers, and paneled walls present a vivid contrast.

One must remember that Samaria was the capital, and that Megiddo, Hazor, and Tirzah were royal administrative centers. They were therefore atypical. The actual and probable descriptions of Mizpah, although in Judah, are nearer to the average standard of living in Israel. Prosperity visited upon the land by the Omrides further exaggerated the distinction between rich and poor and thus flew full in the face of the desert egalitarian ideal and undercut tribal traditions. Hebrew society, particularly in the north, could not reconcile its ideals and traditions with the realities of its settled life. This basic situation was further irritated by the trappings of royal power. Carvings of various types were suspicious to a people whose religious laws forbade graven images. The presence of foreign women in places of power —women who brought with them strange priests of alien cults—could not have pleased a people who traditionally made little place for women to exercise authority. Taxation and conscript labor gave to these things and others a daily relevance not calculated to strengthen loyalty to the crown. The same factors with variations had caused the northern tribes, whose faithfulness to the house of David had no historical roots, to go their own way after Solomon's death. Now these tribes were again confronted with old, familiar grievances, only this time perpetrated by a homegrown monarchy. Their frenzied response was to reach out and brutally exterminate the kings they had set over themselves.

Familiar household items during the time of the Divided Monarchy were artifacts such as the cooking pot above, and the type of lamp on the right.

15. DECLINE, RECOVERY, AND FLAWED PROSPERITY

In the year 849 B.C., two kings of the same name, Jehoram (Joram), came to the thrones of Israel and Judah. Neither proved equal to the situations confronting them. The Jehoram of the south, son, coregent, and then successor to the able Jehoshaphat, showed himself particularly inept. In spite of the overriding scorn which obscures the religiously offended Chronicler's account of his reign, it is still possible to see the king as a person, albeit a fumbling one. In the west Libnah and presumably some of the Philistine border area were lost to Judah (II Kings 8:22b; II Chronicles 21:10b), while in the east Edom gained its freedom (II Kings 8:20-22a; II Chronicles 21:8-10a) and with it Ezion-geber and the rich mines of the Arabah. This no doubt had serious economic consequences. During Jehoram's attempt to reassert authority over Edom, the hapless monarch allowed himself and his officers to be surrounded in the night. While the leaderless Judahite army fled homeward, the king and his commanders fought their way to safety. This is the only account given of his military prowess, and it is perhaps as well for Judah that he had no other foreign adventures.

At home he fared even less well. Asa, his grandfather, and Jehoshaphat, his father, had been able to tone down if not uproot the politically disruptive paganizing effects of Solomon's religious policies and his Phoenician-style Temple. The increasingly provincial kingdom had therefore been without major internal strife for some time. Jehoram, however, did not share his forebear's undivided loyalty to the Hebrew God nor his sense of political appropriateness. His marriage to Athaliah, an extremely capable daughter of Ahab and Jezebel, did not help matters. His murder of his brothers when he came to the throne (II Chronicles 21:13)

may indicate religious opposition within the royal family. At any rate, he introduced or at least gave royal patronage to the cult of Baal in Jerusalem and supported worship at "high places" in the hill country of Judah. Within his own kingdom the wrath of his enemies was strengthened by support from Elijah and the party which actively sought the overthrow of the Omrides in the north. It is little wonder that when opportunity presented itself the regicide which visited Israel touched the Judahite royal family also.

The Jehoram of the north, a son of Ahab, who came to the throne when his brother was fatally injured in a fall from the second floor of the palace at Samaria, made an effort to meet the demands of his opposition and thus to scale down the level of hostility which was rapidly reaching the flash point (II Kings 3:2). Still, he was unwilling and indeed unable to meet all the demands of Elijah and his followers. Absolute conformity to one tradition was just not possible in a kingdom varied in population and pluralistic in religion. Moreover, the fanaticism of the opposition to the king's policies had placed meaningful communication and reason beyond the realms of possibility. Furthermore, foreign affairs commanded much of the king's time and energies. So in spite of his efforts the domestic situation worsened; all that was needed was an opportunity to unleash the pent-up hatred.

The Israelite king inadvertently provided the occasion. With Moab lost, he went up to contest the Syrians once more for Ramoth-gilead and sovereignty over northern Transjordan. Accompanied by Ahaziah, his twenty-two-year-old nephew and the newly crowned king of Judah, Jehoram achieved some success in his campaign, but was wounded and withdrew to Jezreel, his winter capital, to recover. Behind him in Ramoth-gilead he left the army under a council of commanders one of whom was Jehu, a chariot officer with a reputation for personal recklessness. At this point Elisha actively entered the picture as the driving force behind a secret revolutionary plot. He sent a prophet to Ramoth-gilead and had Jehu quietly anointed king over Israel and commissioned with these ominous words:

And you shall strike down the house of Ahab your master, that I may avenge on Jezebel the blood of my servants the prophets, and the blood of all the servants of the Lord. For the whole house of Ahab shall perish; and I will cut off from Ahab every male, bond or free, in Israel.
II Kings 9:7-8

The apparent ease with which Jehu won over his fellow officers (II Kings 9:11-13) is an indication of the hardly submerged hostility toward the house of Omri. Events moved rapidly. With a company of men the usurper drove like the wind toward Jezreel where the wounded king lay. With Jehoram were his royal nephew and the Queen Mother, Jezebel. Again there is an indication of tension and the expectation of storm. Twice the king in Jezreel sent messengers to the approaching Jehu to ask, "Is it peace?" Twice they did not return but joined the revolt. Finally, rising from his bed, he mounted his chariot and, accompanied by Ahaziah in a separate vehicle, went out himself to meet Jehu. It took only a moment in face-to-face confrontation with his chariot officer for Jehoram to learn his intentions and to yell to his nephew to join in flight. With attention centered on the Israelite king, the young ruler of Judah managed to escape for the moment. An arrow from Jehu's own bow "shot Joran (Jehoram) between the shoulders, so that the arrow pierced his heart" (II Kings 9:24). His lifeless body sank into his speeding chariot. Seeing this, Ahaziah now urged his horses forward in earnest. In the chase that followed he was able to reach Beth-haggan some four miles south of Jezreel and turn northwest up the Ascent of Gur headed for the safety of Megiddo. Why

he did not go directly across the plain or why he did not seek shelter in Beth-haggan we do not know. Perhaps neither option was open to him. At any rate, he did reach Megiddo, but in a serious condition. In the Ascent of Gur an arrow from his pursuers had found its mark. After being hit, the king had come another four or five miles in the bumping and jumping chariot. He died of his wound at Megiddo. His youthful body was carried to Jerusalem to be buried in the royal tombs (II Kings 9:27-28).

Jehu, intent upon further murder, came to Jezreel to seek his prize. Jezebel heard of the events, put on her makeup, fixed her hair, and waited his coming. From a window near the city gate she greeted him as "you Zimri." [1] Thereupon he shouted back asking who was on his side. Two or three of the eunuchs who attended the royal women seized Jezebel and threw her from the window killing her. Before he went in to eat and drink at the king's table, Jehu trampled her body with his horses. When later he ordered her buried—"for she is a king's daughter"—it was found that ravenous dogs had devoured her remains save for her skull, feet, and palms of hands (II Kings 9:30-37).

Jezebel was no more. The kings of the north and of the south lay dead. Jehu occupied the palace at Jezreel. But what of Samaria? And what of the other Omrides? Ahab had seventy sons. So far only multiple murder had taken place. There were other elements of the army to reckon with, and there were fortified cities whose loyalty had not been tested. Jehu now hit upon a clever plan. He wrote to the elders of Samaria and told them to select the best of the king's sons, crown him, and support him in the field against the revolutionaries. He thus invited them to become his mortal enemies, he who had not hesitated to raise his hand against two kings and the powerful Queen Mother.

[1] See p. 161.

They refused. Now they were his. A second time he wrote saying if they were really loyal they would send to him the heads of the remaining sons of Ahab. It was done (II Kings 10:1-10).

This was the beginning of a bloodbath which finds its historical parallel in the senseless horror of the Reign of Terror of the French Revolution. Anywhere, everyone who had connections with the Omrides was exterminated. Officials, friends, priests, even foreign visitors—the lot; they all fell before Jehu and his fanatics. From the desert came the most reactionary religious element in Israel, the Rechabites, who joined in the triumphal, bloody march to Samaria. Jehonadab ben Rechab, the leader of the group, rode in the chariot with Jehu in order, as Jehu said, to "see my zeal for the Lord" (II Kings 10:16). "Zeal" in this case meant acts of such terrible butchery that a hundred years later Hosea looked back upon them as the darkest blot on Israel's past (Hosea 1:4-5).

The religious aims of the revolution were, of course, not realized. This could perhaps have been anticipated had not the conspirators, like almost all such people, been blinded to reality. Yet few could have foreseen the utterly disastrous economic, social, and political consequences of the overthrow of the Omrides. In the south Athaliah, her son and brothers murdered in the north, seized the throne with a display of brutality on her own part (II Kings 11:1; II Chronicles 22:11). She, the only woman ever to rule in either kingdom, had no legitimate claim to succession in a country where royal inheritance by birth was inviolable. After seven years Joash (Jehoash), a baby when saved from the killing that accompanied his grandmother's coup d'état, was enthroned. The priestly party that hid him and saw this Davidide safely to his rightful place put Athaliah to death. Unlike their counterparts in the north, however, they did not proceed in anger against others.

For Israel the revolt of Jehu was not merely the interruption of a dynasty. It meant almost the end of the nation. A Phoenician princess was dead at Jezreel, and the new government and its religious supporters were intent upon removing Tyrian influence from the land. Its king slain and Queen Athaliah, an Omride, on the throne, Judah did not wish Jehu well. The foreign policy of recent years was at an end. To the continuing hostility of Syria were added the ill will of the Phoenicians and the hatred of Judah, easily rekindled. At a stroke Jehu had surrounded his land with enemies. In the same year of the tumultuous events in Israel, moreover, Hazael, a singularly capable ruler, came to power in Damascus. Henceforth for half a century Syria was ascendent while the shrinkage of Israel's territory was exceeded only by the diminution of its power. Internally the shock of a sudden fall from a position of strength with its attendant economic consequences was amplified by continuing religious struggles. The campaign against the cult of the Tyrian Baal had perhaps removed one danger, but it could not change the characteristic religious pluralism of Israel. Furthermore, in power Jehu retained the national cultic centers at Dan and Bethel which prompted the writer of II Kings 10:31 to say that "Jehu was not careful to walk in the law of the Lord the God of Israel with all his heart; he did not turn from the sins of Jeroboam, which he made Israel to sin." This understatement does not do justice to the fact that Jehu, a dashing and opportunistic chariot officer, had little interest in religious reform, although his reign had begun with a dramatic slaughter of the priests of Baal and desecration of a sanctuary dedicated to that god. Such "religious reforms" were for political reasons, as he apparently understood even if his more fanatic followers did not. Once in power he had neither reason nor wish to continue such "reform." Religious abuses with all their corollary economic and social inequities were still in abundance after his death, as the words of Amos and Hosea eloquently testify.

The Assyrians Come to Israel

Into this mare's nest of troubles was introduced still another factor which bode ill for beleaguered Israel. Recovering from Qarqar, Shalmaneser III had come west nine times between 849 and 841 B.C. Syria had been made vassal. Hazael, playing on national resentment toward the conqueror, came to power by defying the Assyrian king. Shalmaneser determined to punish this upstart and in events not described in the Bible came against Damascus striking a glancing, but serious blow at Israel. In a battle in the

A panel on the Black Obelisk of Shalmaneser III gives us our only contemporary picture of a Hebrew king. Jehu is shown bowing before the Assyrian king while the Israelite's servants bring gifts as tribute.

mountains northwest of Damascus the Assyrians overcame the Syrians but failed in a siege of Damascus itself.

Shalmaneser's movements after the unsuccessful siege have long been a matter of dispute. The inscription on the Black Obelisk of Shalmaneser III, found at Nimrud by Layard in 1846, says in part:

I marched as far as the mountains of Hauran, destroying, tearing down and burning innumerable towns, carrying booty away from them which was beyond counting. I (also) marched as far as the mountains of Ba'li-ra'si which is a promontory and erected there a stela with my image as king. At that time I received tribute of the inhabitants of Tyre, Sidon, and of Jehu, son of Omri.[2]

The reference to Ba'li-ra'si has often been taken to refer to the headland by the Nahr-el-Kelb, the famous pass along the Dog River just north of Beirut. On the side of the cliff face there are several rock-cut inscriptions including those of Shalmaneser III, Ramses II, and even of a British expedition which passed that way during the First World War. This identification would suggest that the Assyrians moved from Damascus northward to the coast. But the mountains of Hauran are considerably south, even south of Hazor, although some sixty miles to the east. The logical route from this point to the coast would have been due west up the Valley of Esdraelon to Mount Carmel. If this was the line of march it would place an Assyrian army in Israel for the first time. Archaeological evidence tends to confirm this. Hazor, among other sites, contains a destruction level which is tentatively dated to this time. Furthermore, for some years it has been conjectured that *Ba'li-ra'si* was a form of *Baal-rosh*, "Baal of the headland," and thus a reference to Mount Carmel, long a center of the worship of Baal. A fourth edition of the annals of Shalmaneser found at Assur and

[2] *Ancient Near Eastern Texts*, p. 280.

translated by Fuad Safar, director of archaeological research in Iraq, has convinced many that this is a correct conjecture. According to this text, after receiving tribute from Jehu, Shalmaneser proceeded north toward Mount Lebanon and the Dog River where "I set up my royal image beside the image of Tiglath-pileser, the great king, my predecessor." [3]

Shalmaneser illustrates part of his Black Obelisk with scenes of his meeting with "Jehu, son of Omri," thus giving us our earliest picture and only contemporary representation of a Hebrew king.[4] Thirteen attendants of Jehu bear gifts as tokens of submission. These are identified as golden buckets, bowls, vases, cups, silver and gold itself, tin, and a royal staff, in addition to other items. The bearded Jehu wearing a sleeveless mantle over a long fringed tunic is bowed with his face to the ground before the Assyrian king. A greater contrast between this scene and Shalmaneser's facing Ahab the Israelite with his 2000 chariots and 10,000 foot soldiers could hardly be imagined.

Shalmaneser claims to have had no fewer than twenty-one campaigns "across the Euphrates." After the events of Mount Carmel he made no more. Affairs in other parts of his vast empire commanded his attention and that of his son, Shamshiadad (824-811 B.C.). For almost forty years the Assyrians did not return in force to Syria and Palestine. It was, however, little comfort to Israel. Damascus, free from Assyrian pressure, turned again to face its old enemy, and a wounded Israel, ruled by a bloody usurper turned inept king, suffered an unprecedented decline. "In those days," says II Kings 10:32,

[3] F. Safar, "A Further Text of Shalmaneser III from Assur," *Sumer*, 7 (1951): 11-21.

[4] For over a hundred years the Assyrians referred to Israel as "the land of Omri," and anyone who ruled over it was in their eyes a successor to the king who had made it great. The phrase "son of Omri" does not imply a physical relationship.

"the Lord began to cut off parts of Israel." All Israelite Transjordan, so long in contention, passed into Syrian hands along with its Hebrew population and control of much of *The King's Highway*. Amos looking back refers to Gilead being "threshed . . . with threshing sledges of iron" (1:3). Hazael's forces crossed the Jordan and roamed virtually unchecked through much of Israel. Hazor, judging from another destruction layer immediately on top of that of Shalmaneser, suffered again. Ranging south along the coast, the Syrians destroyed Gath and turned inland to make their way into the mountains and Jerusalem.

Joash of Judah (837-800 B.C.), now about thirty years old and according to II Chronicles 24 fully matured in the apostasy of his grandmother Athaliah, gathered together all the gifts and gold he could find in the Temple and Palace and sent them to Hazael. Thus persuaded, the Syrian king spared the Judahite capital and contented himself with making the southern Hebrew kingdom a vassal. Israel was also made vassal. Its army had been a particular object of a Syrian revenge conditioned by historic animosity and years of armed clash. Because Hazael made the army of Israel "like dust on the threshing floor" (II Kings 13:7), Jehoahaz, Jehu's son, could command but ten war chariots. At the apex of its power Syria laid a heavy hand upon its neighbors and especially upon the wretched kingdom which Jehu had made.

"The Lord gave Israel a savior," says II Kings 13:5. He was Adad-nirari III (811-783 B.C.), grandson of Shalmaneser, who now returned to some unfinished Assyrian business with the king in Damascus. Successful in a heavy punitive expedition, Adad-nirari relieved Syrian pressure on the Hebrew kingdoms and took from Damascus booty including that listed upon the Saba'a Stele now in Constantinople:

2,300 talents of silver (corresponding to) 20 talents of gold, 5,000 talents of iron, garments of linen with multi-colored trimmings, a bed (inlaid) with ivory, a *nimattu* couch mounted and inlaid with ivory, (and) countless (other objects being) his possessions.

Tribute was also received from the Hebrews, but before any really serious damage was done to Israel or Judah, the Assyrians were once more drawn home by internal affairs and disputes with northern neighbors. Damascus, greatly reduced, now found its hegemony in the area challenged by Hamath to the northwest. An inscription of Zakir of Hamath, found twenty-five miles southeast of Aleppo in 1904, tells of a Syrian siege of Hatatikka, his capital, and of a subsequent overwhelming victory by Hamath. The Syrian withdrawal from the city became a disaster of considerable proportions. Retreats had a tendency to become routs in ancient days even as has been the case in more modern times. The fragmentary inscription notes an extension of Zakir's power and territory, doubtless at the expense of Syria. Thus in the first half of the eighth century B.C., events conspired to give to the Hebrew kingdoms an opportunity which, coupled with the fortunate appearance of capable kings in each country, produced a renewed flowering of prosperity.

Both Hebrew kingdoms now extended their borders. Reversing an earlier situation, Israel fell upon a wounded Syria and in a series of battles described in II Kings 13 and 14 and alluded to in Amos 6:13 regained not only northern Transjordan, but pushed its authority into Syria itself, perhaps even reaching the northern limits of David's kingdom. Israeli archaeologists think they have found evidence of this fighting in the destruction layers at 'En Gev. Further excavation will determine the correctness of this. Be that as it may, Damascus was occupied and *The King's Highway* from Moab to Hamath was in Israelite hands once more.

Even as Israel was crushing its traditional enemy, Syria, Judah was moving south and east against its old and persistent foe, Edom. Victorious in a battle in the Valley of Salt southwest of the Dead Sea, the Judahite king, Amaziah (800-783 B.C.) besieged and took the crag-encompassed royal city, Sela (Petra), and extended his authority over northern Edom (II Kings 14:7). But the southward thrust of Judah was momentarily halted by a dispute and finally a war between the southern kingdom and Israel. Apparently Amaziah invited Jehoahaz to a meeting to discuss a marriage alliance. The Israelite king responded with stinging words which contain a hardly veiled threat and show his slight regard for Judah:

A thistle on Lebanon sent to a cedar on Lebanon, saying, "Give your daughter to my son for a wife"; and a wild beast of Lebanon passed by and trampled down the thistle. You have indeed smitten Edom, and your heart has lifted you up. Be content with your glory, and stay at home; for why should you provoke trouble so that you fall, you and Judah with you?

II Kings 14:9-10

Amaziah seems not to have got the point. His persistence led to a battle at Bethshemesh (Tell er-Rumeileh) in which his army was defeated and he was captured. An offer of alliance, however demeaning it may appear, is hardly an occasion for war. There were certainly other factors involved; factors we do not know. Whatever the reasons for the conflict, one result was the partial sack of Jerusalem which 'had neither army nor king to defend it. Booty was seized from the Temple and Palace and some hostages were taken. A large section of the north wall of the city was pulled down. Having satisfied himself, Jehoahaz withdrew his army without further damage to Judah.

Archaeologists have found no evidence of this destruction of the walls of Jerusalem. Indeed, there is not even agreement on the location of the north wall. The reasons for this have to do with the history of Jerusalem as explained in a previous chapter. Scholars differ widely in their interpretation of the materials from Beth-shemesh, where one minor and two extensive excavations have been undertaken. There was a general destruction of the city in the late ninth or early eighth century, but few will commit themselves to a precise occasion on which this occurred. It cannot with any confidence be attributed to Jehoahaz' victory over Amaziah.

Uzziah's Empire

There is, however, considerable biblical and archaeological evidence indicating that this battle and the subsequent sack of Jerusalem had only a short-term effect upon the fortunes of the southern kingdom. After Amaziah was assassinated at Lachish (II Kings 14:19-20; II Chronicles 25:2-7), Uzziah[5] (783-742 B.C.), his sixteen-year-old son, came to the throne. Under him Judah successfully renewed its expansionist policy and achieved its greatest limits. Judahite rule extended south to the Gulf of Aqaba where, once more, Ezion-geber was refurbished and made into a port and major way station for the Arabian trade (II Kings 14:22; II Chronicles 26:2). The Edomite conquest of nearly seventy years earlier had destroyed Jehoshaphat's construction, and sands had covered the ruins. So far as archaeologists have been able to determine, the Edomites did not seek to exploit the site during that time. But the Judahites, ever mindful of Solomon's successes, returned as soon as political and military circumstances permitted. They built a settlement which bore more resemblance to the towns of the day than to the industrial-military base which two previous Hebrew monarchs had constructed there. This is not to suggest, however, that the function of this third settlement differed markedly from the

first two. Among the ruins of this last Hebrew town to occupy Ezion-geber was found a seal signet ring bearing the inscription "belonging to Jotham." The reference is thought to be to Uzziah's son who ruled as coregent with his leprous father during the last eight to ten years of Uzziah's fifty-two year reign (II Kings 15:5; II Chronicles 26:21).[6] Beneath the inscription is a horned ram and another object which N. Avigad, an Israeli scholar, has identified as bellows. If this identification is correct, the ring, belonging probably to the governor of the area, testifies to a revitalization of Hebrew mining in the Arabah and related activities at the renewed port.

Uzziah's operations were by no means restricted to Edom and Ezion-geber. Commander of a large, well-equipped, imaginative army, he struck in every direction except north, reducing his neighbors and establishing his authority over them. In the west he tore down fortifications of some major Philistine cities and established Hebrew settlements on Philistine soil. From the east came tribute from the Ammonites who had been free from such burdens since Solomon's death. In the light of recent archaeology, perhaps his most interesting accomplishments are spoken of in II Chronicles 26: "he built towers in the wilderness, and hewed out many cisterns, for he had large herds, both in the Shephelah and in the plain, and he had farmers and vinedressers in the hills and in the fertile lands, for he loved the soil" (vs. 10). The pioneering work of Woolley and Glueck and the later work of Aharoni and Rothenberg among others have shown that this verse refers in part to the Negeb. Upward of 500 Judahite sites, many if not most of them from the time of Uzziah, have

[5] This monarch is also known as Azariah.

[6] Compare the length of Uzziah's reign with the sixty-four years Queen Victoria sat upon the throne of Great Britain. Both monarchs presided over several generations of subjects and saw their nations reach a pinnacle of power and stability not known before or since.

been located there in addition to amazingly well preserved cisterns, some of which are still watertight and are to this day performing their original function. Before the First World War, Woolley in collaboration with T. E. Lawrence excavated a Hebrew fortress at Ain el Qudeirat (Kadesh-barnea). Strikingly located on top of a small hill in the center of the most fertile valley in the entire region, this fort shows the characteristic header-and-stretcher construction of the period. Its rectangular plan, approximately 165 feet by 100 feet, was enclosed by a casemate wall to which military engineers had now returned, perhaps because they were relatively inexpensive and because they were as effective (or ineffective!) as any other. At each corner and in the middle of each side of the walls was a tower. Pottery from the ruins leaves no doubt that it comes from the time of the Divided Monarchy. A powerful fortress in an ancient oasis, this was the military and administrative center for the region.

In 1957 Aharoni unearthed a similar fortress at Khirbet Ghazza in the northeast corner of the Negeb near Arad. This structure, about 125 feet by 100 feet, had latterly been enlarged to enclose about 125 feet by 165 feet, giving it almost the same dimensions as the structure at Ain el Qudeirat. Unlike Ain el Qudeirat which has an occupational history stretching back at least into the Middle Bronze Age, Khirbet Ghazza reveals no settlement prior to the construction of the fort. The strategic location of this site, which blocks the way to Edom and the Arabah, suggests a fortification guarding the southern approaches to Judah proper. In the past, invaders had threatened Judah from this direction and along this way. The idea that this was part of a strategically located defense system is strengthened by the fortification at Kadesh-barnea which guards the Way of Shur leading into, and from, Egypt.

These two forts have been mentioned because of their importance and because they are typical of Judahite constructions found in the Negeb, not because they are the only ones. Glueck, indeed, has identified a whole line of fortresses extending into Sinai, and there is no question that Judah not only extended her borders to the Brook of Egypt, but also sought to secure them with strongholds on almost every strategic hilltop. Uzziah, who made a good deal of this, was not the first to employ it. This may be assumed on the basis of remains of an oval fortress at Ain Qadeis, south of Kadesh-barnea. More than two miles from the nearest spring, it sits high on a hill and commands a number of roads that ran nearby. Casemate walls of header-and-stretcher construction enclose an area of about eighty-two feet by 115 feet. There are no towers; a simple gate penetrates the wall on the south. This crude structure is a border fort, an outpost. In addition to its oval form, pottery remains indicate that it is perhaps somewhat older than the constructions at Kadesh-barnea and Kirbet Ghazza. This may be a Solomonic fortress reacquired and refurbished by Uzziah.

More was going on in the Negeb than merely building fortresses to protect trade routes and to guard the southern approaches to Judah. Uzziah's "love for the soil" was made concrete in the form of agricultural settlements. Again in imitation of Solomon's policy, this later king had undertaken to make the desert bloom. Even today, in many wadis ancient terraces can be seen still serving the minimal agricultural needs of the Bedouin. While these flat areas probably owe their present form to the Roman-Byzantine period when cultivation in the area reached its greatest limits, those who have carefully explored the region widely assume that many of the terraces were originally carved out during the times of Solomon and Uzziah.

It is now possible to see, thanks to archaeology, that much of the prosperity which brought Judah to new heights under Uzziah was based upon several of the elements formerly enriching Solomon and his subjects: tribute, trade, and the mines of the Arabah. To this latter source of revenue Uzziah was also able to add some of the mining operations in Sinai. Also like Solomon, but not on the same scale, Uzziah paid attention to the requirements of royal Jerusalem. According to II Chronicles 26:9, he "built towers in Jerusalem at the Corner Gate and at the Valley Gate and at the Angle, and fortified them." These references have not been positively identified, but some of them certainly refer to restoration of the fortifications destroyed by Jehoahaz. From the Jerusalem of Uzziah's day also comes an interesting object which may have biblical connections. An inscription on a tomb lintel now in the British Museum refers to a Shebnayahu, a "servant of Uzziyau" (Uzziah), who "is over the house." This latter phrase indicates a royal steward, and the length of the entire inscription, third longest in archaic Hebrew, reinforces the idea that this Shebna was a person of considerable importance. Isaiah 22:15-16 uses almost the same language as is on the lintel in identifying a Shebna who is derided for hewing out a pretentious tomb for himself. The Shebna to whom Isaiah refers was, however, the chief steward of Hezekiah. If this is the same man whose tomb lintel now rests in London, he either came to Uzziah's service late in that reign and was an old man when he filled the same position under Hezekiah, or the greatness of Uzziah had given to his name something of the same meaning that "Omri" came to have in Israel.[7]

Prosperity and Prophecy in the North

To the north, Jeroboam II (786-746 B.C.) had inherited Israelite borders at least as large as they had been under David, and, like his fellow monarch to the south, followed policies of Solomon. As in Judah, they were the path to unprecedented but flawed prosperity, a prosperity feeding upon economic and social injustice. Tribute from conquered neighbors, control over major trade routes, and restored relations with Phoenicia, now in the last stages of its ascendency, gave to many of Jeroboam's subjects a higher standard of living than had been known in Israel. It also produced a curious although common religious reaction wherein many saw the nation's prosperity as a sign of God's approval of the current national and personal morality. "Is not the Lord in the midst of us?" Micah 3:11 quotes the people as saying, "No evil shall come upon us." This kind of self-righteousness which denies the independent judgment of God produced a furious counter-reaction. It is enshrined in the words of the great eighth-century prophets.

The everyday commercial life of Jeroboam's Israel has been uniquely illuminated by written documents recovered from the excavations at Samaria. Sixty-three ostraca[8] were found on the summit in what was apparently a royal storehouse. The date of these documents is a matter of some debate. The building in which they were discovered was part of a new construction in the royal quarter. Of irregular plan and poor execution these structures were built against the casemate enclosure and their erection neces-

---

[7] The Russian Archaeological Museum on the Mount of Olives was in possession of a funerary inscription which Professor E. L. Sukenik identified as coming from the tomb of Uzziah himself. This inscription, written in Aramaic and generally dated to about the time of Christ, is apparently evidence that Uzziah's remains were removed to another location after having lain for many years in a tomb said by II Kings 15:7 to have been "in the city of David."

[8] An ostracon is a piece of broken pottery which has been used for writing. In the absence of paper and without an abundance of cloth on which to write, something cheap and readily at hand was sought. Broken pottery suited the purpose and was widely used not only among the Hebrews but other ancients as well. Indeed, the word *ostraca* is Greek, and our English word *ostracize* comes from the classical Athenian practice of writing upon potsherds the name of a person found deserving of banishment.

sitated destruction of much of the handsome wall that had graced the majestically conceived and beautifully built royal quarter. In place of carefully hewn, immaculately laid walls were put broken stones, ill set. The exact date of this ruinous work cannot be assigned to the reign of any given monarch. Its pottery and the utter lack of any Phoenician influence along with the poverty of its material make it certain, however, that it belongs to the early Jehu Dynasty, perhaps to the time around 841 B.C. when Jehu came to the throne. Disfiguring the capital city is in harmony with what he did to the nation as a whole.

The documents, which are receipts for taxes or for crown property,[9] are dated from the ninth to the seventeenth years of the reign of a certain king.[10] A few scholars say this ruler was Jehoahaz (813-796 B.C.), since it was not until eight to nine years into his reign that the Syrian yoke was removed from Israel, thus making it possible for taxes to be collected internally. For the majority of scholars, however, these receipts are slightly later, probably from the time of Jeroboam. If this is correct, the ostraca can be dated 778-770 B.C. The documents are in any case not continuous. They refer to the ninth, tenth, fifteenth, and seventeenth years of the reign. What we have is a partial list or perhaps several lists. More than one list is suggested by two different formulations which occur. A few scholars have been led by this to say that the reigns of Jeroboam and his predecessor Jehoash are referred to.

While the question of specific date is a matter of some controversy, the relative date is agreed upon. Israel had recovered from the aftermath of Jehu's rebellion. Corn, wine,

and fine oil from as far away as eighteen miles was coming into the royal storehouse at the Palace.[11] Of particular interest are the names of the senders and recipients. Almost one third of the theophoric personal names are compounds of elements of *Baal*.[12] The others are some form of the elements of the name of the Hebrew God. This is occasionally cited as evidence for a large continuing Canaanite population with its traditions preserved intact. That is doubtless correct, but a closer look may reveal more than this. The vast majority of the names containing references to the Hebrew God are found among the recipients. Baal names predominate among the farmers and vinedressers. Is this evidence of a Hebrew-urban, Canaanite-rural division? If so, it is a reversal of an earlier situation. Be that as it may, here is considerable evidence of a mixture of religious traditions; they do not merely exist side by side. The prevalence of the adoration of Baal and the admixture of this with Hebrew worship is precisely one of the major themes of Hosea, whose ministry, if not contemporary with the Samaria ostraca, is certainly not long after.

The writings of Amos and Hosea show us the unprecedented prosperity of Israel as seriously, even fatally, flawed. Amos, probably an employee at the royal sanctuary in Bethel, was not a native of Israel. He was a Judahite from Tekoa, approximately six miles south of Bethlehem, from the edge of the harsh Judean desert that falls from there toward the Dead Sea visible in the distance. Amos was a good deal less blinded to the facts of international power politics and to the reality of God than the other Israelites of his day. He correctly reasoned that Assyria was but momentarily distracted from

[9] Typical is the notation on ostracon no. 18: "In the tenth year. From Hazeroth to Gaddiyau. A jar of fine oil." *Ancient Near Eastern Texts*, p. 321.

[10] Of the eighth-century Israelite kings, only Jeroboam II ruled as long as seventeen years. It seems reasonable to assume that receipts mentioning the seventeenth year come from his reign. His seventeenth year was 770 B.C.

[11] These ostraca, many carefully noting the place from which various items were shipped, are of considerable importance for establishing the geography of the region in that period.

[12] Interestingly, no known documents from eighth-century Judah bear Baal names.

its real interests which lay in the south, across Palestine and into Egypt. Moreover, his vision of God made him realize that the nation's prosperity was not a sign that the Eternal had bound himself to the interests of a political entity, not even of Israel. Thus while the people enjoyed their strong international position and congratulated themselves on their wealth, paying but lip service to the details of worship, Amos saw in them only a society cleft in two by injustice and pride. In his so-called "Temple Sermon" (Amos 1–3) the prophet indicts Israel not only for serious breaches of international morality, but for economic, social, alcoholic, sexual, and religious abuses. Like any great prophet, Amos understood the difficulties to be not merely individual, but endemic to the society and built into the structures of the nation's life. The courts, for example, were not places where poor men were dealt with honestly; anyone who called attention to this fact was an outcast in a rich man's society (5:10-13). Many of the outwardly religious merchants spent their time at the sanctuaries thinking of how to make sure that the poor continued to pay higher prices than most for the necessities of life (8:4-6). Such worship, condoned in the sanctuaries and the shrines, is itself a corruption of the people (5:21-24). The women of Samaria, "cows of Bashan" who encourage their husbands in their evil (4:1-3), and the royal priests who try to silence the Word of God (7:10-17), will be the first to feel the coming judgment. And, says Amos, judgment *will* come, for it is the Eternal to whom the people by their life and worship have offered insult. This God, the maker of heaven and earth, calls Israel to the same bar of justice as her enemies:

> Woe to those who are at ease in Zion,
> and to those who feel secure on the
>   mountain of Samaria,
> the notable men of the first of the
>   nations,
> to whom the house of Israel come!

> Pass over to Calneh, and see;
>   and thence go to Hamath the great;
> then go down to Gath of the Philistines.[13]
> Are they better than these kingdoms?
>   Or is their territory greater than your territory,
> O you who put far away the evil day,
>   and bring near the seat of violence?
>
> Amos 6:1-3

Indeed, judgment upon Israel will be even more severe than that upon other nations, for God has walked with Israel all its days and has sought by drought, famine, and other means to turn a perverse people to the ways of righteousness. While the Israelites looked pridefully for God's judgment upon their foes, Amos warned that the days of indirect chastisement were over: "You only have I known of all the families of the earth; therefore I will punish you for all your iniquities" (3:2). It was Israel's existence and not God's honor that was at stake. Exile, death, and the destruction of the nation were as sure as the justice of God. This idea of the judgment of a national God upon his own country was a radical thought in the ancient east and is one reason why many scholars date the beginning of universalism in Hebrew theology with Amos.

In temperament Hosea was very different from Amos. A younger contemporary, he was a native of Israel. He was, in fact, the northern kingdom's only great ethical prophet. While Amos barely touches upon the need of returning to God for the salvation of people and nation, a brokenhearted Hosea makes it his major theme and pleads as only a loyal son could do for his fellow countrymen to avoid the consequences of the path upon which they were embarked. Basing his argument partly upon history, Hosea presents an appalling contrast between the purity of Israel's former life in the desert and the degradation of its present society. This kind of

[13] The references are to territories conquered by Israel.

argument tends to overlook the struggles and errors of the past and to hold up the former days of a nation or group as better by far than the present. His thinking shows him to be more immersed in the old sacral ways than any other major prophet.

For all his distorted glorification of the desert past, Hosea did correctly point to a considerable change in Israel's social structure. Once an egalitarian tribal system, however imperfect, it had become under monarchical economic policies influenced by Canaanite ideals a society of vast distinctions. Religious solidarity as expressed in the Covenant had given way to social disunity as expressed in class interests. Like Amos he was aware of the international situation and warned his people against Assyria (8:1), but for him the great danger was internal and lay in Israel's faithlessness to Covenant responsibilities. In his eyes it was Canaanite religion and its fertility cult which had played a large role in alloying Israelite worship and destroying Hebrew social ideals. To combat this influence Hosea did a daring thing. He used the imagery of the fertility cults and sought to turn it against Canaanite religion. At the same time he was bold enough to attempt to transfer this imagery, which was basically incompatible with Hebrew religion, to the Covenant relationship itself. Israel is described as a harlot whose passion for Baal is nothing other than going "after her lovers" (Hosea 2). Speaking directly of idolatry (4:12), cult prostitution (4:14), golden bulls (8:5-6), agricultural imagery associated with fertility worship (10:12), and other expressions of what he sees as Baalism, Hosea implores his people to return to the Lord and to seek righteousness in Covenant loyalty and a close relationship with the God whose love hovers over them. Otherwise, those who have sown the wind "shall reap the whirlwind" (8:7). Exile and destruction are to be the lot of a people whose "deeds do not permit them to return

to their God" (5:4).

For Amos and Hosea worship and ethics are inseparable. Corruption of the former had had its inevitable effect upon the latter. The judgment of God in the form of exile was not far off. How much influence these men and their points of view had in their day is a matter of speculation. Amos aroused the hostile interest of the officials at Bethel, but only when he uttered a threat directly against the royal family (Amos 7:10-17); of Hosea's reception we have no word. The king and his ministers, we may safely assume, were little interested in either man or in what each had to say. It was economics, treaties, and finding a way to fend off the coming blow from Assyria that commanded their attention. The inner harmony between worship and ethics concerned them even less than did the need for court reform to which they seemed to have paid precious little attention.

16. "A VULTURE OVER THE HOUSE"—THE FALL OF ISRAEL

Within a year of Jeroboam's death (746 B.C.), Tiglath-pileser III seized power in Assyria.[1] This able monarch rekindled once more an old Mesopotamian dream: the subjugation of Egypt. Having made firm his hold over Babylonia and Urartu (Armenia), traditional foes in the northern valley, he crossed the Euphrates as Assyrian armies had done before. Only this time they had not come to raid, but to stay and to prepare a base for the decisive assault upon the Land of the Nile. The "Vulture" of which Hosea spoke (8:1) was indeed over the house of the Lord. Israel spent the greater part of its last half century seeking by one means or another to avoid its deadly clutches. But in the two-hundredth year of the northern kingdom the end came. Israel succumbed and was no more.

[1] This king is known to the Bible and to Babylonian records as "Pul" or "Pulu."

The threat was massive, total, final. Unlike his predecessors this Assyrian king was not interested merely in tribute. His goal was to incorporate conquered lands into his empire. His policy was deportation. Vast numbers of the leaders in every phase of government, business, and society in general were shifted to another and strange part of the empire. Those capable of leading uprisings thus found themselves without a natural following. Such a policy has its own inner rationale. If it was also cruel, it was surely no more brutal than many other practices of conquerors before and since. Its finality as regards the state made it unique, however.

In those times and with such terror on the horizon, Israel's slim chances of survival depended on internal solidarity and considerable political wisdom. In fact, just the opposite came to be the case. Without Jeroboam's firm hand the injustice and debauchery of which Amos and Hosea speak so eloquently combined with the traditional political instability of Israel and literally blew the kingdom apart. The Assyrian threat aside, Israel collapsed from within. The empire of Jeroboam had been put together in a remarkably short time; it came crashing down even more quickly.

Zechariah (746-745 B.C.), Jeroboam's son, became the fifth and last member of the house of Jehu to sit upon the throne at Samaria. Within six months he was dead at Ibleam, fittingly near the place where his notorious ancestor's men had mortally wounded King Ahaziah of Judah ninety-seven years earlier. Zechariah's murderer was Shallum ben Jabesh (II Kings 15:10) of whom we know only that he managed to hold power for a month before falling before another assassin. Civil war was now fully upon the land. Not all peoples and towns eagerly switched their allegiance to Menahem ben Gadi of Tirzah (745-738 B.C.), the murderer of the murderer. Tappuah, a city not yet satisfactorily identified, refused to support the new king. It was sacked with the most horrible atrocities visited upon its inhabitants (II Kings 15:16). This may well be an indication of the struggle between Shallum's forces and those of Menahem as most commentators take it to be. It is also possible that events had moved entirely too quickly for many in Israel and the resistance of Tappuah indicates support for the Jehuites who had, after all, ruled for almost a century. However the incident is understood, a picture of growing anarchy is clear enough. Hosea, whose ministry continued in the midst of the rapidly changing fortunes of the people, saw the end of the process:

I will destroy you, O Israel;
 who can help you?
Where now is your king, to save you;
 where are all your princes, to defend
 you—
those of whom you said,
"Give me a king and princes"?
I have given you kings in my anger,
 and I have taken them away in my wrath.

Hosea 13:9-11

Tiglath-pileser was firmly establishing himself in northern Syria and was receiving tribute from numerous states in the area who sought by so doing to postpone, if not evade altogether, the gathering storm. From the Assyrian royal annals found among the ruins of Nimrud we know that two of those who tried in this manner to assuage the conquering king were Rezin of Damascus and "Menahem of Samaria." II Kings 15:19-20 says that the Israelite tribute was heavy and tells how it was raised. There is also the hint that Menahem may have used the occasion to strengthen his somewhat shaky hold on power by an Assyrian alliance and also by weakening some of the monied interests who could effectively oppose him. Tiglath-pileser's records make it clear that Menahem had little choice in the matter. He speaks of overwhelming the Israelite king "like a snow-storm," and of sending him fleeing "like a bird, alone." For considerations of gold, silver, and linen garments with multicolored trimmings he allowed Menahem to resume the throne in Samaria. Israel was from this time a vassal.

Also in the Assyrian annals is an enigmatic reference to "Azriau of Iuda." This king was leader of a futile coalition which opposed the Assyrian advance into Syria. While there is no proof, this seems to be a reference to Uzziah (Azariah) who, although leprous, retained the power in Judah, now the most stable and powerful of the small states in the area. If this assumption is correct, a change in Judahite foreign policy took place upon Uzziah's death or perhaps upon the failure of the coalition. Aided by the fact that its geographical situation made it neither a barrier to Assyrian ambitions nor a necessity to them, Judah did not offer opposition, but followed a shrewd and extremely successful policy which allowed it to outlive Assyria, if not always with complete independence.

Menahem's submission and the financial burden this entailed for many Israelites did not meet with universal acceptance. There were a number of different opinions as to the best course of action; among them the view of the military advocating stern opposition to the Assyrians and their demands. It was this potentially disastrous position which eventually held the day, plunged the country into a senseless war with Judah, and threw Israel helpless before the Mesopotamian juggernaut. Again it was murder and coup d'état by the military that brought one of their own to power. Pekah ben Remaliah (737-732 B.C.) now set about to implement anti-Assyrian policies. Allying himself with Rezin of Damascus,[2] who had suffered and

who continued to feel the heavy hand of the overlords, Pekah meant to form a coalition supported by Egypt and thus to attempt to repeat the success of Qarqar. This would perhaps block Tiglath-pileser's southern expansion and force his interests to turn elsewhere. It was, of course, absolutely necessary to have Judah as a member of the alliance. Her power was important, but her strategic position between Israel and Egypt was paramount. Jotham (742-735 B.C.), son and successor to Uzziah, wanted nothing to do with this scheme and refused to join. Judahite foreign policy was to appease Assyria, not to offer her military opposition. At this crucial juncture the king died and his son, Ahaz (735-715 B.C.), came to the southern throne. He shared his father's view that the best way to keep the nation safe was to offer no offense to Assyria. He also refused to join Pekah and Rezin, whereupon the troops of Israel and Syria invaded Judah, not to conquer, but to overthrow the government in Jerusalem and to replace the house of David with a Syrian, a man named ben Tabeel. The fear that filled Ahaz was such that "his heart and the heart of his people shook as the trees of the forest shake before the wind," says Isaiah (7:2), who was not only witness to these events but an advisor to the king. Isaiah counseled Ahaz to stand fast in the face of the threat from "these two smoldering stumps of firebrands." Like Amos and Hosea, Isaiah was a keen observer of international affairs. He knew that Egypt, divided into factions and even into rival kingdoms, was hardly a trustworthy ally and still less a solid foundation upon which to base an alliance. Also, many smaller nations of the area, concerned mostly with petty self-interest, had little interest in larger affairs. As for Israel and Syria, it was only a matter of time until the Assyrian heel ground them to dust:

Behold, Damascus will cease to be a city
and will become a heap of ruins.

[2] Inscriptions from the Nabu Temple at Nimrud note that Rezin was also allied to the Tyrian king who, like a more famous ancestor, was named Hiram. This is not only what we should have expected, but it also partially accounts for a decline in Phoenician fortunes a short time later.

Her cities will be deserted for ever;
　　they will be for flocks,
which will lie down, and none will make them
　　afraid.
The fortress will disappear from Ephraim
　　(Israel),
　　and the kingdom from Damascus;
and the remnant of Syria will be
　　like the glory of the children of Israel,
　　says the Lord of hosts.

　　　　　　　　　　　　　　　　Isaiah 17:1-3

Since he held this view, the prophet could do no other than press upon Ahaz a course of strict neutrality. In the later realm the choice was up to Ahaz, but on one level he had no freedom of movement. The Edomites and the Philistines, either acting in concert with the Israelites and Syrians or seizing an opportune moment, struck at Judah from the south and west. Large parts of Edom, including the Arabah, reclaimed independence (II Kings 16:6; II Chronicles 28:17). At Ezion-geber, as archaeological excavations there show, the Judahite buildings were destroyed and replaced by Edomite construction. Not again in ancient times was the mineral and mercantile wealth of this area to come into Hebrew hands. For their part the Philistines, who had not been a serious factor since the days of David, reclaimed considerable territory in the northwestern Negeb and in the Shephelah of what had been western Judah (II Chronicles 28:18).

With Pekah and Rezin before the gates of Jerusalem and with traditional foes making significant inroads into Judah's territories and sources of wealth, Ahaz took exception to Isaiah's advice, if he ever followed it at all, and sent what wealth he could scrape together to the Assyrian king, pledged that he would be his vassal, and earnestly requested an immediate attack upon Syria and Israel (II Kings 16:7-8; II Chronicles 28:16). Tiglath-pileser required little urging. It was time to prepare the base for an assault upon

Egypt.[3] Isaiah's vision of Damascus as a "heap of ruins" finds its parallel in the Assyrian annals where Tiglath-pileser speaks of the sixteen districts of Syria and says: "I destroyed making them look like hills of ruined cities over which the flood had swept." Israel fared but slightly better. Its northern and Transjordanian areas fell before Assyrian arms. The plume-crested soldiers paused just long enough in these regions to deport the leaders of its population (II Kings 15:29), and then pressed southward slaughtering, destroying, conquering.

At Hazor archaeologists have found evidence of the thoroughness of the work of Tiglath-pileser's forces around the year 732 B.C. The entire area of the city of Jeroboam II was blanketed by a layer of ashes and debris which averaged about three and a half feet in depth. At the same time the excavators were able to establish that the attack had not come as a surprise to the defenders. It seems the people of the city had torn down a number of buildings near the walls in a hurried effort to build additional offsets and insets into the defensive structure. Nothing availed as superior might moved forward with hardly a respectful pause before the substantial fortifications which had earlier been so carefully planned and built at such costs of manpower and money. Thereafter this great site, which had been a major center of Hebrew interest since the days of Joshua, was merely a border fort for whatever power happened to control Palestine at a given moment. There was an Israelite settlement after the eighth-century destruction, but it was without walls and lasted only so long as the Assyrians wished.

Megiddo fared better. It likewise was looted and destroyed, but was rebuilt and made the administrative center for those areas of Israel which were now annexed to

---

[3] The actual invasion of Egypt did not take place until approximately sixty-five years later, during the reign of Ashurbanipal.

the ravenous Assyrian empire. Of rough and robbed stone, the new city was laid out in a Mesopotamian manner, unusual for Palestine. Its domestic areas were in blocks with houses backed against one another. Totally ignoring the lines and dimensions of older construction at the site, a large fortress, some 220 feet by 160 feet, was constructed on the eastern side of the hill. With walls averaging seven feet in thickness, it was probably the citadel barracks of the governor and his soldiers. It is interesting to note that the religious objects recovered from the Assyrian levels at Megiddo do not differ greatly from those of preceding levels. We know from II Kings 16:10-16 and II Chronicles 28: 22-25 that Ahaz adopted or was forced to adopt Assyrian-Damascene worship in Jerusalem. Elsewhere things seem to have continued much as they had been. And what they had been was—at least in terms of recovered cult objects—Canaanite! At Megiddo the incense altars and seven-light lamp could have been used in the worship of the Hebrew God. But can the same be said of a red-colored bovine skull with horns, of representations of a phallus, and a number of female figurines, pregnant and holding an object over one breast? Several of these latter come from the same mold and suggest a temple object given or sold to the worshipers much as crosses and other objects were given or sold to Christian pilgrims in the Middle Ages.

Many other cities, towns, and villages less well known than Hazor and Megiddo nonetheless suffered equally. At el-Khirbe, on the northern bank of the Yarkon River near Tel Aviv, excavators have found one such place. Originally a Philistine port, el-Khirbe became Israelite during the time of David. It was a center of various industries including metallurgy, dye-making, and weaving. The casemate wall defending these industries and enclosing much of the port lasted from David's reign until the coming of Tiglath-pileser. Although el-Khirbe was settled until

Arab Mamluke times, it never attained any distinction after the Assyrian had passed by.

As Tiglath-pileser himself tells us: "The town Samaria only did I leave." The capital of the smashed and all-but-finished kingdom was saved by a pro-Assyrian coup (II Kings 15:30). In his annals Tiglath-pileser claims to have had a part in this, which may well have been the case. In any event it did not matter who had a part in what or, for that matter, even who was on the throne or what his policy was. Israel was finished. Only the death agony was to be played out. Hoshea, who managed to rule in the hill country of Ephraim for eight years (732-724 B.C.), was merely a puppet; his reign and kingdom depended upon every whim of the Assyrian monarch. For his part Tiglath-pileser was satisfied for the moment to leave this minuscule state and its larger sister to the south as they were, obedient and relatively powerless. Much of the Philistine area was in Assyrian hands, and preparations were afoot to bring Mesopotamian might to bear along the Nile.

Judah was surviving only by the most abject kind of submission. Ahaz, commanded to appear before Tiglath-pileser in Damascus, returned to implement Assyrian-Damascene religious practices in Jerusalem and other parts of Judah (II Kings 16:10-16; II Chronicles 28:22-25). The writers of Chronicles saw in this little more than an expression of Ahaz' personal apostasy. It may have been that, but it was also an example of the ancient practice of worshiping the gods of your conquerors as being stronger than your own deity or deities who had failed to protect you and give you victory. Moreover, Ahaz' altars and high places and his incense burned before alien gods neither fathered nor constituted the majority of the disaffection from the Hebrew God which was prevalent in Judah in that day. Micah suggests the extent of the apostasy:

I will cut off sorceries from your
   hand,
and you shall have no more
   soothsayers;
and I will cut off your images
   and your pillars from among you,
and you shall bow down no more
   to the work of your hands;
and I will root out your Asherim
   from among you
and destroy your cities.

Micah 5:12-14

From western Judah, in the low, rolling hills near Lachish, came Micah, a man of the soil whose heart belonged to God and whose prophetic vision was more withering than any of his predecessors. A contemporary of Isaiah who may have been influenced by the thought of Amos, he was witness to the death throes of Israel and spoke in a moment when the Assyrians had reduced that recently proud nation to a small area around Samaria. If others thought the policy of Hoshea could long succeed or could long restrain the anti-Assyrian feelings in the land, Micah had no such illusions:

I will make Samaria a heap in the open country,
   a place for planting vineyards;
and I will pour down her stones into the valley,
   and uncover her foundations.

Micah 1:6

From this prophet's point of view this inevitable event was not lamentable, but a sign of the wrath of God upon a people who had worshiped false gods and who oppressed the poor, those without power and influence, and their neighbors. Samaria, so soon to be the heap he envisaged, was to him the symbol of the corruption of Israel (1:5). But this tough-minded man, who looked unflinchingly upon the Assyrian fist as the wrath of God visited upon a deserving people, did not reserve his words for Israel and Samaria alone. His gaze fell upon his own people, his own nation, his own capital. "And

what is the sin of the house of Judah? Is it not Jerusalem?" (1:5). Israel and Judah, Samaria and Jerusalem, each alike was found wanting. Micah does, perhaps somewhat chauvinistically, blame the sins of Judah upon Israel (1:8-9). Yet once the wound has come to Judah it is incurable and must be dealt with the same way as in the northern kingdom. With all the sarcasm of Amos he speaks of those who cannot sleep because they must use the time to think up new ways to defraud others; even their moments of rest are devoted to devising wickedness. Likewise, the Lord is devising evil for such people; evil which will remove their pride and the possessions so wrongly gained (2:1-5).

Micah was hardly the first prophet to speak of doom, but he was the first to speak of the doom of Jerusalem and to see in its inevitability the judgment of God. Just as Amos and Hosea provide a unique insight into the life of Jeroboam's Israel, so Micah makes Ahaz' Jerusalem live again. The dryness of II Kings with its political interests and of II Chronicles with its unbroken religious condemnations are momentarily infused with the noise of people, the haughtiness of rulers, and the insults and hurts of injustice:

Hear this, you heads of the house
   of Jacob
   and rulers of the house of Israel,
who abhor justice
   and pervert all equity,
who build Zion with blood
   and Jerusalem with wrong.
Its heads give judgment for a bribe,
   its priests teach for hire,
   its prophets divine for money;
yet they lean upon the Lord and say,
   "Is not the Lord in the midst of
     us?
   No evil shall come to us."
Therefore because of you
   Zion shall be plowed as a field;
Jerusalem shall become a heap of
   ruins,

and the mountain of the house a
wooded height.
                              Micah 3:9-12

The themes of Micah are those of Amos and Hosea. Judah had learned little from the plight of its northern twin. And that plight was now desperate. In the circumstance Hoshea made a fatal misstep. Tiglath-pileser died in 724 B.C., and with his passing the Assyrian grip momentarily loosened in Palestine. After faithfully performing the duties of vassal and paying his ten talents of gold and thousand talents of silver year by year, Hoshea saw the opportunity to get out from under this burden. He withheld payment from the new king, Shalmaneser V (727-722 B.C.), and sought to ally himself with a man whom II Kings 17:4 calls "So, king of Egypt." From both Egyptian and Assyrian records it seems that this man was at best one of a number of rivals for the Egyptian throne. At worst he was little more than a military officer holding sway over a portion of the Nile Delta. This is the man and the power in whom the king of Israel placed his faith. "Woe to those who go down to Egypt for help," said Isaiah (31:1), perhaps thinking back over the ill-conceived alliance of Hoshea.

Shalmaneser was soon upon Israel. Having consolidated himself in power he moved west and south as fast as feet and wheels could carry his men and weapons. The remaining countryside, towns, and villages of Israel were ravaged as Assyrians poured over the land. From the excavations at Tirzah has come vivid evidence of the work of these soldiers. Over the entire area was a burned layer not unlike that left at Hazor by Tiglath-pileser a few years earlier. Immediately on top of this was new construction containing large quantities of non-Palestinian pottery.[4] It is Assyrian, identical with

[4] Examples have been found at Samaria and Dothan in the north, at Tell Jemmeh near Gaza, and at Amman in Transjordan. Is this evidence of widespread Assyrian settlements? It seems likely.

materials recovered recently at Nimrud. Perhaps it found its way to Tirzah with the army. More likely it came with or was made by settlers whom the Assyrians brought to replace deported natives. When Tirzah was resettled the conquerors, making sure the new people would not become a source of trouble, tore down part of the the city wall, blocked the city gate rendering it useless, and built a completely unprotected entrance.

Apparently Hoshea saw the gravity of his error and sought to make amends by appealing to the new Assyrian king in person. Of this we do not know for sure and can only speculate. What is clear is his imprisonment prior to the siege of Samaria, and one wonders how the king was taken if the city was able to hold out for three years. The horrors of this siege can only be imagined; none of the survivors was in a position to recount them. Perhaps a description of the later, considerably shorter siege of Jerusalem offers a hint:

Happier were the victims of the
     sword
   than the victims of hunger,
who pined away, stricken
     by want of the fruits of the field.

The hands of compassionate women
   have boiled their own children;
they became their food
   in the destruction of the daughter
     of my people.
                        Lamentations 4:9-10

Shortly before the Assyrians stood victorious upon the summit of the hill of Shemer, Shalmaneser died. His successor Sargon II (722-705 B.C.) did not falter in pressing the gallant but hopeless defenders to their limit. Something of the military strength this monarch had at his disposal is known from a tablet recently found in the Fort at Nimrud. It gives a routine, utilitarian inventory of archers available for duty.

Those at Nimrud alone reached upward of 30,000! Excavators have surmised that 70,000 to 100,000 soldiers were garrisoned at Nimrud, the chief arsenal of Assyria. These unexaggerated figures are an indication of the astonishing might Sargon was able to hurl at the embattled mountain in the hills of Ephraim.

"In the ninth year of Hoshea," says II Kings 17:6, "the king of Assyria captured Samaria, and he carried the Israelites away to Assyria . . . ." Excavations have shown that the royal summit of the city was totally destroyed. Everywhere was evidence of severe burning; thick layers as at Hazor and Tirzah. Among the debris and ashes were broken ivories, the remains of looting. Parts of the large casemate wall survived to be reused by the Assyrians, and by the Greeks and Romans after them. But little else escaped. The city inside the walls was literally leveled; few foundations exist above the ground. The fate of the residences of the common people who lived beyond the protection of the walls is unknown. Those areas have not yet been excavated.

In annals unearthed at Sargon's new capital at Khorsabad the conqueror gives a few more details of the aftermath of his victory. He tells of deporting 27,290 inhabitants and of taking fifty chariots which he integrated into his own mobile forces. He then rebuilt the city, "better than it was before," he says, and settled in it peoples from other conquered countries. Pottery evidence of their presence has come from Samaria (see p. 190, n. 4). Sargon adds that So (*Sib'e* in the Assyrian records) finally did appear to fight about a year later when the Assyrians moved south along the coast to reestablish their authority in Philistia. "Sib'e ran away, afraid when he (only) heard the noise of my (approaching) army, and has not been seen again." Such was the man to whom Hoshea had literally entrusted the safety of his realm.

17. "THE GOLD HAS GROWN DIM" —THE FALL OF JUDAH

The devouring flames that engulfed Israel licked at the foundations of Judah. Ahaz' vassalage offered little protection when various cities of the south stood, or were thought to stand, in the way of Assyrian plans. The fortress at Gibeah, practically within sight of Jerusalem itself, was put to the torch. And as the invaders strengthened their positions around Gaza they moved into western Judah. Assyrian policy toward Judah emerged. A greatly reduced kingdom was allowed to remain a more or less independent vassal; it was neither annexed nor occupied. However, as a guarantee of its loyalty and servility, certain fortresses defending its capital from the north and from the southwest were destroyed and major roads were left relatively undefended. This allowed the Assyrians to lay immediate siege to Jerusalem in the event of rebellion. Such was the kingdom inherited by Hezekiah (715-687 B.C.), Ahaz' son. As often, a profound shift in political fortunes produced other changes with their attendant reactions. It was a combination of these that brought forth from Hezekiah a defiant policy radically removed from the servility of his father.

Judah, more isolated and provincial than Israel, had not seen foreign influences erode so deeply into the social and religious fabric of the nation as had its northern neighbor. It is true that the struggle with Canaanite culture had continued unabated and that royal patronage of various cults had not helped the situation. Nonetheless, this patronage had not been supported by a thoroughgoing foreign and economic policy as in Israel. Moreover, the naturally conservative bent of the Judahite mind had preserved a recognizably Hebraic view of the relations between religion, society, and politics. The pro-Assyrian policies of Ahaz had threatened this. He had accepted, or had been forced to accept, a new culture: the Aramaic culture which was rapidly replacing the influence of Phoenician civilization now ground down and disappearing as an independent force. Canaanite factors were subsumed by neo-Assyrian elements which were carried on the wings of Assyrian military might to the far reaches of the ancient east. The lasting strength of this new culture can be seen in the fact that the native language of Palestine in Jesus' day was Aramaic. There were other consequences besides speech. The social and religious abuses to which Isaiah and Micah pointed were accelerated by Ahaz' introduction of the official Assyrian cult into the country. Religion and politics were, of course, never separated in the Hebrew kingdoms. Now in Judah religious reaction combined with national pride to force the new king into an anti-Assyrian policy, or perhaps to support him in a position which he had already reached. Hezekiah was also strengthened by a sudden although not disastrous shift in the fortunes of Assyria. Just as the power of Mesopotamia seemed to be poised for a leap into Egypt, revolts broke out in several parts of the empire. The most serious of these was in Babylonia where Merodach-baladan seized control. For approximately twelve years Sargon was in difficulty and found it necessary to quell first this and then that nest of rebels. In his ferocity the Assyrian king not only reconquered but utterly destroyed city and state one after another, razing structures and deporting populations. While this had the immediately desired effect, it proved fatal in the long run for it removed most of the buffers between Mesopotamia and many of the barbarian areas to the north. Further to complicate Sargon's problems, a strong dynasty had arisen in Egypt and had restored a relative position of strength in the south. Assyria had momentarily missed its best opportunity to realize an old dream. Yet the situation could only be temporary. Assyria possessed

unprecedented might, and it was a matter of time until it would pour down like a flood across the fields bordering the Nile.

Meanwhile, that strength was employed elsewhere and Judah was invited to join a coalition headed by Egypt. Two years after Hezekiah came to the throne Azuri, king of Ashdod, refused to pay tribute to Assyria. According to documents excavated at Assur, this set off intrigue involving not only Egypt, Philistia, and Judah, but Edom and Moab as well. Isaiah, wholly opposed to Judah's joining in this undertaking, not only counseled a negative response to Egypt (Isaiah 18), but paraded naked and barefoot through the streets of Jerusalem to show what would become of a people who made "Ethiopia their hope and . . . Egypt their boast" (Isaiah 20). The prophet and others of his persuasion seem to have won the day. When Sargon smashed a friendless Ashdod—no one came to her aid—Judah was not harmed.

Hezekiah Revolts

Yet a clash between Judah and Assyria was inevitable. Hezekiah had embarked upon an ambitious program of religious reform (II Kings 18:3-6; II Chronicles 29, 31) which embodied and indeed depended upon a strong and increasing nationalism. Among the cult objects destroyed was "the bronze serpent that Moses had made, . . . it was called Nehustan" (see p. 103). But it was the high places and other local shrines that were particular targets of this reform. Foreshadowing Josiah's Deuteronomic reform by a century, Hezekiah seems to have desired to make Jerusalem the only as well as the central focus of devotion. That some success was attained is indicated by counteracting efforts made by the Assyrians. In an attempt to draw attention away from Jerusalem, an Israelite priest was brought back from exile to reinstitute worship at Bethel (II Kings

17:27-28). When Assyrian emissaries later came to Jerusalem, they tried to win the people's loyalty from Hezekiah by pointing out that it was he who had taken away the high places (II Kings 18:22).

The most serious political implication of these reforms arose, of course, from abolishing the Assyrian religious practices instituted by Ahaz. That these may have involved the fiery sacrifice of children (II Chronicles 28:3; see pp. 105-6) may have made it all the easier for those bent upon purging them from the soil sacred to the Hebrew God. But this, were it so, did not change the complexion of repudiation as an act of rebellion. To deny the gods of Assyria was to deny the power and authority of the conquering state. When Sargon died in 705 B.C. and was succeeded by Sennacherib (705-681 B.C.), a less capable ruler, Hezekiah withheld tribute, thereby making formal his already implied state of insurrection (II Kings 18:7).

Bible and archaeology combine to show that Hezekiah did not take this step precipitously. Close to Isaiah he was also influenced by the preaching of Micah (Jeremiah 26:16-19) and probably took steps to correct some of the economic and social injustices in the land. At least this is suggested by the discovery at various locations of jar handles stamped with the words "to the king" and the location of a city. These are widely interpreted as state attempts to standardize weights and measures. Such practice would have removed one of the more serious structural abuses referred to by all the prophets of the eighth century. At Tell Beit Mirsim (Debir), the most complete Judahite town yet excavated, there is no evidence of the kind of social stratification which de Vaux found at Tirzah. There was, however, abundant evidence of different quarters of the city devoted to spinning, weaving, and dyeing woolen cloth. Excavators think these may be the remains of craft associations or guilds,

like those mentioned in II Chronicles 2:14, and in Jeremiah 24:1. Although Hezekiah was by no means the founder of such guilds, their flourishing existence in his reign is another part of the circumstantial evidence suggesting that he sought to strengthen the fabric of Judah. The internal collapse which marked Israel's response to external pressure was therefore considerably less likely in Judah.

Other preparations more directly related to war were implemented. A census determined the manpower and other resources available. It also sought to identify and to remove elements which might have reason to try to take advantage of the impending situation (I Chronicles 4:38-43). Considerable building at this time certainly had military implications even if this was not its primary purpose (II Chronicles 32:27-29). Jerusalem, of course, commanded attention as it was here that the Assyrians, if not turned back sooner, would surely come. Its walls, none too strong, were hastily bolstered by stones taken from nearby houses destroyed for this purpose (Isaiah 22:8-10).

The most spectacular of Hezekiah's preparations was the building of a new water system for Jerusalem (II Kings 20:20; II Chronicles 32:30; Isaiah 22:11). The Jebusite tunnel had not been a viable defense structure for many years and the waters of Gihon had long ago been diverted to royal gardens on the eastern slope of Ophel (II Kings 25:4). The question of refurbishing the old structure or of tapping into any of the other numerous canals joining the spring was in any case not relevant since the dimension and plan of the city had changed radically in the intervening years. Therefore an almost entirely new tunnel running completely under Ophel was carved out of the rock. In a feat of astounding engineering combined perhaps with a large measure of good fortune, groups of workmen started toward each other from the east and from the west. As projected, the passageway would slice through the hill from the northeast to the southwest, approximately sixty feet below the surface. This would bring water from the Kidron Valley flowing into the Tyropoeon. When the work was completed the shaft, following a winding path through hard rock, was 1749 feet long. After some six to nine months of effort the two crews, operating without accurate magnetic instruments, had met. This in itself was no small accomplishment as their path through the stone could hardly be described as anything other than blind groping in a general direction. Few ancient remains have more effectively preserved evidences of the effort and emotions of the men who constructed them. False starts were made here and there; the rock in places was very difficult to penetrate. This was more true of the workmen coming from the southwest than those coming in the other direction, even though the latter met with more material resistance. Perhaps the group coming from the northeast had more perseverance or a sterner foreman. Surely perseverance and sternness were needed in abundance. In spaces so small that only one man could work at a time and where air and light were at a premium, the primitive tools at hand could at best produce frustratingly slow results. Indeed, even today it is not clear how the need for oxygen was met. There was an air shaft 459 feet from the southwestern entrance, but none elsewhere. Workmen clearing the tunnel in 1910 could labor only for short periods before needing fresh air. Very likely Hezekiah employed many men for short periods and thus solved the breathing problem. How adequate light was secured is also a mystery. Triangular notches, probably for lamps, were cut into the walls at irregular intervals. Yet under the best conditions these could provide only minimal illumination, and it is likely correct to assume that for the most part work was carried on in darkness or semidarkness.

As the two groups of workmen drew close together and began to hear the thud of each other's efforts, their excitement grew. Vivid evidence of this is the erratic course of both ends of the tunnel for the last sixty-six feet of digging. Not only did the two shafts vary from side to side, but both tended to rise slightly as they drew closer together. When finally they met, a measure of fresh air was able to come through the tunnel, but, contrary to the Siloam Inscription,[1] there was no water. Not only had the last frenzied efforts of the workmen produced an effective dam in the middle of the construction, but the reservoir end was considerably higher than the source of the water. Judging by the fact that the walls in the middle of the tunnel were not smoothed like the rest, it seems as if all attention was directed to making the flow. While it is barely possible for a grown man to stand in most of the shaft (its average height is slightly over five and a half feet), at the southwestern end it is over seventeen and a half feet high. This is accounted for by the necessity of lowering the floor level. Finally a number of other canals tapping Gihon Spring were blocked, and water began to pour into the Pool of Siloam. A fall of approximately seven feet had been accomplished, and Hezekiah had his defensive water shaft.

After the destruction of Jerusalem by the Babylonians, the tunnel gradually filled with debris although water continued to flow through it. Eventually the source of the water was forgotten and the Pool of Siloam was referred to as a "spring." Such was the case in New Testament and later times. Beginning in the sixteenth Christian century, a few visitors to Jerusalem noted a connection between Gihon Spring and Siloam. Early in the nineteenth century there were attempts to explore the shaft. By 1866 a complete plan of it was produced. A year

[1] See p. 195.

later Charles Warren made detailed measurements which needed substantial correction only in the matter of the fall.[2] It is strange that with all this interest in the tunnel and its various measurements the most important item should have been missed until a group of boys accidentally discovered it in 1880. In that year some lads bathing in the Pool noticed an inscription on the eastern wall about twenty feet inside the tunnel mouth. This was the famous Siloam Inscription written in beautiful classical Hebrew prose. It is now in Istanbul where it was taken by the Turks then in political control of Palestine. Prior to the authorities' seizure of it a Greek merchant, in hopes of receiving a higher price by selling it in fragments, broke it into half a dozen pieces. Almost all were recovered, and the virtually complete text as given by Father J. Simons[3] tells of the moment when the two crews met:

(This is?) the boring through. This is the story of the boring through: whilst (the miners lifted) the pick each towards his fellow and whilst three cubits (yet remained) to be bored (through, there was hear)d the voice of a man calling to his fellow, for there was a split in the rock on the right hand and on (the left hand). And on the day of the boring through the miners struck, each in the direction of his fellow, pick against pick. And the water started flowing from the source to the pool, twelve hundred cubits. A hundred cubits was the height of the rock above the head of the miners.

It has long been assumed that the purpose of Hezekiah's undertaking was to bring an adequate supply of water inside the walls in order to strengthen the city against siege. E. J. Bliss and E. C. Dickie, excavating on Ophel from 1894 to 1897, reported they had found a wall crossing the tip of the valley, at that point 170 feet wide. According to them it formed an angle with another wall going up the eastern side of the western ridge. This would easily enclose the Pool of Siloam. From 1961 to 1966 Miss Kenyon reexamined the area in question and found no trace of Iron Age walls. Indeed, her findings have led her to think that this part of the western ridge was not incorporated into the city until the first Christian century. This has been one of the more perplexing matters to come out of the most recent excavations in Jerusalem. If Miss Kenyon is correct, the Pool of Siloam was outside the walls of Hezekiah's city! Is this possible? Why would one go to all the trouble of bringing water over 1700 feet through solid rock if the supply was still not immediately and safely available in time of war? Miss Kenyon speculates that it flowed into a rock-covered cistern and "all that had to be defended was the access to it, probably by steps in a gallery or by a shaft." [4] This idea flies in the face of all previous notions and, while intriguing, needs a good deal more evidence than has been offered to support it. Unfortunately, as the excavator herself is the first to point out, Roman and Byzantine construction at and above the Pool have combined with previous archaeological excavations to remove the materials that are needed to verify this new suggestion.

[2] Warren thought there was no fall, but later measurement shows it to be about seven feet.

[3] J. Simons, *Jerusalem in the Old Testament* (Leiden: E. J. Brill, 1952), p. 184.

[4] Kathleen Kenyon, *Jerusalem* (London: Thames and Hudson, 1967), pp. 70-71, 77.

Istanbul Museum

The Siloam Inscription which is a contemporary account of one of the most remarkable engineering feats of ancient times.

For a while Hezekiah rested secure in his preparations. After coming to power Sennacherib was occupied for some time with subduing Merodach-baladan who had once again led the Babylonians into revolt. Apparently at that time this ambitious Babylonian courted the favor of Hezekiah (II Kings 20:12; Isaiah 39:1). His intention was to support and to draw support from the growing southern coalition against the new Assyrian king.[5] But the fateful day came when the Assyrian crossed the Euphrates as his predecessors had done and marched at the head of his army to meet the open rebellion of a southern coalition backed by Egypt.[6] Sennacherib's annals, now in the Oriental Institute of the University of Chicago, enlarge the accounts of this campaign as described in II Kings 18:13-16 and Isaiah 36. First moving down the Mediterranean coast, Sennacherib overthrew the king of Tyre, who had a hand in organizing the coalition, and then reduced the Phoenician ports. This proved to be the end of the period of cultural and mercantile greatness for the Land of the Purple. The Phoenician and Transjordanian parties to the rebellion now collapsed. Either destroyed or rushing with gifts and tribute, they were erased as combatants. Philistia, momentarily dominated by Judah (II Kings 18:8), determined to fight alongside Egypt. Sennacherib moved steadily down the coast. Ekron, its king deposed by the people and sent to Jerusalem as captive, was his primary target. Victorious against city after city, he came at last to Ekron only to find that the inhabitants had

[5] Some scholars place this incident during the earlier revolt of Merodach-baladan against Sargon. But it seems more reasonable at this time when an opposition coalition was actually forming with Hezekiah in a leading role.

[6] The following account assumes only one major campaign by Sennacherib against Judah. Many scholars, however, are of the opinion that there were two expeditions, accounts of which have become conflated in the biblical record. The Assyrian annals are not decisive in settling the question.

called upon the Egyptians to honor their pledges. "They actually had come to their assistance," says Sennacherib with a note of surprise. No matter. At Eltekeh, near Ekron, the Egyptians fought valiantly, but were defeated. Nothing defended the remaining Philistine cities including Ekron. No ally stood with Judah once the Assyrians had finished their work in Philistia. All had collapsed, were defeated, or were destroyed. Now it was Judah's turn.

I laid siege to 46 of his [Hezekiah's] strong cities [says Sennacherib in his annals], walled forts and to the countless small villages in their vicinity, and conquered (them) by means of well-stamped (earth-) ramps, and battering-rams brought (thus) near (to the walls) (combined with) the attack by foot soldiers, (using) mines, breaches as well as sapper work. I drove out (of them) 200,150 people, young and old, male and female, horses, mules, donkeys, camels, big and small cattle beyond counting, and considered (them) booty. Himself I made a prisoner in Jerusalem, his royal residence, like a bird in a cage.[7]

Over 200,000 people were driven out of their cities, towns, and villages; how many more were slaughtered? Isaiah speaks of the country lying desolate, of cities burned with fire, and of aliens devouring the land (1:7). The truth of this and the awfulness of the butchery accompanying it is all too clear from excavations at Lachish. At Nineveh Sennacherib commemorated his victorious Palestinian campaign by causing a large relief to be made depicting his successful attack on Lachish. Among the debris on the lower roadway at Tell ed-Duweir (Lachish) excavators found the crest of a bronze helmet identical with those shown on the mural. But other evidence, and a good deal grimmer than remains of armament, spoke of Assyrian presence. Burned debris containing arrowheads, slingshots, and spearpoints was

[7] *Ancient Near Eastern Texts*, p. 288.

Oriental Institute, University of Chicago

Lachish as it is thought to have looked in Israelite times (above). Sennacherib sits on his throne
before the massive walls of the Judahite city (below), while his army attacks those walls with
battering rams and scaling ladders (below, left).
Both illustrations are from a bas relief found at
Nineveh. At left are trephinated skulls from the
mass burial pit.

Palestine Archaeological Museum

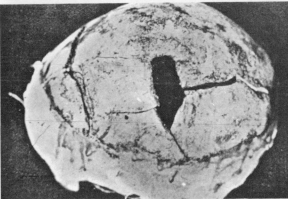

everywhere.[8] There is also no doubt that the invaders camped there after the battle. From a pit which they used for trash, excavators have removed what was left of no less than 1500 bodies. Judging from many burned bones and decapitated skeletons, these were presumably defenders or inhabitants and not attackers.[9] It is also interesting to note that a partially finished water system, not unlike the Siloam Tunnel, was uncovered. Perhaps Hezekiah also meant to furnish Lachish with water in order to strengthen it against siege. If so, the project was unfinished when the blow came.

With fortress Lachish in ruins, the western approaches to Jerusalem lay open. The bird was in the cage and little hope there seemed for him. Micah lamented the destruction of the towns and cities of his native western area (1:10-15), while Isaiah, who had never agreed with Hezekiah's policy in the first place, counseled surrender (1:5). There seems to have been some negotiating, possibly while Lachish was under siege, over terms for capitulation. This may have been when Padi, king of Ekron, was released by Hezekiah and was restored to power by Sennacherib. At any rate, Hezekiah sent gifts to the Assyrian king who in turn sent three envoys to Jerusalem. These men proceeded to appeal to the Judahites in the capital to overthrow their king (II Kings 18:17–19:13). The moving and very human scene described in the Bible did not end in success

for the envoys. The terms for peace which they conveyed to Hezekiah were equally unfruitful in outcome. They were all but unconditional, and the Judahite king balked. In a sudden turn of position Isaiah supported him (II Kings 19:29; Isaiah 14:24-27; 17:12-14; *et passim*). The prophet felt that Assyria had overreached herself as an instrument of divine punishment and that God who had delivered his people from the hopelessness of Egyptian bondage in another age would deliver seemingly hopeless Zion. "Like birds hovering," said Isaiah, "so the Lord of hosts will protect Jerusalem" (31:5).

Hezekiah held firm. Siege began in earnest. Then a very strange thing happened. II Kings 19:35-36 says: "And that night the angel of the Lord went forth, and slew a hundred and eighty-five thousand in the camp of the Assyrians; and when men arose early in the morning, behold, these were all dead bodies. Then Sennacherib king of Assyria departed, and went home, and dwelt at Nineveh." In his annals Sennacherib implies that Hezekiah's fear coupled with troop desertions caused him to "buy-off" the besiegers:

Hezekiah himself, whom the terror-inspiring splendor of my lordship had overwhelmed and whose irregular and elite troops which he had brought into Jerusalem, his royal residence, in order to strengthen (it), had deserted him, did send me, later, to Nineveh, my lordly city, together with 30 talents of gold, 800 talents of silver, precious stones, antimony, large cuts of red stone, couches (inlaid) with ivory, *nîmedu*-chairs (inlaid) with ivory, elephant-hides, ebony-wood, boxwood (and) all kinds of valuable treasures, his (own) daughters, concubines, male and female musicians. In order to deliver the tribute and to do obeisance as a slave he sent his (personal) messenger.[10]

This boast of the Assyrian raises several questions. Why was the tribute sent *later?* Were there agreed-upon terms of surrender

---

[8] Debir (Tell Beit Mirsim), eight miles from Lachish, yielded similar evidence from the same period and doubtless fell to the Assyrians besieging Lachish.

[9] Three skulls from this pit indicate something of the surprisingly well developed state of medical knowledge in late Judah. Trephine operations, surgery to remove circular discs of bone from the skull, had been performed apparently to relieve pressure on the brain. One skull shows signs of renewed growth, and it can be assumed that the operation was somewhat successful. The other two display crude saw marks conspicuously. No healing had taken place. Likely the patients had died during or immediately after the operation.

[10] *Ancient Near Eastern Texts*, p. 288.

involving heavy payment for the lifting of the siege and the withdrawal of the army? If so, and Hezekiah was in the role of a "slave," why did he not do obeisance in person as Jehu had done before Tiglath-pileser some years before, or as Manasseh was later to do before a northern king *in* Mesopotamia? The implication is clear and in accord with the statement in II Kings: the bird was not seized in his cage; Jerusalem was never taken. The Assyrians withdrew without fully accomplishing their purpose. Why? Were they bought off? The size of the tribute as reported by Sennacherib suggests that this may have been so. But was it the only reason? The ancient Greek historian Herodotus relates an account of a plague of rats infesting an Assyrian army "near the border of Egypt." Many have taken this to be the situation spoken of in II Kings 19: 35-36. For whatever reason, plague or otherwise, the invaders were unable or unwilling to maintain their stranglehold on the capital. They struck a bargain with the beleaguered Judahite king, and went home where they received the items and people promised them. However its details are conceived, it was a miraculous deliverance.

Jerusalem was saved, but Judah was in woeful condition. Its western portions were for the moment annexed to those Philistine cities and kings loyal to Sennacherib, and of what remained, all but the capital lay in ruins. Information regarding the next twenty to twenty-five years in Judah is extremely scanty. The utter devastation and the necessity of raising heavy annual tribute were sufficient to occupy the full attention and resources of the people for a generation. No doubt as these people surveyed their ravaged land, returned to their burned cities, buried their dead, and began the tasks of impoverished rebuilding, the anti-Assyrian policy of Hezekiah did not seem so wise as it did at one time. A slow, predictable reaction set in. When the light of history falls once again

full upon Judah, Hezekiah's son, Manasseh (687-642 B.C.), is on the throne, pro-Assyrian, encouraging every tendency that might shore up his country in its tender international position, and discouraging every voice and group that had had a hand in his father's disastrous policy. Among the latter were those zealous for the Hebrew God to whom religious purity and national strength were one and indivisible. No prophet spoke with impunity during this time (II Kings 21:16). This was partly due to the new king's views, but also, one suspects, because the people could bear neither a message of judgment nor one of hope. Judgment, if it were that, had been severe; hope was for another day. Yet the future of Judah was not so bleak as it appeared in those grim days.

Manasseh reigned longer than any other ruler in either Hebrew kingdom. During this time the Assyrians under Esarhaddon (681-669 B.C.) and Ashurbanipal (669-633 B.C.) returned continually to the areas around Judah. The Tyrians proved difficult to keep under control; tribute was slow in coming from the Transjordan areas; and Samaria became an armed camp while the staging base farther south in Philistia was once more prepared for an assault upon Egypt. Toward the middle of the century the cherished Mesopotamian dream was realized; Assyrian arms controlled the Nile. Thebes was sacked in 663 B.C., and the pharaoh and his ministers bowed their faces to the ground before Ashurbanipal. Great international events were transpiring. Assyrian records are full of boasts, lists of conquered peoples, and accounts of booty carried in a continuous stream north. Yet in the midst of all this Manasseh's name appears only twice, both times indicating that he was a faithful vassal who did what was required of him. A third reference to Judah is in an incomplete text of a receipt of tribute brought from Palestine. Its date is uncertain, and its statement noting "ten minas (about twelve and a half pounds) of silver from the inhabitants of Judah" indicates a small tribute. It is not clear from the reference whether this was an annual payment, which is unlikely, or for some shorter period of time.

II Chronicles 33:11-13, on the other hand, shows the Assyrians heavy-handed in managing Judahite affairs. On one occasion Manasseh was dragged in chains to Assyria. But on the whole the wounded nation was left to heal and to regain a measure of stature and stability. Worship of the Assyrian gods was, of course, reinstituted even to the extent of building "altars for all the host of heaven in the two courts of the house of the Lord" (II Kings 21:5). This refers to the astral deities whose cult was then popular in Mesopotamia. Other contemporary Assyrian practices also found their way into Judah, for instance those of soothsaying, augury, mediums, and wizards. Not unknown in the Hebrew past, these pagan practices and persons now enjoyed considerable popularity. In addition royal patronage of old Canaanite ways brought a reversal of the religious practices of Hezekiah. Many high places, so recently defiled, were restored as were altars to Baal and Asherah. A carved image of the latter was set up in the Temple itself. The sacral tradition of the Hebrews was neither banned nor discouraged; still its unique character among the other religions of its time was threatened as it seemed that under pressures such as those of Manasseh its God would become one among many. The situation was not unlike that in the northern kingdom under the Omrides, and the writer of II Kings 21:1-15 was not completely amiss in comparing Manasseh to Ahab.

Amon (642-640 B.C.) was twenty-two when he succeeded his father on the throne. After only two years of following Manasseh's policies, he was cut down in the palace by members of his own retinue. Even though Assyria had now clearly overreached herself and was beginning to show signs of disintegration, it was not yet time for rash action. The regicides were executed and Josiah, an eight-year-old son of Amon, was enthroned under the control of advisors who guided the nation on a cautious course, until such time as the international situation clarified and the king came of age (II Kings 21:19-26; II Chronicles 33:21-25).

While Josiah was king (640-609 B.C.), Judah underwent the most extensive reformation of its religion it had at any time during the monarchical period. This process was aided and indeed made possible by the collapse and final destruction of the Assyrian Empire. Even before the death of Ashurbanipal in 633 B.C., Egypt had been united under a strong pharaoh. Closer home, Babylon under Nabopolasser had become independent once more. This time the Assyrians would not be able to subdue them. Throughout the reign of Josiah, Babylon was marshaling the strength which by 609 B.C. would cause it to replace Assyria as the dominant force in the ancient East. As these events took shape, Assyria first sought to use Judah as a buffer against resurgent Egypt, and then abandoned the area altogether leaving Judah free by default. According to II Chronicles 34:3, in the eighth year of his reign Josiah was able to begin his reforms. Significantly, this was the same year in which Ashurbanipal died.

The need for reform was underscored by the prophecy of Zephaniah whose ministry for the most part took place during the early years of Josiah's reign. According to this prophet, the worship of alien gods was rampant in the land. Like some of his predecessors, the young reforming king sought to root out these foreign and Canaanite practices and to restore purely Hebrew worship. This attempt is reported in some detail in the Bible (II Kings 22:2-23:25; II Chronicles 34:3-35:19). One would hardly think that archaeological evidence of this sort of thing would remain. Yet in 1958, S. Yeivin, the director of the Israeli Department of Antiquities, put forward the interesting idea that some artificial mounds at Manahat near Jerusalem were not ancient burials as had long and widely been assumed, but high places desecrated and stoned during the reformation of Josiah. Beneath piles of rocks were found pavements of flagstones with deposits of ashes and broken animal bones on them. The pavements were raised by a seventeen-sided polygonal ringwall of undressed stone. All the pottery recovered indicated the site was in use in the eighth and seventh centuries B.C. These were certainly not burial mounds (as was once thought), and the date fits the time of Josiah. The enormous conical pile of packed rubble on top of the pavement could easily have been a means of insuring that sacrifices could not be offered there again.

Most important to the reformation and of immeasurable lasting significance was not the destruction of pagan cult objects and shrines, however, but the formal institution of a written law which gave structure to the radical reforms. According to the Bible (II Kings 22:3-13; II Chronicles 34:14-21), while the Temple was being cleansed and repaired an ancient writing was found in the Treasury. This document, which forms the core of the book of Deuteronomy, represented itself as a sermon of Moses. It was, in fact, considerably more contemporary, perhaps from the time of Manasseh or even Josiah. Shot through with the insights of the prophets, it is a priestly attempt to concretize ideal ethical purposes. Among other provisions it decreed the centralization of worship in the Temple in Jerusalem and the destruction of all other shrines, sanctuaries, high places, pillars, altars, and the like (Deuteronomy 12). This institutionalized the centuries-long struggle against non-Hebraic practices in worship and greatly strengthened the hand of those who fought against Canaanite and Assyrian ways. At the same time, the consternation it must have caused to the inhabitants of Josiah's kingdom can only be imagined. The local shrine, Hebrew, Canaanite, or a mixture of the two, was the focus of personal and communal life. To uproot this was to bring about a fundamental change. Still, many have seen in all this a providential preparation for what was soon to come. Scarcely thirty-five years later the Babylonian Exile was a reality, and the Hebrews so far from home, although given almost all the rights of other citizens, were denied their own sanctuary and functioning priests. Because of the Deuteronomic reforms, this blow was not what it might have been, and a new institution, the synagogue, appeared.

With the Assyrians receding and the Egyptian tide not yet at flood stage, Judah under Josiah found itself able to expand, particularly northward, and dreams of a united Israel, not entirely unlike the days of Saul, David, and Solomon, could be realistically entertained. Whether Josiah was able to extend his dominions into Transjordan is an open question. But there is no doubt that substantial areas of the old kingdom of Israel west of the Jordan came into his hands. Bethel with its royal sanctuary was one of the main targets of his religious reforms (II Kings 23:4, 15), and farther north in the Plain of Esdraelon he established Judahite authority at Megiddo (II Kings 23:29; II Chronicles 35:22). At the latter site an excavated large fortress administrative center built over remains from Ahab's time is sometimes credited to Josiah. It is, however, more likely to have been an Assyrian structure used by the king of Judah when he organized the area which extended almost sixty miles farther north, beyond Dan. Under Josiah the Hebrew kingdom was once more "from Dan to Beer-sheba," as in days of old. It included a large stretch of the Mediterranean shore between the Philistine lands in the south and those of the Phoenicians north of Mount Carmel. The Judah-Phoenician border was, as a matter of fact, that established by Solomon in his dealings with Hiram of Tyre many years before (see p. 150). Proof of Judahite presence along the coast was discovered at Mesad Hashav-yahu, a seashore fort west of Jerusalem. From there in 1959 an ostracon was recovered which indicated the fort was once in the hands of Josiah's men.

Days of renewed greatness were few for Judah. In 612 B.C., the Babylonians captured Nineveh, delivering a mortal blow to the already reeling Assyrians. It provided an occasion for many who had suffered at the hands of the Assyrians to vent their exuberant pleasure at seeing the tables turned and captors led captive. Among these was the prophet Nahum:

> Behold, I am against you,
>   says the Lord of hosts,
>   and will lift up your skirts over your face;
> and I will let nations look on your nakedness
>   and kingdoms on your shame.
> I will throw filth at you
>   and treat you with contempt,
>   and make you a gazingstock.
> And all who look on you will shrink from you
>   and say,

> Wasted is Nineveh; who will bemoan her?
>   whence shall I seek comforters for her?
>
> Nahum 3:5-7

Hoping to avoid annihilation and looking in growing desperation for some way to stem the resolute advance of the Babylonians, the Assyrians fell back toward the west. Pharaoh Necho (609-593 B.C.), one of the survivors of the Assyrian sack of Egypt, now found it in his interest to lend aid to his former conquerors lest Babylonian power sweep into Syria and Palestine where a revived Egypt once again had ambitions. Marching along *The Way of the Sea* to join Assyrian forces opposing the Babylonians in the Carchemish-Haran area, the Egyptians of necessity passed through Judah's new northern territory. For reasons which are not entirely clear to us at this distance, Josiah decided to try to block the passage of the Egyptian army. Near Megiddo, *The Way of the Sea* turns inland around Mount Carmel and passes through narrow, winding valleys. At this relatively defensible spot Josiah determined to make his stand. According to the narrative of II Chronicles, Necho sought to avoid battle and sent to Josiah saying, "What have we to do with each other, king of Judah?

The pass between Megiddo and Taanach. Through here the Way of the Sea turns inland to avoid Mount Carmel. This "Thermopylae of Palestine" was the scene of many battles in ancient times, including the one in which Josiah fell in 609 B.C.

I am not coming against you this day, but against the house with which I am at war" (35:21). Josiah paid no heed and arrayed his troops for battle, even disguising himself and mounting a war chariot in order to be in the thick of the fray. The Egyptians, forced to fight their way through, carried the day. In the course of the battle Josiah was struck down by archers from the Nile. Removed from the conflict he was transferred to his own chariot which hastened toward Jerusalem. II Kings 23:30 says he was dead before the royal carriage left Megiddo. Good king Josiah was buried among the tombs of his fathers while Judah, led by Jeremiah, lamented.

Fitting were the laments, too, not only for Josiah, but for Judah as well. The stage was now set, and the last act of the drama of national independence was about to be played out. Necho and his allies were not successful in preserving a viable Assyrian presence in Mesopotamia. The Babylonians could not be dislodged from Haran; Assyrian power was at an end. Necho's strategy paid off handsomely for Egypt, however, and for a time his fortunes did not suffer. Forced to withdraw somewhat he was nevertheless able to hold sway over much of the land west of the Euphrates. This included Judah. Jehoahaz (609 B.C.), who only three months before had ascended Josiah's throne, was summoned to Riblah in Syria to appear before the pharaoh who was returning home. Necho deposed this twenty-three-year-old king, put him in irons, and sent him hostage to Egypt. In his place he established Eliakim, another son of Josiah. Eliakim, who took the throne name of Jehoiakim, was saddled with the necessity of raising tribute of a hundred talents of silver and one talent of gold to pay the man who had placed the royal scepter in his hand and the crown upon his head. This obligation forced Jehoiakim to levy a heavy tax in Judah (II Kings 23:13-35; II Chronicles 36:1-4).

Judah was an Egyptian vassal. Although no definite proof can be given, her borders seem to have been reduced to what they had been before Josiah. Internally, religious reforms, so lately heralded as the bulwark of nationalism, were now seen by some as the reason for national disaster (Jeremiah 44:17). Whether he held this view or not, the king cared little for preserving the religious work of his father. A pagan reaction spread through the population upon whom swift-moving events crowded with accelerating confusion.

In the midst of all this, Jehoiakim's major concern was to build a new palace. Not only so, but he used forced labor since the royal treasury could not stand the expense of paying workers' wages. For the sensitive and insightful Jeremiah, already offended by the king's religious views or lack of them, this was the last straw. With the nation's political and financial situation worsening, and with social ills calling out for justice, Jehoiakim, in Jeremiah's view, offered only ineptitude and irresponsibility:

> Woe to him who builds his house
>   by unrighteousness,
> and his upper rooms by injustice;
> who makes his neighbor serve him
>   for nothing,
> and does not give him his wages.
>   Jeremiah 22:13

After further excoriating the king by contrasting his dishonesty, oppression, and violence with the compassion and justice of his father, the prophet continues:

Therefore thus says the Lord concerning Jehoiakim the son of Josiah, king of Judah:

> "They shall not lament for him,
>   saying,
> 'Ah my brother!' or 'Ah sister!'
> They shall not lament for him,
>   saying,
> 'Ah lord!' or 'Ah his majesty!'

203

With the burial of an ass he shall be buried, dragged and cast forth beyond the gates of Jerusalem."

Jeremiah 22:18-19

Jehoiakim built his palace in spite of financial troubles and prophets. Over 2500 years later, archaeologists recovered that same palace from the Palestinian soil. At Ramat Rahel (biblical Beth-Haccherem?), on the high mountain ridge halfway between Jerusalem and Bethlehem, five seasons of excavations between 1954 and 1962 established almost beyond all doubt that this was the location of substantial royal buildings of the late Judahite period. Not occupied before the eighth or seventh century B.C., the complex in question was burned by the Babylonians in 587 or perhaps even 597. When during this time is there occasion for, or reference to, construction of greatly expanded royal quarters? The answer is given by Jeremiah in his condemnation of Jehoiakim. Judging from the magnificence suggested by the remains, Jeremiah was justified in speaking out against such extravagance in times of national crisis.

This singular fortress palace, situated high enough to see Jerusalem two miles away, was enclosed by a rectangular casemate wall some 300 feet by 165 feet. The quality of this wall is extremely fine, rivaling that known at Samaria. It is, in fact, of the same type of construction and workmanship. Samaria would, of course, have been in ruins at the time of the building of Ramat Rahel, but Solomon's Jerusalem was immediately available and was of the same craftsmanship as Omri's capital. Was the splendidly cut, carefully laid stone of Ramat Rahel in imitation of the techniques of Hiram's Phoenicians? If so, is it a clue to Solomon's city, now beyond recovery?

Similarity to Samaria and to other well-known royal buildings, such as those at Megiddo and Hazor, does not end with the perfection of the walls. Ramat Rahel has

yielded more proto-Aeolic capitals than any other site except Megiddo. These carved tops of columns are known from Samaria where it is thought they lined the inside of the ornamental city gate (see pp. 163-4). Whatever their exact location in the various cities, they were, so far as we know, associated with royal structures. Miss Kenyon's recent discovery of two such capitals on Ophel at Jerusalem has led to the suggestion that all the building activity of Solomon was not restricted to the platform area where the Temple and Palace stood. The remains at Ramat Rahel, however, show that it is not necessary to date structures early on the basis of fine Phoenician or Phoenician-type design and craftsmanship. On the contrary, Ramat Rahel indicates that in the case of royal buildings, at least, the techniques and designs introduced into Israel by Solomon and Omri changed little if any during the lifetime of the Hebrew kingdoms.

A further Phoenician feature in Jehoiakim's palace, and one which may be reflected in Jeremiah's reference to decorated windows (22:14), is a partial balustrade recovered from the ruins. This consisted of a row of small columns with carved petals (known in the Old Testament as "lily work") and topped by small proto-Aeolic capitals. While the discovery of the actual balustrade is unique in Middle Eastern archaeology, its use is well known from Old Testament references (Judges 5:28; II Kings 9:30; II Chronicles 6:16; Proverbs 7:6; and others) and from pictures on ivory plaques which have been found at several places including a few in Palestine (Samaria, for example) and Syria and a number in Mesopotamia. It functioned not merely as architectural decoration, but also as a safety factor to prevent falling from an upper window.

Yohanan Aharoni, the director of excavations at Ramat Rahel, thinks that two other features identified by Jeremiah have been found. The prophet mentions that the ceilings of the palace were cedar and that vermilion paint was used. On top of the recovered capitals are holes into which wooden beams (cedar?) may have been set. On some of the stones there are traces of red paint. Perhaps the conspicuous decoration of the palace made a lasting impression on all who saw it—including the prophet who scathed the king who built it.

In the fourth year of Jehoiakim's reign (605 B.C.), the balance of power in the area shifted radically. Nebuchadrezzar, then a prince of Babylon, defeated the Egyptians at Carchemish [11] and drove them away from the Euphrates, through Syria and Palestine, and back upon the Nile. "And the king of Egypt did not come again out of his land," says II Kings 24:7. Upon the death of Nabopolasser, Nebuchadrezzar was made king. He moved swiftly down the coast, conquered Ashkelon and established Babylonian power along the Brook of Egypt, a riverbed traditionally the northeastern border of Egypt. With a massive hostile army literally on three sides, Judah was thrown into dismay. Jeremiah, harassed and threatened with death by certain Jerusalemites, saw that among other things this could only mean war for Judah, faithful vassal to Egypt (46:2-28). Habakkuk, not having the disloyal image attached to Jeremiah, was able to speak somewhat more openly. Speaking of God's action in raising an enemy against evildoers in Israel, he described the potential calamity whose pall cast a lengthening shadow over the land:

> For lo, I am rousing the Chaldeans,
>   that bitter and hasty nation,
> who march through the breadth of
>   the earth,
>   to seize habitations not their own.
> Dread and terrible are they;
>   their justice and dignity proceed
>   from themselves.

[11] Excavating at Carchemish in 1912-1914, C. L. Woolley and T. E. Lawrence showed that the city was burned about the time of this battle.

> Their horses are swifter than
>   leopards,
>   more fierce than the evening
>   wolves;
>   their horsemen press proudly on.
> Yea, their horsemen come from afar;
>   they fly like an eagle swift to
>   devour.
> They all come for violence;
>   terror of them goes before them.
>   They gather captives like sand.
> At kings they scoff,
>   and of rulers they make sport.
> They laugh at every fortress,
>   for they heap up earth and take it.
> Then they sweep by like the wind
>   and go on,
>   guilty men, whose own might is
>   their god!

Habakkuk 1:6-11

In the circumstances Jehoiakim hastily changed his allegiance and pledged his loyalty to Nebuchadrezzar. But he did not make a very good vassal; his heart and hope still lay with Egypt. When in 601 B.C. the Babylonians were fought to a stand-off by Necho in a battle on the Egyptian frontier, Jehoiakim took Babylonian withdrawal as a sign of weakness. He rebelled. Necho had, however, only prevented an invasion of Egypt. He had not crippled Nebuchadrezzar's ambitions in Palestine. While occupied elsewhere for the next three years the Babylonian king harassed Judah by means of his allies and loyal vassals (II Kings 24:2; Jeremiah 35:11). When the time of reckoning came in 597, Jehoiakim was dead. His eighteen-year-old son, Jehoiakin (598-597 B.C.) reigned in his stead.[12] This young man, mentioned on a seal found at Ramat Rahel, reigned only three months. During most of that time, according to the Babylonian Chronicle, Jerusalem lay under siege. In

[12] Jehoiakin was eighteen when crowned, as II Kings 24:8 says, not eight as stated in II Chronicles 36:9. He is mentioned in archaeologically recovered documents from Babylon as having fathered five sons by 592 B.C.

March of 597, the city was surrendered. This act may have saved what was left of Judah. At least it momentarily preserved the capital. Instead of sacking and burning the city and taking vengeance upon its population, Nebuchadrezzar merely deported the king, most of his family, many of the skilled craftsmen, and all those influential leaders who were suspected of being anti-Babylonian. Jehoiakim's brother, Mattaniah, was established in place of his nephew. To his chosen man Nebuchadrezzar gave the throne name of Zedekiah.[13] This king, who reigned over the last decade of Judah's existence (597-586 B.C.), was certainly willing enough to do the bidding of his Babylonian overlords. But he was an unfortunate choice in that he was unable to deal with the smoldering hatred his subjects held for Babylon. Perhaps no one could have done better. At any rate, the situation was hardly improved when Jerusalem was stripped of its treasures, leaders, and skilled men (II Kings 24:13-16). Judah had survived—barely. Yet, instead of being cowed by humiliation, the spirit of the people was thinly veiled defiance. The restoration of Jehoiakin, alive and well in captivity,[14] if not a valid hope was at least a substantial rallying point for the opposition (Jeremiah 28:1-4). The years of Zedekiah's reign were difficult ones in Judah, and in his ninth year, when Egypt offered material aid in an anti-Babylonian cause, the king of Judah could no longer resist the pressure. He rebelled against Nebuchadrezzar to whom he owed his throne.

Once more the Babylonians were in force before the gates of Jerusalem. True to their word on this occasion, the Egyptians marched northward and actually caused the siege of the Judahite capital to be lifted temporarily (Jeremiah 37:5). Yet this did not basically alter the situation, as Jeremiah correctly understood (37:7-10). All was folly from beginning to end. The Egyptians were hardly a match for the Babylonians who soon returned to strangle Jerusalem and destroy Judah. As the capital lay in increasingly pitiable condition, the invaders from the north spread out over the land plundering, destroying, killing, and reducing various fortresses to ashes. At length only three fortified cities remained: Jerusalem, Lachish, and Azekah (Jeremiah 34:7).

From the excavations at Lachish has been recovered one of the most remarkable of all archaeological finds: letters, some of which report the last weeks, perhaps even the last days, of the Babylonian siege of that city and of Azekah. In a room in the city gate on a floor covered with ashes and debris, eighteen fragmentary texts were found in 1935. In 1938 three more were recovered. These ostraca are of first importance in a number of ways. Where a paucity of private written material exists, they have greatly enlarged our knowledge of the Phoenician-Hebrew alphabet in use during the last years of the monarchical period. They also show that writing was the skill not of a very few highly trained persons, but enjoyed wider usage, certainly at least among those in the royal service. These letters are not from or to Jerusalem, but originate in a provincial context and, although dealing mostly with one man, are from a number of hands. These famous "Lachish Letters" suggest, moreover, the original epigraphic form of much of the Old Testament, particularly the books of Kings and a number of the prophetic writings from Amos to Habakkuk and Obadiah. The biblical works would, of course, have been written on rolls of

[13] Zedekiah was Jehoiakin's uncle, as II Kings 24:17 says, and not his brother as stated in II Chronicles 36:10.

[14] Jehoiakin was treated with kingly respect in exile. The statement in II Kings 25:27-30 is supported by archaeological discoveries made in 1925 in the vicinity of the Ishtar Gate at Babylon. Several tablets were recovered which list allotments of oil and grain made to captives between 597 and 570 B.C. Among those enjoying the bounty of the royal treasury was "Yaukin, king of the land of Yahud."

papyrus or even leather (Jeremiah 36:4, 23) and not on broken pottery. Even so, as original documents contemporary with early biblical scrolls, these hastily written letters are invaluable for a study of the paleographic history of the Old Testament.

The content of these extraordinary documents gives a unique view of the tumultuous internal situation in the last days of Judah, days filled with intrigue, accusation, and

Herbert G. May

Azekah (above) was one of the two remaining fortresses defending the southern approaches to Jerusalem. With its fall, dramatically indicated in Lachish letter number four (below), only Lachish stood between the capital and the invaders. Soon the Babylonians were before Jerusalem itself.

fear. One of the letters appears to be a military order from Yaosh, the commander of Lachish, to Hoshaiah who was in charge of an outpost between Lachish and Azekah, twelve miles distant. Fourteen letters are from Hoshaiah to Yaosh. The remaining ones are lists of names or are so fragmentary that no content has satisfactorily been established. Throughout, Hoshaiah seems to be defending himself against some charge, perhaps the loss of a position to the Babylonians, perhaps an intrigue involving his tampering with official correspondence. The question of intrigue is raised not only by the possibility that official dispatches have been read by unauthorized persons, but also by the mention of opposition by a prophet whose name unfortunately is now illegible. Only the last syllable of the prophetic name remains. It could be that of Jeremiah, who was an active protagonist in the struggle against state policy. It could also be that of the unfortunate Urijah who shared Jeremiah's view and spoke openly with increasingly detrimental effect upon the people's morale and willingness to follow the king. Forced to flee for his life, he was spirited out of Egyptian sanctuary by agents of the Judahite king, put to death, and buried without honor (Jeremiah 26:20-23). One of these agents was "Elnathan." Letter III from Lachish speaks of an "Elnatan" who went down to Egypt. Harry Torczyner, primarily responsible for the excavation report publication of the Lachish Letters, speculated that the passage in Jeremiah and the reference in Letter III speak of the same incident and that Hoshayahu was involved in a prophetic conspiracy. Furthermore Torczyner held the opinion that the Lachish Letters were in the room in the gate because there trials were held. This correspondence is what remains of a dossier of evidence in the case of Hoshayahu, charged with treason. Of this there is *at best* circumstantial evidence enhanced by a good deal of informed guesswork. There was considerable opposition to the policies of Jehoiakim, Jehoiakin, and Zedekiah; there can be no doubt of that. Yet the reference to a prophet need not necessarily point to Jeremiah or Urijah since it is by no means certain that either of these is the illegible name. Many other common names in that day are equally possible. Moreover, Elnatan may have gone to plead for Egyptian aid which, in fact, did come in a futile gesture to lift the Babylonian threat. All the same it needs to be said that whatever the considerable weaknesses of Torczyner's view, it has not done violence to the spirit of the times.

The most dramatic of the messages is in Letter IV. On one side of the ostracon Hoshaiah speaks of carrying out orders and replies to an apparent question of Yaosh noting that some important personage, Semachiah by name, has been taken to Jerusalem by one Shemaiah. So far all seems fairly routine. But on the reverse of the sherd are four lines and part of a fifth which bring vividly to life the mortal struggle in which Judah was then engaged. It is a tense moment for the defenders of the outpost. Azekah had either just been overrun or was so close to defeat that the signal fires had gone out. Anxious eyes now looked toward Lachish. "We are watching for the signal-stations of Lachish," writes the apprehensive commander, "according to all the signs which my lord gives, because we do not see (the signals of) Azekah."

How long Lachish was able to hold out after the fall of Azekah is unknown. The site (Tell ed-Duweir) is one of the largest in Palestine, encompassing some eighteen acres.[15] Archaeologists have established that, when the Babylonians stood before the walls over a century after the coming of the Assyrians, the city had not recovered from the destruction wrought by Sennacherib. The

palace had not been rebuilt nor had much of the residential area. If there were major administrative structures after 701 B.C., they have not as yet been uncovered and identified. The massive double casemate walls which greeted the Assyrians and were pulled down to their foundations certainly had not been rebuilt on the same scale. Nebuchadrezzar had to contend with much less. There was, all the same, a system in imitation of the older walls and incorporating a measure of strength. Strangely these defenses were almost all there was of the city between 701 and 587. Unoccupied for some time after its earlier destruction, the city was fortified probably by Manasseh or Josiah with the apparent intention of resettling it and seeking once more to raise it to its former glory. But few houses were built; the palace and administration structures continued to lie in ruins beneath almost three feet of ash. The failure to revivify Lachish may have been one of the results of the turmoil that marked Judah's last century. At any rate, the "city" was little more than a large fortification when Nebuchadrezzar turned to work his vengeance upon Zedekiah. There is, moreover, some evidence from the gate area that the walls had suffered partial burn slightly earlier, perhaps in 597 when the Babylonians first reduced Judah. Erosion at the site makes it difficult to establish the course of events with certainty. Lachish was, in any case, only a shell of its former self and strength when it was struck a final, fatal blow.

Unmistakable is the havoc wrought by that blow. Breaches in the walls, hastily repaired, were torn open once more. At almost every point on the defensive circuit there is evidence of burning, while at the gate the flames were so intense as to make a liquid stream of the masonry which flowed over the road and there cooled and consolidated into a white mass streaked with red. The same ferocity has been noted in the excavations at En-gedi by the Dead Sea, and at Arad, Debir,

[15] Compare this with the eleven and a half acres of Jerusalem and the thirteen acres of Megiddo.

Beth-shemesh, Beth-zur, and Ramat Rahel where the brief career of Jehoiakim's splendid palace was brought to an end. From this archaeological evidence it appears that Judah south of Jerusalem suffered almost total destruction. Lachish was no exception. It did enjoy a brief revival under the Persians a century and a half later, but never regained its former stature. By the second century B.C., it was relatively desolate although undefended settlements continued there until the seventh Christian century.

No longer could the signals of Azekah be seen; the inferno that had been Lachish gradually cooled; only Jerusalem was left. Judah had no allies.[16] In increasingly desperate straits, the capital held out through the winter, the spring, and into summer. "Zion stretches out her hands, but there is none to comfort her," says Lamentations 1:17 commenting on the situation. With the city and its population wasting away around him, the writer of this work turned for solace to the once-splendid Temple. But its abject condition and the human suffering at every hand inspired him only with anguish:

> How the gold has grown dim,
>   how the pure gold is changed!
> The holy stones lie scattered
>   at the head of every street.
>
> The precious sons of Zion,
>   worth their weight in fine gold,
> how they are reckoned as earthen
>   pots,
>   the work of a potter's hands!
>
> Even the jackals give the breast
>   and suckle their young,
> but the daughter of my people has
>   become cruel,
>   like the ostriches in the wilderness.

> The tongue of the nursling cleaves
>   to the roof of its mouth for thirst;
> the children beg for food,
>   but no one gives to them.
>
> Those who feasted on dainties
>   perish in the streets;
> those who were brought up in purple
>   lie on ash heaps.
>
> Happier were the victims of the
>   sword
>   than the victims of hunger,
> who pined away, stricken
>   by want of the fruits of the field.
>
> The hands of compassionate women
>   have boiled their own children;
> they became their food
>   in the destruction of the daughter
>   of my people.
>
> Lamentations 4:1-5, 9-10

In the midst of filth, with starvation beginning to produce cannibalism, Zedekiah was urged by Jeremiah to surrender the city. The king was caught between the supernationalists on the one hand, and those of Jeremiah's persuasion on the other. His independent power of action was sorely eroded by circumstances and the clash of partisan interests. However he turned, his own life was already forfeit (Jeremiah 38:14-23).

In July of 587, the Babylonians breached the walls. Zedekiah's soldiers, perhaps the only people in the city who had eaten in days, fled by night through the gate "by the king's garden," probably a reference to the southeastern side of Ophel (II Kings 25:4; Jeremiah 39:4). They safely slipped past the Assyrian lines. Among those who deserted the city was the king himself who dashed toward the Jordan River apparently trying to reach Ammon, the nearest region opposed to Nebuchadrezzar. Captured near Jericho, Zedekiah was taken to Riblah in Syria where he witnessed the death of his sons, was blinded, placed in chains, and taken to Babylon to die in prison (II Kings 25:2-7; Jeremiah 52:3-11).

---

[16] Tyre was besieged after Jerusalem. There was also an expedition against Ammon. Neither had offered Judah any effective aid earlier. It was a matter of "divided we fall."

The prostrate survivors of the unspeakable horrors of the siege fared little better. Nebuzaradan, the captain of Nebuchadrezzar's personal bodyguard, arrived in Jerusalem a month later with orders to remove the population and destroy the city. With frightening precision this was done. The city was looted. The pillars of bronze, large and small implements, and even the decorations on the walls were stripped from the Temple. Everything of value was taken from Temple, Palace, home, and shop. The city walls were pulled down and fires set. Arresting numerous political, military, and religious leaders, Nebuzaradan sent them to Riblah where they were slain in the presence of the Babylonian king. Eight hundred and thirty-two who escaped this fate were taken away into captivity following those Judahites who had already been ten years beside the waters of Babylon (II Kings 25:8-21; Jeremiah 52:12-29). Jeremiah, treated kindly by the Babylonians and not taken away, did not fail to note that "Nabuzaradan, the captain of the guard, left in the land of Judah some of the poor people who owned nothing, and gave them vineyards and fields at the same time" (Jeremiah 39:10).

Desolate Zion, once splendid, was mourned:

> What can I say for you, to what
> compare you,
> O daughter of Jerusalem?
> What can I liken to you, that I may
> comfort you,
> O virgin daughter of Zion?
> For vast as the sea is your ruin;
> who can restore you?
> Lamentations 2:13

VII: INTO THE NEW TESTAMENT

18. FROM JUDAH TO JUDEA

Jesus was born some six hundred years after the Babylonians overwhelmed Jerusalem. Filled with almost constant warfare and characterized by a succession of foreign rulers, these intervening centuries were turbulent ones for Palestine. The empire of Babylon "dread and terrible," whose "horses are swifter than leopards, more fierce than the evening wolves," lasted less than a half century after its victory in Judah. The Hebrew exiles, who Ezekiel tells us were along the River Chebar (Ezekiel 1:1, 3; 3:15, 23; 10:15, 20, 22; 43:3) and whom archaeology shows also to have been in Nippur and other Mesopotamian cities, were allowed to return to Zion. Cyrus, the Persian who now established his rule from India to the borders of Greece and from southern Russia to the borders of Egypt, reversed the deportation policies of the Assyrians and Babylonians. Instead of transporting peoples and seeking to root out their customs, he returned them to their former lands and encouraged their native ways, particularly in matters of religion. Foreshadowing Roman provincial ad-

ministration, this enlightened monarch believed that a contented people would be less likely to revolt than a population ruthlessly suppressed. On a famous clay cylinder now recovered, Cyrus tells of magnanimity toward former enemies and ends by speaking of the return of various divine images to sanctuaries looted by the Babylonians. In the course of the passage he notes that "I also gathered all their former inhabitants and returned to them their habitations." Ezra, who was probably an official of the Persian government, preserved the edict which allowed the Jews[1] to return to Judah carrying with them sacred vessels from the Temple as well as permission to rebuild the holy edifice so lately destroyed (Ezra 1:2-4).

"When the Lord restored the fortunes of Zion," recalled those who braved the long

[1] Strictly speaking this term becomes applicable only during and after the Exile. While continuity with the pre-exilic Hebrews and their religion is obvious, Judaism—whose adherents are Jews—is a religion characterized by synagogue, rabbi, and authoritative Scripture, all three of which either originated or gained distinctive status during the period of captivity. The word *Jew* is derived from *Yehudi* (Judea) and indicates the descendants of those carried into exile from Judah. It is thus not merely a religious term.

journey, "we were like those who dream. Then our mouth was filled with laughter, and our tongue with shouts of joy" (Psalm 126:1-2). The dream proved to be more nearly a nightmare. Nebuchadrezzar had shattered the country, denuding, depopulating, devastating. In the aftermath, Edomites, Moabites, Ammonites, Philistines, and other ancient foes had crowded in upon a Jerusalem lying broken upon the Judean hills. The curt refusal of Jewish leaders to accept the help of the Samaritans[2] in rebuilding the Temple added yet another enemy to a list already too long. Calamity compounded; hopes for restoration of the Davidic monarchy came to an end when Zerubbabel, Jehoiachin's grandson, proved an inept leader and disappeared from history. Furthermore, the tiny community of the returned found themselves unable by reason of poverty to rebuild the Temple in spite of aid from Persia. Foundations were laid amidst shouts of joy mixed with sobs of old men who either compared the miserable prospect of this edifice with the glory of the former structure they had known, or wept when they recalled the disaster of 587 (Ezra 3:10-13). Foundations there were, but little else. As a measure of prosperity began to be wrested from their few opportunities, the people, joy and zeal dimmed by the heavy hand of reality, thought little of the House of the Lord. First their survival and next their comfort became paramount. Then came the word of the prophet: "Is it a time for you yourselves

to dwell in your paneled houses, while this house (the Temple) lies in ruins?" asked Haggai (1:4). Under his continued urging and that of his more visionary contemporary, Zechariah, the Second Temple was completed and dedicated in March 515 B.C., some twenty-four years after the return.

While not to be compared with the magnificence with which Solomon adorned Zion, this edifice was hardly the wretched structure it is often held to have been. Partly financed by Cyrus' policy of rebuilding destroyed sanctuaries and also by the largesse of Darius (Ezra 6:4, 8), it was large and so well built as to serve as a fairly successful fortress on several occasions over the next five hundred years. The longevity of this Temple[3] and the fact that the Maccabees undertook only strengthening of its defenses and no thoroughgoing rebuilding bespeak of adequacy and also of accumulated splendor. When Pompey captured it in 63 B.C., its treasury contained a king's ransom (see p. 219). Beyond these matters our extant written sources are vague, and, unless other documents are brought to light, we shall be able only to conjecture about this building that served so long and so well. Herod's work in constructing the Temple known to Jesus completely obliterated any architectural feature of the Second Temple yet recognizable.

What is true of the Second Temple is, in fact, true of almost the entire period in which it stood. Palestine from the fall of Judah to the coming of the Greeks under Alexander is relatively unknown to us in any detail. Surprising as it may be, there is little reliable documentary evidence and not a great deal of archaeological material available. Biblical information ends with the work of "the Chronicler": I and II Chronicles, Ezra-

[2] These people were descendants of the mixed population which resulted from the implementation of Assyrian policy in Israel following the conquest of 722 B.C. (II Kings 17:24). The narrowing views of the returned Jewish exiles caused them to view the Samaritans as racially and therefore religiously impure. An extreme position in this matter was taken by Ezra (9, 10) and Nehemiah (13:23-30) and seems to have become normative, although there was opposition as the books of Ruth and Jonah show. The Samaritans responded by opposing further settlement of Jews around Jerusalem and the rebuilding of the Temple. Bitter hostility between the two groups continued into New Testament times.

[3] It stood longer than any other Hebrew Temple. Solomon's building lasted about four hundred years; Herod's less than a century. By comparison, the Dome of the Rock which now occupies the site has remained virtually unchanged for almost twelve hundred years.

The tomb of Cyrus, founder of the Achaemenian dynasty and the man who allowed the Jews to return to Zion, at Pasargadae in Iran.

Nehemiah. These writings, particularly the latter, have provided scholars with matters for endless disagreements. At best the author of this material carries the story down to the middle of the fifth or perhaps even the early fourth century B.C. The books of Ruth and Jonah, in part protests against prevailing racial views, are from this time, as are Job and Ecclesiastes, likewise protests, but challenging current theological ideas and formulations. In any case, none of these books adds to our detailed knowledge of the course of events. The same is true of the somewhat more abundant apocryphal and pseudepigraphical writings. Materials from Mesopotamia and Egypt increasingly enhance our understanding of Jewish communities there. But it is not until 175 B.C., at least two centuries after the Chronicler, that literary works speak once more of historical events in Palestine. Yet these—I and II Maccabees—cover only thirty-eight years. Daniel, the youngest book of the Old Testament, was also composed about this time or shortly before and encouraged godly martyrs to hold fast to their confession, sure in the knowledge of their reward and the downfall of the wicked. For the last years

of the Hasmonean rule and the days thereafter our primary witness is Josephus,[4] the turncoat Jewish general, whose Wars and Antiquities do not always or even often commend themselves to modern historians as being entirely trustworthy.

Archaeologically there are sufficient remains to indicate that Palestine was focus for the vicissitudes of empires which crowded upon one another in the years following the fall of Babylon. The Persians, the Greeks, the Ptolemies, the Seleucids, and finally the Romans swept back and forth over the land, not merely conquering and destroying, but in some cases building and even glorifying. Yet at first there was little building and less glory. So destructive had been the Babylonian conquest that Palestine did not recover for several centuries. This seems particularly to have been the case south of Jerusalem. Lachish, perhaps a singular exception, was revived during the Persian period as an administrative center. A fifth century B.C. repair of the Hebrew walls and erection of a splendid house on this scarred site were probably not Persian, however, but the work of Geshem of Arabia.[5] This man,

[4] Flavius Josephus was a Jewish general and historian. Of Maccabean descent, he was born ca. A.D. 37 and died early in the second century. Commander in Galilee during the First Revolt (A.D. 66-73), he won Vespasian's favor after being captured by the Romans. Titus made use of his services during the siege of Jerusalem in 70. After the war he received large estates and was able to devote himself to writing two massive works, Concerning the Jewish Wars and The Antiquities of the Jews. The Wars, in seven volumes, details the period from Antiochus Epiphanes and the outbreak of the Maccabean War to the close of the First Revolt. Antiquities, in twenty volumes, covers the history of the Hebrew people from earliest biblical times to the eve of the events of A.D. 66. An eyewitness to many events described in the Wars, he drew on a variety of sources for Antiquities. Both works were written for Roman readers (in Greek!). Josephus sought not only to justify himself for his part in the Revolt, but made a brilliant apology for the Jewish people. The Revolt, in his view, was the work of an extremist minority that was in no way motivated by heritage or by traditional Jewish religion.
[5] Geshem was King of Kedar. He is mentioned on an inscription found at Hegea in Arabia.

The workmanship and materials used in depicting this soldier on the palace frieze at Susa justifies Darius the Great's claim to have brought artisans and the finest materials from various parts of the world in order to do justice to the glory and power of the Persian Empire.

like Sanballat of Samaria and Tobiad of Ammon, sought, with some success, to carve his own little empire out of what had formerly been the kingdoms of Israel, Judah, Edom, and Moab.

Even in a generally penurious period archaeological material from fifth- and fourth-century B.C. Palestine is strikingly meager. Various locations have yielded a number of inscribed jar handles, some coins after the Greek style, a few silver bowls, and a considerably larger collection of other vessels and pottery—not much when compared with the recovered artifacts from other times. This very lack, significant in itself, indicates the poverty and hardship of the time. Yet to the trained eye the few items recovered yield cultural information out of proportion to their numbers. It is clear from them that Greek influence, popularly thought to have come with the conquests of Alexander the Great, was well established in Palestine in the centuries prior to the coming of his armies and the settlement of his veterans on the soil. From the increasing abundance of Aramaic both on jar handles and in some biblical writings (Jeremiah 10:11; Ezra 4:8–6:18; 7:12-26; Daniel 2:4b–7:28), we can see that in this period this official language of the Persian Empire was gradually replacing Hebrew as the native tongue of Palestine. Moreover, certain of the inscriptions on jar handles taken together with coins bearing the word *Yehud* (the Persians used this Aramaic name for the area) are thought by many scholars to indicate a semi-autonomous status for the small Jewish community huddled in the hills around Jerusalem.

In 334 B.C. Alexander the Great began his swift conquest of the ancient east and much more besides. At Tyre, after a siege of seven months, he built a causeway over which to assault the former island stronghold. With the fall of this center of Phoenician power came hegemony over all Palestine and an open road to Egypt.[6] Primarily interested in the Land of the Nile at this time, he did not neglect his new territories along the Jordan. Loath to give offense to any religion, he was particularly kindly disposed toward the Jews and did much to cultivate their loyalty. In addition, Samaria, of greater strategic importance to him than Jerusalem, became the home of Andromachus whom Alexander appointed governor of his newly organized province of Syria-Palestine. Unfortunately for Andromachus, and for Samaria as it turned out, the local inhabitants set fire to his official residence burning the governor to death. Josephus says they were motivated by anger over privileges granted to the Jews. They may have been, or there may have been other causes instead of or in addition to this. Whatever the case, Alexander, now in Egypt, responded with characteristic decisiveness. Samaria was destroyed, its population transported into slavery, and some six thousand veterans of the Macedonian army settled on and around the Hill of Shemer. Henceforth, until the coming of the Arabs in the seventh Christian century, the city was Greek or Greco-Roman.

Frank Cross of Harvard University is of the opinion that the spectacular discoveries in the Wadi Daliyeh in 1962/63 are to be associated with the death of Andromachus and the destruction and resettlement of Samaria.[7] In the spring of 1962, some Ta'-amireh Bedouin offered for sale through their perennial middleman Kando (see p. 255) a number of papyrus fragments. The material came to the attention of Yusef Sa'ad of the Palestine Archaeological Museum who shared them with Father de Vaux of the *École Biblique* and Paul Lapp, then director of the American School. Lapp identified the writing on one fragment as about 375 B.C.[8] After considerable study all the materials from the Wadi Daliyeh proved to be dated between 375 and 335 B.C. Some documents even bear precise dates. For example, the largest papyrus roll has the words: ". . . on the twentieth day of Adar, year 2 . . . the accession year of Darius the king, in Samaria. . . ." The date is March 18, 335 B.C., and on that day, according to this document, a slave named Yehohanan was sold to Yehonur by Hananiah. Interestingly, all three names contain the designation of the Hebrew God. Also of importance, these documents predate almost all, if not all, the materials from the Qumran caves.

Through purchase from the Bedouin and excavation of the cave by Lapp, parts of approximately forty documents are in the find.[9] About half this number are substantial. Some are mere fragments. None is complete. Samaria seems to have been the origin of all of them. They are legal and administrative writings occasionally bearing such well-known names as Sanballat and Nehemiah (no specific references to the biblical figures of the same names).

The content of the documents taken in conjunction with some of the artifacts from the cave where they were found indicates persons of some wealth. Since the cave (Mugharat Abu Sinjeh) is in the desolate wilderness about nine miles north of Jericho and some seven miles west of the Jordan River, questions have been raised of how these documents and the various ornaments,

---

[6] Gaza alone proved a serious obstacle of Alexander's march into Egypt. The city was able to withstand the Macedonian for two months before falling to the twenty-four-year-old genius who never knew military failure.

[7] Frank Moore Cross, Jr., "The Discovery of the Samaria Papyri," *The Biblical Archaeologist*, 26, no. 4 (1963): 110-21.

[8] His hurried judgment proved to be quite accurate. Further study showed the particular material on which he worked to come from the reign of Artaxerxes III (358-338 B.C.).

[9] In addition to written fragments, Lapp and his fellow workers recovered seal rings (three of gold), other personal jewelry, bits of cloth, remains of food stores, and quantities of pottery. A number of bullae (seals for official documents) were also found. Some 128 bullae from this cave are now in the Palestine Archaeological Museum.

including gold rings, got there. There is also the matter of the perhaps two or three hundred skeletons in the vast cave (it extends over 210 feet into the cliffside). Cross thinks the answer to such questions lies in the death of Andromachus, which was not merely murder but the first sign of revolt in the area. Alexander, as was his habit, acted personally and quickly. Having punished those guilty persons whom he had caught, and having destroyed Samaria, he went to Babylon leaving Perdiccas to round up the rest of the implicated Samarians and to rebuild the city as a Macedonian colony. Many patricians escaped the earlier massacre by fleeing down the Wadi Farah and into the terrible wilderness just slightly to the south. The Wadi Daliyeh, so difficult of access,[10] became the hiding place of those people whose status and affluence is attested by their gold, seals, and by the contents of the documents from Mugharat Abu Sinjeh. Perhaps betrayed by a fellow Samarian, they were mercilessly slaughtered. Hence the large number of random skeletons.

The materials from the Wadi Daliyeh are of considerable importance in illuminating an otherwise almost completely dark period in Palestinian life. Together with archaeological evidence from Samaria and Shechem, they show how events transpired to make Samaria a Hellenistic island and a center for carrying out the purposes of Alexander the Great.

Alexander dreamed of a unity of the world, a universal brotherhood of man based upon a common cultural bond—Greek language and learning. And one of his methods for implementing this was to establish Greek-style cities at various places, settle his veterans in them, and marry these men to native wives. By so doing he hoped to create islands of Hellenistic culture which would in time influence the surrounding areas. He is said to have founded over seventy such cities of which about twenty-five have been positively identified. Some were military camps having a history not dissimilar to some cities of the American frontier such as Dodge City, Leavenworth, or Fort Smith. Others, Alexandria in Egypt being the most famous example, were of completely new foundation. Still a third type was older cities refurbished, rebuilt, and endowed with Greeks and with Hellenistic institutions.[11] Marisa (Tell Sanda-hannah), about fourteen miles west of Hebron, and Samaria are known Palestinian examples of this last. Marisa reached its highly developed Hellenistic character slightly later, perhaps in the mid-third century B.C. Samaria, on the other hand, became a thoroughly Hellenistic city as a result of the action of Alexander himself. The summit, crowned by a fort, and a good deal of the gently falling eastern slope were occupied by smallish structures, likely houses. Two large and obviously important buildings have been discovered; their use remains unknown. Black-glazed ware characteristic of Athens and widely imitated among devotees of Greek culture was in abundance. This was true not merely of the more highly prized ornamental pieces, but of commonplace items of everyday use such as cooking pots, lamps, and so forth. In addition over two thousand Rhodian and other stamped jar handles were found, indicating that Aegean wines had a ready market here. But the most spectacular reminders of Alexander's presence and influence and "the finest monument of the Hellenistic age in Palestine" are massive round towers built

[10] Some thought Lapp would be unable to excavate there unless he were supplied by helicopter. A circuitous route was found, however, which allowed donkeys to bring in the needed materials.

[11] The Seleucid successors to Alexander in Syria shared his dream and continued many of his policies, including that of establishing cities as centers of Greek culture. The attempt of Antiochus IV to do this at Jerusalem was one of the causes of the Maccabean War. I Maccabees is an almost contemporary source for this attempt and shows the considerable division among the local population over the issue of hellenizing. Antiochus was not without his Jewish supporters, especially and perhaps surprisingly among the priesthood.

into older defensive structures. Noted by the Harvard Expedition before World War I, examples were not laid bare until the British School of Archaeology worked there from 1931 to 1935. Built into Ahab's then five-hundred-year-old Israelite wall, the remarkable tower on the northwest excavated in 1935 is over forty-two and a half feet in diameter. At one point nineteen courses of carefully hewn and fitted stone rise over twenty-eight feet. When first completed it was somewhat taller, as its rough top and two other towers dug by Paul Lapp and the Jordanian Department of Antiquities in 1966 suggest. These towers, by the city gate on the west, have a small portion of Hellenistic wall running northward and traceable for over one hundred and fifty feet. It is possible that Hellenistic Samaria was enlarged along the lines of the known Roman extension. Much of the Hellenistic work was destroyed by later construction, particularly by that of Herod the Great who lavished much attention, money, and energy upon this city where he was married (see p. 238). There is also no question that much of the Greek work at Samaria was removed by the Romans who greatly valued the site and carried on extensive building activities there. For example, on the northern slope of the summit opposite the Greek fort, there are remains of a Roman temple dedicated to Kore and the Dioscuri. Beneath it archaeologists have discerned a temple to Isis dating from Hellenistic times. There is little doubt that Samaria in the Greek period was a cosmopolitan island, a symbol of universal culture in the midst of a vast provincial sea. Whatever influence this particular city had in liberalizing the life and attitudes of the people of the surrounding area was offset by the offense it presented to many whose particularistic religious outlook and sense of nationalism was outraged by this expression of paganism and foreign rule. Little wonder that John Hyrcanus, builder of Jewish empire in

the Maccabean period, made Samaria an object of peculiar hostility, taking and destroying it in 107 B.C. after a siege of two years.

When Alexander died in 323 B.C., his dream unfulfilled, the empire taken by arms and abortively consolidated by culture rapidly broke up. This process, noted in the enigmatic language of Daniel 8:8, resulted for Palestine in almost two centuries of continuing unrest. The area became an arena for the clashing ambitions of Alexander's generals in Egypt and Syria. Ptolemy I, who seized the Nile breadbasket, betrayed his friend Seleucus Nicator with whom he was allied against other Macedonian officers who wished to keep Alexander's empire intact under their leadership. Seleucus, who ruled in Syria, was to get Palestine. But Ptolemy, sensing the military importance of the land for the defense of Egypt, did not remove his armies after fighting in the north. Wise beyond his *ca.* thirty-five years, possessed of personal courage, imagination, unscrupulous generosity, and aflame with a desire to fulfill Alexander's dream, Seleucus thought it more important to get on with the work of hellenization than to contest his "friend who took more than his share."

Loathsome as the Egyptian-Greek overlordship may have been to the Jews of Palestine, it was, for all its materialistic emphasis, better for them than that of the Seleucids. Not that the dictatorial harshness of Ptolemaic Egypt was worthy to be compared with the more enlightened world of Seleucid Syria; yet the northern rulers were bent on hellenization as a way to brotherhood and latterly for more base purposes. For the Jews this raised the specter of assimilation, the extinction of uniqueness. So long as taxes came in from Palestine and all was quiet and militarily secure, the Ptolemies left the people more or less alone. Attempts at thoroughgoing hellenization of Palestine were postponed until after the battle of Pancas in 198 B.C. when Antiochus III ("the Great") added Palestine to his Syrian kingdom. Thirty-four years later under the rule of his less-wise son, Antiochus IV ("Epiphanes"), the Maccabean War began in a Jewish attempt to halt and then to overthrow a deliberate, harsh, and total policy of assimilating the culture and religion of Palestine with other oriental and Greek elements.

Few undertakings have begun so inauspiciously, succeeded so brilliantly, or come to such a sorry end as the Maccabean revolt. Religiously motivated, it achieved undreamed-of political success and foundered on imperial ambitions and dynastic squabbles. At the last it had irreparably fragmented the Palestinian Jewish community and brought about occupation by the Romans. It began as a struggle for religious separatism. Given the exclusivistic nature of Judaism and the ecumenical nature of Hellenism, friction was inevitable: one was a direct contradiction of the other. Under certain conditions creative coexistence was possible, as the large Jewish community in the midst of the Hellenistic metropolis of Alexandria testifies. Yet in Palestine the situation was entirely different. Whatever the influence of urban Hellenism on areas immediately adjacent, the countryside as a whole saw a dull and obstinate clinging to ancestral ways—not merely in Palestine, but throughout the entire ancient east where immemorial folk ways remained relatively unchanged until the intrusion of transistor radios, rapid mobility, and other "blessings" of modern times. So long as there was no thorough, consistent effort to overthrow these ways, the Jews, forced to give up neither language, racial ties, nor ancestral religion, lived in peace. When Antiochus IV, smarting from a Roman refusal to allow him to fulfill his dreams of empire, decided to stamp out Judaism which he correctly saw as a barrier to hellenization, revolt erupted in Palestine.

Mattathias Maccabee and his five sons waged an incredibly successful struggle against Syria until each in turn was struck down. But by the time of the death of the last son, Simon, in 135 B.C., the land had been wrested from the Syrian-Greeks and the stage was set for the conquests of John Hyrcanus (126-104 B.C.). He extended a burgeoning kingdom into the Negeb, beyond the Jordan, to the Mediterranean coast, and far north into Samaria and even into parts of Galilee. In spite of growing conflicts between Sadducees and Pharisees which eventually caused civil war, John left his son Aristobulus a prosperous kingdom. In the one year of his reign (104-103 B.C.) this man conquered most of the rest of Galilee and began a crash program to settle Jews there. Before his early death, Sepphoris had become a completely Jewish town among others. Alexander Jannaeus (103-76 B.C.), brother and successor to Aristobulus, presided over a kingdom "from Dan to Beer-sheba," in addition to the Transjordanian heights. As so often in the past, however, at its apogee the Hebrew state contained the seeds of internal disintegration. Alexander, beset by religious and political struggles with the Sadducees and Pharisees, used extreme cruelty to suppress what was no less than a state of rebellion. His widow, Salome Alexandra, was able to contain the centripetal forces for ten years after her husband's death in 76 B.C. But when she passed from the scene, each contending party found a champion within the royal house and by civil war sought to determine whether Hyrcanus II or Aristobulus II would mount the throne. Jerusalem fell under siege from a Jewish army.[12] Pompey, the Roman general then campaigning in the east, commanded the two contenders to order a truce and to appear before him. They obeyed. Hyrcanus was favored by Pompey because, some said, he was the weaker. While Hyrcanus was certainly passive of character, this reasoning is probably parti-

[12] Nabatean troops of King Aretas III supporting Hyrcanus were also involved.

san slander. As elder brother he was the rightful heir.[13] No matter, Aristobulus determined to fight rather than accept the Roman's judgment. Pompey was not long in teaching him how unwise it was to disobey a Roman general who had an army in the field. Surrounded at the Alexandrium, a summer palace fortress in the northern Jordan Valley, Aristobulus surrendered and with his family was exiled to Rome. Some of his followers (including his sons) holding Jerusalem chose to continue resistance. Aided by supporters of Hyrcanus within the walls, the Romans quickly secured almost all the city. Only the Temple, a veritable fortress after Hasmonean additions (I Maccabees 4: 60), was unconquered. For three months it withstood siege until in the early autumn of 63 B.C. it too fell to the legions. Pompey personally inspected the holy precinct, entering the Temple and even the Holy of Holies. On his orders nothing was touched, not even the treasury which at that time contained over two thousand talents.[14] The final onslaught, fiercely contested, had brought death to many of the defenders, but at least the Temple, its appointments, and its treasury had been spared.[15]

The Hasmonean kingdom fared less well. Hyrcanus was allowed to exercise high-priestly authority, but civil government was placed in the hands of an Idumean, Antipater, Herod's father and "a man," says Josephus, "distinguished for piety, justice and devotion to his country." The Roman general meanwhile proceeded to dismember the kingdom, assigning various parts to different administrative control. Judea shrank once more to the central highlands, although a portion of the Transjordanian heights was retained. Most serious of all, the Romans had come to stay. In the Roman civil war which began shortly thereafter, the Jews in general and Palestine in particular profited considerably since Caesar and his successors, victors in the fraternal combat, had courted and received Jewish support in the struggle against the Republic. Yet civil power in Palestine eluded Jewish hands. Caesar himself conferred upon Antipater Roman citizenship, strengthened his authority, and did not object to appointment of Antipater's two sons, Phasael and Herod, to be governors of Jerusalem and Galilee respectively. Herod's later friendship with Marc Antony, a result of the close ties between his family and that of Caesar, almost proved the future king's undoing. Antony found himself on the losing end of the continuing civil war from which Octavian—Augustus Caesar—emerged as the sole ruler of Rome and her empire. Yet Herod, consummate politician and man of considerable ability, survived even this and went on to earn the name by which he is known to history: "Herod the Great."

Archaeological remains of the Hasmonean period are scarce, bespeaking perhaps the considerable drain on energies and funds demanded by almost constant warfare. A few sites which are mentioned prominently in I and II Maccabees and in the writings of Josephus have been excavated and some of these—Beth-zur, Shechem, Sepphoris, and Jerusalem for example—have yielded evidence of the tumultuous times. Beth-zur, on the watershed ridge four and a half miles north of Hebron,[16] was an important center

---

[13] There is some evidence that Aristobulus had tried to seize the throne from his mother a year before her death. In this he was supported by the Sadducees who later backed him against his brother. Hyrcanus would probably have turned over the throne to his younger brother had it not been for Antipater who provided backbone for the otherwise spineless king.

[14] Whether silver or gold we do not know. It was an enormous sum in either case since a talent is equal to 75.558 pounds U. S. avoirdupois.

[15] Ten years later the accumulated wealth lavished upon this building by Jewish piety proved too much for Crassus, a Roman popularly known from Shakespeare's *Julius Caesar*. He pillaged the Temple.

[16] Kirbet et-Tubeiquah, ancient Beth-zur, is 3,325 feet above sea level and is the highest ruined city in Palestine. See p. 122 for a general description of the area around Hebron and Beth-zur.

before the Hebrew settlement in the land (Joshua 15:58) and was one of the fifteen cities fortified by Rehoboam at the dissolution of the United Monarchy (II Chronicles 11:7; see p. 155). In Hasmonean times it reached its zenith in importance and was fought over more than once. His victory here in 164 B.C. allowed Judas Maccabee to proceed to Jerusalem sixteen miles to the north where he rededicated the Temple, an event henceforth commemorated among Jews as the Feast of Hanukkah. According to I Maccabees 4, Judas fortified both the Temple mount in Jerusalem and Beth-zur. But his occupation of both was short-lived. Within three years Bacchides, the Syrian-Greek commander, was firmly in control of most of Judea and had driven the insurgents from their stronghold in the Gophna Hills northeast of Jerusalem into the Judean desert south of Tekoa. Here, like Bar-Kochba and his revolutionary followers two centuries later, they lived among the rocks and caves. To guard the approaches to Jerusalem and contain the uprising, Bacchides strengthened a number of existing forts and built others. Among those whose defenses were improved was Beth-zur, particularly vulnerable as it was nearest to the new center of rebel activity.

In 1931 and again in 1957, excavations were undertaken at Beth-zur mainly under the direction of Ovid R. Sellers of McCormick Theological Seminary in Chicago. The earlier dig, in which Sellers was assisted by W. F. Albright, established that the Ptolemies and Seleucids had made extensive use of the town, perhaps as an administrative center. When Judas strengthened it, he did so by rebuilding parts of the ancient walls, some as early as the Middle Bronze Age (2100-1550 B.C.). In addition he added a second wall, roughly built but of considerable strength. Within this double stronghold the central fortress was rebuilt. This work probably suffered much damage in Bacchides'

Excavations on Mount Gerizim in 1966 uncovered the Samaritan temple below the foundations of a Roman temple.

capture of the city, since about three years later he constructed large fortifications there without reference to the earlier plan. Within twenty years this too was severely battered by Simon Maccabee who recaptured the strategic point. When Alexander Jannaeus extended his frontiers farther south around 100 B.C., Beth-zur lost its military importance and its garrison of soldiers. The town declined and was soon abandoned.

Excavations at Shechem in the north reveal a similar history of violence. When Alexander the Great destroyed Samaria in 331 B.C. and settled it with his Macedonian veterans, the native people of the area looked once more, as many of their ancestors had done, to the ancient and honored city of Shechem which they now rebuilt and refortified. Apparently at the same time they constructed their famous temple on the pinnacle of Mount Gerizim, a sanctuary dramatically discovered in 1966 by a group of American archaeologists primarily concerned with the work far below at Shechem. From excavated evidence including datable coins, it is clear that Shechem suffered in the wars that followed Alexander's death. Its walls destroyed in these struggles, the city nonetheless continued to be heavily occupied and had notable prosperity. About 128 B.C., according to Josephus, John Hyrcanus fell upon the city, destroying it and the Samaritan temple on Gerizim. A destruction layer followed by immediate reoccupation is thought by those who dug the site to be evidence of this event. Approximately twenty years later havoc was again wrought on the population and its town. At this time tons of earth were used to cover much of the fortifications with the desired result of rendering the place utterly defenseless. This may have been the work of John Hyrcanus when he moved against Samaria in 107 B.C. Having had to take Shechem twice, he may have determined to see to it that he would not have to do so again. Whether it was Hyrcanus or some other Hasmonean, the literal burial of its walls and northwest gate successfully reduced this ancient and distinguished city to an insignificant village which it has remained for two thousand years to this day.

Sepphoris, a city four miles from Nazareth, is not mentioned in the Bible. Since it was at best thinly populated and of little importance prior to Hellenistic times, it is not surprising that it is not noted in the Old Testament. But it was a Jewish city of considerable importance during the time of Jesus, and afterward was second only to Jerusalem in all Palestine. Its striking location[17] and visibility from Nazareth has led

at least one scholar to say that Jesus' words in Matthew 5:14 ("a city set on a hill cannot be hid") arose from his frequent sight of this brilliant city crowning a prominent hill near his childhood home. This is a matter of merest conjecture. The surprising fact is that Sepphoris is not mentioned by name in the New Testament either.

Josephus was the first to write of the city, and he refers to it during the reign either of Aristobulus or of Alexander Jannaeus when the Maccabees extended their sway over Galilee (ca. 104-100 B.C.). Archaeology shows the city was founded as a major site not many years previously. Just when is a matter of conjecture since, unfortunately, the considerable adornment of the city by Herod Antipas in the middle of the first Christian century removed much evidence of earlier times. But whatever does remain, e.g. the contents of tombs and cisterns, does not indicate anything of significance before the Hellenistic period. It was, at any rate, a major center of first-century B.C. Jewish life in Galilee, a role which expanded a century later after the destruction of Jerusalem by the Romans.

Maccabean power had been felt in Galilee as early as 144 B.C. when Jonathan, then acting as a partisan of Antiochus VI in his struggle against Demetrius for the Seleucid throne, defeated the latter's forces on the plain of Hazor. Some have suggested that the fortress on the summit at Hazor was constructed at this time. It is possible, however, that it may have been the work of Alexander Jannaeus whom Josephus reports to have built a number of fortifications throughout the land, particularly north of Joppa (modern Tel Aviv). Indeed, near Tel Aviv in 1950 was discovered a small Hasmonean fort not unlike that on the citadel at Hazor. The structure near Tel Aviv contained a large cache of coins from the time of Alexander Jannaeus, but this, it must be admitted, is only evidence of occupation at

[17] Some early Jewish scholars understood its name to derive from a word suggesting a bevy of birds perched on a hilltop.

221

that time, not proof that it was constructed then as some have taken it to have been. Likewise Masada, "the Gibraltar of the Dead Sea" (see pp. 232-37), was invested by soldiers of Jannaeus, but the Hasmonean remains there are somewhat older, perhaps again from the time of Jonathan. At Masada as elsewhere the life and time of these Jewish rulers cannot be substantially illuminated by archaeology because of later construction.

Jerusalem is no exception. We know from I Maccabees and from Josephus that both Judas and Jonathan undertook considerable work around the Temple area paying particular attention to its defenses. All this, of course, was swept away by the monumental work of Herod. Yet elsewhere in Jerusalem archaeologists have been more fortunate in identifying the effects of the Hellenistic rulers and the Hasmoneans. This was the time when the city expanded considerably beyond the limits of Nehemiah's walls and spread across the Tyropoean Valley to cover the western hill. Here Antiochus IV established a citadel which proved to be such an effective fortress that it withstood numerous Jewish attempts to dislodge its garrison even when the rest of the city had fallen. The presence of this stronghold may, in fact, have been the impetus for the fortification of the Temple which stood opposite it across the valley. The weak point of the Temple defense was on the northwest where the ground slopes gently. Here an ancient tower known to Jeremiah (31:38) was strengthened and used as a palace by the Hasmoneans. This is the location of Herod's Fortress Antonia (see pp. 226-30) where Jesus, in my view, was tried, scourged, and condemned.

In 1927, J. W. Crowfoot, directing British excavations on western Ophel and in the Tyropoean Valley, discovered beneath the debris of Byzantine houses a massive gate with parts of its wall intact. In the gate was a number of coins from the time of Alexander Jannaeus. The coarseness of the construction led Crowfoot to think it a Bronze Age construction in use down to Maccabean days. Subsequent work in the area in the 1960s by another British undertaking combined with information from elsewhere, such as Sepphoris, has led to a revision of Crowfoot's judgment. There is now no reason to suppose the work anything other than Seleucid or more probably Hasmonean and evidence of the expansion of Jerusalem in the first or second centuries before the birth of Jesus.

The years between the fall of Judah and the coming of the Romans were, on our meager evidence, violent ones for Palestine and witnessed the helpless frustration of one foreign rule after another as well as approximately a century of brilliant if not lasting revival of national fortunes. The land was fulfilling its historic and geographical function as never before: It was a highway between great centers of commerce and culture. More cosmopolitan than perhaps at any time in its history, it was by Jesus' day a polyglot of languages, customs, religions, and cultures. Even had the Hasmoneans succeeded in their political undertakings, their religious aims were doomed from the first as witnessed by prior centuries of struggle against alien cults. Whatever goals they did achieve were almost entirely undone by the interparty strife that arose in Judea during their rule and by the policies of the Roman client king who followed them. Over a period of almost forty years this man turned Palestine, outwardly at least, into a Graeco-Roman land whose architectural monuments rivaled any of its day. Already a vastly different world from pre-exilic Israel, the life and culture of Palestine when Herod finished with it would hardly have been recognized by an Ezra, still less by a Josiah. Into this world Jesus was born.

19. HEROD AND HIS LAND

Herod easily deserves the title by which he has been known over the centuries—"the

Great." By any reckoning he was one of the outstanding men of antiquity. Extraordinarily competent, daring, possessed of personal courage and vigor, faithful to his friends, occasionally magnanimous toward enemies, he was one of the most eminent builders of the Roman era, second only to that prodigious architect, the Emperor Hadrian. Strange, then, that his name should have become almost synonymous with cruelty and baseness. Yet this man who did more than any other for Judaism in his time has been scorned by Jewish writers and is known to Christians as the mad king who ordered the execution of the innocents at the time of Jesus' birth (Matthew 2:16-18). It would doubtless have been better for Herod's reputation had he died before illness ruined his once athletic body[1] and grief over execution of a faithless wife[2] destroyed his reason.

[1] Josephus, who devotes one sixth of his voluminous writings to Herod and his reign, twice describes the horrible symptoms of an illness which racked the king's body in his later life (*War*, I, xxxiii, 5; *Antiquities*, XVII, vi, 5). Two modern Jerusalemite doctors, Norman Manson of St. John's and Vicken Kalbian of the Augusta Victoria Hospital, have ventured the opinion that what Josephus described is the condition and behavior of "an aged arteriosclerotic." For further information on this matter, see Stewart Perowne, *The Life and Times of Herod the Great* (London: Hodder and Stoughton, 1956), pp. 185-86.

[2] This was Mariamme I. Herod had ten wives, the legal number in his place and time. Two were named Mariamme. The wife in question here was a Hasmonean whom Herod married at Samaria shortly before his conquest of Jerusalem. Her adulterous behavior was notorious but was apparently forgiven by the king who satisfied himself with putting her lovers to death. On one occasion it was Herod's own uncle, brother-in-law, and friend, Josephus, who was thus punished. Finally Herod was convinced of her infidelity with Sohaemus, his best friend to whom he had entrusted her safekeeping while he went off to Rhodes to meet Augustus. Sohaemus was summarily executed. Mariamme was condemned by a rigged court over which Herod himself presided. Even so, he refused to put his beloved to death until his sister, Salome (widow of Joseph and violently anti-Hasmonean), convinced him that his throne would never be safe so long as the Hasmonean princess lived. No sooner was Mariamme dead, however, than Herod began to stumble from room to room in the Antonia Palace shouting her name and sending servants to summon into his presence that person he had loved more than any other.

Until the last ten years of his lengthy, fruitful reign (37-4 B.C.) this remarkable man had fashioned a record of political and architectural accomplishments rivaled by few in any era. As frequently with men of such caliber, his personality was complicated and his motives mixed or at least veiled from the eyes of more ordinary men. Even in his own day, as Josephus says, "some there are who stand amazed at the diversity of Herod's nature and purposes." Little wonder that opinions of him tend to be partisan and his vast accomplishments little appreciated.

Herod was born in southern Palestine during the reign of Queen Alexandra, probably in the year 73 B.C. He was an Idumean, today we might say an Arab. His family was by religion, however, Jewish. This was the work of John Hyrcanus who, upon conquering the south, the land of the Idumeans and Edomites, had forced its inhabitants to accept Judaism upon pain of death. Herod was thus a Jewish Arab, a man who in power effectively played a self-defined role as the protector of Jews wherever they were to be found in the Roman Empire. As a passionate builder he crowned his justly renowned achievements by erecting an unparalleled temple to celebrate the glory of the Hebrew God. Nothing withstanding, many of his Jewish contemporaries regarded him as an outsider, a view which the passing of years has done little to correct.

Antipater, his grandfather, rose from humble birth in Ascalon to chief administrative officer of Idumea under Alexander Jannaeus and Alexandra. His son, also known as Antipater,[3] was the strength behind an otherwise weak Hyrcanus II (see pp. 218-19) and the real power with whom the Romans dealt. As was their way, these conquerors from Italy unerringly sought out ability and

[3] He is occasionally called Antipas, but is not to be confused with Herod Antipas of New Testament times who was his grandson, the eighth child of Herod the Great.

loyalty in natives to whom they turned over the administration of their provinces—or as much of it as they could. In Palestine their man was Antipater. While the Roman legate in Syria was the ultimately responsible provincial officer, as many matters as possible were left in the hands of this Idumean who was not only able, but who also took the opportunity to install two of his sons in important posts, Phasael, his oldest, in Jerusalem, and Herod, his most capable, in Galilee. They ruled under their father's guidance, and upon him was the ever-watchful eye of the Roman eagle.

From the moment the Romans came to Palestine the destiny of Herod's family was tied to Roman fortunes in the east. And it was no one-sided affair. Various men and factions in the Roman civil war[4] sought to win the favor of Herod, rapidly emerging after the death of his father in 43 B.C. as the most capable man in the region. Not that Herod was always in power. The year 40 B.C. found him in exile in Rome, driven from his own land by his enemies, the Hasmoneans, who found his ambition and connections with the Romans a threat to their own dynastic claims. Roman armed might carried him home, to a wedding with a Hasmonean princess (the ever-unfaithful Mariamme), to Jerusalem, and to a crown. Antony, imperator of Rome along with his brother-in-law, Octavian, provided his close friend Herod with two legions in order to bring order to a

Palestine divided and deteriorating in the clash of civil unrest become open war. Forced to assault Jerusalem itself with alien soldiers, Herod sought to induce the defenders to surrender by showing his clemency in advance; he had food sent into the surrounded and sealed city to prevent starvation. Characteristically, mercy was seen as weakness. The opposition stiffened. Given no other choice, Herod took the city and the Temple by force. Sosius, the Roman general, ordered that no quarter should be given. Nothing could have suited the Jewish defenders better as they, too, were in a fierce mood. In spite of Herod's efforts to stem slaughter, blood flowed in the narrow, hilly streets. In the Temple area defenders and attackers alike found fighting difficult as the bodies and blood of comrades caused stumbling and slipping.

Following its inevitable success, the Roman army, supported by Sosius, claimed the city by right of conquest and eagerly anticipated loot and women. Herod, however, invoked his own rights and admonished the Roman general not to leave him king of a desert. Reasonable and even threatening words were not enough. Herod showed his willingness to fight the Romans for the city, at the same time wisely offering Sosius and his army almost his entire considerable fortune if (1) they would withdraw without further damage to Jerusalem or its inhabitants, and (2) if they did not profane the Temple. Sosius offered a golden crown to the Hebrew God and withdrew with his army—and Herod's wealth. Herod had prevailed, not for the first time nor the last, and reigned as King of Judea, bankrupt apart from the considerable hatred his new subjects held for him. The year was 37 B.C. Herod was thirty-six.

The Roman civil war was at its height. Antony, friend and protector, had fallen under the spell of Cleopatra of Egypt who had designs on Herod's lands. Out of interest

---

[4] Insofar as it was fought on one level or another in almost every part of the known world, the Roman civil war may be described as the original "world war." There were major battles between contending Roman parties in Italy, Greece, and Egypt. In addition there were numerous struggles in other places involving provincial interests who sought to win for themselves a stronger position in their own areas regardless of who secured the dominance of the Empire. Against this vexed and troubled background, Hasmonean power ended in Palestine and Herod came to the throne. A part of these provincial power politics, of course, was the ability to see who was winning the major prize and to be on that side when it most affected the fortunes of one's own area. In this game Herod had no superiors and few peers.

for his domains and because his Machiavellian sensitivities told him that Antony was losing the struggle with Octavian, Herod courted the favor of the latter whom he had likewise known from older, more carefree days in Rome.[5] At the same time he was keeping his fences mended with the powers-that-be or that-might-be, he set about to fill the two roles in which he saw himself. The first was as protector of Jews living outside Palestine. When in Rome in 40, he had won from the Senate (through the good offices of Antony) not only the title "King of Judea," but also the right of Judaism to be practiced anywhere in the Empire as a *religio licita*, that is, as a legal religion. For the Romans, religion was not true or false but legal or illegal. Unless the Senate had specifically granted its adherents the right to practice their faith, worship was a violation of law and was punished as such.[6] Judaism, monotheistic in a polytheistic world and involving unique habits with reference to diet, the Sabbath, and other matters, needed further exemptions. These were granted thanks to Herod's zeal. Had he not pursued the matter, Judaism like Christianity might have found itself an object of persecution in Imperial Roman times—which would have radically changed the history of both faiths. In power, Herod, friend of the Emperor and of the closest and most powerful imperial advisor,[7]

saw to it that the rights of Jews in the Empire were not violated. In addition he gave considerable financial aid to far-flung Jewish communities in a number of instances.

Herod's Building Schemes

Zeal and even friends in high places, however abundant, do not guarantee greatness. It was in his second role, as glorifier of Judea and indeed of much of the Roman east, that Herod gained the title by which he is remembered. Bankrupt when he came to power, he was soon in a position to command immense funds which were almost at once expended upon colossal building schemes. Once the Romans had withdrawn and left him in Jerusalem, Herod's immediate need was to find or to construct a royal residence. That which had served the Hasmoneans was not available to him because it was primarily a holy site, the home of the high priest and the place where sacred garments were kept. As an Idumean who could by no means lay claim to priestly descent, the new king could not usurp the high-priestly office as the Hasmoneans had done. The strongest and most luxurious palace fortress in the city was thus closed to him. He found himself in the relatively small, inhospitable palace on the western hill, the place where Queen Alexandra, also unable to assume the priesthood, had reigned. Alexandra, however, did not have to live with the multitude of Herod's in-laws who now descended upon Mariamme and Herod to enjoy the revival of family fortunes. The king was soon looking for another place. His solution—a foreshadowing of what was to come—was to rebuild the high-priestly palace. The old building was in considerable need of repair. But repair was hardly what Herod's mind entertained. He had the whole thing torn down. Thus came to an end a structure possibly first conceived by Solomon, rebuilt by Nehemiah, and graced

---

[5] Like most Jews, Herod had sided with the anti-republicans in the Roman civil strife. This threw him in the company of Antony and Octavian and gave him friendships of incalculable value. As one indication of the closeness of these relationships, Octavian as Augustus Caesar was pleased to show unusual favor to Herod's sons when they came to Rome for their education.

[6] For this reason Christians were punished in the Roman Empire. Christianity was not a *religio licita*, and once it had clearly emerged from Judaism it no longer had the protection of law. Many other factors played a role in Roman persecution of Christians, but this was the basic legal ground for such actions.

[7] Herod was perhaps Marcus Vipsanius Agrippa's best friend, and Agrippa was the mind and often the power behind Augustus.

or cursed by the tread of various Hasmoneans to whom it was the royal palace.

Sixty feet to the north, sufficiently far to remove it from contact with the sacred Temple precinct, rose the first of Herod's dazzling structures and one which would provide the setting for poignant scenes in the life of Paul and possibly of Jesus as well. The Fortress Antonia, honoring Marc Antony, was situated on a precipice which at bedrock towered seventy-five feet above the surrounding area. Faced with slippery flagstones, this slope provided an almost perfect glacis. On this natural site were placed the sixty-foot walls of massive blocks, hewn with care and distinguished by marginal drafts which were hallmarks of Herod's architects and masons. At each of the four corners was a tower; three seventy-five feet high, and one, that nearest the Temple, one hundred feet. The height of this building, at one point 235 feet, was but one of the amazing features of the Antonia. Its longest side was 375 feet. On the interior was an enormous tower, larger

Convent de Sion

Herodian construction in Jerusalem, as elsewhere, was on a massive scale. The Antonia (above in model) was said to be a city unto itself. The huge stones of the temple platform are typical of Herodian masonry (left), and are further characterized by the deeply cut drafted margins (below).

but the same effect as the Norman Keep at the Tower of London.

Here was a complex with space not merely for the priest and his vestments, for the king and his retinue, but also for extensive courts, porticoes, baths, and barracks easily capable of accommodating 500 men at one time. It was nothing less than a palatial palace stronghold. Josephus was not far wrong in referring to it as being "like a city." Its military function, however, differed markedly from that of its predecessor. The Antonia did not face northward to protect Jerusalem from enemy assault; rather, it looked inward to provide a point of central control over the city itself. The tallest tower overlooked the Temple area, a likely source of civil unrest. It was joined to the holy precinct by two grand staircases. On one of them Paul was to make a defense of his actions before a mob (Acts 21:35).

These however were not the only means of access to the Temple from the palace fortress. Herod caused a subterranean passage (traces of which remain) to be built from the eastern gate of the inner Temple to the Antonia, thus providing himself with a means of escape should a hostile mob trap him at worship. It also made possible the sending of troops into the Temple without delay. This king who saw himself as a good Jew and the champion of Judaism was not ignorant of the hatred of his subjects for him, nor of their feeling that he was a foreign usurper of a throne which rightly belonged to the Hasmoneans whose reputation, sorely tarnished, tended to brighten with the passage of years.

Twelve years after the death of Herod, Judea came directly under the control of a Roman governor. The Antonia became the principal Roman stronghold in Jerusalem. It was a sort of police station, administrative center, and possibly residence of the governor on those occasions when he came to the city from Caesarea, his permanent head-quarters. There is no question that on one occasion Paul was confined here for his own safekeeping until he could be transferred to Caesarea to appear before the governor (Acts 23:10, 16-24). There is, however, considerable debate whether this was also the location of the trial of Jesus before Pilate. Some scholars hold that this trial took place at the Citadel, Herod's new palace, where a Roman governor, clothed in all the majesty his provincial post could afford, would most likely have resided when in Jerusalem. On evidence from the Four Gospels, Jesus' trial before Pilate was held at dawn. Would the governor have traveled across the city at that hour to take part in a hearing the outcome of which had been decided beforehand? And what about the apparent proximity of Pilate's wife to the scene (Matthew 27:19)? The Gospels seem to indicate that the trial was held at the same place the governor was residing. Would this not have been the most palatial building in the city?

A number of objections, however, prohibit the easy identification of the Citadel as the place of Jesus' trial before Pilate. First, there is abundant evidence to show that Roman officials began work at daybreak. If he needed to travel from his residence to his "office," he would have done so at this hour as a matter of course. There is nothing unusual in this detail from the Passion Narrative. Second, there is no reason why Pilate and his wife would not have found the Antonia's magnificence equal to any pretensions they may have had. It adequately housed Herod for twelve years, and Herod knew the splendors of Rome and settled for no less or not much less. In any event, contrary to the popular view, Matthew does not say that Pilate's wife was actually present, only that she "sent word." Third, and with more force, archaeological work at the site has produced striking evidence that the Antonia, not the Citadel, may be the location described by the Gospel of John. "When

Pilate heard these words, he brought Jesus out," says John 19:13, "and sat down on the judgment seat at a place called The Pavement, and in Hebrew, Gabbatha." There was, then, in Jesus' day a court so famous for its covering that it was merely known by the descriptive Greek name, *lithostroton* (literally, "Stone Pavement"), and an Aramaic term, *gabbatha* ("elevated ridge").[8] For a number of years, beneath the Convent of the Daughters of Zion and the Convent of the Flagellation, two of the numerous buildings now occupying the site of the Antonia, Franciscan and Dominican Fathers labored quietly to investigate the relation of the so-called *Ecce Homo* Arch over the *Via Dolorosa* to various other ancient constructions. In 1929 Father L. H. Vincent determined that the constructions had no relation to the arch which was in fact later, from Hadrian's building of Aelia Capitolina in A.D. 135. But other works were Herodian. One was a very large (8200 square feet) stone pavement. Father Vincent, perhaps the greatest researcher into Jerusalem's past, established to his satisfaction that this was the grand court of the Fortress Antonia. Its drains and cisterns are still in place and are used. The large and carefully fitted stone, now some eight feet below the level of the modern streets, was ridged on top to prevent horses from slipping. On several stones are clearly visible marks of *basilicus*, a game popular among Roman soldiers who thus whiled away their time. Here, in Vincent's view, is the *lithostroton*, the pavement where Jesus stood before Pilate.

For twelve years Herod lived at the Antonia. In 23 B.C. he began a new palace. As a site he chose the western hill, highest point in the city and location of the Syrian fort which had resisted so many Hasmonean efforts and was one of the last areas taken by Herod and Sosius. Three stout battle towers were added to the older castle. On a rock outcropping thirty feet high, these towers rose, from west to east, 128, 135, and 72 feet respectively. Fashioned by his superb masons into almost solid cubes, they were forty-five, sixty, and thirty-five feet square at their bases. Herod named them Hippicus for a friend who had fallen at his side in battle, Phasael for his older brother who had died at the hands of the Parthians, and Mariamme—just which Mariamme is not clear. His habitually unfaithful Hasmonean wife had been dead for some years. Josephus says that this tower, however, commemorated Herod's undying love for her. But the king had just married another Mariamme, a young girl of renowned beauty whom Herod is said to have adored at first sight. Surely, whatever was in Herod's mind in naming the tower, the second Mariamme must have been flattered by thoughts that it honored her.[9]

The three towers were essentially fortifications. Yet Herod's architects did not neglect other possibilities, nor leave them with that unadorned functionality common to military architecture in all ages. On the outside, at least, Phasael suggested, or was suggested by, the famed Pharos, the lighthouse of Alexandria. Within, on its lower story, it contained a cloister, while above a bath was surrounded by splendid rooms. Hippicus, slightly smaller, was given over in its lower levels to a cistern thirty-five feet deep. The use made of its upper story is not known. It likely was purely military. The gem was Mariamme, the smallest, whose interior was resplendent. Yet for all their magnificence,

---

[8] Such designations are familiar in history. Louis XIV's "marble court" at Versailles was one. A current example of such usage is the common Russian word *kremlin* ("fortress") to single out the particularly important and famous fortress in Moscow. And there is, of course, the "White House" in Washington.

[9] Herod-Philip, son to Herod and Mariamme II, was the father of Salome who demanded from him the head of John the Baptist (Matthew 14:3-12; Mark 6:17-29).

On the western hill of Jerusalem Herod built a new palace. The base of the Phasael Tower can still be seen (below). What some scholars thought it looked like in Herod's day (model, below, left) is in contrast with the Citadel as it appears today with its Crusader glacis and its mosque (above).

these structures were not strictly speaking a part of the royal palace itself. That building, so large as to be compared to the Temple, rose immediately to the south of the tri-towered Citadel. Paneled with marble,[10] ceiled with extraordinary wood from Lebanon, decorated with silver, gold, paintings, and sculptures after the fashion of the times, the crowning achievement of the interior of the palace proper was two enormous and lavish apartments. These he named Agrippium, for Marcus Vipsanius Agrippa, and Caesareum, for Augustus. Significantly Herod moved from the Antonia to the Caesareum. It was after the Battle of Actium and when the political balance in Rome had shifted decisively. Herod never tired of naming buildings and cities after his friends and allies. Caesar, as might be expected, was most prominent in this connection. But Herod had buildings and cities in abundance, and there seemed to be enough to honor all, including at least one for himself—which he chose to be his final resting place.

The Roman conquest of Jerusalem in A.D. 70 and the subsequent leveling of the city destroyed most of Herod's monuments there; the hippodrome, theater, Antonia, Temple, and the royal palace. It has long been assumed that ashes of the palace are beneath the present-day Citadel, parts of the Armenian Patriarchate, and other structures in the area. Miss Kenyon's diggings at the Patriarchate have not shown this to be so, but she dug at only one spot and that probably was too far south to have been included in Herod's palace. One need not wonder, however, whether or where there are remains of the three towers. When Titus destroyed

the city he ordered that these strong works be pulled down. Mariamme came down almost entirely, as vestiges discovered in 1901 in the courtyard of Christ Church, Anglican, show. Hippicus also yielded to destructive efforts. C. N. Johns, a British archaeologist, was able to recover parts of it in excavations from 1937 to 1948. Its hollow center (the reservoir) made it possible to reduce it fairly easily to ground level. Phasael was something else. Stalwart, it proved an immovable rock. The battlements and the upper story gave way, but the massive stones of the base and lower level were too much for men working in days before blasting powder. Josephus says Titus left it as a monument to his victory. In truth he could not tear it down. Today these stones, still reflecting the skill and care with which they were hewn and laid, survive in the lower courses of the so-called "Tower of David," that immense structure dominating the western part of Old Jerusalem.

At the same time the palace was being built, royal tombs were constructed some 650 yards to the west. Herod never intended that he himself should rest there. Grander plans were made for his burial. Discovered in 1891, his family tomb—vacant except for two empty sarcophagi—bears resemblance to some of the tombs of Petra, so familiar to Herod. Four burial chambers oriented to the major points of the compass flank a large central room. Considerably less elaborate than the royal tombs of Egypt but no less carefully or beautifully done, the interior is finished with fine masonry. On the outside, columns grace an entrance which was sealed by a large rolling stone set in a groove after the common manner of Jerusalem in that time. Grave robbers have long since done their grim work. We do not know how many of Herod's family were buried here or with what artifacts. One of the sarcophagi from this tomb has survived and for some reason has found an honored position in one of the

[10] Josephus, again, is our authority for the decoration of this palace. He also reported that Herod had decorated his residences at Masada with marble. But recent excavations there reveal that Josephus' "marble" was common stone painted in imitation of the scarcer material. It is probable that the same was true in the palace in Jerusalem. Such was the fashion in Rome itself and was one of the architectural features of the Augustan Age.

chapels in the Church of the Holy Sepulchre where it may be seen today.

The new palace in Jerusalem was but one of a number of royal residences scattered throughout the kingdom. The most frequented of these was the winter palace at Jericho; the most spectacular was that recently recovered at Masada. Two miles from Tell es-Sultan, Old Testament Jericho, is Tulul Abu el-'Alayiq, Herodian Jericho. The site was well chosen, for there the Wadi Qelt flows out of the Judean hills on to the plain and toward the Jordan. The valley through which this stream runs is the only one in the area abundantly supplied with springs. Excavations at the site in 1951 showed that Early Stone Age man sought to take advantage of these attractions. The Bronze Age saw another settlement, but it was not until Hasmonean times that substantial buildings were constructed. These were destroyed by Pompey in 63 B.C. as he secured the country. Shortly thereafter Herod began his work of magnificence there. The stream served as focal point for this little Graeco-Roman masterpiece. The sumptuous restoration of the Hasmonean palace along the northern side of the Wadi would have dazzled its original architects. To the south were grand buildings reflecting Herod's successful attempt to imitate some of Augustus' new works along the Tiber. A staircase 150 feet long graced one building. Another structure bordered the stream for 400 feet. There was an enormous sunken garden with places for over fifty statues. In addition other parks as well as date and balsam groves separated oversized civic buildings, splendid villas, theaters, and even a mammoth hippodrome. Everywhere there was water. Not only was the Wadi Qelt cleverly employed, but at least five large springs in the area were tapped by aqueducts through which water ran to cascade into the numerous pools and fountains of Herod's winter palace which knew no rival in the Roman world until Hadrian built his beloved villa at Tibur in the hills above Rome.

The excavations at Herodian Jericho in 1951 proved to be exceedingly disappointing insofar as they failed to recover much of the grandeur of 2000 years ago. A number of walls allowed various structures to be traced in their foundational outline at least. Here and there indications of vivid paint of different colors were found. Two extensive mosaics and fragments of another are still in a good state of preservation. Otherwise that portion of the site excavated was in a ruinous state. One large building (approximately 163 feet by 255 feet) was recovered. In form it was a large courtyard once apparently surrounded by a colonnade giving way to numerous rooms including a typical Roman bath of considerable size. Several suggestions were offered as to its original function. The idea that it was Herod's winter palace did not gain credence, since at the time there was no similar structure with which to compare it apart from the western palace at Masada then not fully investigated. It was noted by the excavators at Jericho that the Masada palace "is quite different in plan from our structure." The best guesses were that a Hellenistic-style gymnasium or palaestra had been uncovered. Subsequently Masada has been dug. A number of details from both the western palace and the northern villa coincide with features of the large building at Herodian Jericho. It is now clear that Herod was extremely fond of Roman baths and had them close at hand. The size of the Jericho one does not necessarily indicate that the building that housed it was public. It is not so big as the large bath at Masada. Even more striking are mosaic fragments from the hypocaust at Jericho. They are identical in design and execution with the mosaic border of the antechamber of the throne room of the western palace at Masada. None of this proves that the building unearthed at Jericho is Herod's winter palace. But it does indicate that such an

232

The spectacular position and contour of Masada (opposite top) offered Herod the opportunity for an unparalleled royal residence. He surrounded the summit with a casemate wall and among other things built vast storehouses, a palace, and state apartments on the top of the rock (opposite, bottom left). The masterpiece of his creation was the three-tiered northern villa which combined genius of conception with extraordinary engineering ability (opposite, bottom right). The remains amply testify to Herod's love for personal comfort and the lavishness he insisted upon even in this remote spot. His personal bath (right) had mosaics similar to those found in the western palace (below right). The plastered columns and painted walls (below) were so skillfully done that Josephus thought them to be monolithic and marble respectively.

Y. Yadin

Y. Yadin

Y. Yadin

233

identification must once more be seriously entertained.

Masada, after Jerusalem and Jericho Herod's favorite, was very different from either. It was primarily a military fortification and as such bore semblance to a number of places which Herod refortified and on which he bestowed a measure of grandeur: the Alexandrium on the summit of Qarn Sartabeh in the central Jordan Valley; the Hyrcania northwest of the Dead Sea; and Machaerus, that desolate spot in Transjordan where John the Baptist spent his last days. *Masada* means "mountain stronghold"; no place was ever more aptly named. A mesa roughly 1900 feet by 650 feet whose flat top comprises twenty-three acres mostly of soil, it is a sheer rock cliff 820 feet above the valley on the east and 600 feet on the west. The shore of the Dead Sea is 1300 feet below. Before the Romans constructed an enormous assault ramp in A.D. 73, access to the top of the rock was solely by way of the "Snake Path" whose designation suggests the difficulties of ascent. Known as "The Gibraltar of the Dead Sea," the site is spectacular. What Herod did here was nothing less than stupendous.

For eleven months, from October 1963 to May 1964, and again from November 1964 until April 1965, Yigael Yadin led a team of Israeli archaeologists and a large contingent of volunteers from twenty-eight countries in excavating 97 percent of Masada. Only the great cisterns and parts of the remains of Roman camps were left untouched. Among other things it was discovered that Early Stone Age peoples, whose material remains are similar to those known from other parts of Palestine, had inhabited some of the caves in the great rock as early as the fourth millennium B.C. A small amount of Iron Age pottery indicated that during the time of the Hebrew monarchies the summit was visited. But there is no evidence to suggest that there were any buildings there at that time. Numerous coins struck by Alexander Jannaeus show that this Hasmonean king[11] or an immediate successor had interests here. But as Yadin says, "we discovered no structure which could with certainty be attributed to any period before that of Herod."

Whatever the pre-Herodian history of occupation at Masada, it was not until Herod's grandiose ideas were applied to the site that it emerged as a major settlement, which it remained for over a hundred years, until the Zealots put the torch to many of its structures in the revolt of 66-73. This was done in the last heroic moments of the lengthy siege of the rock when the Jewish defenders chose suicide and the torch rather than allow themselves to be captured or the buildings to fall intact into Roman hands.

The number, types, and character of the buildings excavated by Yadin vindicate the judgment of Josephus that for Herod Masada was both special and personal. It was a refuge where he and his family could be safe either from his own subjects or from the covetous Cleopatra, and could continue to live in a manner to which they had become accustomed in Jerusalem. Nowhere else do we have so intimate a glimpse of the pomp and splendor of this man and so clear an insight into what he thought fitting for his royal presence. The work on this great rock above the Dead Sea was thus not just another of his gifts to his land; it was Herodian in the truest sense in that its silent stones still bespeak his energy, vision, tastes, and personal luxury.

Except at the northernmost tip where the three-tiered villa was located, the summit of Masada was completely enclosed within a casemate wall, a wall 4250 feet in total

[11] The excavators are of the opinion that Alexander Jannaeus is probably the "Jonathan the high priest" who Josephus says erected buildings on Masada. See Y. Yadin, *Masada* (London: Weidenfeld and Nicolson, 1966), p. 205.

length. According to Josephus this wall was twenty feet high, of gleaming white stone, and had thirty-eight towers each over eighty feet high. Doubtless the angle of vision looking up made wall and towers appear higher than they actually were. Numerous pieces of plaster with which the structures were covered have been found showing that on the white appearance of the fortress Josephus was correct.

Almost all the southern and eastern portions of the mesa were left open to allow for growing food in the still fertile soil. The northern tip was covered with buildings of various sorts. On the western verge, almost equidistant from north and south, was the largest structure: a ceremonial and administrative palace, in part two stories high, self-contained, and decorated in the finest Graeco-Roman mode. Here amid superb mosaic floors similar in design to Greek examples found at Delos and walls painted to resemble different types of stone were Herod's throne room and various chambers connected with other official functions. Administrative offices, not only for Masada but on occasion for the whole kingdom, were in this building. Herod's private apartments were no less grand than the public rooms. Even the passageway to his ingeniously heated bath was paved with a brilliant mosaic which survives virtually complete. The whole was surrounded by storerooms (one of which was the largest room found at Masada: 210 feet long) and servants' quarters, and was equipped with an independent water supply.

Within a radius of 375 feet of the southeastern corner of the western palace were three other houses, royal residences whose total living space was more than that of the large palace itself. These were badly damaged by the Zealots who occupied them during the First Revolt. Large numbers of families were then housed in these struc-

tures, and poorly built interior walls were constructed to the serious detriment of the original plan. In Herodian times their use was doubtless to house the many members of Herod's family and their relations. Two similar dwellings are in the northern complex. Five in all, they provided considerable space for the royal family and were so planned as to take advantage of the hillocks on the summit. Each commands a breathtaking view of the surrounding hills and of the Dead Sea.

Toward the northern end Masada rises and narrows, suggesting the bow of a large ship. Here most of the Herodian structures were concentrated. The southernmost of these was a large rectangle, some 135 feet by 90 feet. On the interior was a courtyard flanked by nine "apartments," each consisting of a smaller court with two rooms side by side at the far end. In addition there were five other rooms of considerable size, two over thirty feet square. There is no doubt that this was a dwelling, probably quarters for high-ranking officers of the local garrison and certain administrative officials.

Immediately north of the "apartment building," Yadin and his staff came to grips with a mass of large dolomite stones, weighing four to five hundred pounds apiece. They lay in clearly discernible rows, thrown down by earthquakes which regularly shake the Jordan Valley. There was never any doubt that these were the remains of storehouses similar in design to others from the time and region. Separated by a central street, Herod's storerooms consisted of fifteen long, narrow chambers each apparently given over to a single item such as grain, wine, oil, or perhaps even weapons, although understandably in light of Masada's role in the First Revolt none of the latter was found here.

In addition to storerooms of considerable

capacity,[12] the northern complex contained an administrative building somewhat larger than that in the western palace, a big bathhouse in the finest Roman style, and the gem of Masada: the wondrous three-tiered villa of Herod. Judging by its remains, the administrative building was relatively undistinguished, large, unadorned, becomingly workmanlike. The bathhouse, on the other hand, was decorated floor, wall, and ceiling by artists who also labored on the villa. It rivals the finest examples of Roman baths known from Pompeii and Herculaneum, and surpasses in lavishness although not in design the Roman works at Bath in England. The instructive difference between Bath and Masada, however, is the abundance of water: steaming hot water from natural springs deep in the earth at Bath, as contrasted with the dry, arid conditions that prevailed on Masada. Bath, where the Romans first built within a half century of Herod's work beside the Dead Sea, is a natural spot for enterprises requiring great quantities of water and was so recognized centuries before the legions came to Britain. Few men would have conceived of doing the same thing on an arid rock over 600 feet high and all but inaccessible. Only a Herod could have accomplished it.

Amazing as his other buildings were at Masada, nothing there surpassed or even rivaled the private villa for imagination, sheer exploitation of location, and difficulty of execution. For a long time few thought that Josephus' description of a palace "within and beneath the walls of the citadel, but inclined to its north side" referred to anything other than the western palace. To be

sure a number of details mentioned could not have possibly applied to that structure, but then, Josephus had been wrong about details on other occasions. The strange ruins on the northern tip were well known to be a part of the fortifications of the site. Then, in the early 1950s, two young Israeli mountain climbers scaled the northern wall of the rock, examined the ruins close at hand, and concluded that this, not the western palace, was the building described by Josephus. Subsequent archaeological work has proved them correct. Here indeed the great king dwelled amid an opulence which would have done honor to Caesar, and with views so striking that even the Emperor would have been envious.

Across the narrow northern tip of Masada was a high wall, plastered white and still gleaming when uncovered in 1965. It provided privacy. At its western end graceful steps were found leading to the highest point on the rock, the location of the upper terrace of Herod's villa. Four lavishly decorated, moderate-sized rooms divided by spacious corridors formed a living unit designed for the king alone or perhaps with one or two of his favorites. But the most striking feature of this upper terrace was not the dwelling itself, however splendid it may have been. In front of it was a semicircular terrace, colonnaded and provided with a roof. From this vantage point 1300 feet above the level of the sea below, Herod and his guests enjoyed an unparalleled view northward toward En-gedi, and west where the scorched hills and wadis of Judea stretch in seemingly endless grandeur. The most magnificent sight of this truly superb panorama is east, across the blue of the Dead Sea to the majestic hills of Moab often shrouded by a halo of heat mist.

From here Herod could descend by hidden stairs carved from living rock to the middle terrace, a circular structure clinging to the cliff sixty feet below the summit. At this

---

[12] Josephus says that large quantities of food placed there by Herod and weapons "which had been treasured up by the king, and were sufficient for ten thousand men" were found by the Romans when they captured Masada in A.D. 73. Even though almost a century had passed, the food that remained (probably dried fruits) had "not corrupted all that while"—this again on the word of Josephus.

point the natural outcropping is extremely narrow. With ingenuity and considerable daring, Herod's engineers extended the foundation, at the same time leveling out a platform on which they erected two rows of pillars supporting a roof over the entire area. With structural insight presaging the double walls and buttresses so familiar in medieval cathedrals, they built two lines of walls to distribute the weight more evenly. Paucity of embellishment here is accounted for by the fires set by the Zealots. Extensive damage was done to this level and increased its exposure to the ravages of nature. Little of its former resplendence is left. Nonetheless, the stupendous engineering feat required to provide the king this place of relaxation needs nothing else to command our admiration.

The same may be said of the lower terrace which literally hangs on the face of the precipice. Joined to the middle level forty-five feet above by another hidden stairway, it is supported from beneath by an enormous wall in places over eighty feet high. When one realizes that archaeologists examining this retaining embankment had to be secured by ropes after the manner of mountain climbers, the effort involved in constructing it begins to come into view. And what was so important as to command this mammoth and dangerous effort? By now we should not be surprised to learn that it was yet another area given over to the pleasures of a monarch to whom architectural achievements unthinkable to the ordinary mind were commonplace. Not only was there a spacious terrace where logically none belonged, one whose columns and frescoes are still impressive after 2000 years, but also a complete Roman bath. Surely no such structure ever sat in a more improbable location. It was, however, but one feature of this wondrous villa. Most of the platform was occupied by a square building, colonnaded about with a smaller square of columns in the center. Very likely these once supported a roof. Many columns remain, particularly those sheltered against the rock face. Josephus, duly impressed, had noted that they were monolithic. As in the case of the "marble" panels on the walls, he had been deceived by Herod's craftsmen. Here as elsewhere in Masada, the columns were stone drums fitted together after the time-honored fashion of the Greeks and plastered over so as to appear of one piece. This plaster was fluted and, on the lower terrace at least, topped by Corinthian capitals.

On the lower terrace Herod, virtually isolated from his retinue and garrison, could enjoy his bath and emerge to banquet with companions in an unparalleled setting. After eleven months of laboring in the relentless sun and struggling against the prevailing south wind that blows off the hot sands, Professor Yadin noted two advantages of the site chosen by Herod for his private retreat. The slight rise of the northern tip of the rock tends to shade the middle and lower terraces early in the day. Moreover, located sixty and 105 feet respectively below the summit, they are shielded from the hot blasts that rake the surface. The cliff face was forbidding, but considerations of comfort coupled with the prospect of spectacular achievement moved the undaunted builder to set his engineers and architects to their plans and his masons and craftsmen to a mountainside which more than any other monument remaining today reveals the character of Herod.

Many factors motivated Herod's building schemes—comfort, religious interest, necessity, as well as a desire to glorify himself amid a people who would not allow statues and other means by which rulers commonly sought to remind their subjects and posterity of their greatness. Many today would readily agree to Herod's selfish motives but refuse to recognize an admixture of religious devotion. His personality, although perhaps not so complicated as that of David, was nonetheless not so clear-cut as some take it to have been. The Temple complex which Herod built in Jerusalem was perhaps the most magnificent single structure of its day. If the king enjoyed the reflected glory of this sanctuary built to the honor of the Hebrew God, he did not, like Solomon, build his own palace abutting it. And what personal glory did he receive for greatly enhancing that other holy place which enjoyed his royal favor: Abraham's traditional grave at Hebron? For Herod this place involved ethnic heritage as well as religious tradition. From about 586 B.C. until Judas Maccabee utterly destroyed it in 164 B.C., Hebron had been occupied by Idumeans, the stock from which Herod sprang. These Semitic people as well as the Jews reverenced not only the Cave of Machpelah but also nearby Mamre, Abraham's traditional home. On both sites Herod caused enormous, even pretentious structures to be built. At Mamre several courses of the carefully hewn, marginally drafted stone still stand, while in Hebron itself the huge mosque dominating the modern city contains vast quantities of Herodian masonry whose beauty contrasts sharply with the work of later days.

Necessity, not sentiment, demanded the rebuilding of Samaria and the founding of a major seaport at Caesarea. But the character of the king determined that magnificence and not mere functionality would mark both cities. Samaria, its Hebrew glory erased by the Assyrian debacle, had been considerably revived and embellished by a series of conquerors: Assyrians, Babylonians, Persians, and Greeks. Yet when the Romans came to Palestine toward the middle of the first century B.C., the city was in abject ruins and all but deserted. With his unerring Roman eye for strategic importance, Aulus Gabinius, the provincial governor of Syria, resurrected Samaria in 57 B.C. Some modern scholars are of the opinion that the Roman forum at the site as well as the handsome Doric

stadium were laid out during this time. However, given the modest scale on which Gabinius built, it is more likely that these structures as well as many other arrangements which survive are in form at least Herodian.

In the year 30 B.C. Augustus gave the city to Herod. But before this, the King of Judea had deep personal ties with the place. Here he had left his family for safekeeping when he fled the land ten years earlier. Here, too, he had married his beloved Mariamme I upon returning to claim his kingdom. Moreover, the city had lent material aid in his struggles with the Hasmoneans. Herod belonged to Samaria before Samaria belonged to Herod. Not one to forget such things, he lavished wealth, privilege, and handsome buildings upon the city and its inhabitants. Not one to forget the importance of Samaria in his rise to power, he took further steps to insure its loyalty in the future. About 25 B.C. he repeated the action of Alexander the Great by settling 6000 of his mercenaries there. These men, Gauls, Thracians, and Germans, had no sympathy with Jewish national aspirations and could be counted on to support the continuing presence of Graeco-Roman influence and power in Palestine.[13] To accommodate this increased population it was necessary to expand the limits of the city. The line of the two-and-a-half-mile circuit of walls erected at this time is still visible. Within this the orderly plan of Gabinius—houses and shops laid out in blocks—was extended somewhat into the valleys at the

[13] This is, in fact, what happened. The city's loyalty never wavered, and it was here rather than in Jerusalem that Herod entertained Agrippa. After Herod's death Samaria was the one center in Palestine on which the Romans could rely. During the reign of Claudius (A.D. 42-54) five cohorts of infantry and one squadron of cavalry were raised here for the Imperial service. Not surprisingly the city was one of the first objectives of Jewish revolutionaries in A.D. 66 when it was ravaged by heavy fighting. After the war it became even more important to the Romans and as late as the third Christian century was enjoying all the pleasures of a prosperous Roman provincial center.

238

base of the hill. On the summit, near where the palace of Omri and Ahab had stood, Herod caused a large temple to be built. Its nave was approximately 213 feet by 246 feet. Entrance to this sanctuary was by means of monumental steps. They are still there and suggest this glorious temple whose gleaming white walls could be seen as far away as the coast. This building Herod dedicated to his benefactor, Augustus, and on an altar before the steps he placed a statue of the Emperor. A marble torso, thought by many to be this very representation, has been recovered by archaeologists.

The temple, although the dominant feature of the city, was by no means the most revered holy place there. Since Hellenistic time Kore (Persephone), the goddess of the underworld, had been worshiped by the non-Jewish residents of this city. It is difficult to know when her shrine there was first built or at what periods the various rebuildings identified by archaeology took place. Yet it was certainly in use during Herod's day, as was also a sanctuary dedicated to the Capitoline Zeus, known to us along with the temple of Augustus from coins struck at Samaria. In matters of religion as well as everything else the city was thoroughly Graeco-Roman before Herod. He recognized it as such, intensified it as such, and glorified it as such, providing not merely temples, but a theater, hippodrome, forum, and porticoed shops. To complete the process and to express gratitude for its gift to him by the Emperor, he changed its name to Sebaste (from *Sebastos,* the Greek equivalent of *Augustus*). By this name it was known throughout Imperial Roman and later times; even today the name survives in the designation of the Arab village there: Sabastiya.

Strato's Tower, an ancient, minor harbor twenty-four miles northwest of Sebaste likewise had its name changed. It became Caesarea and is still known as such today. In 22 B.C. work was begun here to provide a new and somewhat more worthy seaport for a kingdom brought from insignificance to a Graeco-Roman showplace and thrust into the mainstream of the life of the Empire. Joppa with its shoals and reefs, its ugly buildings and generally depressing appearance, was Herod's sole water access to Greece, Rome, and Egypt. It afforded so sorry a haven, Josephus tells us, that even a slightly fresh wind was enough to blow ships upon the rocks. For this reason no sailor going from Phoenicia to Egypt would risk dropping anchor there. Strato's Tower, thirty-four miles to the north (twenty-eight miles south of Mount Carmel) seemed even less promising. Never very important, its harbor was little more than a relatively unprotected anchorage, and the town associated with it was in a ruinous condition. A Herod asked for no more. Here, in a spot whose possibilities had gone unrecognized by centuries of Palestinian rulers who had longed for a good port, would be his *Caesarea-by-the-Sea.* Here, unrestrained by earlier constructions or by Jewish religious sensitivities, would be his wholly Graeco-Roman masterpiece. Here his engineering feats would surpass the work at Masada and even rival the accomplishments in Jerusalem.

It took twelve years to complete. When Herod came to Caesarea to celebrate the twenty-eighth year of his reign and to dedicate the city, he looked out upon a circular harbor, artificial, but larger than the Piraeus, the port of Athens. It struck Josephus that Herod had literally overcome nature by lowering limestone blocks, some 50x9x10 feet into twenty fathoms (120 feet) of water. The entrance, on the north where the winds are more gentle, was flanked by six gigantic statues, three to a side. Landward was a seawall 200 feet wide; half was used by commercial houses, warehouses, and lodging places for sailors. On this wall were a number of towers the largest of which was named Drusium, after Drusus, Caesar's stepson and potential heir. Above the haven the city itself was no less grand. Laid out on a grid after the manner of Alexandria, its main streets were oriented to the harbor joining it with a magnificent forum, theater, and amphitheater overlooking the sea. Dominating all was a temple dedicated to the "Divine Caesar." It enclosed two colossal statues, one of Augustus modeled after the Zeus of Olympia, and one of Roma copied from the great Hera at Argos. All was in limestone, glistening white, and enhanced by many fountains copiously supplied by water brought from the hills several miles away. In the midst of beauty, sanitation had not been neglected. An intricate drainage system underlay the streets.

In 10 B.C. Herod inaugurated the city with splendid games dedicated to Augustus who had given him the site. Livia, the empress, sent pieces of her personal furniture as a gift to the city and as decoration for the games which were to be but the first of a series held every five years in Caesar's honor. No others were held. Herod's body deteri-

orated and his paranoia prospered in the following years. By 5 B.C. he was in no physical or mental condition to preside over, much less to plan, olympic-style games. But Caesarea did not decline; it became a bustling port, the official residence of Roman governors in later days,[14] and the scene of Cornelius' vision (Acts 10:1-33) as well as a place of imprisonment for the apostle Paul (Acts 23:23–27:2).

As late as 1884 large sections of a Roman wall could be traced at Caesarea, and the remains of temples, theaters, a hippodrome, and an aqueduct were clearly visible. Today, however, considerably less is to be seen although fortunately a large golf course occupies much of the ancient site. Yet in spite of sandy soil and easy accessibility Caesarea is uninvestigated to a large degree.[15] Aerial photography has been helpful in identifying many notable ruins such as the amphitheater

[14] In 1961 Italian archaeologists working at Caesarea found a stone inscribed with Pontius Pilate's name.

[15] Some work has been done on Crusader ruins.

The aqueduct at Caesarea was built by Herod to bring water to his splendid new city. One hundred and fifty years later Hadrian doubled the size and thus the capacity of the structure.

where Herod inaugurated the city and where Titus enjoyed gladiatorial contests between Jewish captives from Jerusalem. Pictures taken from the air have also shown quite clearly the outline of Herod's harbor. In 1960 an American underwater archaeological team explored and plotted much of the sea bottom there. They confirmed Josephus' measurements of the stones, and also think they have found parts of the lead bases on which some of the colossal figures stood. The bottom of the harbor, clay and stone in Herod's day, is now covered with from five to fifteen feet of sand. But with the use of a suction airlift, the divers were able to move enough sand (particularly near the harbor entrance where water and sand are deepest) to diagram a portion of the stone tumble. On the basis of this they concluded that an earthquake destroyed the seawall, and tentatively pointed to the tremor of A.D. 130 as the one that may have brought down Herod's magnificent constructions. One other matter of some importance was discovered. Submerged just off shore were numerous Roman pillars, walls, and foundations. This indicates that some of the city once on land is now covered by water. Again, earthquake activity that has caused portions of the northern Palestinian coast to rise and others to fall is the probable culprit.

The Temple

Herod's masterpiece among many notable achievements was the Temple in Jerusalem. The structure built by the returned exiles and dedicated in 516 B.C. (see pp. 212-13) was hardly a worthy one. In the eighteenth year of his reign, 20-19 B.C., Herod determined to tear down the Second Temple and replace it with what Josephus tells us the king considered to be "the most glorious of all his actions." "It really was," adds Josephus with awe. But then, ever unsympathetic to Herod, he goes on to say that it was constructed as a sufficient and everlasting memorial to the king himself and not to God. Doubtless Herod's motives were mixed. Certainly his name did come to be associated with the fabulous Temple complex which he caused to be situated on the holy mountain in Jerusalem. Yet, there is no more sufficient ground for consistently questioning his motives than there is for assuming that David always or even usually acted in good faith. Herod, who as a layman could not and never did enter certain parts of his new structure, was nonetheless content to proceed with what should be numbered among the wonders of the ancient world.

It was no easy thing, in the first instance, to convince the religious community of Judea that they should allow their sacred area to be destroyed and totally remade. Many scholars cite Herod's Idumean background and his treatment by Jewish writers to suggest that the opposition to his grandiose scheme was based on the suspicion that he did not mean to rebuild the Temple, or if so, that he intended to dedicate it to a pagan god, perhaps even to Augustus. Suspicion there surely was, but a large measure of it was doubt that the plans which Herod had for the site could be brought to pass. So vast was the design, says our ever-present witness Josephus, that the king knew that he would find little support among the multitudes. In order to win them over and to show his intention to carry through his plan, Herod made extensive preparations including training 1000 priests as masons and carpenters so that profane hands would not defile the holiest portions of the sacred area. In addition, he readied 1000 wagons to carry the hewn stone the short distance from the famous quarry near the present-day Damascus Gate. This had the effect of assuring his opposition that, once the old building came down, all the stone for the new structure could be moved in completely and at once.

Two well-known parts of Herod's platform wall. The Pinnacle of the Temple, towering high above the Kidron Valley (right), is mentioned in the Temptation narratives. The Wailing Wall (above) is a part of the western wall.

What was this vast design? There was only so much he could do with the Temple proper.[16] It could be made—and was made—into a splendid Hellenistic building, but its dimensions were mostly determined by those recorded of Solomon's earlier structure. It was a different matter with the sacred enclosure in which the sanctuary was to stand. This Herod meant to enlarge, even double in size, and to adorn with splendor unmatched anywhere by anyone. The site today, the Haram es-Sharif,[17] is deceiving, and the vastness of Herod's plan and accomplishment does not at first commend itself. Mention has previously been made of the natural contours of the hill (see p. 137). Whatever modifications were necessary for the construction of Solomon's Temple and

Palace, it would appear that the essential pear shape of the site was left as it was. On the northeast corner the hill fell steeply away for 162 feet, at the southwest the drop was 163 feet, while on the southeast it was 150 feet. Herod proposed to construct an enormous platform over all this. What this man proposed, he did. When the 10,000 laborers withdrew eighty-six years later, they left a flat area covering approximately thirty-five acres. Although the northern limit of the present haram was extended sometime later, perhaps by the Emperor Justinian (A.D. 527-565), the other sides of this structure are those which first commended themselves to Herod's mind.

What the execution of this colossal conception entailed can readily be grasped by an examination of its walls which in total circumference are only forty-six yards less than a mile. Although thoroughly restored by Suliman the Magnificent in 1585, it is still easily possible to see in this wall the large, carefully cut, marginally drafted Herodian masonry. In places it extends twenty-two courses above present ground level. The fullest and best description of this type of crafted stone is that given by Father Vincent:

Herodian construction favors the use of regular and homogeneous materials; each block is of large size and the edges are dressed after the practical and ornamental manner of drafted masonry, leaving the face projecting as a bevelled

[16] The sacred area consisted of two major parts, the Temple proper (naos in Greek) and the larger enclosure within which it was located (hieron in Greek). Although the distinction between these two is not made in the Old Testament, the New Testament usually maintains the difference (Matthew 26:55; 27:40; Mark 14:49; 15:29; Luke 21:37; John 2:19; 7:28) as do Josephus and later Jewish sources. But none of these is entirely consistent. Matthew 27:5 and John 2:20, for instance, seem to speak of naos when indicating the totality of the sacred complex. This is in line with Old Testament usage.

[17] Cf. the discussion on pp. 137-38.

Arches known as "Solomon's Stables" (below) are actually Herodian supports for the southeastern corner of the temple platform, the Pinnacle. Excavations at the southwestern corner of the platform have unearthed a massive master course stone, some thirty-five feet in length (above).

Convent de Sion

panel. Sometimes this face is smooth and lightly pricked all over, with a delicately-chiselled border; sometimes it is rough-hewn with the quarry face jutting out boldly and giving to the stone an impression of strength. Both these forms give at once vigor and relief to the face of the wall by producing an effect of light and shade and correcting the defects of perspective. The blocks are jointed without mortar and laid in regular courses of often more than a meter in height. In the interior of the wall the ends of the blocks are carefully fixed to each other with very hard mortar, the use of rubble being scrupulously avoided. The foundations are embedded in the rock-cut trough, not necessarily deep but sufficiently so to give the stones a firm and immovable base. Sometimes this may be further strengthened by a layer of cement or other packing proof against all pressure. The varying height of this packing corrects any un-

evenness in the level of the rock. Above the regulation course the wall is made up of continuous rows of blocks, set back according to the requirements of the building and the slant of the terrain.[18]

The southeast corner of the platform is even today spectacular, although like the rest of the structure it is but a hint of its former grandeur. Here is the "Pinnacle of the Temple" (Matthew 4:5; Luke 4:9) which Josephus describes as being so high that one could not see the valley below. In fact, this corner, the singularly most imposing part of the wall, in its full glory was surmounted by a portico and tower which raised it 450 feet above the valley floor. Because of Muslim religious sensibilities it has not been possible to excavate within the sacred precincts, and until June 1967 it was almost impossible to work even in the vicinity of the walls. Charles Warren's extensive work in the middle of the nineteenth century was a singular exception. Until finally stopped by the religious authorities, he carried out large-scale excavations at various points around the walls. His method was that of shaft and tunnel. Working at this southeastern angle, he was able to determine that, in addition to the fourteen courses of Herodian masonry visible above the ground, twenty-one more are below the surface. Nine shafts at various other places showed the same thing: Herod had founded his platform on bedrock.

At the southeastern corner the master course is still in place, five courses above the surface. This line of particularly large stones is on a level with the entrances to the Double Gate and the Triple Gate, the access from the south, and with the floor of the so-called Solomon's Stables. This latter construction, a series of vaults supporting the southeastern section of the platform,

[18] Louis-Hughes Vincent, "La troisième enceinte de Jèrusalem," Revue Biblique, 37, no. 3 (July 1928): 332.

is Crusader in its present form and may have got its name from the quartering of horses here during the time of the Latin Kingdom of Jerusalem (A.D. 1099-1291). The first written reference to these vaults as "Solomon's Stables" is even later. Mejir ed Din, an Arab writer, seems to have given them the name in 1521. Originally the work of Herod it served to support the interior ground level of the sacred enclosure. In no case does it have any known connection with Solomon.

Along the western wall Herod constructed a number of gates, three of which have been positively identified by archaeology. The population of the city had shifted from the south, where the bulk was as late as Nehemiah's time, to the western hill. Between this hill and that on which the Temple stood was the Tyropoeon Valley, subsequently filled to a large extent but in that day in places as much as eighty feet deep. Across this chasm bridges were erected on large arches so that movement between the city and the Temple would be easy. Robinson's Arch, named for Edward Robinson who called attention to its existence and significance in 1838, is approximately forty feet from the southwestern angle. Today it consists merely of parts of springers of an arch whose span has been calculated at forty-two feet. Its width is about forty-three feet.

Along the western wall 550 feet north of Robinson's Arch is the Gate of the Chain, main entrance to the present Muslim sanctuary. The Street of the Chain which penetrates the wall at this point joins the *haram* with the western hill. In Herod's time this route connected the Temple with that part of the city containing the royal palace. Today's street appears to be on ground level. In fact it crosses the central valley, the Tyropoeon, by means of a series of subterranean vaults about ten feet below the surface. The contemporary paving stones over which hundreds of the devout walk

daily are in fact almost eighty feet above bedrock. Bearing the main weight is an arch identical in span to that projected for Robinson's Arch, forty-two feet, and similar in width, about forty-three feet. This is Wilson's Arch, named for Sir Charles Wilson who in 1864 was the first to explore it scientifically. In his words it is "one of the most perfect and magnificent remains in Jerusalem." Observing the splendid masonry of its construction, Wilson immediately noted its similarity of workmanship to the Wailing Wall which is only a few feet to the south. Such a connection would indicate a Herodian structure.

Three years after Wilson first saw the arch, Warren began its extensive examination. This second young officer sank a shaft through the relatively modern concrete floor which once formed a reservoir beneath the arch. This not only showed the depth to bedrock, but revealed remains of what was apparently an earlier arch some twenty-four feet below the existing structure. These obviously earlier remains plus the ruinous state of Robinson's Arch as compared with the perfect condition of Wilson's led Warren to the assumption that the latter was in whole or in part of later construction. At first he thought its present appearance the result of rebuilding in the fifth or sixth century A.D., perhaps by Justinian. A few years after venturing this opinion Warren revised his view slightly; the arch could have been as early as the fourth Christian century.

Recent major excavations have shown that the arch and many of the surrounding structures are, in fact, Herodian. Had Warren been able to continue his work, he might have corrected his own view. But the governing authorities in Jerusalem in 1870 were fearful that the infidel would excavate under the holy enclosure itself. Such an occurrence might produce serious consequences, even civil disorder. Thus while the young Englishman was away at Jericho, the Turk-

Exploration under ground in Jerusalem has increased our knowledge of the Herodian city. W. F. Stinespring (above left) looks at Robinson's Arch before its recent excavation

Scholars conceived in a model what this Herodian bridge over the Tyropoeon Valley may have looked like in biblical times (above, right; note the double-arched bridge by the Temple platform). Stine-spring's success in reaching Wilson's Arch resulted in the first photograph of a Herodian bridge intact (below). This arch has since been excavated and is accessible as is the passageway leading from it. This passage was perhaps Herod's underground access to the Temple from his palace on the western hill.

W. F. Stinespring

ish governor seized the opportunity to close the entrance to Wilson's Arch with a stone wall. Dismayed, his investigation hardly begun, Warren turned his attention elsewhere. "Presumably the pasha's wall is still there," said Father J. Simons commenting on the event in his *Jerusalem and the Old Testament* (p. 365), "waiting to be removed by a yet greater diplomat than Charles Warren."

Such a man gained access to Wilson's Arch in the summer of 1963, and returned in 1965 and 1966. W. F. Stinespring of Duke University was the first person in almost a century who was allowed to investigate underground Jerusalem near the holy enclosure. With a view to studying some of the major chambers in the area and to determining whether or not Wilson's Arch is Herodian, this scholar entered into sensitive, seemingly endless negotiations accompanied by the inevitable countless cups of jet black coffee. In the end the Muslim Council agreed to allow him to explore. A difficult and somewhat dangerous path to the arch was opened. It involved scaling walls, dropping into dark pits, clambering over the ruins of ages, and, worst of all, encountering the debilitating effects of ancient dust which earlier had laid Warren low. Stinespring was no more fortunate and had to suspend operations temporarily to recover from illness. The whole matter was made more unpleasant by fleas which stoutly resisted the intrusion.

Having at last overcome both objections which had kept a century of scholars at bay as well as the health hazards of the subterranean chambers, Stinespring set to work. He tentatively established the Hellenistic reconstruction of Jerusalem under Antiochus IV as the likely date of certain structures. Turning to Wilson's Arch itself, he removed some of the plaster, probably Turkish in origin, to reveal the juncture where the southern edge springs from the platform wall. The first courses of the arch were found

Excavations at the southwestern corner of the platform have revealed a rich occupational history from the time of the Hebrew monarchy to the Byzantine period. Massive Herodian masonry is visible in the lower courses of the wall. The dome is that of al-Aqsa Mosque.

to be an integral part of that wall. This wall is a continuation of the Wailing Wall which is a part of Herod's great work.

In 1965 Stinespring had mainly charted, measured, and photographed. Some of his photos—first ever of the subject—appeared to show evidence of rebuilding, thus substantiating Warren's argument for post-Herodian dating. But in 1966 Stinespring found that the apparent indications of reconstruction were nothing more than plaster applied in relatively modern times to make the area watertight in order to incorporate it into a large cistern nearby. The wedge-shaped stones comprising the springers of the arch are identical with those in the wall and show no indication of repair or rebuilding. The arch is bonded to the wall. Stinespring concluded that as it now stands it is an architecturally planned part of the retaining wall surrounding the platform of Herod.

In the summer of 1967, following the June War, the government of Israel cleared out a large number of homes near the Western Wall in order to give easier access to the Wailing Wall and to form a plaza in front of that site holy to Judaism. Among the dwellings destroyed were those abutting

Wilson's Arch. One result of this operation was to expose a large portion of the wall toward the north. This newly exposed part extended up to the arch. Indeed, today the section of the wall under the arch is continuous with the Wailing Wall and is a place of prayer for the devout. Another result was to confirm Stinespring's conclusion that the arch was a part of the original Herodian wall. There is now no question that Wilson's Arch is one of Herod's bridges which joined the Temple with the western part of the city where the king's new palace stood.

At the same time clearing was being done at the Wailing Wall, there was some preliminary exploration of the maze of chambers and passageways associated with the arch. Formal and careful excavation was not undertaken until later, however, and is still in progress. Much of the construction is Turkish; some is earlier, Arab, Crusader, Byzantine, Roman, and perhaps Herodian. There is a large tunnel running westward from the arch. This may be one of the two underground passages which Herod built to allow quick access to the Temple by his soldiers—and also a means of escape lest a mob entrap the ruler in his Temple! Herod's son had to use just such a means of escape on one occasion. The tunnel in question, if it is the Herodian one, ran to the Western Palace, the present site of the Citadel. The other and as yet unrecovered tunnel joined the Temple to the Antonia.

In 1968 Benjamin Mazar, president emeritus of Hebrew University, undertook massive excavations outside the walls on the southwestern corner of the platform. Among other things this work has shown that the area was not merely occupied, but was the location of attractive and occasionally monumental architecture from the time of Herod (who apparently first developed it) until the Abbasids (ca. 9th century A.D.). When Hadrian rebuilt the city following the Second Revolt (A.D. 135), the area seems to have

been residential. Dwellings may have been placed there in the preceding period, between the first (A.D. 70) and second (A.D. 135) destructions of the city when nondescript structures occupied the site. Prior to that, in the time of Herod, the area likely resembled a Roman plaza with terraced marble streets in the valley and beside the walls of the platform. Towering above was the twin of Wilson's Arch: Robinson's Arch. The springer of Robinson's Arch can be seen built into the wall of the platform. Mazar's excavations have laid bare the piers on which the arch stood in the valley. It was, contrary to what had long been thought, a bridge with several arches. The excavators found debris from the destruction of Herod's Temple lying on the pavement of the Herodian streets.

In addition to what has already been mentioned, four other matters worthy of attention have been found in the Western Wall excavation. (1) By the late summer of 1970, over 20,000 coins had been recovered from the area. These range in almost unbroken succession from Alexander Janneus (2nd century B.C.) to French Crusader (12th century A.D.) coins. (2) A Hebrew inscription has been found rudely carved on the Western Wall near the corner. It is a quotation from Isaiah 66:14. This was cut into the stone after the destruction when the pious were looking longingly forward to a gathering of God's own people into the Holy City. (3) Halfway along the southern wall, at the eastward extreme of the excavations, a column drum was uncovered. The excavators believe that it is from the Royal Portico that surmounted the southern wall during the time of Herod (see p. 249). (4) On the excavated slope of the hill that faces the Western Wall, a number of tombs have been found. Pottery associated with these indicates that they are eighth-century B.C. tombs. This area, then, must have been outside the city during the time of the Hebrew monarchy. This supports Miss Kenyon's earlier suggestion that the western hill was not a part of the city before Maccabean times. Are these newly discovered tombs royal tombs? Some excavators think so, but the pottery from them is undistinguished. Would not royalty have been buried with something out of the ordinary? Even if the tombs were robbed, would not some trace of grandeur survive? These questions cannot be answered. At least they cannot be answered on the basis of evidence now available. But the excavation at the Western Wall continues, and Mazar intends to extend his work westward and thoroughly excavate the tomb area.

Between Mazar's excavation and the Wailing Wall is an unexcavated area which includes Barclay's Gate, buried up to the lintel. From the interior more of this gate can be seen. The lintel is almost twenty-five feet across, and contains five enormous stones. Above it is vaulting. From this gate may have been the steps which Josephus describes as descending to the level of the valley some seventy feet below. A fourth entrance to Herod's Temple from the west was called in antiquity *Coponius*. Its location is a matter of debate. The origin of the name is likewise not agreed upon. The first Roman governor of Judea bore that name, but it is not likely that he, having replaced Herod's ousted son, Archelaus, would have been honored by having a sacred gate named for him.

Only one gate pierced the north wall. It was called *Tadi,* a word which denotes darkness. Its function seems to have been to allow rapid passage from the holy place by a priest who had incurred defilement. It is also possible that this was the place through which sheep were brought into the shrine for use in the sacrifice. If so, it is the Sheep Gate mentioned in John 5:2. In any event no trace of the gate remains as all was carried away by a later extension of the northern limits of the platform. It is interesting to note, however, that today one of the northern gates bears the name *Bab al'Atm,* "Gate of Darkness."

The eastern wall also had only one gate. Those who knew it in Herod's day called it *Shushan.* Today it is known as the Golden Gate. In its present highly decorated form it is Byzantine and is but one bit of evidence indicating, contrary to a widespread view, that Christians were uninterested in the Temple area. While this structure was refurbished and adorned in later times, it has retained its essential Herodian features. In order that traffic might flow easily it was double, as were all the major entrances to the Temple enclosure. Anyone who has tried to pass quickly through the Damascus Gate or any of the present gates to Old Jerusalem can appreciate the wisdom of Herod's "divided highway" traffic pattern at the gates. The long porch of the Golden Gate and its bays and vaulting are also structurally from the original and were necessary to accommodate Solomon's Porch, the double portico which ran along the top of the eastern wall. Through this gate Jesus is thought by some to have passed in his triumphal entry into the city (Matthew 21: 1-9; Mark 11:1-10; Luke 19:28-38; John 12: 12-19). According to local lore with Jewish, Christian, and Muslim variations, it is this gate which will play a prominent role in the Last Judgment. Blocked since the late twelfth century, this entrance will, in the piety of Muslims, open to admit Allah who will weigh the souls of men in the numerous arches on the raised stage supporting the Dome of the Rock.

There were porticoes along all the walls. Those on the east, north, and west were double, approximately sixty feet wide. That along the eastern wall, Solomon's Porch, was the setting for the Fourth Gospel's narrative of Jesus' dramatic winter confrontation with certain of his enemies (John 10:23; see also Acts 3:11 and 5:12). Its name is a matter of debate, and there are those scholars who follow Josephus in maintaining that it had some connection with the old King of Israel himself. This is most unlikely, given the fact that the eastern wall of Herod's enclosure was, of the four, the one which probably followed a new line. Yet, on the evidence of the New Testament it certainly seems to have been known as "Solomon's Porch" when it formed a part of Herod's Temple.

It has already been noted that the most spectacular aspect of the walls was from the south. There, where the three valleys meet, waters from Siloam give the area an almost continual green. Moreover, the gradual slope of Ophel makes it impossible to see the bottom of the wall until very close, thus giving to the part visible from the valley an illusion of floating and lightness. In this setting Herod chose to place the masterpiece of his creation. Here was the Royal Portico, so named apparently because it rose above the site of the palace of Solomon and his successors, the kings of Judah. Dividing the thirty-foot-wide aisles known to the other porticoes was a third aisle of fifteen feet. The roof of this middle portion was almost 100 feet above the top of the wall, twice the height of the coverings of the side aisles. The whole was colonnaded, with the interior elevation made possible by columns resting on architraves, a feature familiar in medieval cathedrals. Each of the 162 columns in this portico was surmounted by a Corinthian capital. Its wooden roof was richly carved, and in the best Roman style further decorated by sculpture. On the east this portico ended at the tower which dominated the Pinnacle of the Temple. On the west it may well have been integrated architecturally with the southernmost viaduct over the Tyropoeon of which the sad stump of Robinson's Arch is our sole reminder today. Nowhere in the unparalleled achievement of Greek and Roman culture was there a passageway to rival this Royal Portico, not in conception, setting, design, or execution.

Sir Charles Wilson, writing in *The Recovery of Jerusalem* (pp. 7-8), tried to recapture something of what it was like:

It is almost impossible to realize the effect which would be produced by a building longer and higher than York Cathedral, standing on a solid mass of masonry equal in height to the tallest of our church spires; and to this we must add the dazzling whiteness of stone fresh from the mason's hands.

Such was the setting Herod provided for the House of God.

Strictly speaking, the Temple proper is not a matter of archaeological consideration since only one stone from it and parts of another can be positively identified. Ironically these fragments are warnings which were built into a stone balustrade dividing the Temple complex from the much larger esplanade popularly known as the Court of the Gentiles. The complete inscription was found in 1871 in a cemetery at Jerusalem. It instructs non-Jews not to enter the sacred areas; if they do they accept the risk of death.[19] A portion of another stone bearing the same inscription was found to the east of the city, near St. Stephen's Gate (again in a cemetery) in 1938.

No one knows exactly what Herod's Temple looked like. Many designs have been suggested. A number have been drawn; most are utterly incredible. We know it was in the vicinity of the Dome of the Rock, that it was a Hellenistic building, and a handsome one. "Whoever has not seen Herod's Temple," said the rabbis, "has never seen a beautiful building." Like many other sanctuaries be-

[19] It is not clear if this refers to the danger of mob action or if legal action is being threatened. In the view of many New Testament interpreters the presence of these warnings on the balustrade was in Paul's mind when he spoke of "the dividing wall of hostility" in the second chapter of Ephesians. According to the account in Acts 21:27-36, Paul was the object of mob hostility because he had ignored these warnings and had taken Greeks into the Temple (*naos*; see p. 242, n. 16).

fore and since, it was a series of enclosures which became more sacred and thus more exclusive as one drew nearer to the inner sanctum, the Holy of Holies. To the best of our knowledge there were six enclosures: the vast open space now commonly known as the Court of the Gentiles; the Court of the Women; the Court of Israel to which only Jewish males were admitted; the Court of the Priests in which the great altar of sacrifice stood; the Nave of the Temple; and finally the Holy of Holies, a completely empty cube which was entered once a year, on the Day of Atonement, and then solely by the High Priest.

The Temple was oriented east and west with the five inner enclosures occupying an area probably exceeding 475 feet in length and just under 400 feet in width. Approaching from the east, one passed through the balustrade with its warnings and moved toward the first major barrier, a wall perhaps as high as sixty feet. Eight gates at the top of five steps penetrated this; the one on the east was the most massive and the most highly decorated. Enormous, double, and covered with sheetings of bronze from mines near Corinth, it was appropriately known as the Corinthian Gate. Its gorgeous appearance may, however, have given it another name, one preserved for us in Acts 3:2: "that gate of the Temple which is called Beautiful." Inside was a large space, the Court of the Women, which occupied almost one third of the total area of the sacred enclosures. In this were located the chests which received the monetary offerings of those who came to worship. It was probably here rather than in the Temple Treasury proper (a place neither readily nor easily accessible to the public) that Jesus taught his disciples by the example of the widow's mite (Mark 12:41-44; Luke 21:1-4).

From this area fifteen steps, semicircular in design (not unlike those at the mosque in Hebron), gave access to the Court of Israel.

The gates at the top of these stairs were the most massive in the sacred complex. Twenty men, it is said, were required to open or shut them. Decorated in gold, they were named *Nicanor* for the Alexandrian Jew who either made them or gave them. At any rate, their association with him distinguished his family for several generations. The courtyard in which the worshiper now stood surrounded the sanctuary on three sides. But between it and the building was another open space, the Court of the Priests, wherein stood the altar of sacrifice. This structure, itself of enormous proportions, could easily be seen when the Corinthian and Nicanor Gates were open. It was thus possible for nonpriests and women, neither of whom could directly approach the altar, to participate to a degree in the offering of a sacrifice which they had provided.

Twelve further steps led into the Temple building itself. A structure perhaps somewhat reminiscent in profile of old Coventry Cathedral, it was compared to a lion whose body was in repose but whose head was held high. Its porch was indeed considerably higher than the roof over the nave. It was also much wider and gave the opportunity to surround the inmost sanctuary with a series of rooms as had Solomon's Temple. A feature not known in either of the earlier structures on the site was a large room above the sanctuary (or more likely only in the towering porch) which could serve as an assembly hall for priests. The wooden roof was virtually encrusted with gilded spikes whose purpose was to prevent birds from settling where they might soil the holy edifice.

An embroidered tapestry from Babylon hung before the twenty-foot-wide doors which gave entrance into the Temple. Above these doors was not only a golden vine complete with grapes, but also an eagle which for some reason Herod thought appropriate. This latter, needless to say, was scandalous to the more orthodox who conspired to have it destroyed when premature reports of Herod's death circulated through the city. Once inside the building, the priest was greeted by a large, dim chamber perhaps twenty-eight feet wide, fifty-six feet long, and as much as 162 feet to the ceiling. In an atmosphere thickened by the smell of incense, one could see the seven-branched candlestick, the table for the Bread of the Presence, the silver trumpets, and other objects vividly recorded to us on the Arch of Titus in Rome.[20] At the far end of the nave, separated from it by a thick veil (Matthew 27:51; Mark 15:38), was the Holy of Holies, a twenty-eight-foot cube, empty of objects, but for the faithful the place of the awesome presence of God.

After less than a year and a half of work, the Temple proper was dedicated in the summer of 18 B.C. Elaborate preparations had been made for its swift construction. Herod himself offered a sacrifice of 300 oxen on the occasion. The enormous platform, walls, and porticoes were unfinished, indeed, they were hardly begun. At Herod's death they were not yet completed, nor even thirty years later when Jesus in the fullness of his manhood walked there (John 2:20). It was not until A.D. 64 that the whole design was accomplished. This included among other things reconstructing a part of that which holy but unskilled hands of the priestly masons had originally built. It had collapsed sometime during the reign of Nero, probably in the late 50s or early 60s of the first century. Yet even in its unfinished state the Temple and its setting were one of the most remarkable sights of the ancient world, easily challenging the so-called "seven wonders."

[20] This monument, standing at the head of the Sacred Way in the Imperial Forum, celebrates the victory of Titus over the Jews in the war of A.D. 66-73. The future emperor's triumph through the streets of Rome is shown in various scenes including one where his soldiers are carrying booty from the Jewish Temple in Jerusalem. Prominent is the large seven-branched lampstand as well as the silver trumpets.

The Arch of Titus in Rome depicts Roman soldiers bearing sacred vessels from Herod's Temple (above). Another relief from the arch (below) shows Titus in triumph. Near the Temple site in Jerusalem bricks bearing the stamp of the Tenth Legion (bottom) indicate that other Roman soldiers stayed behind.

It elicited unusual praise from Tacitus and Pliny who was moved to speak of Jerusalem as the most famous city of the Roman east. Josephus who knew it in detail and Titus who made every human effort to preserve it in his conquest were awed by its strength and magnificence. Situated on a high hill on the spiny mountainous ridge of Judea, its gleaming white stones, unweathered by the passing of time, could be seen for miles in almost any direction. Whatever his motive for this marvel, Herod had provided a shrine that quickened with pride the heart of every Jew and whose glories were celebrated by the rabbinic writers long after they had forgotten what it looked like and when it had become commonplace to ignore the "outsider" who had built it. It is one of the tragedies of history that this structure, so splendid, should have lasted only six years after its completion. It was accidentally but perhaps inevita-

A fragment of a wall just north of Jerusalem (above) has long been a matter of controversy. It is now thought to have been a part of Titus' wall of circumvolution. At Bethlehem a portion of Herod's aqueduct is visible (below).

bly burned in the siege of A.D. 70. Smoke like a sickening pall hung over the Judean hills for days. Shortly thereafter what remained was pulled down. Literally not one stone was left upon another. Only the platform remained.

Herod died in 4 B.C., the same year in which Jesus was born. On the verge of suicide, he sought relief for his gangrenous, pain-racked body in the warm springs beside the Dead Sea. Carried from spa to spa on a litter, he found no alleviation, not even through terrible baths in hot oil as prescribed by his physicians. Always capable of cruelty, his mind of genius, now seriously eroded by the horror of constant physical suffering and the terrors of paranoia, was easily capable of the deeds reported in Matthew 2:16. It was at this time that he ordered the death of his son and heir, Antipater, thereby prompting Augustus Caesar's remark that he had rather be one of Herod's pigs than one of his sons.[21] Five days after the burial of his eldest son, Herod, aged seventy, thirty-four years king of Judea, was dead at Jericho. Another son, Archelaus, succeeded him and gave his father a fitting funeral, one worthy of any monarch. Followed by what remained of his family, at least five regiments of his mercenary army in full battle dress, and 500 servants bearing spices, Herod's body in royal regalia was borne on a golden bier draped in purple across the Wilderness of Judea to the Herodion, near Bethlehem. There on a towering cone-shaped hill he had created by placing one mountain crest on top of another, he was buried in a round castle surrounded by gardens and pavilions and reached by a very steep marble stairway. From the Herodion, gleaming Jerusalem was easily visible. For

[21] Herod had previously ordered the deaths of two other sons, Alexander and Aristobulus, sons by Mariamme I. These awful things occurred in the familial hatreds involving Herod's sister, Salome, and certain of his wives, especially Mariamme I. In the end Salome succeeded in destroying almost the whole of the lineage represented by this Hasmonean Mariamme and her offspring.

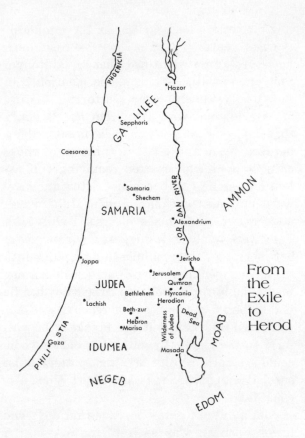

20. THE DEAD SEA SCROLLS

The Original Discovery

"A PHENOMENAL DISCOVERY," announced *The Biblical Archaeologist* to its readers in May, 1948. *"The most important discovery ever made in Old Testament manuscripts . . ."* began the article which went on to state that four scrolls from the Syrian Orthodox Monastery of St. Mark in Jerusalem had been identified by scholars of the American School of Oriental Research as the book of Isaiah, a commentary on Habakkuk, and a sectarian writing. The fourth scroll, of tightly rolled leather, had not been opened because of advanced deterioration. Word of these manuscripts had earlier been given in a routine ASOR Newsletter sent out on March 7 by Millar Burrows, then director of the School in Jerusalem. In a special news release a month later, April 11, 1948, Burrows announced publicly the date assigned to the Isaiah Scroll—at least the first century B.C.! From America the astounding news traveled to Europe and around the globe. Thus did the world come to learn of the amazing existence of what are now commonly called *The Dead Sea Scrolls,* manuscripts whose biblical materials predate previously known Hebrew sacred texts by a thousand years.[1] On April 26 an Associated Press dispatch from Jerusalem announced that other scrolls believed to be of similar character and date had been acquired by the Hebrew University and were being studied by E. L. Sukenik.

Behind these dramatic statements did not lie the usual story of patient scholarly inquiry, nor days and weeks of hard, often frustrating digging in the hot Palestinian

those who mourned this man or perhaps merely recalled his accomplishments, the vision would not cease with what the eye could behold on the holy hill just to the northwest. His many monuments at Hebron, Samaria, Caesarea, Masada, Machaerus, Jericho, and elsewhere would have come to mind. Beyond his borders his vision and generosity had graced Ptolemais, Damascus, Tripoli, Sidon, Tyre, Beirut, Antioch, and a host of other cities as far away as Rhodes. "Fortune," said Josephus in summary, "was very favorable to him." And so it was.

Looking back today, one cannot but wonder whether those who stood in Herod's funeral train on the Herodion and considered his benefactions and failures may have glanced down and slightly to the west, to a pasture near Bethlehem which Christians now know as "Shepherds' Field," the place where according to tradition the angels announced the birth of Jesus.

---

[1] The Nash Papyrus, a small fragment of Deuteronomy from *ca.* 100 B.C., is the sole exception. This fragment containing the Ten Commandments and the *Shema* (6:4) was liturgical in origin and not from a manuscript of the book of Deuteronomy itself. The Nash Papyrus was valuable in dating the newly found texts.

sun. The events which brought the scrolls to light, established their date, and led to their first publication and final disposition were almost incredible; a mixture of chance, intrigue, doggedness, courage, accusation, and subterfuge. No writer of mystery stories would have invented so improbable a tale lest it not be believed. Yet the fascinating sequence of events is not only true but was played out against a background of increasing violence, bloodshed, and finally open war. After almost two years at the center of the storm surrounding his possession of four of these invaluable texts, Metropolitan Athanasius Yeshue Samuel, Syrian Orthodox Prelate of Jerusalem,[2] could not recall exact dates on which various matters connected with the scrolls took place. Dates, it turns out, are hardly the only matters now unclear. The principals are not in agreement on who was involved, when or what was said, inferred, or promised, and on what authority. Furthermore, the astounding public interest in these sensational finds has produced a veritable flood of books and articles, some very good, some not. Innumerable magazine and newspaper stories appeared, often serving narrow partisan interests and hence doing little to untangle an already complicated situation. Compelling in their simplest retelling, the events have become enhanced and somewhat romanticized in various accounts.

It all seems to have begun innocently enough in the winter of 1946-1947. Three Bedouin of the Ta'amireh tribe which inhabits the forbidding wilderness between Bethlehem and the Dead Sea were grazing their sheep and goats by the cliffs one half mile north of some ancient ruins northwest of the Sea. Known to the Old Testament as "the City of Salt" (Joshua 15:62), these remains have acquired another name over the years: Khirbet Qumran. Archaeologists made

[2] Now Syrian Metropolitan of the United States and Canada.

test digs there as long ago as the middle of the last century. Not much was concluded, however. Some identified it with a Roman fort, others with various places mentioned in the Old Testament, even Gomorrah. If any of this history was known to the Bedouin that day, it was far from their minds. Shepherding sheep and goats in the area of those cliffs is a difficult matter requiring full attention. As he climbed about after his wayward animals, one man, Jum'a Muhammed, noticed two small holes in a solid cliff face. They were too high to suggest a normal cave, but there they were. Jum'a flung a stone into the lower opening. When it struck he scrambled quickly for a look. He later said that he did so because what he had heard was not rock striking rock, but the breaking of pottery. In the gradually gathering darkness he could see nothing. But breaking pottery must surely mean jars. Treasure! Gold! What else could it be?

Jum'a did not enter the cave that day. The lower opening was entirely too small; the higher one might be large enough for a slender man. Could he get out if he once got in? What dangers might surround a hidden fortune? And, oh yes, those sheep and goats. He called his two cousins up to examine the opening. Khalil Musa was older than Jum'a. Muhammed Ahmed el-Hamed (called "edh-Dhib"—"the Wolf") was younger, in his teens. They decided they would investigate further, but later. Every other day they had to take their flock to Ain Feshkha, a couple of miles south, in order to give them water. It was already getting dark, and they needed to gather their animals in preparation for the short journey to the spring the next day.

The next afternoon, with their flocks watered, they returned to the foot of the cliffs beneath the cave. There they made their beds for the night beside their sheep and goats. Edh-Dhib was the first to awake the next morning. He scaled the 350 or so feet up to the openings. By ingenuity and agility he was able to enter the upper opening feet first. He came down upon a floor littered with broken pottery and other debris. The darkness dispelled as his eyes adjusted to the light. In the dimness he saw a number of long, fairly narrow jars standing against the sides of the cave. A few jars had bowl-shaped covers. An eager hand went into one jar, then another, and another. Nothing! Eight proved to be empty. A ninth was filled with dirt. But from one, edh-Dhib extracted two bundles wrapped in a greenish cloth. A third bundle was a roll of leather with no covering. This was all the crestfallen Bedouin took down the hill with him that morning when he went to rejoin his sleepy cousins. John Trever, who was the first to make a thorough investigation of all the Syrian Monastery material, is of the opinion that what this boy had under his arms as he half ran and half slipped down toward the Dead Sea that winter morning was the great Isaiah Scroll containing the whole biblical book, as well as the Habakkuk Commentary and the Manual of Discipline.

In the eyes of Jum'a and Khalil these decaying rolls were worthless. Where was the gold edh-Dhib had surely found while they slept? Where had he hidden it? Most of the rest of the morning and probably some more days as well were spent dealing with these kinds of question. The three men did remove some of the jars from the cave, but these were left just outside once they had been thoroughly searched. When the Bedouin returned to the Ta'amireh center near Bethlehem, Jum'a carried the scrolls with him in a bag. When he reached home he hung them on a tentpole and practically forgot about them. They were occasionally passed around among members of the tribe as a sort of curiosity. Some damage was done to the Isaiah Scroll in this process, but it seems to have been restricted to the cover. The text was not hurt. It is possible that the Manual of Discipline which reached St. Mark's in two

pieces was torn apart in Bedouin hands. But this is by no means certain. It could as well have been ripped in ancient times. The break was not such that this could be determined with any assurance.

Maybe the rolls were worth something after all, thought Jum'a. In the next weeks the Bedouin returned to the cave several times and removed a number of scrolls. But who was going to buy them and for what price? Perhaps it was not worthwhile to bother with these things. In Bethlehem they would find out.

Bethlehem, the birthplace of Jesus, is the principal market town of the Ta'amireh. Saturday, the day after the Muslim holy-day, finds the small market area crowded with Bedouin, some buying, some selling, all talking noisily. It is the weekly social occasion for these people who spend most of their days in the lonely desert. Often in the middle of this was Kando—Khalik Iskander Shahin, a Christian (Syrian Orthodox) Arab merchant known and trusted by the shepherds. He eventually became the middleman in selling the manuscripts, but almost by chance. Jum'a and Khalil had taken three scrolls and two jars to Ibrahim 'Ijha, a Bethlehem carpenter who dabbles in antiquities. He showed them to Faidi Salahi, another antiquities dealer. Salahi cautioned 'Ijha that these might be stolen materials and that serious trouble could result. Early in April 1947, the carpenter-merchant returned the manuscripts to the Bedouin saying they had no value.

A little later in the market area Jum'a, carrying the scrolls, met George Ishaya Shamoun who was often found in Bethlehem on Saturdays selling cloaks to the Bedouin. He said he would sell the manuscripts for Jum'a. As they talked, a Ta'amireh friend of Jum'a entered the conversation and suggested that they all go along to Kando's shop and talk with him. Serious negotiations ensued. Khalil was found and became a party to the discussions. It was finally agreed that Kando and George would handle the sale and that they would get one third of the selling price whatever it was. Jum'a and Khalil were given five Palestinian pounds ($14.00) as a guarantee, and the scrolls were left with Kando.[3]

A few days later, during Holy Week, George, also Syrian Orthodox, mentioned the manuscripts to the Metropolitan at St. Mark's Monastery in Jerusalem. Three months later, through a series of adventures and misadventures, Samuel had four of the scrolls in his possession. Along with many others in war-torn Jerusalem he did not know that Professor Sukenik also had some writings from the same source—through Salahi who had apparently changed his mind about there being thievery involved in the Bedouin acquisition of the materials.[4]

The authenticity of the scrolls was much debated for some time. While the vast majority of scholars was convinced that they were first century B.C. or earlier, a few demurred. In the face of mounting evidence to the contrary at least one prominent scholar doggedly held they were medieval. Another maintained the whole thing was a hoax, while a third is reported to have spoken of the materials in Metropolitan Samuel's posses-

sion as "St. Mark's garbage." Today few doubt the judgment of the vast body of international learning that has focused upon these scrolls. They are in the main from the first two centuries before Christ and originated from a Jewish sectarian community based at Khirbet Qumran on the northwestern shore of the Dead Sea.

The Contents of the Scrolls

The original find in what is now known as Cave One contained seven manuscripts.[5] Sukenik had three: the *Warfare Scroll,* the *Thanksgiving Hymns,* and the remnants of an Isaiah Scroll (1QIs^b) containing about one third of the biblical text. Samuel had four: the *Manual of Discipline,* a *Commentary on Habakkuk,* the *Genesis Apocryphon,* and the most magnificent and best preserved manuscript of all—the *Isaiah Scroll* (1QIs^a) containing the complete book.

Although a vast number of biblical texts and fragments of texts were later recovered, the original find contained only one complete scriptural writing: Isaiah. Twice in the New Testament where accounts are given of people reading from the Scriptures it is Isaiah. Once Jesus (Luke 4:16-20) and on another occasion an Ethiopian eunuch (Acts 8:26-39) had the words of that prophet before them. Isaiah was a very popular book among the Jews of Palestine, and the residents of Qumran were no exception. Although apparently much used in ancient days, the *Isaiah Scroll* from beside the Dead Sea is still in superb condition. Twenty-four feet long by an average of 10.2 inches high, it is formed of seventeen sheets of parchment (of vary-

[3] Four scrolls were sold in 1954 for $250,000, and at one point the purchasers were prepared to offer a great deal more, perhaps as much as $400,000 for the Isaiah Scroll alone! Kando received $97.20 for the materials; two thirds went to the Bedouin. He kept about $32.

[4] The story of the intricately tangled web of events surrounding the Scrolls which came into the hands of Samuel and Sukenik is extremely fascinating. It is, however, a tale in itself and cannot be told here. Furthermore, many details concerning the earlier finds from the time of their discovery in 1948 until they came to rest at Hebrew University in 1954 are debated. The interested reader should refer to Yigael Yadin, *The Message of the Scrolls* (London: Weidenfeld and Nicolson, 1957); John Trever, *The Untold Story of Qumran* (London: Pickering and Inglis, 1965); and A. Y. Samuel, *Treasure of Qumran* (Philadelphia: The Westminster Press, 1966). All three accounts should be taken into consideration in making a judgment.

[5] It was thought at first that there were more than these. But one of the scrolls Sukenik had (the *Thanksgiving Hymns*) and one from St. Mark's (the *Manual of Discipline*) were in two parts. When these were joined, seven, not nine, manuscripts were present. Excavators found fragments of the *Thanksgiving Hymns* in the cave, but neither this nor breaks on various parts of the rolls established whether the damage had occurred in ancient or modern times.

ing lengths) carefully sewn together with linen thread. The entire sixty-six chapters of the book are contained in forty-four columns of approximately thirty lines each. The scribe was prone to a number of mistakes, although he almost always corrected them himself. There are, however, evidences of other hands correcting and marking in the margin here and there. The date of this manuscript is usually given as the second century B.C., perhaps toward the end of the century.

The great value of this scroll, as of all the other biblical material from the finds, lies not merely in its antiquity (a thousand years older than the Masoretic text), but also in the fact that it comes from a time before the text was standardized. In the Masoretic text we have the accepted Hebrew text used by scholars today. It dates from the ninth and tenth Christian centuries and was produced by a group of Jewish scholars (the Masoretes) who sought to provide the finest standard text they could. In so doing they made judgments among a number of readings, at various points disregarding some and accepting others. Those disregarded were lost. The Septuagint, a Greek translation of the Hebrew Scriptures made in Egypt in the third century B.C., survives in fourth-century A.D. versions. For purposes of establishing the history of the text, it has been helpfully compared with the Masoretic text. But it is not a simple one-for-one identification since the versions are in different languages, and the Septuagint's value in this regard is limited.

Comparison of the *Isaiah Scroll* (1QIs*) with the Masoretic text has shown a number of things. It is, on the whole, substantially

The beginning of the great Isaiah Scroll (1QIs*) from Cave One. The average height of the columns is ten inches.

John C. Trever

the same, indicating that standardization did not involve a question of major variants.[6] Yet there are numbers of minor variants often pointing to a rejection of archaic spellings and grammar on the part of the Masoretes. Since ancient Hebrew had no vowels, the Masoretes used a system to preserve vocalization in a time when Hebrew was no longer a living language. It is interesting to note that the *Isaiah Scroll* has something of the same sort and, indeed, indicates a much richer range of vowels than the Masoretic system. There are, in addition, certain passages where variants may make a difference in interpretation. There are upward of thirty-four differences in the Servant Song in Isaiah 52–53. Commentators, until now dependent upon the standardized text, will have to consider whether subtle theological viewpoints caused the Masoretes to prefer a certain reading. These are extremely delicate matters. Yet along with these increased difficulties the Dead Sea Scrolls have brought considerable enrichment to our knowledge of the Bible.

The shorter Isaiah Scroll (1QIs[b]), also of parchment, is in a seriously damaged condition, and it was some time before it could be unrolled. Further to complicate the problem, the leather had begun to disintegrate, causing an opaque deposit to cover much of the text that had survived. Infrared photography succeeded where the naked eye failed. The upper part of the last third of the canonical book is present, along with some fragments. In all only six columns, some in poor condition, remain. These contain approximately thirty-six lines each. From all the recovered pieces, those purchased by Sukenik and those recovered by archaeologists at Cave One, it is clear that once the scroll contained the entire book of Isaiah. The writing is particularly graceful, better

than on the *Isaiah Scroll* (1QIs[a]). But the date is approximately the same.

The shorter Isaiah differs from the larger scroll in that it stands much closer to the Masoretic text. This in itself is important in showing that there was no standard Qumran text of Isaiah. Yet the readings are not entirely the same as the Masoretic and provide enough variants for us to say that where there was only one Hebrew text of Isaiah prior to the discovery of the Dead Sea Scrolls, there are now three. This introduces a new era not only in the study of this great Old Testament prophecy; it also provides new material for understanding the development of text and canon.

The *Habakkuk Commentary* is of two strips of soft leather, together four and a half feet long and a little over five inches high in its present condition. Its biblical passages (only chapters one and two are present[7]) show about sixty variants from the Masoretic text. It has, therefore, important implications for a prophetic book long neglected. But of perhaps greater immediate interest is the light it sheds on the history of the Qumran sect. The commentators associated various events in the prophecy with matters in their past and with problems they faced. Hence, to cite one example, where the wicked and the righteous are contrasted in Habakkuk 1, the Qumranites say the figure of the "Teacher of Righteousness" and the "Wicked Priest." The Teacher seems to have been the founder of the sect, while the Priest (the high priest at Jerusalem? Alexander Janneus?) was his bitter enemy. This sets the tenor for the entire commentary. The Priest rejected the prophetic message of the Teacher, forsook the true ways of God, and delivered himself to a search for wealth. His power grew along with his conflict with the Teacher who at

---

[6] The same cannot be said for the book of Samuel which, although not a part of the original find, was recovered later in perhaps a third-century B.C. Hebrew form.

[7] Some have thought that chap. 3 had not yet been added to the biblical book. The end of the scroll from Qumran is preserved, showing that it, at least, never contained a third chapter.

length was persecuted (made exile from Jerusalem?). But God is on the side of the righteous, and the unjust will fall into the hands of their enemies, lose their ill-gained wealth, and bring the nation to devastation.

This commentary shows a temporizing and localizing of the prophecies of Habakkuk in terms of the founding and history of the community. At the same time it betrays an allegorizing tendency on the part of the interpreters and a strong (messianic?) faith in the eventual triumph of the Teacher of Righteousness and his cause.

The *Genesis Apocryphon* is another scroll of the original find which forms a bridge, so to speak, between the purely biblical materials and those primarily sectarian in nature and function. When John Trever photographed the four scrolls from St. Mark's in 1948, he did not try to open one roll. It was in an advanced state of deterioration, and Trever was afraid that an attempt to open it outside a laboratory would do further harm. One fragment from the scroll had already fallen off in the process of recent handling. This piece Metropolitan Samuel had brought to be photographed along with the other materials. From this, Trever determined that the document was written in Aramaic, not Hebrew. Further, he deciphered the name *Lamech* on it as well and the name *Bit-Enoch*, the wife of Lamech. Both are mentioned in the Book of Jubilees. Trever assumed that he had identified the lost *Apocryphal Book of Enoch* known to us only in a Greek list of such works.

During the time Metropolitan Samuel had the scroll in the United States, he refused to allow it to be opened until it along with the other three had been purchased. Then the owner could do with it as he pleased. The purchaser turned out to be the State of Israel, and the manuscript was taken to Hebrew University where it proved extremely difficult to unroll.

Much of the text was ruined, not by those who opened the scroll, but by time. Some inner parts of the scroll were well preserved. It was not *Lamech*. Rather, it had to do with Genesis. There were interpretations of themes from the first book of the Bible as well as stories, mostly related to the biblical narrative, but with more detail and unknown names. There is at one point a first-person account by Abraham describing how the pharaoh took his wife, Sarah. This includes, in the mouth of an Egyptian prince, an account of the beauty of Sarah, a matter implied in the biblical narrative. In addition to such things the somewhat detailed topography of Palestine given in the *Genesis Apocryphon* not only shows a considerable knowledge of the land by the writer(s), but has proved valuable to the modern scholar in his efforts to establish the locations of sites mentioned in the Bible.

Writings similar to this Aramaic document were subsequently discovered. Yet the Apocryphon from the first batch of manuscripts to appear remains the outstanding example of midrashim[8] from the centuries prior to the birth of Jesus, and before the destruction of the Temple produced a decisive change in the orientation of Judaism.

Three of the scrolls from the original find were more clearly sectarian writings: the *Warfare Scroll*, the *Manual of Discipline*, and the *Thanksgiving Scroll*. The *Warfare Scroll*, also known by the more descriptive title, "The War of the Sons of Light with the Sons of Darkness," is nine and a half feet long and a little over six inches high. In its present condition it contains eighteen and a half columns averaging seventeen lines, but again the bottom of the scroll, like the *Habakkuk Commentary*, has been damaged by moisture that settled in (or came through) the bottom of the jar. It may once have contained more lines, perhaps as many as twenty to a column.

[8] Jewish commentaries and explanatory notes on the Scriptures.

259

It is a remarkable document giving a detailed plan for the final war between the Sons of Light and the Sons of Darkness. This is to be not merely a moral struggle, but a battle for the nation, for "Israel." This aspect of the thought of this scroll has been primarily responsible for the view of a few scholars that the Dead Sea Scrolls are first century A.D. and reflect the struggle between the Zealots and the Romans. But the Sons of Darkness are not merely Romans, and the Sons of Light were surely only members of the community. "Israel" in this scroll does not mean the nation in the religio-political sense conceived of by Zealots, but draws nearer to Paul's use of the term as designating those who are saved. In this sense the nationalism of the Qumranites was more narrowly drawn than that of the Zealots.

A number of discernible influences have shaped the actual plan of the work. It reflects the tradition of holy war in the Old Testament as well as the continuing influence of the Maccabean War on nationalistic thought of the time. The author(s) was also well aware of the equipment and tactics of the Roman army of his day. All this is blended together in a framework of apocalypticism.

The basic assumption of the author(s) seems to be the thought of Daniel 12:1 which speaks of the coming of Michael who will stand up for the people and deliver them at a time when there was "trouble, such as never has been." They were to prepare themselves and their weapons, and to learn their religious and military lessons well. The time of deliverance was near, perhaps at hand. What then follows in the scroll is a description of actual military paraphernalia and their proper use, a plan of war with detailed instructions for the deployment of various troops, as well as religious requirements to preserve the purity of the soldiers. Chosen, armed, deployed, and sanctified, the holy army is sure of victory, victory given by the God of battles, whose *two* armies insure success:

For with Thee in heaven are a multitude of holy beings, and armies of angels are in Thy holy abode, to serve as Thy legionnaires; and down on earth Thou hast likewise placed at Thy service the elect of an holy people. The roster of all their host is with Thee in Thy holy habitation, and (?) in Thy glorious abode. And the benefits of Thy blessings and Thy covenant of peace hast thou inscribed for them in a charter of Eternal life—an assurance that through all the epochs of time Thou wilt be their king, and that when Thou contendest in judgment against the upstarts of the earth Thou wilt muster an army of these Thine elect, in their thousands and tens of thousands, side by side with Thine holy beings and Thine angels, and that they shall prevail in battle and along with the heavenly elect be triumphant.[9]

The *Manual of Discipline* is a sectarian document of very different character and, judging from the recovery of portions of eleven other manuscripts of it,[10] one of considerable importance to the community. The beginning of the scroll is missing, but over six feet of it remains.[11] Almost nine and a half inches high, it has eleven columns of twenty-six lines each. These contain rules for the holy life of the community. It is, in short, somewhat analogous to the later Christian monastic *Rule*.

Detailed requirements for entrance are set forth along with blessings and curses used in a ceremony of initiation. The new Son of Light was required to give up everything he had to the community—knowledge, strength, and wealth—and pledge himself to faithful adherence to the rigid schedule of the group, including its special religious

[9] Theodore H. Gaster, trans., *The Scriptures of the Dead Sea Sect* (London: Secker and Warburg, 1957), p. 275.

[10] The oldest is from the beginning of the first century B.C.

[11] It was in two pieces. John Trever, who joined them, thinks the rent was caused by the rotting of linen thread at one point.

calendar. There follows in the scroll a condemnation of those who refuse to join the community, and then the writer(s) returns to the theme of the struggle between Light and Darkness. This section, to which considerable space is given, treats the matter quite differently from the *Warfare Scroll*. Rather than a clearcut conflict between two groups, the *Manual of Discipline* speaks of two spirits struggling for each man:

Now, this God created man to rule the world, and appointed for him two spirits after whose direction he was to walk until the final Inquisition. They are the spirits of truth and of perversity.

The origin of truth lies in the Fountain of Light, and that of perversity in the Wellspring of Darkness. All who practice righteousness are under the domination of the Prince of Light, and walk in the ways of light; whereas all who practice perversity are under the domination of the Angel of Darkness and walk in the ways of darkness. Through the Angel of Darkness, however, even those who practice righteousness are made liable to error. All their sin and their iniquities, all their guilt and their deeds of transgression are the result of his domination; and this, by God's inscrutable design, will continue until the time appointed by Him. Moreover, all men's afflictions and all their moments of tribulation are due to this being's malevolent sway. All of the spirits that attend upon him are bent on causing the sons of light to stumble. Howbeit, the God of Israel and the Angel of His truth are always there to help the sons of light. It is God that created these spirits of light and darkness and made them the basis of every act, the (instigators) of every good deed and the directors of every thought. The one He loves to all eternity, and is ever pleased with its deeds; but any association with the other He abhors, and He hates all its ways to the end of time.[12]

The abhorrence of God is reserved not merely for those who constantly associate with the Angel of Darkness, but especially for the Son of Light who leaves the community. The scroll makes this quite clear. In addition, the *Manual* is concerned with the way the community disciplines itself internally, selects its leaders (whose conduct is regulated), and holds the Law (Torah) in high regard. Such were some of the theological and practical issues dealt with in this extremely functional writing which governed every action of the community and its inhabitants.

The remaining sectarian document in the original find is the *Thanksgiving Scroll*. Like the *Manual of Discipline* it was in two pieces. But unlike that other document it is in a sad condition. One so-called part is in fact a large number of detached fragments pieced together. The better-preserved portion contains three sheets with four columns each. But happily the columns are unusually high for the Qumran materials and contain thirty-five to forty-one lines each. In Cave Four (see p. 270) fragments of five similar manuscripts were found and to a certain degree have filled in gaps in the main scroll.

The document is a collection of psalms and receives its name from the typically introductory formula, "I give thanks unto Thee, my Lord," the customary opening words of a thanksgiving hymn. The might of the God of creation is contrasted with the folly and impurity of man, a prominent theme found also in the other sectarian writings. So also is the awareness of a holy community in a hostile world which fills the days of the faithful with troubles and woes. Yet God has not abandoned the loyal ones and has already revealed to them the nature of paradise where they shall be as trees planted by living waters. Allusions to the psalms of the Old Testament are everywhere, yet this work shows a pious originality and an abiding awareness of the transitoriness of the present coupled with unshakable trust in the faithfulness of God.

[12] Theodore H. Gaster, trans., *The Scriptures of the Dead Sea Sect*, pp. 53-54.

I give thanks unto Thee, O Lord (says Qumran
    Psalm 13),
    for Thou hast cast not my lot in the congrega-
       tion of the false,
    nor set my portion in the company of dis-
       semblers.

Behold, in Thy mercy I trust,
    in Thy pardon confide,
    and on Thine abundant mercies I lean,
    when all just judgments are passed upon me.

For Thou dost tend me as a mother tendeth her
       babe,
    and like a child on the bosom of its nurse dost
       Thou sustain me.
Thy justice holdeth firm for ever,
    for Thou dost not abandon them that seek
       Thee.[13]

The ancient community at Qumran centered its life on work, meditation, and the
study of the Scriptures. Night and day, continuously, some members were devoting
themselves to the Sacred Word seeking to
learn, and to care for their souls. Their
scrolls were a priceless possession, and the
seven documents described here were a part
of that collection. Such was the material
discovered by some shepherds on a spring
morning in 1947.

Further Discoveries and a Monastery
Excavated

The summer and fall of 1948 were frustrating ones for scholars in Jerusalem. An
unparalleled discovery had been made. Yet
the Arab-Israeli war, which had suddenly
exploded into full-scale hostilities, made it
impossible to engage in archaeological work.
The claimed origin and authenticity of the
materials needed to be confirmed. If the cave
could be excavated, at least the context in
which the scrolls were found could be dated.
More importantly: Were there other manuscripts waiting to be found? Among the
Bedouin word had spread that manuscripts

were bringing respectable sums. Fragments
were being sold by the square centimeter.
Kando alone had received over 1000 pounds
Sterling for scraps and bits. A good deal of
Ta'amireh time was being spent looking for
salable items. In Jerusalem scholars were
immobile due to travel restrictions imposed
by the belligerents. In the minds of all were
the frightening cases of the Moabite Stone
and the Siloam Inscription which had been
found virtually intact, but were broken up
in hope of receiving a better price by selling
piece by piece. Such a thing could more easily
happen with fragile parchment than with
large stones.

The American School was being used by
United Nations mediators. Ovid R. Sellers,
director for 1948-1949, and his wife were
the sole Americans remaining. With considerable courage they faithfully performed
their duties under extremely difficult conditions. When limitations eased early in 1949
and it was possible to move around the
country to some extent, Sellers at once set
in motion plans to visit and to excavate the
cave from which the manuscripts had come.
Archbishop Samuel was away at the time,
but Father Sowmy, a Syrian monk, introduced a man who offered to lead the way to
the still somewhat mysterious and not yet
easily found cave. But this guide wished a
considerable advance payment. In addition
he demanded further handsome fees for any
work he might do, and insisted he was to
be given a share of any of the finds. The
influence of the secretary of the Palestine
Archaeological Museum and of the Major
of Jerusalem failed to change the nature of
these demands. Sellers rightly refused to
agree and the matter was dropped. But the
professor did interest a young Belgian UN
observer, Lieutenant Philippe Lippens, in the
manuscripts and the cave while the officer
was stationed at the American School. When
Lippens was shortly transferred to Amman
he proposed to some officers of the Arab

---

[13] *Ibid.*, pp. 163-64.

Legion that they take steps to find the cave and safeguard it. Captain Akash Bey of the Legion went to the area, explored a number of caves, and finally found what he thought correctly to be the one in question. There he posted a guard to prevent further looting. In one sense it was too late. Not only had the Bedouin been there a number of times, but others who should have known better had come seeking to find something with which to enrich their pocketbooks.

These unauthorized excavators had opened a sizable hole lower in the rock face to make it possible to enter the cave—and to carry things out!—more easily. G. L. Harding, director of Antiquities for the new Kingdom of Jordan, was on the site a few days after Captain Bey. On February 8 he began a systematic exploration of the cave along with Father Roland de Vaux of the *École Biblique* and three highly trained Arab workmen. Recent treasure hunters had left the place a shambles. Excavation was further slowed by the meticulous care with which Harding and his associates worked. Small hand tools, usually pocketknives, were used exclusively. When these men finished on March 5, they had gone far to determine the occupational history of this cave, now known as Qumran Cave One. About a thousand more manuscript fragments had been found. These were taken to the Palestine Archaeological Museum, there to become parts of a gigantic jigsaw puzzle, the subject of countless scholarly hours. From the pottery and coins recovered, there is absolutely no question that the cave was in use during Hellenistic times. Among other things the identifiable remnants of some fifty large Hellenistic jars were found, along with two lamps from the period. These yielded a date up to and including the early Roman occupation of Palestine. There were also a few Roman sherds, including parts of a pot and two lamps. Some have connected these with the report of Greek and Hebrew manuscripts being found near Jericho during the reign of Septimius Severus, about A.D. 217. If that is correct, this may indicate that the early Christian scholar Origen was in Cave One. He is said to have used such materials for his *Hexapla*. But this connection is only speculation. The evidence fits the story, but there is nothing to tie the two inseparably together. All one can say for sure is that the cave was entered by someone sometime during the middle Roman Empire, about the time of Severus. There is, however, considerably less uncertainty about the third period represented by finds in the cave. Cigarette stubs, modern cloth, roughly contemporary newspapers still showing signs of food that was wrapped in them, and a device for rolling cigarettes were unmistakable indications of the clandestine digging that had taken place in November 1948. Those who did this are known, and Harding returned to its owner the gadget for making cigarettes when he confronted the culprits.

The context in which the scrolls were found agreed with the paleographic[14] evidence. The archaeologically established range of dates is roughly 200-50+ B.C. Furthermore, linen which once covered some of the scrolls was found in the cave. A portion was sent to W. F. Libby of the Institute for Nuclear Studies of the University of Chicago. Using Carbon 14 tests, he determined its date as A.D. 33 plus or minus 200. The linen is from the early second century B.C. to the early third century A.D. Here was a third confirmation of the dating. Paleography, archaeology, and Carbon 14 tests agree on the two centuries before the birth of Jesus as the date of the Dead Sea Scrolls.

While exploring the cave, Harding and de Vaux made a number of visits to the ruins at Qumran, less than a mile away. They suspected that these might have some connection with the manuscripts. But a super-

[14] Paleography is the study of ancient writings and forms of writing.

ficial survey convinced them otherwise. However, P. Kahle, writing in the distinguished Dutch journal, *Vetus Testamentum,* argued strongly that it was indeed the inhabitants of ancient Qumran who had placed the scrolls in the cave. A full-scale archaeological undertaking at the site would, in Kahle's view, show the connection. So convincing was the argument, and so swift their recent survey, that Harding and de Vaux did return to Qumran from November 24 to December 12, 1951 to conduct the first of a series of excavations to establish the history of the site and its relationship, if any, to the manuscripts from the cave.

Archaeological work proved the wisdom of Kahle's view. Pottery and other artifacts were found to be identical with those from the cave. Furthermore, the complex of buildings covering an area approximately 262 feet square was found to have an occupational history in four phases covering nine centuries. The first was from the seventh and eighth centuries B.C., the time of the Kingdom of Judah. A rectangular structure with roughly built casemate walls stood near a large and deep round cistern. To the south, one and a half miles distant from the plateau on which the main ruins are located, there is a small plain. There, at Ain Feshka, another Judahite enclosure was found. Larger than the early ruins at Qumran, it was perhaps for animals. Ain Feshka was at that earlier period as later an agricultural area supplying the needs of the community at Qumran. A number of precise dates have been suggested for these Iron Age constructions. Perhaps that best suited to the archaeological data and biblical materials is the reign of King Uzziah (II Chronicles 26:10; see also p. 179).

During the political and religious unrest which was an accompaniment to the establishment of the Hasmonean kingdom, at least one group withdrew from the Temple in Jerusalem where the high-priesthood had been usurped by the new dynasty. These people, whom it seems correct to identify as Essenes, came to Qumran, the old "City of Salt," then in a sad state of disuse. The cistern was cleaned and two others, rectangular in shape, were added. Some of the old casemate rooms were used for various purposes. A potter's kiln was built, the fields at Ain Feshka recultivated, and in all respects the religious community sought to become self-sufficent. Silver coins from this stratum of ruins are Seleucid and indicate occupancy from about 130 B.C. In addition, some fifteen bronze coins from the reign of John Hyrcanus (135-104 B.C.) reinforce numismatic indication that the first, somewhat smallish group of Essenes at Qumran were there in the second century before Christ.

Toward the end of the reign of Hyrcanus a great change took place in the size of the community. The entire complex of buildings was rebuilt and considerably enlarged. The religious struggles in the kingdom, mainly involving Pharisees and Sadducees, also drew into their orbit other groups of varying opinions. Judging from the reconstruction at Qumran, many more Essenes withdrew to this isolated spot on the northwestern shore of the Dead Sea. Expanding south and west, the complex was distinguished by two and perhaps three stories in some places. The older water system was found inadequate for the new numbers. A dam was therefore built in the marl cliff at a point where the spring rains collect and drop in a waterfall into the Wadi Qumran many feet below. From this barrier an aqueduct and a long trench cut into the stone brought large amounts of water inside the walls of the settlement and into a storage system with seven large cisterns (including the older ones). Interestingly this aqueduct system is identical in date and very similar in design to one at Hyrcania (Mird) not far away. Located variously within the buildings, the cisterns at Qumran served not only the necessities of drinking and bathing, but also the rites of many lustrations which were a part of the Essene ritual. Moreover, these plaster-faced storage tanks were linked together so that they filled consecutively, that nearest the water source first, that farthest last. There was also an overflow arrangement to prevent any excess (should that condition happily occur in so arid a climate) from coming into the buildings.

John C. Trever

The effects of an earthquake can be seen in steps at Qumran (above).

Increasing numbers of inhabitants meant that the community could no longer be self-sustaining, if indeed it ever really was. Fields and grazing lands at Ain Feshka were not large enough, especially to supply the needed grain, and there were no other areas reasonably handy. Some scholars are of the opinion that the stables at Qumran (with room for nine or so animals) were for the beasts on which the Qumranites rode to Ain Feshka and back. A more likely explanation for these structures which appear at this time is the need to bring food and perhaps other supplies from Jericho and some of the small villages then existing in the Judean wilderness.

Two disasters overtook this phase of the settlement. It may have been a double dis-aster, or it may have been two separate events. At any rate, fire destroyed a considerable portion of the buildings. Evidence of it is widespread. It is also clear that the canals ruptured causing mud to settle where the water overflowed inside the monastery. At one point this mud is almost twenty-nine inches deep, indicating either a very large spillage or more likely a continuous overflow for a longer period. If this latter is the case it may be that the buildings were not extensively used for some time, or perhaps even completely abandoned.

The other disaster which may support the suggestion that the buildings were temporarily in disuse during the Herodian period was an earthquake which caused extensive damage. Josephus reports that in 31 B.C. a serious quake struck Judea and particularly the Jordan Valley (the valley is an earth fault). At Qumran the present ruins show clear evidence of a strong earthquake. The entire eastern edge of the plateau dropped some twenty inches, producing a large opening in the earth which ran over 180 feet right through the buildings. Steps leading into one of the cisterns were literally torn in two from top to bottom, with half dropping over a foot below their original level. Walls of the various buildings were weakened and doubtless a number gave way causing roofs to collapse onto floors below. This may have been the occasion when the scriptorium, which was on the second story, dropped into the room beneath. But this is a matter of debate. Some consider this to have happened when the Romans attacked a century later. When it occurred long plaster tables and benches came crashing through the ceiling. They were found 2000 years later just as they fell. Today they have been reerected in Jerusalem where they may be seen in the Palestine Archaeological Museum. With the tables archaeologists found inkwells bearing stains from the fluid they once contained.

Father de Vaux is of the opinion that the fire resulted from the earthquake. Others think that it was deliberately set in an attempt to destroy the home of the religious community. Still a third view is that already mentioned: The fire was set by the Romans when they captured Qumran in A.D. 68.

Very few Herodian coins were found among the ruins. This has led some to say that Qumran was abandoned after the disaster or disasters which presumably occurred in 31. But there are very few coins from the reign of Hyrcanus II (63-40 B.C.), and no one claims that the site was not inhabited then. On the contrary, it is said that this was the time of its greatest expansion. It would therefore seem wiser to say that the calamity which occurred near the beginning of Herod's reign (37-4 B.C.), perhaps coupled with Herod's favorable disposition toward the Essenes, caused a momentary decrease in activity at Qumran. Not all these sectarians lived at Qumran in any case. Their small groups were scattered throughout the country. The vast majority that were near the Dead Sea did not live in the main buildings. The disasters mentioned would not have deprived them of their dwellings, such as they were. But the strict discipline of the religious community would have been seriously disrupted. Perhaps some saw the earthquake and fire as signs that they should not continue their work there. For whatever reason, it does seem that activity at the site diminished for a time but did not come to an end. The evidence from coins, if sparse at certain periods, is nonetheless continuous from about 130 B.C. until approximately A.D. 100. One cannot with certainty assert that the buildings were abandoned at any time during that period, although it is assumed by some scholars that they were during part of Herod's reign.

Unrest following the death of Herod may have been the occasion for a renaissance at Qumran. A second influx seems to have taken place about this time.[15] Buildings were rebuilt along the lines of previous structures. The cistern damaged by earthquake was cut off from the water system and not used. Higher buildings, such as the tower by the main entrance, were strengthened against future earth tremors by additional courses of stones so laid as to bind the older portions. Certain of the older gates were eliminated by means of a new enclosure on the north. This may have been done to make the complex more defensible. Whether intentional or not, it was the practical result.

In the summer of A.D. 68, the third year of the First Jewish Revolt, the Tenth Legion (Fretensis) and the Fifteenth Legion (Apollinaris) swept through the Jordan Valley destroying the Jewish defensive network there. Any point that might serve the insurgents was taken by the legionnaires. Among these was Qumran. Excavators found seventy-three bronze coins dated to the second year of the Jewish Revolt. Only five from the third year were present. Thirteen Roman coins minted in 67-68 were also in a stratum marked by fire damage and dotted by arrow heads of the three-winged form used by the Roman army. The religionists by the Dead Sea apparently did not give up without a fight. Yet their position was militarily hope-

[15] In 1896 there was recovered from the genizah of the Karaite synagogue in Cairo a manuscript known as the *Damascus Document* or the *Zadokite Fragment*. It was recognized to be extremely old, some said 2nd cent. B.C., others thought it medieval. Without adequate knowledge of paleography it was not possible to say with certainty. The Dead Sea Scrolls, and especially the *Habakkuk Commentary*, now establish it as post-63 B.C. but contemporary with some Qumran writings. The similarity of contents of the *Damascus Document* and the *Manual of Discipline* has convinced many that they arose from the same group. Indeed, A. Dupont-Sommer takes the view that the sect which produced the *Damascus Document* was related to Qumran, but transferred its headquarters to Damascus where the manuscript was written. Within a generation there was a return to Judea and possibly Qumran, thus swelling the numbers and taxing the capacity of the settlement. See A. Dupont-Sommer, *The Dead Sea Scrolls*, trans. E. Margaret Rowley (Oxford: Blackwell, 1952), pp. 53-68.

The spectacular setting of Cave Four which is in a scarpe jutting into the Wadi Qumran. The view is from the monastery.

less, and we cannot assume that they long delayed Roman intentions.

The imperial soldiers cleared some of the debris resulting from their efforts, leveled off a small area near the tower, and built a few barracks. Qumran was not a vital military position, but it was a convenient one, providing watchmen who scaled the cliff with a singularly good vantage point from which to keep an eye on activities in the desert to the west and for some distance to the south along the Dead Sea coast toward Masada itself visible from Qumran on a clear day. Judging from coins found in the Roman remains, the occupation of the site lasted until the last decade of the first Christian century. Then for all practical purposes the site was abandoned except for brief use by the followers of Bar Kochba during the Second Revolt (A.D. 132-135), and the occasional monk or Bedouin who found temporary shelter among the ruins over the centuries.

The first Essene buildings at Qumran covered an area approximately 121 feet by about 98 feet. Twenty rooms surrounded an inner courtyard. There was perhaps a second floor over some parts, but this may have been restricted to the tower by the main (northeast) entrance. There must also have been other structures, such as meeting halls and storerooms. If so, traces of them disappeared when buildings from this period were included in the later expansion. An early portico and colonnade were clearly incorporated as well as the existing water system and guard tower.

At the apex of its importance the community's buildings presented an imposing sight on their plateau above the Dead Sea. More finely built than its predecessor, the complex was also much larger, almost 262 feet square. Even though utilizing a number of walls from the earlier structure, the reconstruction was arranged differently. There was still a courtyard hard by the southeastern corner of the tower. The rooms around it, however, were larger than before and served the major purposes of the community. The kitchen,[16] dyer's shop, scriptorium, and another somewhat enigmatic room (perhaps a council chamber of the elders of the community) took up the larger part of the major building. Two large cisterns were in this area. To the southeast were the laundry, pottery shop, and the largest cistern which was also the final one in the water system. Immediately south was the longest room at Qumran, over seventy-two feet in length and almost fifteen feet wide. Near one end is a small, round stone platform. This is assumed to have been a podium. This room is probably the refectory-meeting hall. From the podium one member of the community read from Holy Writ or gave a commentary on it while the others ate their simple meal. Immediately west of this room was another cistern and the stables. North

[16] I am following the designation of the rooms given by Father de Vaux, the principal excavator of Qumran. If de Vaux is correct about the large northern room of the structure as the kitchen, it does seem to have been an inordinately long distance from the pantry and the refectory.

of the stables and west of the main entrance was the other complex of structures and rooms. Around the Iron Age cistern were two other cisterns and a series of rooms of undetermined function, likely workshops of some sort. As has been noted previously, there were few, if any, areas for sleeping, since caves in the area served that purpose.

On the eastern edge of the plateau, separated from the buildings by a low wall, is a cemetery of over 1100 graves, carefully arranged, each covered with pebbles.[17] Almost all are oriented north and south. Only relatively few of the tombs have been excavated. These reveal skeletons lying on their backs with heads toward the south. Surprisingly, and contrary to Jewish practice current at that time no artifacts were found in tombs containing males. Also unlike Jewish custom in Palestine at the turn of the era, no funeral offerings were buried with the dead. Indeed, it seems that the corpse was buried naked; no sign of garments has been found. A few skeletons were female, giving pause to the easy identification of the community as monastic in the Western Christian sense.[18] Graves containing females did have a few artifacts, but nothing to indicate any degree of wealth. No children's remains have yet been found. One skeleton has been identified as a male about sixteen years old. For the most part the ages ranged from thirty to fifty. But very little of the necropolis has been examined. Further work here will doubtless go far to suggest whether this was a monastic community with a vow of chastity (which does not seem to be the case) and whether children were taken into the order to insure its continuation (as suggested by at least one ancient author). At the moment the cemetery has raised more questions than it has furnished answers.

More Manuscripts from the Desert of Judea

In December 1951, while archaeologists were working at the ruins of Qumran, Ta'amireh Bedouin appeared in Jerusalem with another batch of manuscripts, Greek documents as well as Hebrew. Examination showed them not to be a part of the earlier find. Most of the manuscripts were later, from about the time of the Second Revolt. Reluctant to reveal the place of their new and potentially lucrative discovery, the shepherds vaguely mentioned some sites near Qumran. But Father de Vaux, wise in the ways of the oriental mind, not only succeeded in discovering from the Bedouin the true identity of the new hiding place, but also convinced them that he, Harding, and the police (!) should go there with them. It turned out to be in the Wadi Murabba'at, about fifteen miles south-southeast of Jerusalem, some distance from Qumran. From the end of January to the first part of March 1952, various scholarly groups from Jerusalem explored the Wadi. Four caves yielded manuscripts and other archaeological data. Occupied as early as the fourth millennium B.C., the caves were still in use in the Graeco-Roman period although occupation was not continuous. Among the latest artifacts were two Roman coins countermarked with an emblem of the Tenth Legion (*Fretensis*).[19] Some wooden materials and fabrics from several periods were recovered. This is a rarity in Palestinian archaeology and has happened at only a few sites, among them Jericho and Bab ed-Dhra'.

The texts from Murabba'at may span a thousand years. Some scholars date one papyrus to the period of the Kingdom of Judah (perhaps seventh century B.C.), and

[17] A second cemetery, quite small (about a dozen tomb groups), was discovered in 1955. Located just north of the Qumran ruins, it is from the same period as the larger cemetery and shows the same characteristics.

[18] The Essenes discouraged marriage; they did not forbid it.

[19] There were a few Arab artifacts indicating an itinerant occupation during the Ommayad period (A.D. 661-750).

there are Arab documents on paper from the Ommayad period. Biblical texts from the first and second Christian centuries include portions of Genesis, Exodus, Numbers, Deuteronomy, Psalms, and Isaiah. But these texts are in a very poor condition caused by both man (Romans?) and nature (deterioration and rats). Among the biblical texts should be listed a complete phylactery of as yet undetermined date. Its entire agreement with the Masoretic text of the tenth Christian century probably does not indicate its dependence upon the work of the Masoretes, but more importantly may indicate the antiquity of the textual tradition used by those early medieval scholars. Among the papyri are letters from the Second Revolt mentioning the name of Bar Kochba. One is said to bear his signature.[20] Aramaic and Greek documents are mostly legal contracts of various sorts. Three are dated internally to the second Christian century. The most interesting Greek document is a fragment of what seems to be a history of Herodian times. Salome and Mariamme are mentioned. Unfortunately the text is too fragmentary to help reconstruct the life and times of Herod the Great.

A couple of weeks after the archaeologists went to Wadi Murabba'at, in February, the Ta'amireh Bedouin were back with more fragments. These, they said, came from quite near the now famous cave at Qumran. In this instance they were not trying to mislead. The new cave was just south of the first one. Cave Two yielded only a handful of fragments, all of the same period and content as those from Cave One.

Were there other caves containing yet more documents? This question and the distinct possibility of answering it in the affirmative caused the *École Biblique,* the American School, and the Palestine Archae-

[20] At Nahal Hever and Masada excavators have also recovered letters written or signed by Bar Kochba.

ological Museum to join forces in an investigation of every cave, opening, and hollow within a five mile radius of Qumran. Twenty-five caves contained pottery similar to that found at the monastery. This indicates the domestic quarters of some of the members of the community. Two caves contained manuscript fragments including biblical materials from Leviticus (in Phoenician script), Exodus, Isaiah, Jeremiah, Psalms, and Ruth. Among the finds was the strangest yet found in the wilderness of Judea. Under the direction of William L. Reed, then director of the American School, a team discovered a copper scroll engraved in square Mishnaic Hebrew. Of undoubted antiquity (middle of first Christian century) and connected with the sect at Qumran, it speaks of great hidden temple treasures. Almost all scholars are convinced that the language of the *Copper Scroll* is to be taken figuratively and not literally.

Justly congratulating themselves on the discovery of the Copper Scroll and thinking they had fairly well combed the caves, the scholars devoted themselves to piecing together, translating, interpreting, and trying to figure out a way of unrolling the oxidized copper of their newest find. At about that time, during the summer of 1952, the indefatigable Bedouin came forth with yet another and different group of documents. They said these were from caves in the Wadi en-Nar, an extension of the Kidron Valley. Among the texts were parts of *codices* (books of unbound sheets) including the Gospels of Mark and John, and the Acts of the Apostles. These were from the fifth to eighth centuries A.D. Even more important, portions of the Bible (Joshua, Matthew, Luke, Acts, Colossians) written in Syro-Palestinian were present. This is a type of Aramaic and was the language of Byzantine Christians in Palestine. It was replaced by Arabic in the seventh century. In addition, there were a number of other Greek nonbiblical works,

William L. Reed

The Copper Scroll as it looked when discovered in the cave.

and some fragments of Arabic and Syriac writings offered for sale by the shepherds.

In early August this material came to the attention of scholars at the University of Louvain. Shortly thereafter a Belgian archaeological team was formed to explore the region from which they reputedly came. It was soon established that Khirbet Mird, the Hyrcania of the Hasmoneans and of Herod the Great, was the place of origin, not Wadi en-Nar. In A.D. 492, St. Sabas founded a monastery upon the site. It bore the name *Castellion*, "fortress," and flourished until some time in the ninth century. The library for this monastic community seems to have been in an underground chamber, for it was from a grotto that the Belgians extracted a number of fragments of the same kind as those earlier said to be from en-Nar but later admitted to be from Mird. Among these was a portion of Euripides' *Andromache*. The monks in the wilderness, or at least one of them at Mird, had a taste for Greek drama.

At the same time the Belgians were preparing their campaign (it was not actually undertaken until February 1953) another spectacular find came to light, in some ways rivaling the discoveries from Cave One. On a point jutting into the Wadi Qumran, hard by the ruins which had by then been under excavation for some time, another cache of

manuscript fragments, numbering into the thousands, was found. It seems that one evening in early September 1952, as some Ta'amireh Bedouin sat around their campfire discussing the lucrative trade in old documents, one of their number, an old man, mentioned a cave he had known as a youth. It was full of old jars and such, as he recalled. It was, he said, right at Qumran and very difficult and dangerous to enter. One slip of the foot and serious injury if not death would result from the long fall into the dry creek bed many feet below.[21] Taking careful note of the exact details of how to reach the spot, the younger men set off almost at once armed with rope and primitive lamps. It was not long before their dangerous work was rewarded.

Items were already on sale in Jerusalem before authorities found out the location of their source from a jealous tribesman, one who was not sharing in the new source of wealth. By late September, de Vaux and his colleagues were carefully working their way through the cave. Unlike the earlier grottoes, this one was artificial, carved out of the marl, and by design difficult of detection and even more difficult to enter. Several hundred more fragments were recovered from this place, designated Cave Four. Another cave was found nearby. It yielded about a dozen manuscripts, badly decayed because of dampness. The latter place, Cave Five, was also man-made. A third opening, Cave Six, produced a few documents. Whether these caves were merely or mainly for hiding the precious library of the Qumran community, or whether they served as a place of storage for manuscripts to be sold in Jerusalem (one way the community could earn money), or whether their cool interiors were set aside for study we do not know. There are many theories to explain how the scrolls got into the caves.

[21] At least one tourist seeking to enter Cave Four has fallen to his death.

In Jerusalem, the Department of Antiquities in conjunction with the Palestine Archaeological Museum was trying, often in vain, to buy the fragments earlier removed from Cave Four and now appearing in the thousands. The Bedouin, aware of the growing value of their possessions, were in no hurry to sell. When the first bundle was purchased and came into the Museum, the necessity of acquiring the fragments quickly became apparent. In order to increase the price of the materials, a number of ill-fitting parts had been pasted together—increased size, increased price. In Bethlehem Kando was acting as a go-between and was rapidly getting rich. The Museum, on the other hand, had soon exhausted almost all its funds. Indeed, it was on the verge of bankruptcy (it was then a private institution with a Rockefeller endowment). At this juncture the Jordanian government made a generous grant to allow continued acquisition, as did a number of universities and other scholarly institutions in the United States, Canada, Britain, Germany, and Italy. Among these was the Vatican Library. Even with money in hand, however, the process of securing the fragments was not easy. It took well over eight years to complete the major purchases, and even now one can be fairly sure all are not in scholarly hands. Some are known to be in private collections. Others may still rest in Bedouin houses or tents.

An international team of scholars, invited by the Museum and the Jordanian Department of Antiquities, was chosen to publish the documents from Caves Four, Five, and Six. But before one could publish them, or even read them, it was necessary to assemble them. On long rows of tables in the Museum's basement thousands of fragments were laid out, identified by paleographic techniques, and slowly put together to form the manuscripts which had begun disintegration so long ago and which had of recent date suffered badly. Out of this greatest of all jigsaw puzzles, a remarkable team of men was able to publish Greek and Hebrew biblical fragments, sectarian writings, phylacteries, some Apocrypha in Hebrew and Aramaic, and parts of Tobias in these languages. Up to that time Tobias was known only in its Greek version.

More documents continued to turn up in Jerusalem, including some of Nabatean origin, but no new caves were identified and explored until the spring of 1955. During the fourth season of excavation at Qumran, four more caves once containing manuscripts were discovered. The Bedouin had not emptied these caves, perhaps unfortunately. Nature in the form of erosion and dampness had done the damage. A very few fragments were recovered along with one ostracon. About the same time another scroll, much damaged, was found at Murabba'at by a Bedouin. Once it was a copy of the book of the Twelve Minor Prophets. Now this second-century A.D. scroll contained only a fragment —from the end of Joel to the beginning of Zechariah.

Another remarkable manuscript find occurred early in 1956. Long after the scholars' time and energy had given out, the Bedouin continued relentlessly looking into every crack and crevice in the area of Qumran. A little less than a half mile from Cave One, they found a hermit's cave of two chambers with artifacts dating from three periods: Chalcolithic (ca. 4000-3000 B.C.), Judahite monarchy (ca. seventh century B.C.), and contemporary with the Essene occupation of Qumran. It is interesting to note that the excavated caves and indeed Qumran itself show the same general occupational history indicating that the desert was inhabited at three distinct periods in the history of Palestine. The middle period, the Judahite, seems to have been a part of a deliberate royal policy, while the last period was the result of religious and political ferment. Among the treasures of Cave Eleven was a cigar-shaped scroll on skin hardened and darkened by age.

In late 1959 and early 1960, the busy Bedouin were at it again. They offered for sale in the Old City of Jerusalem some papyrus documents which turned out to be letters from the time of the Second Revolt, the one lead by Bar Kochba. To the shock of Professor Yadin and the dismay of the Israeli Minister of Defense, these manuscripts were reported to have been found in a cave between Masada and En-gedi—in Israel! Yadin was concerned that an important find had left the country. The Minister was upset that the Bedouin could enter the country, explore extremely difficult terrain at leisure, and leave completely undetected. The entire area from Qumran to Masada, it should be pointed out, is a part of the Wilderness of Judea, and the boundary is hardly a natural one. It is doubtful that the Bedouin knew where the border was; if they did know, it is questionable whether they cared about such things.

The Israel Exploration Society immediately dispatched Y. Aharoni and a team to the area. They found a few fragments of writing, but for the most part returned with evidences of recent Bedouin presence. A few days later the Israeli Chief of Staff contacted Yadin saying that security forces in the area had been so vastly increased that it was possible to undertake a large-scale, thorough search to see if anything remained in the numerous caves of the hostile region. Helicopters, mine detectors, electric generators, and sheer physical courage on the rugged cliffs produced results. A cave in the Nahal Hever was found to have been the final hiding place of two of Bar Kochba's officers, Jonathan and Masabala. Reached by means of rope ladders and only with the utmost difficulty, the cave yielded a grim harvest of skeletons. In addition, it contained perfectly preserved Roman cult apparatus (captured by the rebels who had defaced some images on them), woven baskets and mats in superb condition, numerous skeins of wool ready for deft fingers, colored cloth looking as if it had just come from the loom —and a collection of fifty letters and other documents ranging in date from the end of the first century A.D. to the middle of the second century.

Fifteen are military dispatches from "Shimon Bar Kochba, Prince over Israel." Several, including one written on wood (unique in Palestinian antiquities), are actually signed by him. These show, among other things, that En-gedi was an important port and supply base during the Second Revolt. Bar Kochba, apparently in the area of Jerusalem, urges Jonathan and Masabala, commanders at En-gedi, to get on with the business of supplying him. "You sit and eat and drink the property of the house of Israel, and care nothing for your brothers," he complains at one point. Several times he orders his subordinates, under threat of severe penalty if they disobey, to seize the property of some landowners in the area and to present them bodily before him. It would seem from the language and tone of the letters that these persons were not being forcibly brought for punishment, but because their services were required.

The dispatches also show Bar Kochba's concern with the religious requirements of his army. Among the letters was one addressed to "Yehuda Bar Menashe," instructing him to take the two donkeys being sent to him and direct them along with two of his men to Jonathan and Masabala. They will be loaded with palm branches and citrons. At the same time Yehuda is to use other men to gather willows and myrtle which along with the items from En-gedi are to be sent to the army in the field. Supplying a battle group with such things may seem strange until one realizes that these are the four kinds of plant required to celebrate the Feast of Succoth.

Four of the dispatches were written in

Hebrew, nine in Aramaic, and two in Greek. The other thirty-five documents are in Greek, Aramaic, and Nabatean. Fortuitously they are all dated. The earliest was written in A.D. 88 and the latest on the eve of the revolt, A.D. 132. There are papers of a large Jewish family from En-gedi which include marriage contracts, deeds, wills, and even a document specifying guardianship of an orphan son of one of the daughters.

The materials from Nahal Hever are complementary to those from Wadi Murabba'at and go far to bring light to the period between the two Revolts, an important time for which we have little information. Again, the discovery was touched off by Bedouin to whom we owe much.. They are, after all, the ones who in their own curious way have produced the most spectacular discoveries in Palestinian archaeology.

Whether the contents of the caves of the Judean wilderness are exhausted or not remains to be seen. There is now no doubt that writings on various materials can survive for centuries in the Palestinian climate. Only recently on Masada Yadin's excavators unearthed several texts, some biblical and some bearing the name of Bar Kochba. Furthermore, in the aftermath of the war of June 1967, another Dead Sea Scroll came into Yadin's hands. This scroll, whose existence had long been known to scholars, was immediately taken to Hebrew University where it was opened.

Provisionally called the *Temple Scroll*, it is the longest of all the Dead Sea Scrolls, over twenty-eight feet. It contains sixty-six columns; many near the beginning of the manuscript are damaged. The first part is missing entirely, but not much seems to have been lost. It is contemporaneous with the ministry of Jesus or slightly earlier. The contents of the document can be gathered under four headings: (1) religious rules on various subjects, (2) sacrifices and offerings for various festivals, (3) a detailed description of the temple, and (4) instructions for the defense of the king and the nation:

(1) The religious rules are based upon prescriptions in the Pentateuch, but have two significant differences. They are considerably elaborated in a polemical and somewhat stricter sense. They are written in the first person as though God himself were speaking. This latter is a curious characteristic of the *Temple Scroll* and along with other features suggests that the scribe perhaps intended it to be taken as scripture.

(2) The enumeration of sacrifices, offerings, and festivals leaves no doubt that the manuscript is from the Qumran sect. Many of the matters spelled out in considerable detail had been adumbrated in other Qumran materials already known. Moreover, the religious calendar used by the writer of the *Temple Scroll* is the same peculiar one earlier seen in other Qumran ritual writings.

(3) The longest section of the new scroll, the subject of over half the columns, has to do with a description of the temple. This is not an account of an existing or previously existing structure, but a commandment to build one. Detailed instructions are given. In manner and style the narrative depends upon Exodus 35, but it may have been inspired by I Chronicles 28:11 (which mentions a plan of the temple which David gave to Solomon). The people of Qumran, envisioning a new kingdom, may have sought to supply the missing plans to be ready for construction of a House of God which would be the focal point of their coming greatness.

(4) The final section deals with the same theme as the *Warfare Scroll:* the mobilization for war. But unlike the other writing, the *Temple Scroll* envisions a purely defensive struggle, one which will keep the king and his family as well as the people of Israel from falling into the hands of the Gentiles. While the soldiers of the holy army are to be without blemish, "men of truth, God-fearing, hating unjust gain," the author is

quite mundane about the precise stages for mobilization. Everything is to be done in order, with just the right man at the right place at the right time. Here again the writers of Qumran show themselves to be particularly well informed in military matters.

The impossibility of the preservation of early manuscripts, a common view prior to the discoveries of Muhammed edh-Dhib, has been shown to be wrong. There is now the hope and some expectation that more documents from biblical days will be found.

The Importance of the Scrolls

Not all so-called Dead Sea Scrolls are connected with the Qumran sectarians. Those from Murabba'at and Mird as well as some of unidentified locale are for the most part from a later period and deal with subject matter unknown to the Qumranites. It would be better, therefore, to speak of "scrolls from the Wilderness of Judea" or something of the sort. Yet the term "Dead Sea Scrolls," misleading as it may be in several senses, is nonetheless an internationally recognized designation, and one would be wise to retain it. At the same time one needs to be aware that at least two main divisions of material are included: those related to the ruins at Qumran and its former inhabitants, and those with no such affiliation. Within these major categories other distinctions can be made, such as biblical-secular, language, age, etc. With these things in mind it is possible to speak of the importance of the scrolls for our knowledge of (a) the text of the Bible, (b) the history of Judaism, and (c) early Christianity.

(a) Written in ten languages over a period from perhaps the third century B.C.[22] to the eleventh Christian century, the scrolls have

[22] The Wadi Daliyeh materials are even older.

vastly enhanced the science of paleography —our ability to discover the date and possible provenance of a manuscript on the basis of its script. Styles of writing like styles of everything else change. A fairly firm knowledge of the history and development of written script from this period existed prior to the finds in the Judean desert. But these discoveries have filled many gaps and have provided contemporary examples of changing forms of script. This, as we have seen, is of primary importance for the identification and dating of documents. From the caves at Qumran and at Murabba'at and Mird, a variety of texts—legal, personal, sectarian, biblical, and other—has refined and expanded our knowledge of paleography.

The biblical manuscripts have of course drawn most attention. Prior to these finds, the oldest known Hebrew texts of the Old Testament were from the Masoretes, although there were Greek texts from as early as the third Christian century. The extremely important question of the faithfulness of these Greek and later Hebrew texts to the ancient Hebrew textual tradition could not be answered. Whatever their questions and however uneasy they may have felt at certain points, translators could but work with what they had. At one stroke the new discoveries pushed our knowledge of the Hebrew text back a thousand years. For this reason it can be said with truth that the newest translations of the Bible are older than their predecessors—they make use of more ancient texts.

Every book in the Old Testament except Esther is represented in the cave finds, often in many copies and several languages. Fragments of the book of Samuel may be as old as the third century B.C. Daniel, the youngest book in the Old Testament, may not even have been written when the Samuel manuscript was copied. Some of the Daniel material from the Qumran library may possibly be dated within a century or so of the composition of that book. If this is correct, and it seems so, it is truly astounding in the history of the study of the Old Testament. Equally striking, although not wholly unexpected, these newly discovered documents have shown how very faithful were the Greek version and the later Hebrew Masoretic text to their prototypes as found among the writings from the Wilderness of Judea.

There are, to be sure, a number of differences between the new texts and those that have been known. Not surprisingly the vast majority of these differences occur in the biblical manuscripts from the Qumran library (where a number of textual traditions are present) rather than in the finds from Murabba'at and Mird. After the fall of Jerusalem in A.D. 70, a rabbinical group established at Jamnia, west of the destroyed capital, declared canonical the thirty-nine books of the Old Testament as they appear in Jewish and Protestant Bibles today.[23] After Jamnia, of course, the sacred textual tradition became considerably more uniform than previously, and this is reflected in the materials from Murabba'at and Mird. The scriptures of the Essenes at Qumran show that status of the tradition before Jamnia and thus yield a unique picture in the development of a standard text of the Old Testament.

(b) At the same time the sectarian writings from Qumran and the various secular texts from elsewhere in the wilderness add substantially to the mosaic of a complex period in the history of Judaism. It has long been recognized that the period around the time of the birth of Jesus was for Judaism a period of extreme plasticity with a multiplicity of groups representing various religious and political points of view. Yet in the absence of contemporary documents, the pharisaical viewpoint has often and mis-

takenly been seen as normative for the times. The Pharisees were extremely important. After the fall of Jerusalem their views did, with some modification, become dominant if not in all respects normative. They are widely quoted in rabbinical literature and are known (somewhat slanderously) from the New Testament. Still, they were not so paramount as we are usually led to think. The Dead Sea Scrolls are particularly valuable in showing us from their own writings another group, virile, apparently with some influence, with views distinct from those of the Pharisees. These people were not, one hastens to add, set over against the Pharisees, but their emphases were very different. In spite of what the New Testament writers make them out to be, the Pharisees were the liberals of their day desiring to make the Law applicable to and meaningful in every aspect of human endeavor. The Qumranites, on the other hand, while having an equally high regard for the Law, were a fervently messianic community caring little for social reform, since they looked forward with eager anticipation to the appearance of those[24] who would initiate the kingdom of God among men. Moreover, the piety of those by the Dead Sea laid greater stress on the withdrawal of man from the ordinary into a search for more intimate union with God and his angels.

Equally important for our knowledge of the history of Judaism are the discoveries at Nahal Hever, Murabba'at, and Mird, especially Hever. Most of the Jewish manuscripts from these sites are from the Second Revolt. These show among other things that the general Talmudic regulations for the copying of Sacred Scripture were already in effect in the mid-second century. Particularly striking is the way in which the sheets of skin were prepared and laid out, and also the highly stylized form of writing denoting

[23] The Catholic Old Testament includes as sacred a number of books which Jews and Protestants view as apocryphal.

[24] There was the belief in two messiahs, one priestly, the other kingly.

Holy Writ. As previously noted, the scriptures are very selective and do not begin to show the variation seen at Qumran. The messianic fervor found at Qumran is present in the nonbiblical writings from elsewhere and indeed was one of the major factors in the Second Revolt. But again there is a difference. The role of the priestly or Aaronic messiah is considerably pushed into the background, while that of the kingly or Davidic savior has also undergone something of a change. The latter is now seen in an almost purely military sense. Bar Kochba, the leader of the Revolt, is viewed as the Messiah of Israel, the one who will deliver his people from the Romans and will lead them to their rightful destiny. All in all the documents from the second century show the Revolt in an extremely orthodox context with great stress upon Sabbath observance, the purity and centrality of scripture, and the imminent fulfillment of God's promises of deliverance as understood by the faithful.

(c) Undoubtedly a major reason for the unprecedented popular interest in the Dead Sea Scrolls was the light they shed or were said to shed on the background and possible origins of Christianity. But what can be aptly described as "Qumran fever" spread not only through the popular mind; but it infected also certain segments of scholarship. To some, the discoveries had shaken Christianity to its foundations by showing that the story of Jesus of Nazareth was modeled closely upon that reported of the Teacher of Righteousness, the founder of the Qumran sect. On the other extreme were those who suggested that now, finally, we had the proper clues to the mysteries of Christianity. Here, at last, were the documents that would show the Christian faith in its full uniqueness. The views of the adherents of each extreme have been shown to be without foundation. Nothing in the scrolls substantially changes our previous views of the origins of Christianity, and nothing indicates that emergent Christianity was any less indebted to Judaism than had been known or suspected.

A more balanced view of the relation of the thought in the Qumran manuscripts to that of early Christianity takes account of considerable similarities and numerous differences. Christianity did not arise in a vacuum, but grew out of Judaism and particularly out of that part which was strongly messianic. Both the early church and the community by the Dead Sea had collections of Old Testament texts (*testimonia*) which were used as messianic proof texts. Both saw themselves as living in the last days. Yet at Qumran the kingdom of God was anticipated;[25] for the Christians it had come. This is a major difference between the two groups. Christians saw themselves as living in the New Age; Qumranites prepared themselves for it. Other differences in messianic belief, already mentioned, need to be emphasized. The members of the Qumran sect anticipated the appearance of two messiahs, one Davidic (kingly), the other Aaronic (priestly). Neither seems to be the heavenly figure confessed in the faith of the early church where the roles of king and priest were combined with those of prophet and suffering servant into one messiah—Jesus of Nazareth.

Both groups believed in a resurrection, practiced baptism, reverenced the Jewish Scriptures, saw themselves as the "true Israel," and offered similar arguments against marriage (see I Corinthians 7:29-31 for an example). Organizationally both held common property, were ruled by a council of twelve, had community meals, and devoted themselves to prayer and teaching. In each the faithful were seen as struggling with spirits of evil seeking to subvert not only men but the cosmos as well. Yet in almost every one of these things there are striking

[25] This is one of the reasons why some scholars have tended to identify John the Baptist and his movement with the Essenes of Qumran.

or subtle differences. This is due not only to the Christian belief that Messiah had come, but also to the prophetic context of early Christianity as compared with the more priestly approach and organization of the Essenes. The followers of Jesus were considerably less ritualistic than their Qumranite counterparts even though the former, unlike the latter, devoted themselves faithfully to the services at the Temple (Acts 2:46; 3:1). Christianity, of course, did not remain a Jerusalemite-Galilean group, nor even merely a part of Judaism. With its universalistic thrust, it leaped across all human barriers. The community by the Dead Sea, in stark contrast, was never anything other than a Jewish sect. Universalistic tendencies in their thought were countered and canceled by the hostility of these self-identified Sons of Light to the Sons of Darkness whom their *Manual of Discipline* instructed them to hate.

In the Dead Sea Scrolls we are given a unique insight into the minds of certain of the contemporaries of Jesus. Those who wrote these documents are shown to be similar in some respects to the Pharisees and in other ways to the Christians. Yet they are revealed in their own right, with their own distinctives. The value of these writings for the history of Judaism is obvious; for the background of Christianity they are equally important if more debated. Just as an adequate appreciation of the accomplishments of Herod the Great shows us an important element in the cultural world into which Jesus was born and in which he lived, so the recovery of these remarkable manuscripts indicates something of the religious atmosphere of Jesus' day. From these writings we see both the debt of Jesus and the church to the religious movements of the times, and the uniqueness and mystery of the gospel.

VIII: THE NEW TESTAMENT

21. ARCHAEOLOGY AND JESUS

Archaeology has done a great deal to illumine the background of the life and ministry of Jesus. The recovery of Herodian Palestine and the discovery of the Dead Sea
materials are premier examples of this.
Unfortunately, similar success has not been
enjoyed with reference to Jesus himself. No
artifacts related specifically to him have been
found, nor are there any archaeologically recovered structures whose primary association is with Jesus. This is not surprising
since Jesus was a poor man. No Herod, he
left no villas, fortresses, and temples to be
his monuments. Nor is he known to have
written anything. Moreover, two terrible
wars engulfed Palestine within a hundred
years of Jesus' ministry obliterating many
if not most of the places that were familiar
to him, including Jerusalem. These produced
a complete break in the continuity of life in
that unhappy land. Today even the sites of
some of the major events in Jesus' life are
in doubt.

An inscribed stone found at Caesarea in 1961. It
bears the name "Pilatus," and is the first archaeological reference to the famous Prefect.

A. Frova

278

A great many of the places pointed out to tourists are often wholly without claim to antiquity and to any connection with Jesus. In Nazareth, one can be shown two grottoes of the Annunciation, two homes of the Holy Family, a cave said to be Joseph's workshop, and even a stone table where the resurrected Jesus is said to have dined with his disciples. Other locations, hallowed by the pious through the years, are identified by ancient traditions—in almost no case do they predate the Emperor Constantine. But we are not primarily concerned here with either tourist attractions or traditional sites, however distinguished. Our focus is on archaeology, and while this has, for valid reasons, been able to tell us less about the ministry of Jesus than about other major matters in the Bible, it has made a contribution. This contribution lies in the areas of clarifying certain people

A Roman milestone in Moab. The Romans were able to extend their love of order to the roads more easily than to the population.

and events connected with Jesus' life, and supporting the value of the Gospels as historical documents.

Roman Governors and a Census

Pontius Pilate is the most famous Roman governor of all. Every Sunday millions of Christians speak his name as they repeat the Apostles' Creed. Yet apart from coins there was until 1961 no firm archaeological evidence of his presence in Palestine.[1] In that year Italian archaeologists working at Caesarea came across a stone with a half-obliterated inscription. What was left was enough to identify it as having probably come from a public building of some sort dedicated when Tiberius was emperor and Pontius Pilate was prefect of Judea (see p. 313, n. 9).

Sulpicius Quirinius is also well known. It was when he was legate of Syria, according to Luke 2:2, that Mary and Joseph went to Bethlehem "to be enrolled" because of a census. While they were in the City of David, Jesus was born. Matthew dates the event a bit differently, but not in contradiction to Luke. According to Matthew 2:1 "Jesus was born in Bethlehem of Judea in the days of Herod the king." Herod, we know, died in 4 B.C.[2]

There is abundant archaeological evidence to support the view that the census was a regular feature of life in the Roman Empire. These population counts seem to have begun under Augustus and continued for several centuries; in some places they were held at regular intervals of perhaps fourteen years. From Egypt there is papyrus evidence of a census around A.D. 104, when families were required to be enrolled in their ancestral

[1] There are several Roman aqueducts south of Jerusalem. One of these was built by Pilate. Further work is needed to enhance our knowledge of these marvelous systems which carried water uphill from south of Bethlehem to the Holy City.

[2] Jesus was born B.C. There was an error in the calendar. It was corrected in the early Middle Ages by Pope Gregory the Great.

homes. This is exactly the kind of event that took Mary and Joseph from Nazareth to Bethlehem.

But when was the census mentioned in Luke? When was Quirinius governor? From an inscription recovered in one of the Antiochs in Galatia, we know that Quirinius, a Roman senator, was sent to Syria in 10 B.C. He remained there for three years while he quelled disturbances in Asia Minor.[3] He was back as governor in A.D. 6-9. A census was taken at that time and provoked rioting among the Jews of Galilee. But this census is too late to be the one referred to in Luke. There is some evidence suggesting he was governor earlier, in 3-2 B.C., but that is also after the death of Herod and thus too late for the birth of Jesus. Moreover, there is nothing to indicate a census during an earlier governorship. Some scholars have sought to solve the problem by translating Luke 2:2 so as to point to the last census *prior* to Quirinius' service in 6-9. But this clever suggestion does violence to the Greek text and has not been widely accepted. The problem is a difficult one and has not been solved.

Bethlehem, Capernaum, and Chorazin

Almost all the sites associated with the life and ministry of Jesus have been identified by archaeological surveys of Palestine. But as previously mentioned, there are few structures which can be dated to the time of Jesus, much less connected with him personally.[4]

Matthew and Luke tell us that Jesus was born in Bethlehem, in a stable "because there was no place for them in the inn." Since early Christian times a certain cave in Bethlehem has been venerated as the place of the Lord's birth. After the Council of Nicaea (A.D. 325) Constantine built churches at the traditional sites of the Nativity, the Resurrection, and the Ascension. Portions of the one built at the resurrection site are still visible in the Church of the Holy Sepulchre. The ascension church, now vanished, was on the Mount of Olives. The Church of the Nativity in Bethlehem was constructed over the sacred grotto. Very little remains of that early structure. Indeed, there is some question whether the splendid mosaics recently discovered beneath the present floor of the basilica are Constantinian or later.

In the sixth century, Samaritans attacked a number of Christian shrines putting them to the torch. This prompted the Emperor Justinian to engage in extensive rebuilding at various places. One cannot be sure that this is what caused him to rebuild and beautify the Church of the Nativity, but a layer of charred material beneath a part of the mosaic floor strongly suggests it. At any rate, the basilica along its present lines was built at that time and beautified by marble paving, marble and mosaic wall-covering, gilded capitals, carved architraves, and an elaborate roof.

Miraculously the church survived the Persian and Muslim invasions. Both groups reverenced the building, and the latter even insisted that a portion of the southern apse be set aside for Muslim prayers. During the eleventh and twelfth centuries, the Crusaders made many contributions to the structure including new marbles so polished that it was said one's face looked back from every column. So carefully joined was this material that the Crusaders claimed a needle could not be inserted between slabs. The white marble paving of Justinian gave way to colored marble mosaics of renowned brilliance. The roof was covered with precious lead, and a gilded star was afixed on its

[3] Syria was a first-class Imperial province and the primary line of defense against the ever-present Parthians. The legate there was more than a provincial governor. He was the emperor's chief representative in the entire region including not only Asia Minor but Palestine as well. A legate of Syria removed Pilate from office in A.D. 36 and had him sent to Rome to stand trial for misconduct in office.

[4] The well of Sychar may be an exception; see p. 289.

highest point to lead pilgrims to the manger.

That was the apogee of the church's career. Kings were crowned there, and endowment from copious landed estates paid for the considerable upkeep of the building. But it has been mostly downhill since then. The basilica continued to survive the vicissitudes of Palestine's various fates, but time itself took a tremendous toll. The floors were literally destroyed by hundreds of thousands of pious feet. The mosaics of the walls disappeared behind the damaging, accumulated smoke of centuries of oil lamps. The trusses supporting the roof rotted and the ceiling was prevented from falling only by struts hurriedly erected at vital points. Pigeons, sparrows, and other birds easily found entry around the tops of the walls and defaced the whole sanctuary. At the end of the fifteenth century the entire structure was in a perilous condition.

Edward IV of England and the Republic of Venice saw to the church's immediate needs. Among other things Edward provided new lead for the roof. In the seventeenth century, this was found to have been stripped away over large areas. The Greek Orthodox Church undertook new repairs. Almost all the marble was found to be missing, and rain coming through the roof had seriously damaged the remaining mosaics. Again, it was the Greek Orthodox Church that repaired the basilica after an earthquake in 1832. The floor of the choir was paved with marble, and flagstones were laid in the nave. The plaster on the walls today was applied then, but in such a way as to leave visible those pitifully few mosaics that had once formed one of the most gorgeous decorations in Christendom. Unfortunately the sacred cave, gutted by fire in 1809, was left almost completely untouched due to lack of funds. In 1874 the president of France presented hangings which now cover the walls of the grotto. Intermittent repairs have been made

in the past few years. But this hallowed site is much in need of funds to maintain the structural soundness of the building, not to mention the considerable need for refurbishing. It is, all the same, an extremely lovely basilica, pleasing to the eye and of inestimable value to the pilgrim.

At Tell Hum a very different scene greets the visitor. This location is generally considered to have been biblical Capernaum. It has, at least, been so taken since the fourth century when pilgrims began to come there in some numbers. In 1921 Father Orfali unearthed a Byzantine church which was evidently intended to commemorate the holy spot. A Roman cemetery was found at the same time. But the most striking ruin is that of a synagogue. Six of its reconstructed, gleaming white limestone columns still capped by superb Corinthian capitals tower almost twenty feet. It is in basilica form and once had rows of columns supporting a gallery (for the women) around three sides. The ornamentation is reminiscent of later baroque. Reliefs are everywhere and, while human representations are absent, there are numerous lions, eagles, birds, and even centaurs, cupids, and sea horses. Traditional Jewish vines, grapes, ivy, date palms, and the like blend with geometric designs, garlands, rosettes, and other decorations bespeaking of considerable lavishness. The floor is of flagstone, and two-tiered benches are against the side walls. Doubtless men sat also on mats on the main floor.

In Mark 1:21-28 and Luke 4:31-37, there is an account of Jesus teaching in a synagogue at Capernaum and of his cleansing a man with an unclean spirit. It is tempting to assign a first-century date to the existing ruins and to point to the building as the very one Jesus entered on that distant Sabbath. Father Orfali, in fact, did maintain such a dating and has been followed in this by some people. Unfortunately the building seems to

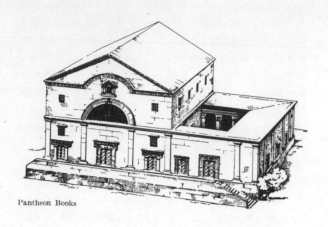

Pantheon Books

The synagogue at Capernaum as its second-century ruins appear today (above), and as it may have looked when in use (left).

be second century at the earliest and was in use for some time after that. About all one can say to connect this with the New Testament story is that it probably rests on the site of an earlier synagogue; it may have been that one which Jesus knew.

Chorazin and Bethsaida were cities familiar to Jesus; he prophesied their doom along with that of Capernaum (Matthew 11: 20-24; Luke 10:12-15). At Kerazeh, the modern site of Chorazin, another synagogue has been unearthed. It is similar to the one at Capernaum: basilica form, benches along the walls, and baroque ornamentation. But this building was later than the other and was in ruins earlier, perhaps by the early fourth century.

Neither of these synagogues can be associated with the life of Jesus, although each stands in a location he would have known well. Archaeology has confirmed what was suspected from our knowledge of the history of the times: These structures were a part of the rebuilding of Jewish houses of worship after the thorough Roman vengeance of the mid-second century (the Second Revolt). That they reflect a kind of synagogue familiar to Jesus is quite possible. Beyond that they have no known New Testament associations.

The Church of the Nativity presents a different case. The structure of Constantine is said to have replaced a Hadrianic shrine of Adonis. Hadrian is known to have constructed Roman temples over Christian, Jewish, and Samaritan sanctuaries. By such practice the emperor may inadvertently have preserved the locations of many holy places. But that is in the realm of conjecture and tradition, not of archaeological fact.

Jerusalem

"When the days drew near for him to be received up," says Luke 9:51 speaking of Jesus, "he set his face to go to Jerusalem." Jerusalem, vital place in the Old Testament narrative, was no less central to the life and ministry of Jesus and to the story told in the New Testament. Several times mention has been made of the particularly frustrating circumstances Jerusalem presents to the archaeologist. To the history of recurrent destructions is added the fact that almost all New Testament Jerusalem lies squarely beneath the present inhabited area. At least a part of the older Old Testament settlement has not had modern houses built upon it and has thus been open to excavation. Nonetheless, for all the problems associated with excavating in Jerusalem, attempts have been made to determine something of the Temple, the Antonia, Herod's Palace, and other major structures of the city Jesus knew.[5]

Some other locations mentioned prominently in the Gospels are well known today, for example, the Mount of Olives and the Garden of Gethsemane on its eastern slope, although we can be sure its present form is hardly as it was in Jesus' day. The Pool of Siloam, where the man born blind washed away the clay Jesus applied to his eyes (and in so doing received his sight; John 9), is no mystery to the scholar. Moreover, within the garden area of the Church of St. Anne's, itself a masterpiece of Norman architecture from Crusader days, excavations have unearthed the twin pools of Bethesda where Jesus healed a crippled man (John 5:2-9). Various traditions have identified other sacred places such as the Upper Room and the houses of Caiaphas and Annas.

Tradition has also pointed to the sites of Jesus' crucifixion, burial, and resurrection. Yet the locations of these momentous events are a matter of considerable debate among scholars. Two places claim to be Calvary and the fateful garden. Either is questionable, if not both.

The so-called Garden Tomb is just north of the Damascus Gate, well outside the present wall of the Old City, near a spot long

Istanbul Museum

identified as "Jeremiah's Grotto." Entering a simple and unspoiled garden, the visitor senses a reverent atmosphere. In the side of the limestone cliff face there is a rock-cut tomb. Within is a chamber with three recesses, each intended to hold a body on its stone shelf. Only one is completely finished. From the small doorway it is possible to look inside and see the completed shelf. In front of the door is a groove which once held a large stone, similar to a millstone, to seal the sepulchre. These features fit well with the biblical narratives that indicate that the tomb in which Jesus was laid was new and cut into stone (Luke 23:53); that the disciples stooping down could look in at the place where Jesus had lain (John 20:5); and that the entrance was sealed by a large stone (Luke 24:2).

It was not until 1842 that a German scholar, Otto Thenius, proposed that this was the true site of Calvary and the garden of the Resurrection. A number of prominent authorities have agreed with this identification. The hill nearby is popularly called "Gordon's Calvary" after the famous British general, Charles George Gordon, to whom the craggy face of the cliff appeared to resemble a skull. The place where Jesus was crucified, we are told in Matthew 27:33, was called *Golgotha*, "the place of a skull."

In 1923 the tomb was excavated and ma-

---

[5] In 1913 evidence of another structure possibly known to Jesus was found on Ophel. It is an inscribed stone from a synagogue dating before the destruction of Jerusalem in A.D. 70. "Theodotus, son of Vettenus, priest and synagogue-president [it reads], son of a synagogue-president and grandson of a synagogue president, has built the synagogue for the reading of the Law and the teaching of the Commandments, and he has built the hostelry and the chambers and the cisterns of water in order to provide lodgings for those from abroad who need them—[the synagogue] which his fathers and the elders and Simonides had founded." Because "Vettenus" may reflect an Italian background, and because of the mention of "those from abroad," this inscription is frequently mentioned in connection with the "Synagogue of the Freedmen" from which Stephen was dragged and stoned (Acts 6:9).

terials were recovered which bore resemblance to objects associated with a shrine of Venus and Adonis. Perhaps, the excavators suggested, these were relics of a Hadrianic Temple of Venus erected over the site of the Crucifixion. This was said to be further evidence of the genuineness of the site. Most archaeologists, however, do not accept this as evidence of the location of the holy site and consider the entire complex to be second century in origin. Today the German Protestants who maintain the tomb and its garden are firmly convinced that it is the place where the anxious women found the stone rolled away and the body gone. And the pious who go there cannot fail to be moved by its reverential atmosphere. Nonetheless, from a purely archaeological point of view and from the perspective of ancient tradition, there is nothing to sustain the claim that this is indeed the place.

Since at least the time of Constantine tradition has firmly fixed upon another spot as Calvary and the garden. This is the Church of the Holy Sepulchre, a sprawling maze of chapels covering under one roof what has long been said to be the site of the Crucifixion, the place of the anointing of Jesus' body for burial, the tomb, and the garden of the Resurrection. There is no question of the antiquity of the church. The fifth-century mosaic map at Medeba[6] shows it in its present position. Moreover, some masonry in the north transept has been identified as fourth-century work. Extensive renovation now un-

[6] In the church of the small town of Medeba, near Mount Nebo, there are extensive remains of a mosaic map which covered much of the sanctuary floor. This map has been helpful in identifying many sites, or at least in showing where they were considered to be by fifth-century monks who made this remarkable chart. Fortunately well preserved is a diagram of Jerusalem showing clearly the outline of Hadrian's city and marking subsequent construction of specifically Christian interest. The church of the Holy Sepulchre was, of course, foremost among these.

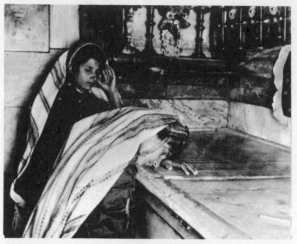

The present main entrance to the Church of the Holy Sepulchre (above right) is Crusader and does not convey the grandeur the church possessed during the reigns of Constantine and Justinian. Conquests, fire, and an encroaching city have combined to reduce the shrine to a sorry state from which it is only now being recovered. The steps in the lower left of the picture once led to Calvary. They are now blocked. Under the dome is the traditional Tomb of Jesus (above), now as for almost twenty centuries the most sacred site in Christendom. The famous Medeba Map (below) is our most authoritative source of knowledge for Byzantine Jerusalem which was built within the conceived limits of Hadrian's *Aelia Capitolina*. The Church of the Holy Sepulchre is clearly visible in the middle of the *cordo maximus*.

der way will doubtless shed more light on this matter.

Today the church is well within the walls of the Old City, as indeed it was in Constantine's day when the first sizable edifice, perhaps the most splendid of all, was erected there. This has been a major factor in the considerable skepticism surrounding the au-

thenticity of the location. Neither Jews nor Romans carried out executions within a city. A Jewish place of stoning was usually just outside the city gate (as is reflected in the traditions about the death of Stephen), while the Romans sought some prominent place where crucified bodies could be left to rot as a warning.[7] Furthermore, John 19:20 states specifically that Jesus was crucified outside the city, and all four Gospels and the Letter to the Hebrews give clear indication that the tomb of Jesus was outside the walls of Jerusalem.

Many a person standing in the hustle and bustle of the streets near the Church of the Holy Sepulchre and noting how it is hemmed in by other buildings rightly wonders about the correctness of the location. Yet the question is not one of today's city or of the present walls. As an example of what has happened in a well-documented period of the Church's history, we should note that the main entrance now is the western door of the southern transept. This is surely strange in itself, and more puzzling given the enor-

[7] In the case of Jesus and those executed with him, it was at Jewish insistence that the bodies were removed (John 19:31).

mous amount of daily traffic. The answer is quite simple, however. A great eastern facade erected by Crusader masons around 1135 has been considerably reduced, and the incursion of other buildings has caused it to be unsuitable as an entrance. The eastern door of the south transept was sealed at the time of Saladin's capture of the city in 1187. It has not been reopened. Thus one battered old wooden door in a somewhat unlikely place opens to permit entry. Such are the happenings in Jerusalem.

Of greater consequence is that the size of the walled city has changed a number of times over the centuries. The present walls are those of Suliman the Magnificent and were constructed in the sixteenth century. That they incorporate older portions of other walls is certain. It is widely and probably correctly assumed that for the most part they follow the lines of the so-called "third wall" built by Herod Agrippa (A.D. 41-44). Agrippa's work not only enclosed a large area north of the city of Herod the Great, but the southern end of the western hill, as Miss Kenyon's recent excavations have shown. When Herod ruled Jerusalem it had an area of 140 acres. Under his grandson, Agrippa, it had grown to 310 acres. The issue bearing upon the possible authenticity of the site of the Church of the Holy Sepulchre is the line of the northwestern segment of Herod's city wall.

Excavating from 1934 to 1940, J. N. Johns established the northwest corner of the Herodian city at the citadel, the place where three massive towers once stood (see p. 236). Slightly earlier, Father Vincent had identified the remains of the Antonia on the northwestern corner of the Platform (see p. 236). But what was the line between these two archaeologically established points? Did it run due west to the general area of the Damascus Gate before turning south roughly ninety degrees to join the triple towers? Or did it turn south after only a shorter distance, drop down until east of the citadel, and then make another ninety-degree angle to link up with the towers? On topographical grounds and from the point of view of military defense, many have argued for the former. This would place the location of the Church of the Holy Sepulchre within the walls of the Herodian city and thus rule it out as the place of the Crucifixion. Still other scholars, Father Vincent among them, have argued from meager archaeological evidence that the second line is really the correct one. In this case, the location of the Church would have been just outside the walls in Jesus' day. New evidence has recently come to light which adds considerable strength to the position of Vincent and others.

Excavating within an urban center is almost impossible even if there is an open space. The question of what to use for a dump soon becomes a pressing matter. Nonetheless, so important is the question of the location of the Herodian walls that Miss Kenyon undertook to dig in a small area (approximately a hundred feet by fifty feet) just south of the Church. When, after two seasons of work, bedrock was reached the uncovered area was only thirteen feet square. But the effort, frustrating and expensive— among other things earth had to be transported out of the city by donkey—was well worth it. After removing a considerable accumulation of twentieth-century debris (over six feet deep), the excavators came upon evidence of the Crusaders: the foundations of massive piers, probably all that is left of the famous Hospital of St. John.[8] Beneath this were Arab buildings, and then some Byzantine and Roman ruins. Below them—nothing. Nothing, that is, except a massive fill. For the greater part of the two seasons, this fill occupied the time and energy of the workmen and the increasingly frustrated archaeologists. All the pottery, and

[8] The Order of St. John still owns the property on which the excavations took place.

there were vast amounts of it, came from the seventh century B.C. and the first century A.D. The only structure in the enormous fill was a Roman drain quite similar to the one that still functions as the main drain of the Old City. The drain and the fill were a part of the same plan; all the ground surrounding them had the same character. Then, after going down over twenty-seven feet through this material from two very different periods, there was a change. There was another fill, but it was all pure Iron Age, seventh century B.C. Then bedrock was struck. When the bottom of the pit was cleared, the rock was seen to be a series of cut steps and ledges —a quarry.

To the unpracticed eye this excavation may seem to have been a considerable waste of time, energy, and money. But a good deal had been learned. The quarry shows that the area was definitely outside the walls during the time of the Judean monarchy. For a considerable distance around this, there was no occupational evidence except for the fill and the drain. Buildings were placed over this. But when? It would seem almost certain that it was in the second century A.D. The drain, halfway down the fill, was planned as part of a development of the area. As early as 1870 Warren had established that the drain later found by Miss Kenyon connected with another continuing into the central valley where it joined the main Roman drain. The only post-first-century occasion known to us when a vast town-building operation took place, involving such a well-planned system deep under the houses and streets, was in A.D. 135. It was then that Hadrian significantly changed the topography of Jerusalem by filling large areas and constructing a new city, *Aelia Capitolina*, on the site. The Old City today is essentially that laid out by Hadrian, although during the Middle Ages it became cluttered and its streets more twisting than the master Roman architect had planned.

Miss Kenyon's conclusion is that the entire area was outside the city until the second century A.D. Not everyone agrees with her. Even if it was open in Jesus' day, as she has conclusively proved, it must not necessarily have been outside the walls. Yet we must admit that her evidence is strong, if not absolutely convincing. Furthermore, it enhances earlier suggestions made by Father Vincent on the basis of his unequaled knowledge of the history of Jerusalem.[9]

Most would agree today that archaeology has gone far to show that the Church of the Holy Sepulchre can be the site of those events which climaxed the earthly life of Jesus and began the Christian movement. Absolute proof has not been given nor perhaps will it ever be. Much still rests upon tradition and upon the word of the early Christian historian Eusebius, who may have been an eyewitness to the erection of the great Church of Constantine. In his *Life of Constantine* he says that the location of Jesus' tomb was marked by a Hadrianic temple of Venus. This was torn down and work was begun on a fitting Christian structure. During the operation workmen discovered the very tomb of Jesus himself. How they distinguished it from other tombs in the area is not said.

Part of the strength of the tradition lies precisely in the fact that the area was within the city walls in Constantine's day. People then were as informed as we of the accounts in the Gospels concerning Jesus' death. They were probably a good deal more aware of Roman practices. At the same time they doubtless knew considerably less of the history of Jerusalem. That a site well within the walls was identified as the place of the Crucifixion certainly enhances the creditability of the tradition.

⁹ Louis-Hughes Vincent, *Jérusalem de l'Ancien Testament* (Paris: Librairie Lecoffre, 1956), pp. 699-725.

The Fourth Gospel and Archaeology

The First Revolt against the Romans radically dislocated Jewish life in Palestine. The Second Revolt practically brought it to an end. Some of the archaeological evidence for this was mentioned in connection with the synagogues at Capernaum and Chorazin (see pp. 281-2). Christianity was affected in much the same way. Christians in Palestine were treated as traitors by Jews, and as Jewish rebels by others. Yet it should be recalled that well before the First Revolt, by 44 if not earlier, the center of this new faith was not Jerusalem nor even Palestine. The spread of Christianity was a unique phenomenon in the history of religions. After a brief struggle of two opposing emphases—Jewish sectarianism and a universalistic thrust—it literally exploded into every part of the known world. It is thus no accident that none of the Four Gospels was written in Palestine.

This raises a serious question of the accuracy of the Palestinian traditions of the Gospels. The issue has been particularly critical in the case of the Fourth Gospel. John's Gospel, perhaps the most sublime writing in the entire Bible, has been something of a stepchild in biblical history. Some of the Church Fathers regarded it as too congenial to certain heretical views; some more recent critics have attacked it as a wholly theological interpretation of Jesus Christ, without substantial historical value. Fifty to seventy-five years ago men of this persuasion looked upon this Gospel as the end result of a long period of theological reflection. It was from the end of the second century, they said, a writing addressed to a sophisticated Greek audience and drawing heavily upon Greek philosophy if not heretical Gnostic materials. Similar views of John are still with us. Now archaeology has demonstrated that such positions, perhaps warranted from one point of view on the basis of limited information once available, are no longer tenable.

To cite a highly developed theology as evidence of a late second-century writing is, on the face of it, invalid. Is this to suggest that Paul's letters, which were the earliest New Testament writings (in the form in which we have them) do not contain a highly developed theology? Moreover, and to the point of archaeology, the sands of Egypt have yielded a fragment of the Gospel of John dated variously from A.D. 110 to 150, but in no case later. This writing, a papyrus fragment now in the John Rylands Library at Manchester, England, is the earliest manuscript evidence of the New Testament. It gives the latest date the Gospel could have been written, not when it was written. Scholars today generally agree that John was composed toward the end of the first century, perhaps around 90.[10]

Archaeology has also blunted another criticism often leveled at the Fourth Gospel: the author was unfamiliar with the geography of Palestine. This was to support the contention that the traditions underlying John's Gospel did not have firm Palestinian roots. Yet an examination of the place-names referred to in John, but not mentioned in the other Gospels, shows quite the opposite.

There are nine such place-names. The Kidron Valley (John 18:1) is well known as the gorge east of Jerusalem and running into the Wilderness of Judea. Cana of Galilee (John 2:1, 11; 4:46; 21:2) has long been associated with Kefr Kenna, four miles northeast of Nazareth, but archaeological surveys of the area indicate that it is probably to be identified with Khirbet Qana, eight miles north of Nazareth. Ephraim (John 11:54) is to be identified with et-Taiyibeh about four miles west and north of Bethel. There also need be no doubts about the location of Solomon's

Porch where Jesus is said by John (10:23) to have walked in the winter. It was the long eastern colonnade of the temple platform of Herod (see p. 249).

This leaves five places: Bethany-beyond-Jordan, Aenon near Salim, Sychar, Bethesda, and Gabbatha. The first two have to do with John the Baptist. According to John 1:28, the Baptist's confrontation with the priests and Levites from Jerusalem took place "in Bethany beyond the Jordan." This has been a troublesome reference. It is usually assumed that John's place of baptism near the Jordan was on the west bank, near Jericho, where tradition says he baptized Jesus. But is there any reason to assume that he had no activity on the east bank, where the Fourth Gospel suggests? On the contrary, there is evidence from the Synoptic Gospels and Josephus that he was active there, in what was then known as Peraea whose ruler was Herod Antipas. Herod (grandson of Herod the Great) was, according to Josephus, fearful of the great popularity of John. Moreover, when John criticized the somewhat involved family relations of this ruler, the prophet found himself an object of considerable hostility not only from Herod but from his powerful and unscrupulous wife, Herodias (former wife of his half-brother, Herod Philip). Some think this deadly opposition caused John to shift his activity northward to Samaria and Aenon near Salim which was under direct Roman jurisdiction. At any rate, John did eventually fall into the power of Herod and Herodias and according to Luke 3:20 was shut up in prison. This prison, Josephus tells us, was Machaerus, a mountain fortress east of the Dead Sea. Here Salome danced before Herod and at Herodias' insistence asked for the head of John the Baptist. All this took place in Peraea, *east* of the Jordan. Here is clear support for the Fourth Gospel's reference to a Bethany-beyond-Jordan, even though the exact site has not yet been identified.

[10] The Gospel of Mark is thought to come from the 60s of the first century, while Luke and Matthew from the 70s or 80s. These are dates usually given for the composition of the books as we now have them. Underlying the Gospels are oral and written traditions from the time of Jesus and shortly after.

Aenon near Salim where, according to John 3:23, John baptized "because there was much water there," was unidentified until recently. Archaeological surveys around Shechem, however, have pinpointed it with some certainty. It is at the head of the Wadi Farah. There is Ainon, doubtless preserving the older Aramaic name which means "Little Fountain." Nearby is Salim, a beautiful spring that gushes from the northern slope of the Wadi. Its abundant water not only supplies the area round about, but runs down into the Wadi to nourish that green carpet which winds its way through the scorched hills and down to the Jordan.

Sychar, where Jesus is reported to have had an amazing conversation with a Samaritan woman (John 4:5), has likewise been identified by work in the Shechem area. The Old Syriac Gospels preserved the name Sychem where most other texts read Sychar. So long as the site of ancient Shechem was identified with modern Nablus, the place-name in John 4:5 presented great difficulties. Some scholars suggested that Askar on the slope of Mount Ebal was a possible location for Sychar. A few still hold to the older view. In the early part of this century, however, Ernst Sellin, German pioneer archaeologist, demonstrated beyond doubt that ancient Shechem was not under modern Nablus, but a mile and a half east, at the end of the pass between Mount Gerizim and Mount Ebal. There, at a mound known as Tell Balata, very extensive excavations from 1956 to 1968 by an American team headed by G. E. Wright confirmed Sellin's view and the history of one of the most famous cities of the Old Testament. At the same time more modest work in Nablus by the Jordanian Department of Antiquities showed it to be of Roman foundation during the First Revolt. Shechem was destroyed about 128 B.C. by John Hyrcanus and apparently not rebuilt on a large scale. The American archaeologists found no evidence of settlement in Roman times. Yet there is an abundant supply of water (it still serves the modern village). It would have been surprising if no advantage were taken of it. Moreover, because of the presence of modern houses it was not possible to dig in the immediate vicinity of the water source or near an ancient well associated by tradition with the patriarch Jacob.[11] It is he who is associated with the story in John 4. There is every possibility that the Sychem of the Syriac Gospels is correct and indicates Shechem.

Bethesda (Bethzatha, RSV) is a pool in Jerusalem. It had five porticoes in which invalids lay hoping to find cure in the waters which were said to have curative powers. John 5:2 says this was where Jesus healed a man who had been ill for thirty-eight years. John notes that the pool was near the Sheep Gate. This gate is mentioned only here and in Nehemiah 3:1 where it is said to have been built by priests. It likely had a ritualistic function (for bringing in sacrifices?). J. Simons locates this "without great difficulty" in the northern wall of the city close to the northeastern corner.[12] This would place it opposite the district of Bezetha from which the pool probably drew its name. Working there in 1888, Conrad Schick excavated twin pools with five porticoes. Excavations in 1923 further opened the site, while archaeologists in the mid-1960s have gone far to lay bare the once splendid nature of the site. Outside the north wall in Jesus' day the area has been a part of the enclosed city perhaps since the time of Herod Agrippa. Today it occupies a large section of the property of the White Fathers whose Crusader "Church of St. Anne's," a fine piece of Norman architecture, stands close by.

The last of the place-names unique to John's Gospel is Gabbatha, the *lithostroton*

[11] Quite close by, only a matter of yards away, is the traditional tomb of Joseph.

[12] J. Simons, *Jerusalem in the Old Testament*, p. 343.

where Jesus was brought before Pilate for judgment. This has been discussed earlier (see p. 228), but we do well to remind ourselves here of the discovery of Father Vincent at the present-day Convent of the Sisters of Zion. He found an enormous pavement (*lithostroton*) which once stood on a rocky ridge (*gabbatha*) above the adjacent terrain. In the view of many, including W. F. Albright, "there can be no reasonable doubt that the place referred to (in John 19:13) lies in the court of the Tower of Antonia." [13]

Archaeology has demonstrated decisively that the writer of the Fourth Gospel was thoroughly familiar with the geography of the country and particularly with the terrain of southern Palestine. Apart from Cana, all the sites unique to John are in the south. This, coupled with reports in John that Jesus was in Jerusalem for at least three Passovers during his ministry, and that he was there the winter previous to his crucifixion, ought to suggest to students of the New Testament that they give more attention to the possibility of a lengthy ministry of Jesus in Judea. From the Synoptic Gospels (Matthew, Mark, and Luke) we know of only one Passover and of a ministry confined almost entirely to Galilee.

Not only did certain scholars some years ago raise questions about the place-names unique to John, but the very language of the Gospel seemed non-Jewish. In particular the dualism of thought—the contrasts between light and darkness, above and below, etc.—seemed foreign. The men who held this view sought the nearest parallels available to them and found them in Greek philosophy, in the works of Philo Judaeus, and with Christian heretics known as "Gnostics." From Greek philosophy came the idea of preexistence which is prominent in the Prologue to the Gospel (John 1:1-18). Philo was a brilliant Alexandrian Jew, roughly contemporary with Paul, who combined Old Testament thought with neo-Platonism in a dualistic framework that seemed particularly compatible with certain ideas in the Fourth Gospel. From Gnosticism came a thoroughgoing dualism. In the eyes of some, the Gospel of John was practically a Gnostic book.

It is likely that the author of John was aware of many of the currents of thought in his time, and that he wrote for a Greek audience. But one need not look beyond Palestine for thought strikingly similar in language and concept to his. From the caves by the Dead Sea have come scrolls—from a conservative, withdrawn, Jewish sect—which furnish all the parallels one needs, to assert that there is no undue Greek or Philonic influence in the Fourth Gospel. The dualism of the Fourth Gospel, as has long been pointed out in reaction to the Greek hypothesis, is ethical, not ontological. There is, in short, no struggle between good and evil for ultimate dominion of the created order (or the totality of all that is), but an ethical struggle within a thoroughly monotheistic context. This is precisely what we find at Qumran, especially clearly in the *Manual of Discipline* but also in the other materials. Moreover, many of the "foreign" expressions in John appear at Qumran: "the spirit of truth" (John 14–16), "sons of light" (John 12:36), "the light of life" (John 8:12), and others, familiar from the scrolls.[14] On the basis of available materials today, the closest parallels to the thought and language of the Johannine Gospel are to be found in the Qumran manuscripts.

---

[13] W. F. Albright, "Discoveries in Palestine and the Gospel of John," *The Background of the New Testament and Its Eschatology*, eds. W. D. Davies and D. Daube (Cambridge: The University Press, 1964), p. 158.

[14] Some of John's words, said to be second-century Greek, have turned up in first-century A.D. inscriptions from Jerusalem. For example, *didaskalos* ("teacher"), a term used of Jesus in John 1:38 and 20:16, was found in 1931 by E. L. Sukenik on a first-century Jewish ossuary unearthed on Mount Scopus. Other first-century ossuaries have been inscribed with a number of names familiar to readers of the Fourth Gospel.

Finally, in 1948, the same year the Dead Sea Scrolls were found, scholars in Egypt recovered over forty different Gnostic texts from the late third and early fourth centuries A.D. These manuscripts, discovered at Chenoboskion in Upper Egypt by natives in 1946, were eagerly read by Coptic experts. The Gnostics no longer were to be known through the eyes of the Church Fathers who attacked them as heretics. Now they could speak for themselves. What was discovered, among other things, is a considerable difference between the thought of the Gnostics and that of the Fourth Gospel. Moreover, such common elements as may exist seem to come from an earlier and shared inheritance. Against the older view that the Gnostics emerged from a Greek philosophical tradition, some scholars have begun to suggest that the movement may have had its origin in a form of Jewish thought! A considerable revision is taking place in Gnostic studies, while at the same time archaeology forces us to reconsider the traditions and influences behind the Fourth Gospel.

22. IN THE FOOTSTEPS OF PAUL

Paul traveled over 12,000 miles in his journeys as a Christian missionary. Today with our high-speed jets this does not seem like a great distance. We can fly from Jerusalem to Athens in just over an hour; to London in five hours. The miles race below. Paul's mode of transportation, though, was by foot or by slow-moving ships whose sole propulsion was fickle winds. The apostle was a tireless peripatetic for the sake of the gospel which motivated his life. To him this message of Good News was the realization of the dreams of both Jews and Gentiles; of Jews because it spoke of the fulfillment of messianic hopes, and of Gentiles because it was the basis for a united humanity as envisioned by Alexander the Great and attempted in the Roman Empire. By land and by sea he pressed this cause, preaching the crucified and risen Christ, gathering into church fellowships like-minded men and women, and nurturing the faithful by his presence and his letters.

Graeco-Roman was the world in which Paul labored; Greek in language and culture, Roman politically and militarily. It was not until the mid-third century after the birth of Jesus that Latin began to predominate in the western Empire. In the liturgy of the western church it became universal or *catholic*. In the east it never succeeded in replacing Greek as the *koine* or common language. The armies of Alexander had spread this Greek across the known world. It had become *lingua franca*, the international language. In every land men in public life knew two tongues: their native one and Greek. With this language went the culture it had borne. Mixed with native elements from the east, this culture was Hellenistic (as distinguished from Hellenic), of a civilization which reached its zenith in fifth-century B.C. Athens and was subsequently submerged in the great Hellenistic tide that succeeded it. (Hellenic life and thought were recovered in the Middle Ages and became the basis for the Renaissance or Reawakening of the values and tastes of ancient and glorious Athens.)

Half by accident the Romans had come into possession of a vast empire encompassing among other things Hellenistic culture which proceeded to conquer the conquerors. Fair laws ably administered, just taxes, and mobile armies gave the world *pax romana*, the Roman Peace, three centuries in which the Mediterranean basin was almost completely free from the clashing of arms and the havoc, hardship, and horror of war. From Greece came an equally important gift: a love of the beautiful, appreciation of nature, contemplation of the nature of man. Insofar as they were able, given the pragmatic character of their heritage, the

Romans profited from what the Greeks had to teach them. Insofar as they were able, given their heritage of contentiousness and strife, the Greeks profited from matchless peace which the Romans gave them. But the creative genius of Attica was spent. The fifth century was its classical golden age; the second century before Christ its Hellenistic silver age. Nonetheless, the twin gifts of Rome and Athens combined to spread throughout that Graeco-Roman Empire of the first Christian century the benefits of splendor and peace not matched again in the history of mankind. This was the world of Paul.

Of the six foremost cities of the early Empire,[1] five heard the tread of this man's feet, and one, Ephesus, was the scene of his longest ministry. It is instructive to note that this city in western Asia Minor (now Turkey) was the only one of the five in which Paul founded a church. Three of the others already had such fellowships, and in the fourth (Athens) his efforts failed if indeed he really intended to evangelize there. Paul, it is clear, was not the first missionary. Others before him had passed through the unparalleled splendor of the Hellenistic cities with their gleaming marble buildings and porticoed streets lined with statuary.

Whatever success Paul enjoyed, his journeys were not exactly triumphant. Once, in writing to the Corinthians, he spoke of some of his experiences:

imprisonments, with countless beatings, and often near death. Five times I have received at the hands of the Jews the forty lashes less one. Three times I have been beaten with rods; once I was stoned. Three times I have been shipwrecked; a night and a day I have been adrift at sea; on frequent journeys, in danger from rivers, danger from robbers, danger from my own people, danger from Gentiles, danger in the city, danger in the wilderness, danger at sea, danger from false brethren; in toil and hardship, through many a sleepless night, in hunger and thirst, often without food, in cold and exposure. And, apart from other things, there is the daily pressure upon me of my anxiety for all the churches.

II Corinthians 11:23-28

Archaeology is unable to recover any direct evidence of the work of Paul. All the churches founded by him were doubtless house churches considerably less elaborate than the earliest similar place of worship known to us.[2] No statues were erected to his honor at that time and no early inscriptions carved to commemorate his work at this place or that. Indeed, many are of the opinion that he died virtually unrecognized for his work and without the active succor of the Christians in Rome. Yet a significant contribution has been made by archaeologists to our knowledge of the background of Paul's journeys and to our understanding of the intellectual, religious, and general cultural context in which he labored

[1] Rome, Alexandria, Antioch, Ephesus, Athens, and Jerusalem. Paul, so far as we know, was never in Alexandria.

[2] In 1931-1932 along the banks of the Euphrates River in eastern Syria, at a place called Dura-Europus, archaeologists found a Christian place of worship in what had been a private home. Three of the rooms had been made one and could seat as many as a hundred people. A smaller room contained a large, ornate baptistry. The walls of this room were painted with scenes taken from the Old and New Testaments. Above the water was a picture of Jesus as the Good Shepherd. He was envisioned as a strong, beardless young man with a sheep on his shoulders and others grazing in peace about him. On a plastered wall of this house was an inscription giving the year it was built: A.D. 232-233. The church obviously can be no older than that, although the fellowship may have met elsewhere earlier. This is, however, the earliest known Christian place of worship and is a superb example of a developed house-church building, perhaps in its latest stage just before the construction of separate buildings for the specific purpose of Christian worship. On the same street as the church was a synagogue from the same period (thirteen years later according to an inscription found there), also in a house, and also with painted walls depicting Old Testament scenes. The baptistry of the Christian church has been reconstructed in the Yale University Gallery of Fine Arts. Damascus Museum houses the synagogue today.

and in which he wrote his letters of which ten and possibly thirteen survive.[3] Though Paul's mind was focused upon "a temple not made with hands," he cannot have been unaware of the gold, silver, and marble which turned many Hellenistic cities into monuments to the skill of man. Nor can he have failed to take note of the massive temples celebrating gods and goddesses whose worship he found vain, empty, and often immoral. In Ephesus, site of the temple of Artemis, one of the seven wonders of the ancient world, a howling mob chanted for two hours "Great is Artemis of the Ephesians," [4] in a successful attempt to drive Paul from the city where he had had a three-year ministry in the shadow of that magnificent shrine. Although much remains to be done, archaeology has gone far to bring alive again echoes of those days and events.

The First Missionary Journey

By the 30s of our era there was a thriving Christian church at Antioch-on-the-Orontes, 300 miles north of Jerusalem in Syria. Perhaps Pentecost had been the very spark that lit this beacon. Whatever the events of its origin, this church soon became for many of the followers of Jesus a more congenial atmosphere than that of Jerusalem where hostility seemed to be the order of the day: Jewish-Christian groups against one another

and almost all against the Romans. Characteristic differences between the two churches appeared. Jerusalem was provincial and defensive; Antioch, cosmopolitan and outwardlooking. The dynamic center of the new faith and that which provided its missionary emphasis was soon by the Orontes, not on the hills of Zion. Here, in a city famous for bestowing nicknames, the disciples were first called "Christians" (Acts 11:26). It was from here that the first organized and largescale attempts were made to evangelize among non-Jews. This was the base from which Paul went forth. As the church in Jerusalem turned in upon itself and became ever more particular about requirements of the Jewish Law, that in Antioch laid emphasis upon the more universal dimensions of the gospel and preached without distinction among that hodgepodge of humanity present in a cosmopolitan center.

From the very beginning this Antioch (there were at least fifteen other cities so named) was by design a mixture of various elements, the center and symbol of that Hellenistic blending of men intended by Alexander the Great. Alexander's dream was shared by only one of his generals, Seleucus I, Nicator ("Victor") who reigned from 312 to 280 B.C. He was the founder and builder of this royal city which he named, for his father and for his son, Antiochus.[5] Situated on the eastern bank of the Orontes River some twenty miles from the sea, it was safe from naval attack although accessible to small merchant ships. Its main outlet to the sea was Seleucia Pieria, one of the finest harbors on the coast. Antioch's advantageous location was further enhanced by its proximity to one of the major overland trade routes in the Middle East: that joining Syria, Palestine, and points south with Asia Minor and Greece. Long appreciated and exploited

---

[3] Although some scholars would admit as genuinely Pauline only four of our canonical letters (Galatians, I and II Corinthians, and Romans), most are of the opinion that at least ten have claim to authenticity. Still others accept the "Pastoral Epistles" (I and II Timothy and Titus) as Pauline, thus giving thirteen. Few today follow earlier scholarship in viewing Hebrews as the apostle's letter. Even if one were to accept all fourteen as his, this number does not begin to approximate what this inveterate letter-writer probably authored. He himself tells us of two others to Corinth (I Corinthians 5:9; II Corinthians 2:4) and of one to Laodicea (Colossians 4:16). The Corinthian correspondence as we have it may be a composite of four letters. We may assume with some confidence that what we have in the New Testament is but a portion of a larger body of material.

[4] Acts 19:34.

[5] The other Seleucid royal city, located near the junction of the Tigris and Euphrates Rivers in Mesopotamia, he named Seleucia, for himself.

by traders, the site was turned into one of the greatest cities of the ancient world by Seleucus around 300 B.C. In addition to a large number of native Syrians, its population contained many Macedonians and Greeks as well as a colony of Jewish veterans retired from the Seleucid army and given land around the capital city as a reward for faithful service. The early population of the city and its extensive suburbs is not known. But it has been estimated as high as 800,000 by the end of the fourth century A.D.

Whatever the size of the population, it was always a mixed bag continuously embroidered by a flow of tradesmen. The city was not without reputation, two reputations, in fact. The first had to do with a civic attitude whose motto could have been, "Eat, drink, and make merry." When the Roman satirist Juvenal spoke of the immorality of Rome, he did so by noting sarcastically that the Orontes had flowed into the Tiber. The second reputation, equally widespread, was for magnificence. The city was in more than one respect the "Vienna of the ancient world."

As in his other royal city, Seleucia, Seleucus first built a splendid palace and then set about to build a city worthy of the royal residence. At Antioch he further emphasized the beauty and dramatic elements (not to mention military gain) of his palace by constructing it on an island in the river. Yet it was not he but a later and infamous successor, Antiochus IV, Epiphanes, who glorified the city, making it the most splendid in the east, if not in the world. Most historians consider it to have surpassed the Rome of its time and to have rivaled Alexandria. It was in any case a place of great beauty whose numerous theaters, temples, gymnasiums, palaestrae, and other public and private buildings were porticoed and placed in a setting of spacious boulevards, parks, and gardens. Antioch was the only city of its day whose streets were lighted

at night. The Garden of Daphne, once in the vicinity and later included within the suburbs, was so beautiful as to be known throughout the world. Many visitors came to its well-watered laurels and cypresses. Notorious also for vice, it drew many from long distances for purposes other than admiring fountains, streams, trees, and flowers. In A.D. 540, the beauty and the vice disappeared together as Persian invaders leveled the city. Its monuments, its gardens, its rollicking love of life moral and otherwise, and its churches passed into history. Rebuilt to a degree and destroyed with some ferocity six more times, it is today Antakya, a Turkish town betraying no hint of the grandeur of bygone days.

Excavations were conducted at Antakya from 1932 to 1939. Unfortunately interrupted by the Second World War before significant remains from apostolic times were found, these efforts nonetheless produced some interesting finds that do nothing to dim the city's ancient renown. Hundreds of mosaic pavements were uncovered. One, the "Mosaic of the Phoenix," covers over 1300 square feet and contains, in addition to over 7500 delicately executed roses, an intricate border of forty-eight ram's-heads. But the focus of attention is a graceful phoenix who with the rocks on which he stands is six and a half feet high. The visitor chancing upon this in the Louvre today will at first think himself gazing upon an oriental carpet of great delicacy in design and execution. While Christians made use of the legend of the phoenix as a symbol to express their faith in the resurrection of Jesus, there is nothing to connect this fifth-century A.D. mosaic with Christianity or even to suggest it was part of a Christian house. The story of the bird who emerges from his own ashes was widespread long before the Christian era and was used in various contexts by authors and poets from numerous localities and traditions.

Other mosaics and artifacts witness more directly and positively to the religious pluralism of Antioch. One of the most vivid is at Seleucia Pieria, partly excavated from 1937 to 1939. A semicircular pavement containing images of twenty-one different animals wandering through woods and foliage provided a peaceful setting for a Christian martyrion. The martyr whose remains lay in this context is unidentified, although archaeologists in dating the building before the earthquake which heavily damaged the area in A.D. 526 have provided at least the hint that it may have been Saint Thekla whose shrine was constructed somewhere in the area toward the end of the fifth century. Another Christian church, this one in Kaoussie, a suburb, yields a somewhat more positive identification. In cruciform design, the structure was built in A.D. 387 according to an inscription recovered in 1935. Its mosaics converge upon a central shrine which is thought to have contained the remains of St. Babylas, martyr-bishop of Antioch who perished in the persecution under the Emperor Decius (A.D. 250). His relics are known to have been moved several times before they came to rest just west of the Orontes in Kaoussie.

Ten other Christian churches of equal age were found in and around Antioch, indicating that the Christian mission which radiated from this place was successful also at home. Unfortunately the excavators failed to find the octagonal structure which was built during the reign of the Emperor Constantine and which is referred to in several early Christian works because of its influence and its beauty. In shape and gilded dome it likely bore resemblance to the later Dome of the Rock which stands today in Jerusalem (see p. 135).

Among the buildings unearthed was one which seems to have been the local center of a mystery religion devoted to Isis and Osiris. This ritual, which told of the death and resurrection of the god through the intervention of the Queen of Heaven, was one of the most popular in the ancient world. Native to Egypt, it was found in every part of the Roman Empire. The mosaics from Antioch which might have gone far in bringing to light more of the secret ritual of this cult were tragically damaged at some point by the laying of a pipeline. One pavement, apparently depicting the god and goddess inducting an initiate into the brotherhood, has a wide and important band obliterated, as if censored by fate.

The Jewish community prospered at Antioch. Given complete religious freedom and even the right to try civil cases before their priests (elders?) they attracted other Jews from various places. Essentially cosmopolitan, this community nonetheless confined itself to certain sections of the city (as at Alexandria). At the time the Christian church was establishing itself in the city, one seventh of the population was Jewish and lived in three widely scattered areas. Josephus, who recorded many interesting details in recounting the history of those times, could not but note the costly offerings which seemed to characterize the gifts of the Antiochene Jews to the Jerusalem Temple. In addition to Jews, a number of Gentiles attached themselves to the synagogues of Antioch as "God-fearers," people attracted to Judaism for one reason or another (often the high standard of ethics) but unwilling to fulfill all the requirements for full membership in the community.

So far archaeologists have recovered only one artifact that can with assurance be associated with that flourishing Jewish community. This is a piece of marble bearing the image of a seven-branched candlestick. Its original context cannot be determined however, and the conclusion that it was Jewish is an assumption albeit a fairly safe one. Another find which some say points to the Jewish community is a sixth-century A.D. mosaic bearing the words, "Peace be your coming in, you who gaze; joy and blessing be to those who stay here. . . ." This quotation is from I Kings 16:4-5 in the Septuagint, the Greek Old Testament; it corresponds to I Sam. 16:4-5 in our English translations from the Hebrew. Yet this could as easily point to Christian influence, since the Septuagint, having literally been taken over by Christian missionaries, was virtually abandoned by Jews by the fourth century. Furthermore, even though it is unmistakably from Scripture, there is no reason to connect the inscription with a religious structure. Glanville Downey may well have been right in suggesting in the excavations publications of the site that it was a greeting which once stood before an inn.

Two other finds are worthy of brief mention. One is a graceful marble statue of *Tyche* (Fortune), the symbol of the city. Placed by Seleucus I, it proved to be prophetic of the prosperity enjoyed by the city for several centuries. Now in the Vatican Museum, its well-preserved state offers hope that more material from the oldest portions of the city and the apostolic period may yet be unearthed.

The other find is a colossal bust of Charon, ferryman on the mythical River Styx (the dividing line between life and death). It is carved on the limestone cliffs northeast of Antioch. The Charonion can hardly be said to have been "dug up" since it overlooks the city, and its sixteen-feet-high bust can be seen from considerable distances. No one knows exactly when it was begun. According to ancient legend it was during the time of Antiochus Epiphanes (175-162 B.C.) when a ruinous plague ravaged the city. The image of Charon high above the dying was intended to relieve suffering and death, and to drive away the evil which had brought disaster to the population. For some reason the bust was never finished.

By the early 40s of the first Christian century, boats sailing from Seleucia Pieria and roads leading from Antioch were burdened with men and women carrying the story of Jesus and the message of salvation. Within a few years this led to a clash with the church in Jerusalem and to the famous conference and compromise mentioned in Acts 15 and Galatians 2. Meanwhile the gospel was spreading far beyond the limits of Palestine and Judaism. One who was won to the cause of the Christ was Barnabas, a Hellenistic Jew of priestly heritage, native to Cyprus, and a man of wealth in a position of influence and trust in the Jerusalem church (Acts 4:36-37; 9:27; 11:22). As Christians gathered beneath the ever watchful but long ignored eyes of the Charonion to make their plans for missionary activity, Barnabas remembered a talented new Christian whom he had met in Jerusalem some years before. He alone seems to have trusted this man who, like himself, was a Hellenistic Jew. In addition to native ability, the convert had the finest rabbinical education Jerusalem could offer. He was, furthermore, a person of considerable zeal. But it was there—precisely there—that difficulty arose. He had employed his enthusiasm against Christians in an attempt to wipe out the church. Once converted, this young man had found it difficult to gain acceptance within the Christian fellowship, much less a measure of trust. At length he withdrew to his home in Tarsus, a hundred miles in a straight line from Antioch, twice that far by road. But a ship from Seleucia Pieria could be found bound for Rhegma. From there it was only twelve miles by road to Tarsus. With luck a ship might be found sailing up the Cyanus River to the very docks of Tarsus. Barnabas wondered whether this man might not be exactly the companion he was looking for, to go with him to evangelize his home, Cyprus. So Barnabas went to Tarsus to find Paul.

Settled as early as the third millennium B.C., important in trade with Troy around 2300 B.C., Tarsus has been almost continuously occupied since Hittite times (*ca.* 1400-1200 B.C.). It suffered heavily from the Sea Peoples at about the same time they were ravaging the coasts of Syria and Palestine and trying to break into Egypt (see p. 87). Sometime thereafter it was resettled by Greeks from Mycenae. Mentioned by Shalmaneser III on the Black Obelisk, it continued within the Assyrian sphere of influence until the fall of that empire in the sixth century B.C. Heir to an ancient and honorable history, Tarsus eventually emerged as the chief city and capital of Cilicia, an important and abundantly endowed district within which lay the Cilician Gates. This pass knifes through the Taurus Mountains and is so strategic that almost every conqueror and would-be empire-builder in the ancient world strove for it at one time or another. Because of its position near that vital opening, Tarsus was a major center for trade and communication passing between the east and Greece or Rome. If you went by land, you went by Tarsus.

In spite of the recovery of many well-preserved coins, not much is known in detail about Tarsus during Hellenistic times.[6] Alexander saved it from the Persians in 333 B.C. One of the Seleucids named it "Antioch," a designation Antiochus Epiphanes preferred for the city. But Tarsus, the name by which it was known to the Hittites, survived and still identifies the place.

[6] Excavations at Tarsus in the spring and summer of 1936 unearthed numbers of 2nd-cent. B.C. terracotta plaque fragments depicting a monument of some sort. It has been suggested that these were offerings made at a local shrine. Moreover, symbolism on the fragments has caused some to think that Tarsus may have been the center of a cult combining a local deity with Hercules. This type of synthesis is known from other sources to have been extremely widespread in Hellenistic times and indeed to have been characteristic of that age. For more information, see H. Goldman, "The Sandon Monument of Tarsus," *Journal of the American Oriental Society*, 60, no. 4 (December 1940): 544-53.

Unfortunately for the city, it became a pawn in the Roman Civil War. Alternating between the extremes of harsh punishment and heavy taxation on the one hand, and lavish gifts and status of free city on the other, it emerged in the end on the winning side. Julius Caesar was there in 47 B.C., and the city took the name Juliopolis in his honor. Three years earlier, Cicero had been provincial governor in residence there. In spite of his apparently superb administration,[7] no love was lost between this urbane intellectual and the inhabitants of this back-of-the-beyonds, this intellectual desert to which he felt himself banished. In this matter Cicero was probably being a snob; Tarsus had a distinguished intellectual heritage and an active one at the very time he was governor there. Be that as it may, the people made no move to name anything after him, and he for his part readily departed for Rome as soon as his term of office expired.

Cassius was in the city in 43 B.C., much to the sorrow of the inhabitants who suffered greatly from his wrath. Marc Antony rescued Tarsus two years later and there welcomed Cleopatra who sailed up the Cyanus on a golden barge. She was suitably dressed as Aphrodite, leaving no doubt of her intentions as regards Antony.

At the end of the war Augustus favored Tarsus with privileges, among them the status of free city. It was perhaps then that Paul's father gained the Roman citizenship he was able to pass on to his son. The Stoic philosopher Athenodorus, one of Augustus' teachers, was from this Cilician city. His direct intervention relieved Tarsus of an unworthy administrator and gave the emperor a personal tie to the city. Athenodorus was not the only distinguished man of letters produced there. Several of the finer teachers in Rome were natives of Tarsus and gained

[7] At least Cicero in his letters never failed to tell his friends back in Rome what a fine job he was doing.

their education in that city which, unlike Alexandria, gave preference to its own inhabitants rather than encouraging outside students. It is perhaps not without significance that Paul's quotation of Hellenistic poetry in his sermon on the Areopagus in Athens contained a line from a Cilician poet, Aratus.[8]

With pride Paul could tell a Roman soldier in Jerusalem that he was "from Tarsus in Cilicia, a citizen of no mean city" (Acts 21:39). Such boasting was fully justified in a day when a fine city rose on both sides of a river adequately bridged. Broad streets with porticoes and a goodly number of fountains gave access to baths, theaters, temples, a gymnasium, palaestrae and other public buildings of note. Unfortunately only three remnants point to a former glory. Just outside the modern town where some excavation has taken place, remains of a Roman theater have been found. For the most part, however, this area has yielded more ancient evidences, some from preliterary times. During the Roman period it was little more than an outpost for the city, and the theater is hardly a major one for the population. A second ruin, and the largest to date, is the foundation of a huge temple. It is Roman and some marble parts of its former walls remain to suggest an erstwhile splendor. But little work has been done to identify this massive ruin with precision. The simple fact is that the major portion of the old city is directly beneath the modern one. Further to complicate the difficulties of excavating in Tarsus, the gradual rising of ground level on the coastal plain has accelerated the buildup of debris left by continuous human habitation. Today the remains of the Roman city lie far below the surface. When foundations are dug for new construction, almost invariably they turn up

[8] Acts 17:28. Aratus was born in Soli in the 3rd cent. B.C. The poem from which Paul quoted was *Phaenomena*.

nothing earlier than Byzantine artifacts (ca. A.D. 300-700). An exception to this occurred in 1947 when excavations for a new courthouse uncovered a large Roman building (function unidentified) with a number of mosaics. Apart from these meager matters, nothing suggests the fine provincial town that greeted Barnabas when he came on his successful mission to seek out Paul. Even the weaving of tent cloth from goat's hair, a trade the apostle learned there, has recently been discontinued. Now a mechanized mill spinning cotton from the fertile Cilician plain turns out over 650,000 yards of high quality fabric per month.

Knowing nothing of such fabric, but pleased to have Paul at his side, Barnabas returned to Antioch. There, together with his friend and fellow Christian, he played an active part in the church devoting himself particularly to teaching. Although the sequence of events is not entirely clear, it seems that word came of famine in Judea and of suffering among the followers of Jesus there. Barnabas and Paul were sent to Jerusalem with relief from the church at Antioch. It was about this time, perhaps the year A.D. 44, that the bitter antagonism of the local Jewish religious and political authorities against the Christians boiled over into open and bloody persecution. At least one of the leaders of the Jerusalem church was put to death. Peter was arrested and put into prison from which he miraculously escaped (Acts 12). Whether or not Paul was actually present in Jerusalem when these events took place, he and Barnabas were shortly thereafter in Antioch with John Mark (from Jerusalem) preparing to sail to Cyprus, some ninety miles southwestward in the Mediterranean.

From Seleucia Pieria, whose once busy harbor is now silted up, they took ship and landed at Salamis, a city beside a shallow but important harbor on the east coast of the island. The capital of Cyprus in former days, it became under Roman rule second to Paphos where the governor had his official residence. There was a Jewish community at Salamis, and in its synagogue Paul proclaimed the word of God (Acts 13:5). Today only a few random stones from what seems to have been a splendid marble forum remain bearing silent witness to early Christian and Roman times.

Paphos, on the other side of the island, was also a natural harbor sheltered by the rocky headlands on the southwestern coast of Cyprus. Of some importance as early as 480 B.C., it was still known in Paul's day as "New Paphos" to distinguish it from a still older city about nine miles to the north. Here the proconsul [9] lived. It was also a Roman naval base. Paul seems to have come into bitter conflict with a certain Bar-Jesus, "a Jewish false prophet" (Acts 13:6). According to Acts, the matter was settled with the temporary blinding of Bar-Jesus and the conversion of the proconsul. We hear of no other activities of Paul and his companions in Cyprus. They set sail for the mainland of Asia Minor and came to Perga.

Eight miles inland from the coast, Perga is some five miles west of the River Cestrus. The major port for the city is Attalia (modern Antalya), but it is not mentioned at this point in the story in Acts. Perhaps Paul and his companions were able to sail up the river and reach the city more directly. What-

ever the case, they came to an extremely ancient city, endowed with many splendid public structures not the least of which were a large stadium now half buried but still to be seen, and a famous temple of Artemis which, like most of the rest of the city, has long since vanished. The main street, over ninety feet wide, is still there however. The early Christian missionaries did not tarry long on this boulevard nor among the buildings gracing it. They pushed inland to the north, to another Antioch, Antioch of Pisidia.

Although strategically located in the rich Pamphylian plain, Perga had, save one time, escaped the vicissitudes and unrest that marked late Hellenism and the Roman Civil War. Fashionable in this prosperous area was an escape from summer's depressing heat to the higher and cooler elevations of the Taurus Mountains in the north. It was perhaps because much of the population was gone that we hear of no activity of Paul at Perga. On the other hand, he may have wished to reach Pisidian Antioch as soon as possible. It is known that John Mark left them at Perga and returned home. This may have caused difficulties which made effective work impossible. Some scholars think Paul fell ill and escaped Perga's stifling climate as quickly as he could. For whatever reason, Paul and Barnabas did go almost at once ninety miles due north, climbing ever upward until they had reached Antioch on the highland plateau.

Founded by Seleucus I, this Antioch served the Syrian Greeks until 188 B.C. when Antiochus III was defeated by the Romans. Declared a free city, it remained so until caught up in the Roman Civil War. In the end it wound up as a part of the Roman province of Galatia (25 B.C.). Called variously Caesarea and Caesarea Antiochea, its population became increasingly Roman as veterans from the imperial armies were settled there. Augustus undertook a major

[9] Acts 13:7 correctly calls the Roman governor, Sergius Paulus, a "proconsul." There were two types of Roman provinces: senatorial and imperial. The former, less troublesome, were responsibilities of the senate. The latter, usually border areas of military importance or those more difficult to rule, were directly under the emperor's authority. Governors in senatorial provinces were called "proconsuls"; those in imperial provinces were "prefects" until A.D. 48 when the Emperor Claudius restructured the civil service and changed their title to "procurator." Thus Pontius Pilate, the world's most famous procurator, was really a prefect. There is a difference only in title. But it is of some importance to note that Acts makes the proper distinctions in speaking of Roman officials who play a role in the Pauline narrative.

effort to turn the city into a thoroughly Roman center of culture and loyalty (much as had been done at Samaria-Sebaste in Palestine; see p. 217). By 6 B.C. two fine roads joined Antioch with its surrounding area. Marble and man power were lavished upon the city itself. As a Roman colony it was given Italian citizenship. When the missionaries came to this place they found themselves in a truly hellenized environment: four major types of inhabitants (Phrygian, Greek, Roman, and a large Jewish community present since Seleucid times) among the temples, theaters, porticoes, and other outward signs of Graeco-Roman life.

Much explored and occasionally excavated, Pisidian Antioch has justified literary claims to former brilliance. Built high above the River Anthius, large sections of its city wall are still intact. At the heart of the city was a large square named for the benefactor, Augustus. Indeed, flanking the square was an elaborate Corinthian-style temple dedicated to the emperor whose cult flourished there during his lifetime. Much ornamental work from this structure has been found. Across the square was a propylaeum (splendid gateway in Graeco-Roman style) commemorating various land and sea battles. From this a monumental stairway descended to a second square, that of Tiberius, smaller but no less grand than the other one. The inevitable theater has been unearthed. It is, however, in a serious state of decay. Yet a sense of grandeur is present in its tumble of carved stone.

Instinctively as well as by conscious design, Paul was drawn to the synagogue on the Sabbath. There, in a sermon recorded in Acts 13:16-41, he exhorted his fellow Jews to acknowledge that Jesus was the Messiah foretold by the Holy Scriptures. Rebuffed and reviled in such attempts, Paul and Barnabas turned their energies toward the non-Jewish population with some success. The universalism implied in the gospel thus became a part of conscious missionary activity. The doors of Christianity were thrown open to the world. But in what was a foretaste of later troubles, the missionaries found themselves the object of the hostility of a riotous mob stirred up by Jewish religionists. Driven from the city and the district, they moved eastward through fertile fields, well watered by swift-flowing streams, until after seventy-five miles and several days' walking they came to Iconium, capital of Lycaonia, focus of trade routes and always with an abundance of plums, apricots, and various grains which grew all around.

The history of Iconium (modern Konya), a much older city than Antioch, was virtually parallel to it in Hellenistic and Roman times. Thoroughly hellenized by Seleucus I, it became a pawn in the Civil War and was at length brought under direct Roman rule in 25 B.C. As in Antioch, Paul and Barnabas made straight for the local synagogue where they found not only Jews but a goodly number of Gentiles, probably "God-fearers." The message of salvation through Jesus the Christ caused division among the population, a division which led to an attempt on the lives of both missionaries. So once more hostility drove them away, but not until they had planted the seeds of a church.

Traveling scarcely twenty miles southeast, the two men left the verdant plains and plunged into a very different region. Not quite a century earlier the patrician Cicero had been at a loss for words to describe the inhospitable land as well as the rustic and for the most part ignorant people of the area. In this case Cicero's judgment was founded on something more than snobbery. The reference in Acts 14:11 to the use of the Lycaonian language indicates not only the tenacity of older ways in the face of a large settlement of Roman veterans, but also the provincial nature of Lystra and Derbe, the principal towns of the region. Paul had come to preach the gospel in an atmosphere which he had probably never before encountered. He also came upon something else he had never dealt with before.

At Lystra Paul caused a crippled man to walk. Almost at once the rustic inhabitants of the city came to the conclusion that Paul and Barnabas were gods "come down in the likeness of men" (Acts 14:11). Paul, because he had done most of the talking, was thought to be Hermes, messenger of the gods. Barnabas, perhaps because of striking looks (?), was taken to be no less than Zeus himself. Even the priests of Zeus, whose temple was by the city gate, wanted to offer sacrifices of oxen. With great difficulty the two were able to prevent the sacrifices from being offered to them, and to convince the people that they were merely humans.

For a time the men were able to go about their work without hindrance. But word of their activities reached hostile ears in Iconium and Antioch. With leadership from the Jewish communities in those cities, certain of the people of Lystra were stirred up against Paul and Barnabas. Paul was seized, dragged out of the city, and stoned, being left for dead. Barnabas and other Christians came, took his bleeding and bruised body into the city, and ministered to him. The next day, aided by Barnabas, he was able to leave Lystra and journey toward Derbe, sixty miles distant. Little is known of Paul's work when he reached Derbe. Acts 14:21 mentions merely that he preached, made many disciples, and left. He seems to have been free to preach without opposition. Acts 20:4 lists "Gaius of Derbe" as accompanying Paul from Corinth to Macedonia on his third missionary journey. But it is not known if he was converted in Corinth or in his native city and, if in the latter, whether now or when Paul returned later.

Archaeologists have not worked at the sites of either Lystra or Derbe. Zoldera, identified today with Lystra, is a large mound whose surface potsherds indicate habitation from the Stone Age through Roman times. Not even that much is known about Derbe whose site was in dispute until recently. At a place called by the Turks Kerti Huyuk, there is a mound somewhat smaller than the one at Zoldera. There a dedicatory inscription has been found. It honors the Emperor Antonius Pius and is dated to the year A.D. 157. According to its words it was set up by the council and citizens of Derbe.

At length the blue waters of the Mediterranean were once more before the apostle's eyes. At Attalia where today broken but beautiful Corinthian columns are lapped by waves and are used as diving platforms by local youngsters, Paul found a ship bound for Seleucia Pieria. As the ship moved slowly eastward and the coast of Asia Minor slipped by and finally began to recede, Paul could look back upon a momentous accomplishment: The gospel had been preached among men in disregard of human barriers. The grace of God as shown in the crucifixion and resurrection of Jesus of Nazareth, the Messiah, was all-sufficient for salvation. There was much to tell his fellow Christians in Antioch. There was much for which to give thanks and rejoice.

The Second Missionary Journey

Reports of the work of Paul and Barnabas among Gentiles as well as Jews were not received with universal rejoicing. From Jerusalem came a rebuke and a suggestion—a demand!—that full adherence to the Law of Moses was necessary for salvation and for admission to the church. Moreover, without circumcision none of this was possible. Full adherence was demanded—nothing less. Debate at Antioch was succeeded by a conference in Jerusalem. The two missionaries told again of Gentile response to the gospel. Further, they refused to budge on the major point regarding salvation and membership in the Christian fellowship. In their view, the grace of God as revealed in Jesus the Christ, and that alone, was sufficient for salvation. When all seemed hopelessly divided, James, head of the Jerusalem church, effected a compromise. Gentiles were to abstain from food offered to idols (the remains of sacrifices were often sold), from unchastity, and from eating strangled animals and blood. Otherwise the church at Antioch was free to pursue its policy toward Gentiles (Acts 15). This was, in fact, an almost complete vindication of Paul's view and was a source of joy when word reached Antioch.

Soon Paul, anxious to visit the fledgling Christian fellowships he and Barnabas had begun, was urging his fellow missionary to join him on another journey to "see how they are." Barnabas agreed. But, ever the friend of the outcast, he insisted upon taking John Mark with them. Paul objected on the grounds that the young man had not proved himself on the first journey. In the end the two agreed to part. Barnabas with Mark returned to Cyprus, while Paul and Silas took the land route north from Antioch toward Tarsus and thus into Asia Minor once more (Acts 15:36-41).

Following the main road, Paul entered his hometown Tarsus but did not tarry. From there the highway went due north, through the Cilician Gates to Podandus (about thirty-five miles from Tarsus) where it turned west to Cybistra and then southwest to Laranda and finally to Derbe, Lystra, and northward once more to Iconium. This route, a good deal less direct than most Roman roads, was, in fact, not originally a Roman road. It was a very ancient route which wound through the great eastern Cilicia plain and then turned north into Lycaonia to avoid the mountains of western or "rough" Cilicia, as it was called in ancient days. About 400 miles in a direct line from Tarsus to Ephesus, it was over 600 miles by road. Yet for caravan travel it was much easier to go around the worst of the mountains than to attempt to penetrate them. Since it was one of the major arteries of the world of that day, the Romans did their best to maintain its normally marble surface in good condition. They also tried to keep the route free of robbers for which it had long been notorious. Very likely experiences on this very road caused Paul to mention "in danger from robbers" among the perils he had faced for the sake of the gospel (II Corinthians 11:26).

Almost 100 years before Paul traveled westward on his second missionary journey, Cicero proceeded eastward by the same way. Leaving Ephesus at the end of July (probably the 27th) in the year 51 B.C., he arrived at Tarsus on the fifth of October. There were a number of stops along the way as he held provincial court first here and then there. From Cicero's numerous letters to his friend and financial advisor, Atticus, we know a good deal about the speed and comfort of traveling the main roads of Asia Minor. "Hot and dusty" is a phrase that reoccurs in the correspondence. But then Cicero was traveling in the hottest time of the year. The Greek geographer Strabo, who was born in Asia Minor in 54 B.C., tells us that during the scorching days of summer the land was so dry, particularly in Lycaonia and western Cilicia, that water was sold for a good price. But all was not so bad. A few hours' travel can change the scenery entirely: the choking dust gives way to the wild grandeur of the mountains; green trees, wild flowers, and even some cultivated fields are on every hand. We are not sure at what time of the year Paul left Antioch with Silas. But we can be sure that climatic conditions rapidly changed along his way. Furthermore, thanks to Cicero we can gain some idea of how fast he was able to travel. Cicero wished to go to Tarsus as quickly as possible in order to establish his authority in a province which, in his view at least, had been in the hands of an incompetent administrator, and because Parthians were threatening the area. He tells

Atticus that, traveling by wagon, he was able to make twenty-five miles a day; thirty if he was not burdened by his retinue.[10] Paul, on foot, may have made half that much on the difficult highway. We must remember that he was not a physically strong person and may thus have proceeded more slowly than normal. To take an example of one part of the road covered by both men, Cicero left Iconium on September 3 and arrived in Tarsus on October 5. This included a three-day lay-over in Cybistra where he concerned himself with pressing military matters.

Paul had no such responsibilities and went as quickly as possible until he reached Derbe. We are not told what he did there. But in Lystra he met young Timothy, a Christian, whose mother was Jewish and father Greek (Acts 16:1-3). From that time until the apostle's death Timothy was an almost constant companion. The missionaries, now three in number, "went on their way through the cities" delivering to the various congregations news of the decision reached by the council in Jerusalem. We do not know what "the cities" were. Doubtless one was Iconium and another was Pisidian Antioch. But what were the others? Paul did not turn south at Antioch and trace his earlier steps from the first journey, but went farther north and west, departing from the road to Ephesus and going in the direction of the province of Mysia and the city of Troas. Were there churches in Philomelium, Ipsus, and other places along the way? If so, who founded them, and did Paul visit them?

Apparently it was Paul's intention to go directly north into Bithynia along the southern coast of the Black Sea. But, according to Acts 16:7, when he attempted to enter Bithynia "the spirit of Jesus did not allow them." So the three proceeded due west (from Dorylaeum) to Troas, on the Aegean

Coast ten miles south of Ilium (ancient Troy). Today ruins of various civic buildings from Roman times in addition to the aqueduct (built after Paul's time) which brought water from Mount Ida are visible. But these meager stones do not begin to speak of the glory of the city that Julius Caesar, Augustus, and Constantine each considered as a site to replace Rome as capital of the Empire. The circuit of the city walls, still traceable, is six miles. To this "renowned city," as Strabo called it, Paul came three times and each time was but briefly there. On this first occasion he had a vision by night. In it a man of Macedonia appeared to him and appealed saying, "Come over to Macedonia and help us" (Acts 16:9). Convinced that this was a call of God to preach on the European mainland, Paul and his companions[11] immediately sought passage for Neapolis. Their ship laid over at the island of Samothrace, and the next day they reached their destination in Macedonia. The gospel had come to Europe and was soon to bear fruit.

Neapolis, seaport for Philippi, had long been an important harbor. Among the many ships it had sheltered were the triremes of Brutus and Cassius in their unsuccessful attempt to defeat Octavian (Caesar Augustus) at the Battle of Philippi (42 B.C.). According to inscriptions recovered there by archaeologists, the port later became a favorite of the rich from Philippi who preferred to live in the charming town away from the hustle and bustle of the larger city. The modern port, called Kavalla,[12] leaves no doubt as to the wisdom of those who were able to live

[10] Where it is possible to check Cicero's movement with some precision, he made closer to twenty-three miles a day.

[11] Were there now four? The "we passages" in Acts begin with 16:10, and many commentators have taken this as an indication of the travel diary of Luke.

[12] *Kavalla* is vulgar Latin for "Horse" and may preserve a memory of the place as the terminus of the horse-borne imperial postal service established by Augustus. The early Christians called it Christopolis apparently to recall Paul's visits and preaching there.

there in other days. It is a very pleasant place, inviting, and with an air of unhurried prosperity. Today the perfume of tobacco pervades all. Kavalla is a major center of the Greek tobacco industry and many thousands of men and women work in the warehouses sorting the strong, dark "Turkish" leaves for baling and eventual shipment from that harbor where Paul landed and where later, on his third journey, he departed for Troas (Acts 20:6).

Neapolis was not Paul's destination. He went at once toward Philippi, one of the most favored of the Graeco-Roman cities of his time and the chief city of the region.[13] It was about eight miles along the Via Egnatia. This highway, still in use by foot traffic today, was built by the Romans in the second century B.C. across northern Greece from Neapolis to Dyrrhachium and Apollonia, two ports on the Adriatic directly across from southern Italy.[14] This direct route through Macedonia cut many days from the earlier ways of communicating with the growing empire in the east. By such means traffic was speeded considerably, so much so that Cicero in Cybistra could marvel that he had written to Rome and received an answer in only forty-six days.

So Paul came to Philippi. On an open plain surrounded by mountains the town, settled perhaps in the mid-fourth century B.C., entered a period of prosperity with the building of the Via Egnatia. Yet it was not until the great battle that took place about a mile west of there in 42 B.C. that Philippi began to enjoy favor lavished upon few cities

of its day. Antony and Octavian smashed the republican forces of Brutus and Cassius. To commemorate the event Antony ordered the town, then small, enlarged and made a Roman colony.[15] Veterans were settled there and the city was named Colonia Victrix Philippensium to celebrate the recent victory. When in the year 30 B.C. Octavian, fresh from his victory over Antony in Egypt, deported many of Antony's supporters from Italy, he allowed them to settle in various places, especially Philippi. The privileges of the city as a colony were reaffirmed and its name changed to Colonia Julia Philippensis.[16] Three years later when the Senate conferred the title "Augustus" on Octavian, Philippi found its name changed as well. It was now Colonia Augusta Julia Philippensis and was so called when Paul came there to speak of the Christ.

A lengthy series of excavations was conducted there from 1914 until 1938 by the *École Francaise d'Athènes*. A superb forum was unearthed. Three hundred feet by 150 feet, it was of balanced design with a temple at each end. An inscription from one of these shrines points to construction during the reign of Antonius Pius (A.D. 137-161) or, more likely, Marcus Aurelius (A.D. 161-180). It seems likely, judging from the symmetry of the whole complex and its various recovered parts, that it was all built at one time. Yet it was doubtless a renovation of an earlier forum and as such identified the site, if not the actual buildings, known to the apostle. The same can be said for the numerous splendid Roman buildings found in the vicinity of the forum: baths, a library, various shrines, columns, porticoes, and all the other architectural monuments associated

[13] Amphipolis and Thessalonica were both politically more important than Philippi in that each was a seat of provincial government. But in economic and social terms the "chief city" was Philippi.

[14] For those wishing to proceed by land, the Via Egnatia turned north at the port of Dyrrhachium passing through what is now Albania and Yugoslavia until it reached Aquileia. Here, at the northern end of the Adriatic, four major Roman highways converged. The Via Egnatia was the most important of the four and was one of the longest of all Roman roads.

[15] This status conferred special rights upon the city and its inhabitants as regards privileges of law and taxation. It was thus a highly practical matter as well as an honor.

[16] Octavian was the grandnephew of Julius Caesar and was named in Caesar's will as adoptive son and heir; hence the Julian family name.

with a splendid Graeco-Roman city. Philippi was not large, but it was a gem, and its population was a cross section of the Empire.

"Outside the gate to the riverside" Paul and his companions went to the "place of prayer" where Jewish women assembled (Acts 16:13). Among those who heard Paul preach on his first Sabbath in the city was Lydia, "a seller of purple goods." [17] This woman believed and was baptized along with her "household." She thus became the first known Christian convert in Europe. It is not possible to identify the site of this preaching and conversion. Some point to a small stream flowing through tobacco fields surrounding the now-deserted city as the place. Others think the "gate" mentioned in Acts is in fact the Roman Arch still standing a mile west of the city. Near this is the Gangites River in which Lydia may have been baptized.

Lydia was not the only woman Paul met at Philippi. A slave girl, thought to have the power of divination, followed him and his companions about the streets crying, "These men are servants of the Most High God, who proclaim to you the way of salvation." Whatever the basis of her continuing activity she proved a source of irritation to Paul who finally turned on her and exorcised the spirit in her (Acts 16:16-18). As her gift had been a source of considerable gain to her owners, they assaulted Paul and Silas, dragged them to the market place (the forum area?), and accused them before the authorities of disturbing the public peace. There was an unruly scene. Because of mob action—or perhaps to prevent it—the magistrates stripped Paul and Silas, had them beaten with rods, thrown into jail, and fastened in stocks (Acts 16:19-24).[18] During the night, as the two missionaries were praying and singing, an earthquake occurred. The jail was shattered

[17] A Latin inscription found at Philippi mentions merchandizing in purple.

[18] The Roman architect Vitruvius, writing shortly before Paul's time, mentioned that the prison of Philippi was beside the forum.

so that it was possible for prisoners to escape. But they did not, and it was the voice of Paul assuring the distraught jailer that they were all present which prevented the jailer's suicide. As a result of this, the jailer eagerly sought to hear the message of the missionaries. He heard and believed. "And he was baptized at once, with all his family" (Acts 16:33).

The next morning the magistrates ordered the pair released. When it was discovered that the two were Roman citizens, publicly beaten and thrown into prison without trial or sentence (all violations of the law), amends were made. But Paul was asked to leave the city. He obliged, but not before visiting Lydia and "the brethren" (there were thus other converts) and exhorting them in the faith. With their public honor restored, the missionaries left Philippi along the Via Egnatia, passed through the cities of Amphipolis and Apollonia, and after seventy-five miles came to Thessalonica, the political capital of the Roman province of Macedonia.

Thessalonica (modern Salonica) was and is the chief seaport of Macedonia. Situated at the head of the largest gulf on the Aegean Sea, it has been a cosmopolitan center of commerce ever since its founding (ca. 316 B.C.) by Cassander who named it for his wife, the sister of Alexander the Great. Construction of the Via Egnatia (which is still the main street of Salonica) considerably enhanced the prosperity of this already wealthy city. As one might expect in a continuously occupied urban center, archaeological activity has been restricted. Such work would require large-scale demolition of existing structures. But working in the town square, excavators have had the good fortune to come down on the ancient Roman forum, as yet of undetermined exact date. Most of the old ruins visible in the city are medieval. An outstanding exception is the splendid triple arch of Galerius (A.D. 292-311) spanning the Via Egnatia. Erected in the early fourth century A.D. to commemorate Roman victories over the Persians, it contains numerous military scenes. More to the point of our purpose, it also mentions *politarchs*. These were civil magistrates and are spoken of in Acts 17:6 as the type of officials before whom Jason and some other Christians were arraigned (*politarchs* is translated in the RSV as "city authorities").[19]

Monks of the monastery of Vlatadon overlooking the beautiful harbor at Salonica claim that their building is on the site of a pagan temple at which Paul sought out Gentiles in order to proclaim the gospel to them. This tradition is of doubted antiquity. Nonetheless, memories of Paul's connection with the city are very much alive today. The church founded by Paul was a continuing source of joy to him. But Jewish opposition[20] to his work produced an ugly riot. "The house of Jason" (apparently the place where Christians were meeting) was attacked. When Paul and his companions were not found, Jason and other Christians were dragged before the politarchs and charged with political revolutionary intentions: "These men who have turned the world upside down have come here also, and Jason has received them; and they are all acting against the decrees of Caesar, saying that there is another king, Jesus" (Acts 17:6-7). Jason and the others, having posted bond, were released. But the danger to Paul and Silas remained. They were therefore spirited out of town at night.

[19] This is a particularly good example of how archaeology can help us understand certain terms in the biblical text. The word *politarch* was unknown apart from its use in Acts 17:6. Then archaeologists found it in the Oxyrhynchus Papyri from Egypt and on the Galerian Arch at Thessalonica. In addition, two other inscriptions from this Macedonian city, one from the reign of Augustus (27 B.C.-A.D. 14) and the other from that of Claudius (A.D. 49-54) contain it. We now know that politarchs were four or five civic officials who made up the governing councils of Macedonian cities.

[20] There was a large Jewish community in Thessalonica in Paul's day, as there is to this day.

The Areopagus in Athens showing the steps leading to the seats of the elders (below) where Paul disputed. The Athenian acropolis (above) is dominated by the Parthenon, dedicated to Athena.

Beroea (modern Veroia), fifty miles by road from Thessalonica, proved considerably more hospitable to the missionaries. Off the main roads, this middle-sized town nonetheless had a Jewish community of some proportions. They accepted Paul, heard him eagerly, and searched the Scriptures to test the truth of his proclamation. As a result many believed the gospel. Paul's success was not confined to Jews, however. A number of Greeks, some of "high standing," also became Christians. Then word of this activity came to Thessalonica. From there some of Paul's Jewish opponents came to Beroea and caused enough difficulty that Paul left, while Silas and Timothy stayed to continue the work so well begun (Acts 17:11-14).

Paul, we are told, went "on his way to the sea" and came to Athens, there to await the arrival of Silas and Timothy. While this does not specifically rule out the possibility that he traveled by land down the coast of Thessaly and into Attica, it is more likely and usually assumed that he went by ship from some small port in the vicinity, perhaps Methone or Alorus. This would have taken him past Mount Olympus, fabled dwelling place of Zeus, and Cape Sounion surmounted by the temple of Poseidon. At length, perhaps after five days, the ship would have entered Piraeus, port of Athens.

Athens, cultural arbiter of the ancient world, was even in Paul's day living already on memories of past glories.[21] Then as now, dominating all was the Parthenon, supreme achievement of architecture. In its shadow the Greeks of Roman times gathered to engage in pretentious conversation, emulating but in no regard rivaling the thoughts of their illustrious predecessors, Socrates, Plato, Aristotle. One group in particular—the Council of the Areopagus—was well known for entertaining and discussing various ideas.

When a new thought came their way, they were particularly glad to hear it.

The Areopagus[22] is a small rock outcropping on the northwestern slope of the Acropolis. The council of elders that held sessions on its top had a distinguished history dating far back into Athenian monarchical times. With the abolition of monarchy, the council became extremely important as the governing body of the city in conjunction with three elected archons. There was a division of power among the leaders with the council acting as guarantor on the part of the people. Abuse of power by the Tyrants led to Draco's publication of the law in 621 B.C. and to its being entrusted to the council. This body alone could hear cases of homicide, for example. Over the years in a complicated political development the group gradually lost power to the *ecclesia* (an assembly of all free men over eighteen) and the *boule* (a representative assembly of the *ecclesia*). The Council of the Areopagus, once advisor to kings, administrative power, court, and protector of public and private rights, was in the end a largely honorary group consisting of old men who solemnly met to discuss ideas old and new.[23]

Paul, as was his habit on the Sabbath, went straight to the synagogue in Athens. He argued with Jews and "God-fearers." On other days he went to the agora to speak of his belief in the resurrection of Jesus and of salvation for all men. On one occasion he became engaged in dialogue with some Stoic and Epicurean philosophers who took him

[21] Of all its archaeologically recovered monuments, only the Areopagus and the agora are more than obliquely associated with the work of Paul.

[22] The name of the hill is originally derived from *arai* (curses) in keeping with its somber functions of criminal jurisdiction. In passing years, *arai* was confused with *Ares*, god of war. Ares' Roman counterpart was Mars; hence the popular English name *Mars Hill*.

[23] Some scholars are of the opinion that Paul's presence before these men was some sort of formal hearing. Apart from the question of the council's authority at this time, the record in Acts simply bears no resemblance whatever to that kind of proceeding.

up to the Areopagus, only a few hundred yards away. There, in one of the most famous speeches recorded in Acts (17:23-31), he made a defense of his views, even citing as support certain of the Greek poets (see p. 298).[24] The reception of his words was hardly equal to their intent. Some listeners began to laugh when he spoke of the raising up of a dead man. Others, perhaps interested or perhaps just wishing to be amused on another occasion, said that they would hear more of this later. For Paul it was a bitter experience and one he did not easily forget (I Corinthians 1:18; 15:12, 35).

Away went Paul—from Athens, its Parthenon, its enormous gold-and-ivory statue of Athena, its laughing elders—southward across the isthmus to Corinth. Unlike modern Athens, Corinth is a short distance from its ancient location. The old city, twice destroyed by earthquakes, was about two miles inland from the Gulf of Corinth on an elevated plateau at the foot of the Acrocorinth, a rocky peak some 1,886 feet above sea level. Today the Corinthian Canal, conceived by Nero but not completed until 1893, joins the Aegean Sea with the Ionian Sea. This makes the lengthy and often dangerous voyage around the Peloponnesus unnecessary. In ancient times this voyage was avoided by transferring cargo to oxcarts and moving it across the narrow waist of land from ship to ship. Corinth, an old and distinguished city, prospered from its strategic location. Known for its wealth, it also had a certain notoriety for the night life and immorality of merchants, sailors, freebooters, and others who congregated there. Depopulated and utterly destroyed after a cruel siege in 146 B.C., it was rebuilt by Julius Caesar exactly a century later (46 B.C.) and settled with freedmen from Italy, orientals, and Jews,

all of whom mixed with numbers of Greeks who came to live in "Colonia Laus Julia Corinthiensis," as it was then called. This mixed population was not only alien to Greece and the scorn of the proud Athenians,[25] but was conducive to the licentiousness already mentioned. In such an atmosphere, as at Ephesus, Paul enjoyed some of his greatest success. The church he founded there was a tumultuous one, however, always ready to misunderstand Paul's words when it suited their more sensual impulses to do so. Paul's numerous letters to this church (there are at least four preserved in what we know as I and II Corinthians) are vivid evidence of the nature of this unruly fellowship. The First Letter of Clement written just before the turn of the century shows that matters in the Corinthian church had not much improved.

Thanks to excavations carried on since 1896 by the American School of Classical Studies in Athens, we have some idea of the splendid city that greeted Paul as he came from Athens. Julian favor and local wealth combined to erect within a six-mile circuit of walls a lavish display of limestone and marble. The Lechaion Road on which the apostle doubtless approached the city was twenty to twenty-five feet wide and flanked by sidewalks. Within the city, raised steps along its borders suggest to excavators that it was not used for wheeled traffic but was designed as a promenade giving easy access to numerous colonnaded shops on both sides. On Paul's right as he approached the agora was a large rectangular basilica and behind it the architectural gem among many treasures: the Temple of Apollo. Built in the sixth century B.C., it was the only structure in Corinth to survive the disaster of 146 B.C. Seven of its original thirty-eight massive

[24] In the form in which we have it, this sermon has been edited by the author of Acts to suit his theological purposes. But the quotation from Aratus and Paul's own bitter memories echoing the occasion point to an actual reminiscence.

[25] Corinth had by this time eclipsed Athens in commercial, political, and military importance. The Athenians however viewed the Corinthians with snobbish disdain.

Herbert G. May

The excavated marketplace at Corinth (above) contains not only the *bema*, perhaps to be associated with Paul, but also the Fountain of Peirene (right). The columns are remains of the Temple of Apollo.

Herbert G. May

columns still stand, twenty-four feet high and six feet in diameter. The Peribolos, a large sacred enclosure, was also dedicated to Apollo. Just south of it and next to the entrance to the agora was the Fountain of Peirene, a natural spring well known in the ancient world.

The agora itself was entered through a propylaea smaller and somewhat less grand than that on the Acropolis in Athens, but nonetheless splendid in its own right. Once inside this, Paul's eye would have beheld a rectangle approximately 200 meters by 67 meters. The agora was divided into two parts with that on the north lower and larger than the part farthest from the entrance. On the elevated southern portion was a stoa, a covered walk with numerous shops, some of which have been found to have wells connecting them with the Peirene spring. Many vessels found in this portion of the agora suggest that much of the stoa was occupied by taverns. Dividing the two sections of the agora was a *bema,* or rostrum, flanked by long lines of shops. This bema of white and blue marble was the focus of the market place and undoubtedly presented an impressive sight at the height of its glory. Here speakers could address a gathered crowd, perhaps here Paul was brought before the Roman governor for

a hearing. Acts 18:12 says, "But when Gallio was proconsul of Achaia, the Jews made a united attack upon Paul, and brought him before the tribunal [*bema*]."

By fortuitous discovery of an inscription at Delphi, we know when Gallio[26] was governor of Achaia. It was the year A.D. 51-52. This is the only firm date we have for the life and ministry of Paul. Acts 18:2 tells us that Aquila and his wife Priscilla had come to Corinth in the general expulsion of Jews from Italy by the Emperor Claudius. We know from other sources that this took place probably in A.D. 49. So Acts 18 gives us a general date and the inscription from Delphi a more specific one. Paul had been in the city with a successful ministry to

[26] Gallio was the elder brother of the famous philosopher Seneca.

Gentiles (he abandoned the synagogue[27] after being reviled) for a year and a half before being taken before the Roman Governor and charged with "persuading men to worship God contrary to the law" (Acts 18: 13).[28] How much longer Paul stayed after this incident we do not know. It was, says Acts 18:18, "many days." [29] Finally he decided to return to Antioch. With Aquila and Priscilla he went down to Cenchreae,[30] seven miles from Corinth. There they took ship for Ephesus. In this great city Paul went to the synagogue where he disputed for a time. Then, leaving Aquila and Priscilla behind, he took ship again, but for Caesarea, not Seleucia Pierea. His destination was Jerusalem, not Antioch.

The Third Missionary Journey

The text of Acts is cryptic regarding the beginnings of the Third Missionary Journey and indeed in speaking of Paul's movements until he arrived once more at Ephesus. Much discussion has taken place seeking to determine Paul's activities in Jerusalem and Antioch. It is best for our purposes simply to follow the account in Acts. Paul "greeted" the church in Jerusalem and perhaps also took the occasion to fulfill the requirements of the Nazirite vow, as he had done in Cenchreae. Indeed, this latter may have been his reason for coming to Jerusalem instead

of going directly to Seleucia Pieria and Antioch. But shortly Paul was back in Antioch, his home church, so to speak, and remained there "some time" (Acts 18:22-23).

His third journey was undertaken because disquieting reports had reached him. Judaizers, apparently Jewish-Christian opponents of Paul, had been active in some congregations he had founded in Asia Minor. These people had been insisting with some success that Paul's view of salvation by grace through faith was not correct. Observance of the Jewish Law, God's ancient revelation of himself, was also a necessary component of salvation and must be pressed upon Gentile as well as Jew. To counter this attack on the sufficiency of Christ's atoning death, Paul set off along the same path he had followed on his second journey: north from Antioch and then west to Tarsus, through the Cilician Gates and into the interior of Asia Minor. It was not a mission primarily to evangelize new areas, but to confirm, teach, and restore.

He "went from place to place through the region of Galatia and Phrygia, strengthening all the disciples," says Acts 18:23. This imprecise reference does not give us much to go on.[31] We may assume from Acts 19:1 ("Paul passed through the upper country . . .") that he was once again well inland, on the arid plateaus of the old Gala-

[27] In 1898 archaeologists working near the propylaea found an inscribed piece of white marble. "Synagogue of the Hebrews" it said, identifying the general location of Paul's unsuccessful disputations with the Jews of Corinth.

[28] Gallio, a learned man cultured in the ways of the Greeks, acted in this case in a manner typical of most Roman provincial governors when confronted with what appeared to be a local religious quarrel. He threw it out of court.

[29] At some point during Paul's stay in Corinth he addressed a letter to the church at Thessalonica. This writing, I Thessalonians, is the oldest preserved Pauline letter and thus the oldest book in the New Testament.

[30] The site is now a ruin, but many ancient remains can be seen identifying this port once famous for its temples and shrines.

[31] It is not clear what *Galatia* means. There are two possibilities. The term may refer to that portion of central Asia Minor settled by Celts in the first half of the 3rd cent. B.C. In 240 B.C., King Attalos of Pergamum limited the territory of these people to lands around the rivers Halys and Sangarios including the cities of Ancyra, Pessinus, and Tavium. A second possibility refers to a much larger area. When in 25 B.C. Amyntas, last king of the Galatians, left his kingdom to the Romans, they made it a province with Ancyra as capital. But this Roman province included in addition to the old Galatian kingdom also Pisidia, Isauria, and parts of Lycaonia, Phrygia, Paphlagonia, and Pontus. Further to complicate the problem, the Romans changed the boundaries of this administrative district a number of times.

tian kingdom and Phrygia. This would place him in the region of Ancyra (modern Ankara) and bring him to Ephesus by way of Gordium, Pessinus, Ipsus, and Sardis. It is possible, of course, that the apostle took a more southern route along the Maeander River. If so, this would have taken him through Colossae, Laodicea, and Magnesia.

By whatever route, he came at last to Ephesus, the first city of Roman Asia Minor, center of proconsular government, major commercial port, and focus of a considerable traffic of religious pilgrims. Here was the home of the worship of Artemis (Roman *Diana*) whose temple at Ephesus, the *Artemision*, was one of the seven wonders of the ancient world. So fabled was this sanctuary that in the mid-nineteenth century the British Museum commissioned an archaeologist, J. T. Wood, to go to Ephesus and find it. Through the years every surface trace of it had disappeared. Wood began his labors on May 2, 1863. Exactly six years later to the day he found a wall of the temple. The clue to this discovery was an inscription found in the Roman theater telling of the route of a religious procession on the birthday of the goddess. Following this ancient sacred way, Wood came upon the sanctuary. Over the years various British and Austrian archaeological expeditions[32] have sought to determine the history and dimensions of the shrine. The temple known to Paul was built in the middle of the sixth century B.C. on the site of an even much older sanctuary. Burned in 356 B.C. (on the very night Alexander the Great was born, according to Plutarch), it was restored along the same lines but with considerably more magnificence. The platform on which it stood was 239 feet wide and 418 feet long. This was reached by ten steps; three more led into the sanctuary itself. The temple was over 180 feet wide and almost 360 feet long. It contained 117 columns, each over six feet in diameter; some thirty-six of these were sculptured to a height of twenty feet. Behind the great altar (twenty feet square) stood the focus of the cult: a "sacred stone that fell from the sky" (Acts 19:35). This probably refers to a meteorite. It is known from sources referring to the worship of the Cybele in Asia Minor that meteorites were considered sacred in that area. In addition to splendidly cut stone, archaeologists have recovered a large number of brilliantly painted fragments. These indicate that skills of painters were combined with those of sculptors and goldsmiths to adorn this splendid structure which some men were fearful would "count for nothing" under the impact of Paul's ministry (Acts 19:27).

About a mile west of the Artemision was the heart of the ancient city lying between two hills and centered upon the harbor.[33] Here were a stadium (does I Corinthians 15:32 refer to activity here?), a theater, a fine agora, and the many glistening public buildings and shops one might expect in a city of Ephesus' importance. The *Arkadiane*, perhaps the finest street in the Roman Empire, in its excavated form was rebuilt by the Emperor Arcadius (A.D. 395-408) for whom it was named. It was thus not yet there when Paul came to the city. However, its width (thirty-five feet) and deep colonnading (fifteen feet) give at least an indication of some splendor in the time of the apostle. This street, lined with carved columns and statues, joined the harbor with the theater.

The theater demands a little more of our attention. It was here that the riot precipitated by the silversmiths took place. In accordance with an ancient custom of selling votive images to pilgrims at shrines (see pp. 80-81), Ephesus, as the center of a wide-

[32] The British worked from 1863 until 1874, and again in 1904/5. The Austrian Archaeological Institute excavated from 1898 until 1913, in 1926-35, and again in 1954.

[33] Ancient attempts to prevent silting up of the harbor disastrously had the opposite effect. The shoreline is now some three to four miles from the site of the old city.

spread worship of Artemis, had a thriving industry in such images. It was the considerable success of Paul's ministry with its resultant decrease in the sale of pagan amulets that brought about the apostle's departure from Ephesus. Demetrius, a silversmith engaged in the manufacture of these items, stirred up his fellow craftsmen against Paul. Through the efforts of these men many people in the city were led to think that the Christians endangered not only a craft, but the very worship of the goddess itself. A riot resulted. "Great is Artemis of the Ephesians," began to ring throughout the streets. Two of Paul's traveling companions were seized and dragged into the theater. Set against a hill, this typically Hellenistic structure held three ranks of marble seats, arranged in twenty-two rows per rank. In all, it could seat 24,000 people. Elaborately decorated with pillars and statuary, it was in keeping with the rest of the city. In this setting on that day confusion reigned. Paul wished to go in and make a defense of his views. Some friends, wiser on that occasion, dissuaded him. At length, after at least two hours, with the hills echoing to the shouts of the mob, the town clerk convinced the people that they were in danger with being charged before the Roman officials for rioting. With this threat and a certain emotional and physical weariness, the crowd dispersed. But Demetrius and his friends had accomplished at least a part of their purpose: Paul soon left the city.

Thus came to an end Paul's longest ministry[34] and one in which he took the opportunity to send other missionaries to various places in the region. Many of the cities of the Lycus Valley were evangelized.

From Ephesus he sailed to Macedonia where he strengthened the churches before proceeding "to Greece," doubtless a reference to the south and Corinth (Acts 20:2). Paul was three months there, until a Jewish plot against his life caused him to leave. Again he went to Macedonia and eventually to Troas. On the Sunday of his week in Troas, Paul preached to the local Christians. Planning to leave on the morrow, he seems to have desired to tell them all that was on his mind. At any rate, he spoke until midnight. Eutychus, a youngster sitting in a window, went to sleep and fell out. Knocked unconscious, he was thought to be dead. Paul himself discovered that this was not so, and they all were "not a little comforted" (Acts 20:7-12).

At Assos (modern Behramkoy), a beautifully situated provincial harbor and home of the Stoic philosopher Cleanthes, Paul boarded a small vessel for passage to the island of Lesbos. There he took another ship and after touching Samos came to Miletus. He had deliberately avoided Ephesus, not out of fear of the silversmiths, but from the sure knowledge that if he went there he would have to spend considerable time with the Christian community. He was in a hurry to get to Jerusalem. But he could hardly ignore the church at Ephesus, doubtless even then a flourishing and highly important center of Christian activity.[35] He summoned the elders of the church there to come to Miletus.

Miletus had four harbors and had been important since before recorded history. When Greek culture blossomed in western Asia Minor, this city was one of the fairest blooms. Its ancient glory, undiminished in Paul's day, has been partly recovered by archaeologists.[36] Among other things its high-rising Hellenistic theater still yields an

---

[34] Acts 19:8-10 says he was in the synagogue for three months and then moved next door to the hall of Tyrannus where he preached for two years. Acts 20:31 notes that Paul labored for three years in Ephesus.

[35] Within a century Ephesus was third only to Alexandria and Antioch in its Christian importance.

[36] Some of the ancient city, including the agora, is flooded by the Maeander River.

unparalleled view of the sea from its upper courses. Little of this was of any interest to Paul as he met an emotional farewell with his friends in Christ. After a speech in which he quoted a saying of Jesus not recorded in the Gospels (Acts 20:35), he took leave of his friends and of Asia.[37]

To Rome

The ship on which Paul had sailed from Miletus visited Tyre and Ptolemais before reaching Caesarea. At Tyre, seven days were required to unload cargo, and Paul spent the time among Christians of that city. They warned him not to go to Jerusalem (Acts 21:4). But when the ship weighed anchor, Paul was once again on board with his traveling companions. After a day with Christians in Ptolemais, he set foot in Judea at Caesarea. There he stayed at the home of Philip the evangelist where he received a dramatic indication of what awaited him should he insist on proceeding up to the Holy City. Agabus, a prophet, bound Paul's hands with his own girdle, saying, "So shall the Jews at Jerusalem bind the man who owns this girdle and deliver him into the hands of the Gentiles" (Acts 21:11). This symbolic act greatly impressed those with the apostle, but only moved him to declare his readiness "to die at Jerusalem for the name of the Lord Jesus" (Acts 21:13). So Paul began to climb into the Judean highlands toward those events which would within two weeks bring him back to Caesarea—in chains.

Upon reaching Jerusalem Paul reported to the church of his many activities and of the receptivity of Gentiles to the gospel. His words were received with rejoicing. At the same time Paul was told that the Jerusalem church had sent a letter to Christian

Gentiles informing them of the earlier decision of the council. Moreover, Paul was warned that word of his activities had reached hostile ears in the city. It was being said that he taught men to abandon the Law of Moses. In order to demonstrate otherwise, suggested some in the church, he should go into the Temple with four men who were under a Nazirite vow, pay their expenses, and thus show to all openly that even the strictest of Jewish vows was honored by this man accused of having no regard for the Law. It took seven days to fulfill the requirements for ending the vow properly. Near the end of this time Jews from Asia Minor saw Paul in the Temple and stirred up a crowd against him. A riot ensued. The apostle was dragged from the sanctuary into the larger courts. Immediately the inner gates were closed to prevent the mob from flowing back into the shrine proper. In a few minutes Roman soldiers, doubtless from the Antonia, were pouring into the sacred area. Some members of the crowd, intent upon beating Paul to death, ceased their efforts when confronted by a Roman officer. It was impossible in the tumult to determine anything. So Paul was placed in chains and led away. On the steps leading into the Antonia (see p. 227) he persuaded the officer to allow him to address the people. His impassioned defense was cut short by angry and mounting shouts. At length he was led prisoner into Herod's fortress (Acts 21:17–22:24).

Roman citizenship kept Paul from the baser kinds of physical punishment. Various hearings followed in the next few days. These included an extremely unruly session before the Sanhedrin in which Paul skillfully played one side against another (Acts 23:1-10). When Paul's nephew discovered a plot against his life, the Roman officer sent his prisoner to Antonius Felix at Caesarea. Felix, appointed governor through the efforts of his brother, Pallas, a favorite of the

---

[37] Paul's ship called at Patara on the southern coast of Asia Minor, but there is no record of any activity there on his part.

Emperor Claudius, was said by Tacitus to govern Judea "with the powers of a king and the soul of a slave." This man professed to be interested in Christianity and had many talks with Paul. But money seems to have been of more concern to him. When no bribe was forthcoming he left Paul—uncharged with any crime—in prison. After two years [38] Porcius Festus came to Palestine to exercise the governorship. He who eventually died in that land far from Rome tried to be just. A good example was his treatment of Paul.

Festus' first step as governor was to go to Jerusalem and confer with the local authorities. He found the Jewish leaders concerned about a prisoner in Caesarea. They wanted this man for trial in Jerusalem. Festus was apparently aware that they planned to see to it that Paul never made it to the city alive. He acted properly for a provincial governor. The Jewish leaders were summoned to Caesarea there to present their case against this man in the presence of the procuratorial court. Paul denied all charges. Not wishing to offend the leaders of the people he had been sent to govern, Festus asked Paul if he wished to return to Jerusalem and be tried by his own people. Paul, as was his right, appealed to Caesar in Rome. This meant that jurisdiction in the matter was taken out of the hands of the provincial governor who was now obliged to see that his prisoner was safely transported to Rome for trial. "You have appealed to Caesar," said Festus after due consultation, "to Caesar you shall go" (Acts 25:12). Along with other prisoners Paul was placed in custody of one Julius, a member of the Augustan Cohort, for transport to Rome. In the harbor at Caesarea was a ship from Adramyttium (modern Edremit) on the northwest coast of Asia Minor not far from Assos. This vessel was calling at ports along the coasts of Syria-Palestine and Asia Minor. Julius decided to use it to reach western Asia Minor and then to find another bound for Italy. After some days, several ports-of-call, and adverse winds, anchor was dropped in the harbor at Myra (modern Kale). [39] An Egyptian ship from Alexandria was there and was bound for Italy. Julius made the necessary arrangements and he and his prisoners went aboard.

The sea captain had intended to hug the coast of Asia Minor, sail across the southern Aegean, and stay in the lee of the Peloponnesus before heading across the open Ionian Sea for Italy. Almost as soon as they left Myra, however, it became clear that a change in plans was necessary. The sailors had not learned to tack against the wind, so that the ship made little headway, and then only with the greatest difficulty. After a number of days, the ship came to Cnidus, the westernmost point of southern Asia Minor. A dash across the southern Aegean was not possible—the winds were against it. Turning south the captain took his ship under the lee of Crete hoping to use this means to reach Greece. Cape Salmone was made with relative ease, but the easterly journey under the lee of Crete was a further struggle against the winds. At length Fair Havens was reached. By now it was obvious to all that they could not continue. Safe shelter must be found until the winter's storm abated. Paul was in favor of staying there (Acts 27:9-10). But Fair Havens, an anchorage about four miles east of Cape Matala, was vulnerable to east and southeast winds. These were just what the sailors now sought to avoid. Risks had to be taken to reach a larger and more protected harbor.

[38] It is not clear from Acts 24:27 if this refers to the two years of Felix' governorship or to the length of Paul's imprisonment at Caesarea.

[39] Myra later became the seat of the fourth-century Christian bishop Nicholas—St. Nicholas—whose fame for generosity is said to have prompted his identification with giving at Christmas.

The owner of the ship, the captain, and the centurion agreed that a run should be made for Phoenix.[40]

Out of the harbor at Fair Havens came the ship in what seemed fortuitous calm breezes. But soon a northeaster struck. The ship was driven away from Crete. The vessel proved first difficult to steer, then impossible. All was completely out of control as the ship passed under the lee of the small island of Cauda (modern Gavhos). Attempts to secure the vessel there only increased the danger of its destruction. Ship, crew, and apostle were storm-tossed into the open Mediterranean. The men abandoned all hope. But on the fourteenth day, with the wind less strong and the waters somewhat calmed, the sailors became convinced they were coming into more and more shallow water. At daybreak strange land appeared. An attempt to keep the ship off the beach failed, and the vessel began to break up. When the soldiers planned to kill their prisoners lest any should escape, Julius prevented it in order to save Paul's life.

The land was the island of Melita (modern Malta), and its inhabitants showed great kindness to the men who washed ashore on boards and debris. As wood was being gathered for a fire, a snake bit Paul who, suffering no ill effects, was taken to be a god. His stature was increased even more when he effected the cure of the father of the chief man of the island, named Publius (Acts 28:1-10). Strangely, we are not told of any specifically Christian work by Paul on Malta, but the population of that island traces its religious faith back to the apostle, probably not without cause.

After three months (perhaps in February) another Alexandrian ship which had wintered at Malta took Paul to Puteoli (modern Pozzuoli) on the Bay of Naples.

Intermediate stops were made at Syracuse and Rhegium, but there is no record of the apostle's activity at either place even though he was three days in Syracuse. At Puteoli he was allowed to stay with local Christians for a week before going northward along the Via Appia toward Rome. Roman Christians, who knew him through his letter to them, heard of his approach and came out of the city to meet him. Some came as far as the Forum of Appius, thirty-three miles south of Rome. Others waited ten miles closer to Rome at Three Taverns where the Via Appia intersected the road to Antium.

Paul had come to Rome.

Considerable mystery surrounds the apostle's stay in the capital of the Empire, and his eventual fate. Acts 28:17-31 reports that he was confined, but in his own dwelling.[41] His extant letters from those days (Colossians, Philippians, Philemon, Ephesians[?], I and II Timothy [?], Titus [?]) indicate that various companions of his came and went freely. Sometimes they brought gifts to relieve certain of the hardships of the situation. He made an appeal to the leaders of the Jewish community of the city to hear him.[42] They came to his house, and for a full day there was discussion. The result was the same as elsewhere: a few believed, but for the most part Paul's gospel was rejected by this group. Undaunted, he turned to the Gentiles of Rome and had an unhindered ministry for two years. With this the narrative of Acts ends.

What happened to Paul? A full discussion of this question falls outside the limits of this book. It is just as well, for there are many theories and few certainties. We know of Paul's desire to work in Spain (Romans 15:24-28) and of a late first-century writing that can be interpreted to mean that he did

---

[40] The reference in Acts 27:12 has not been identified to everyone's satisfaction. It seems reasonably safe, however, to identify it with modern Loutro.

[41] The Romans called this *custodia libera*. We speak of it as "house arrest."

[42] Jews had by this time been allowed to return to Italy and Rome. Among those who came back were Aquila and Priscilla (Romans 16:3).

so.[43] The same passage may support an early tradition saying he was martyred in Rome, and many have taken this as a reference to the Neronian persecution (A.D. 64). If this is correct, he probably was found guilty at his trial and put to death. On the other hand, he may have been released, gone to Spain, returned to Rome, and then have been put to death. Still others think the Pastoral Letters (I and II Timothy, Titus) are evidence for later work in Asia Minor. There are many other views. We simply do not know. He disappears into the mists of history at the end of Acts.

In Rome today there are a number of sites which various traditions connect with Paul. Near the Forum there is a dungeon where visitors are told that not only Paul, but Peter as well was confined. The Church of St. Paul of Three Fountains is claimed to be the place where he was beheaded.[44] Water, it is said, sprang up as his head struck the ground three times in falling from the block. St. Paul's Outside the Walls on the Via Ostiense is a magnificent basilica marking the traditional spot of Paul's final resting place. Beneath its altar is a stone inscribed PAULO. This is thought to have been the work of Constantine in identifying the site. Beside the letters is a round hole through which pilgrims were once allowed to lower various objects to touch the blessed coffin. All these places are identified by traditions, some ancient and strong (the tomb), others less so (the dungeon). None, it should be pointed out, is firmly supported by very early Christian literary evidence, and at none has archaeology made a connection with the apostle himself. While this does not make a difference for the pilgrim, it is a matter the historian cannot fail to note.

[43] I Clement 5:7 says: "He taught righteousness to the whole world, having traveled to the limits of the west; and when he had borne his witness before the rulers, he departed from the world. . . ."

[44] As a Roman citizen he would not have been crucified, as tradition indicates was the fate of Peter.

Archaeology has done much, however, to bring alive many of the actual contexts known to Paul. Graeco-Roman urban splendor with its skillful blending of materials has

Herbert G. May

In the crypt of a church near the Imperial Forum in Rome (above) is an ancient prison said to have held both Peter and Paul. The Church of St. Paul's Outside the Walls (below) contains the traditional tomb of the Apostle to the Gentiles.

been recovered. The brilliance of Pisidian Antioch, of Philippi, and of a dozen or more other cities which greeted his eye can today be seen by our eyes. The streets he walked, the places he was tried, dragged, shouted down—many are known to us thanks to excavations. We can walk there, stand there, even shout there and try out the echoes if we like. Paul's world lives. Yet this is not merely a matter of stones and carvings, of temples, shops, and streets. The complex cultural and religious atmosphere of those days has been made equally visible. Memories of a cosmopolitan Antioch with its religious pluralism and a resplendent Ephesus dominated by the temple and cult of Artemis are more vivid today perhaps than at any time since the collapse of the Empire. They are but two examples of the cultural vitality archaeology has been able to breathe into long-silent stones.

All this is not merely antiquarian interest. "For I am not ashamed of the gospel," Paul confessed, "it is the power of God for salvation to every one who has faith, to the Jew first and also to the Greek" (Romans 1:16). The stones are certainly there. In some cases the very structures he touched are also there. They serve to remind us that Paul was a real man laboring among real people. His confession echoes from the stones and resounds in the structures, for it was this contagious faith that has made him important. It is this that gives the towns and cities described here more than mere historical value. In them Paul preached his gospel, proclaiming salvation for every man. Perhaps at no time in history could a man traveling the 12,000 or more miles he journeyed have seen so much splendor. But his gaze was steadily upon "a temple not made with hands," and in the midst of the perishable he spoke of the imperishable. The buildings are ruins and for the most part were forgotten until the archaeologists came. The gospel abides.

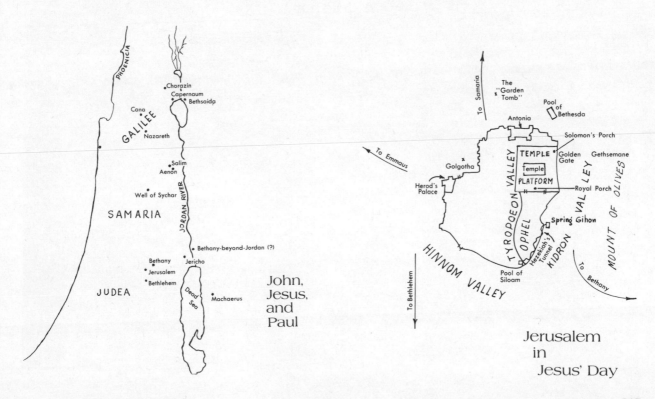

John, Jesus, and Paul

Jerusalem in Jesus' Day

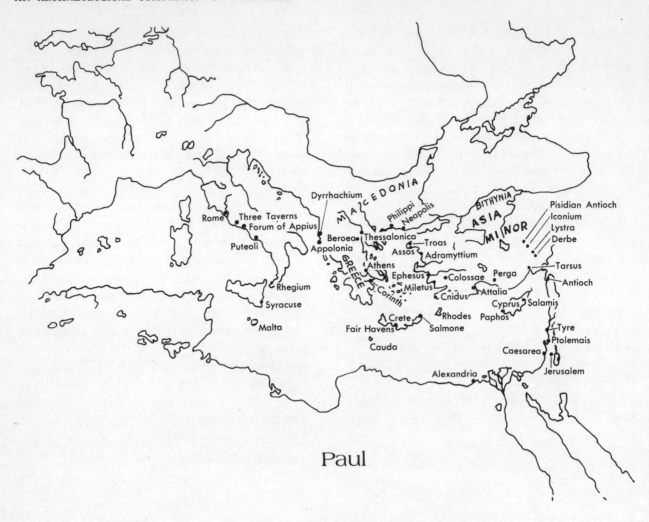

Paul

EPILOGUE: BIBLE, ARCHAEOLOGY, AND FAITH

EPILOGUE: BIBLE, ARCHAEOLOGY, AND FAITH

Much archaeological work in the Middle East has been legitimately motivated by a desire for a fuller understanding and exposition of the Bible. "The one great object of all my investigations," wrote Edward Robinson at the end of his second pioneering survey of Palestine in 1852, "has been *the historical topography* of that country in its relations especially to the Holy Scriptures." In other words, this American scholar wished to learn all he could of the physical setting of the Sacred Story. Little could he have dreamed that his work would prompt the unlocking of a vast storehouse of knowledge of ancient history as well as geography. In the mid-nineteenth century even his fertile mind could hardly have imagined the extent to which archaeology would revolutionize the understanding of the Bible and its context.

Later explorers, although they may express themselves differently and have a wider focus, have not essentially departed from Robinson's stated purpose. In some quarters, however, their work has been misunderstood, and unfounded claims have been made. Some scholars, usually not archaeologists, have seized upon certain discoveries in an attempt to "prove" the Bible. One of the more popular books on Bible and archaeology in recent years is that of a German journalist, Werner Keller. Translated into English under the title, *The Bible as History: A Confirmation of the Book of Books,*[1] it is filled with the excitement of a man for whom a new vista had suddenly opened. At the same time, it is shot through with the idea that now, finally, the Bible has been validated. Indeed, it is possible to render the German title, *Und die Bibel hat doch recht,* as *The Bible Is True After All.* For many people in our own skeptical age, this is what archaeology does. It dispels doubt; it proves. It gives tangible evidence to sustain the intangible. Where faith cannot stand on its own merit, and the

[1] Trans. W. Neil (New York: W. Morrow, 1956). The British edition (Hodder and Stoughton) is subtitled: *Archaeology Confirms the Book of Books.*

319

Bible cannot be taken as a primarily religious document telling of God and his love for man, some people feel more secure and comfortable in their beliefs if a wall, a city, or a manuscript can be produced to suggest that after all the Bible just may be true.

This unfortunate situation—a violation of both Bible and archaeology—is understandable given the nature of biblical religion and the recent history of the interpretation of the Bible. Any serious attempt to understand Old and New Testament thought must take full recognition of its historical character. Every religion, of course, has a history. While it is not always easy to speak with certainty of the origins of the various religions, it is clear that each has come from somewhere and has undergone development and change. Many things are responsible for the complex movements and shifts religions undergo. Social, political, military, and economic factors as well as internal theological dynamics can be cited. To trace out and to understand these factors and dynamics is to search for the history of a religion. Archaeology can be and has been helpful in such undertakings in various parts of the world. Activity in the Shetland and Orkney Islands north of Scotland have immensely added to our knowledge of Norse life and religion. Similarly, Indian ruins in the southwestern United States have been excavated with profit to our understanding of early American religions. Examples could be drawn from almost any part of the world. In the same way as all other religions, biblical religion as well as Judaism and Christianity can be studied as *religions with a history*.

Yet the religion of the Bible and of those faiths which look to the Bible as their principal source of authority are *historical religions* as distinguished from *religions with a history*. For the Jew and for the Christian as well as for the men who lived in Old and New Testament times, history is not merely an account of man's past and the reality of his present. It is also the way through which and in which God reveals himself and his will. This belief is very different from that of the ancient Greek for whom time was understood as a process of decay. Like many people today, the Greek viewed salvation as an escape from time. Not so the man whose faith is rooted in the Bible. History from his point of view is a series of moments given by God. Sustained by the Eternal Creator it has a beginning and a purpose throughout its course. It is the presence of history which makes possible the coming of the kingdom of God. The Bible views history in two ways: as a record of the past and as a medium of revelation. This sets the Bible uniquely apart from other religious writings. It is not merely or mainly moral, spiritual, and ritual teachings, but a story of a people to whom it confesses God revealed himself.

The ancient Hebrew's conception of God was not couched in the sort of speculation or contemplation so well known to us today. Rather, standing before the altar with a sacrifice of grain in his outstretched hands, he said:

A wandering Aramean was my father; and he went down into Egypt and sojourned there, few in number; and there he became a nation, great, mighty, and populous. And the Egyptians treated us harshly, and afflicted us, and laid upon us hard bondage. Then we cried to the Lord the God of our fathers, and the Lord heard our voice, and saw our affliction, our toil, and our oppression; and the Lord brought us out of Egypt with a mighty hand and an outstretched arm, with great terror, with signs and wonders; and he brought us into this place and gave us this land, a land flowing with milk and honey. And behold, now I bring the first of the fruit of the ground, which thou, O Lord, hast given me.

Deuteronomy 26:5-10

In the Early Church as in old Israel, a confession of faith was never abstract. It was a concrete recital of what God had done and was doing in the midst of his people:

In those days a decree went out from Caesar Augustus that all the world should be enrolled. This was the first enrollment, when Quirinius was governor of Syria. And all went to be enrolled, each to his own city. And Joseph also went up from Galilee, from the city of Nazareth, to Judea, to the city of David, which is called Bethlehem, because he was of the house and lineage of David, to be enrolled with Mary, his betrothed, who was with child. And while they were there, the time came for her to be delivered. And she gave birth to her first-born son and wrapped him in swaddling clothes, and laid him in a manger, because there was no place for them in the inn.

These words from the Gospel of Luke (2: 1-7) are not merely the objective account of history which most people take them to be. They are also and profoundly a confession of faith. The Eternal God, says Luke, makes himself known in history, in ordinary times and places: in Bethlehem, when Quirinius was governor of Syria.

The religion of the man whose faith is rooted in the Bible is a *historical religion* as well as a *religion with a history*. At its very heart is the confession that God reveals himself and fulfills his purposes precisely in history. Faith is trusting this kind of God.

It is little wonder, therefore, that archaeology—a historical discipline par excellence —is of considerable importance for understanding the Bible. The problem arises when there is a confusion of *historical religion*, with which archaeology cannot deal, and *religion with a history*, about which archaeology can tell us much. Again, there is reason for the confusion. Until about a hundred years ago the Old Testament existed in virtual isolation. Little was known of the context in which it was written or the times it described; still less was suspected about its

relatively late appearance on the ancient Middle Eastern scene. On the contrary, the history of man on this planet was widely affirmed to have begun with the People of God, and whatever advances there were in civilization were surely due to them. Creation took place somewhere around 3500 to 4000 B.C., depending upon whose reckoning you followed. Then came the geological and biological assertions, based upon fossil remains, of an enormous preliterary period stretching back thousands, perhaps hundreds of thousands, of years. The evidence mounted. By the middle of the nineteenth century, Darwin had put forth his theory of evolution, and the "God or gorilla?" debates, involving healthy misunderstandings of both Bible and science, were joined.

When the results of archaeology began to come into the picture, they were at first not comforting to many defenders of the Bible. The Old Testament was definitely not mankind's oldest document. Hebrew was not the first language. Indeed, the Hebrews had appropriated it! Worse: the biblical account of the Flood had Babylonian and Sumerian antecedents; the psalms praising the God of Israel were similar in form and often language to those extolling Ra, Marduk, and even Baal. The pithy proverbs of the Bible were similar to examples from Mesopotamia and Egypt. Even the Law of Moses was found to have almost verbatim parallels in the law codes of Hammurabi. The historical narrative of the Bible was therefore seen to be limited. As the findings of historical documents multiplied, the originality of the Old Testament came into question. Those bent upon attacking Christianity seized the opportunity. If there was doubt about the originality and completeness of the Bible, was not its "truth" also in question? They failed to see the Bible as religious literature with a purpose, form, and confession at best but partially subject to historical disciplines.

Then the situation began to change. There

was another angle of vision on the vast and continually enlarging body of archaeological materials. The Bible was emerging from its isolation. As its context became better known, students of the Scriptures gained a new perspective on the ancient world as experienced by the people of the Old and New Testaments. Sacred history came to life as real history with people struggling in situations not entirely unknown to us. The shifting foreign policy advocated by Isaiah made sense in light of newly available Assyrian records. It was even possible to have some sympathy for Ahab, once the social, economic, and cultural dimensions of Israelite life came to light. These are but two examples of the kind of human drama and realism that were shown to be on the pages of the Scriptures.

Furthermore, the weight of evidence showed that there were few reasons to doubt the essential correctness of the narrative history in the Old Testament. Of course, certain natural tendencies were present— the nationalistic and religious points of view of the writers of the Bible. They could not bring themselves to admit, for example, that the magnificent Solomon had brought the kingdom to the point of bankruptcy and was forced to cede to his creditor, Hiram of Tyre, what was considered to be native Israelite territory. But the recovery of Egyptian and Mesopotamian records shows that there is considerably less prideful falsifying in the Bible than in neighboring literatures. If the Chronicler makes David appear to be a spotless, holy king, the author of the "Court History" in II Samuel 9–20 does not spare us the darker side of his character.

Almost all the events reported in the Bible are given a religious interpretation. "I will sing to the Lord, for he has triumphed gloriously; the horse and his rider he has thrown into the sea," sang the joyous Hebrews as they escaped from pharaoh's drowning soldiers (Exodus 15:1). Creation was an act of God, as was the birth of Isaac, the gift of the Promised Land, David, the Prophets, as well as punishment, the Assyrians, Nebuchadrezzar; above all, Jesus Christ. Archaeology has indicated sometimes generally and sometimes specifically that biblical interpretations do rest upon real events. Even those matters whose descriptions were not written down until years, even centuries, later have been shown to be contextually correct. This does not mean that we have any extra-biblical information bearing directly upon persons or events mentioned in the patriarchal narratives, for example. Yet the recovery of the Bronze Age cultures of Mesopotamia, Canaan, and Egypt leave no doubt that the background of those narratives as reported in the Bible is Bronze Age and not Iron Age when they were written. The late date of written records does not necessarily mean historical unreliability.

The advantages archaeology provides to biblical study came to be seen as legion. It became possible to trace the organic development of Hebrew society and culture. Comparative materials allow us to distinguish what was essential from what was subsidiary in the revelation enshrined in the Bible. Contrary to destroying the originality of Holy Writ, archaeology tends to highlight the uniqueness of its thought. Many of the forms are the same, but what they enshrine is quite different. Thus not only has the earlier historical skepticism been discredited, but the religious affirmations of the Bible stand out more clearly than ever.

Assertions that the Bible had been "proved" were sure to come. Archaeology was claimed to have settled many questions concerning various events including the Flood (Woolley at Ur) and the Conquest of Canaan (Garstang at Jericho). It did not matter that the field excavators had been considerably more guarded in their conclusions than what was alleged to them. It mattered not at all that later work with better techniques had corrected earlier conclusions. Even worse, it did not seem to matter that the defenders of the "truth" of the Bible were committing the same error the detractors had earlier made: They assumed faith was open to the findings of historical disciplines. Because the general trustworthiness of the narrative had been established, it was widely assumed that the spiritual and moral truths of the Bible had been made credible.

Of course, had the findings of archaeology tended to indicate that the events spoken of in the Bible were fabrications, there would be ground for suggesting that the faith of biblical men was a pious fiction and not a worthy basis for confidence today. But the reverse is not true: The vindication of the historical value of Holy Scripture does not validate the interpretation those ancient men of faith placed upon events. The certainty of faith does not rest upon the conclusions of science, historical or otherwise. Such conclusions, by their nature, are always subject to revision. Faith, the absolute assurance of man's meaningful dependence upon the activity of God, is hardly dependent upon the transitory methodologies of science.

Archaeology has provided a very different orientation for understanding the Bible than was possible a century, or even a generation, ago. In general it has confirmed the narratives. At places it has shown their historical inaccuracy.[2] On some points, such as the conquest of Canaan as reported in Joshua and Judges, the full archaeological story is yet to be told. In such matters it is dealing with a *religion with a history*. There it must be given full range. The Bible requires no "special pleading." As history and literature it is, and should be, examined with all literary and historical tools at our command. When it comes to the faith of the Bible as a *historical religion,* greater appreciation and understanding are possible only to those whose spirits are attuned to matters independent of time and place.

---

[2] For example, the setting of the story in Genesis 26 is Philistine. But the Hebrews involved are Abraham and Isaac. Archaeology has shown that the patriarchs and Philistines were divided in time by a minimum of 300 and a maximum of perhaps 700 years. Here is a story from one age placed in a setting from another. Some years ago many thought this was the case with all the patriarchal narratives, but we now know that Genesis 26 is almost alone in this regard.

INDEXES

SCRIPTURE INDEX

Old Testament

NAME INDEX

Aaron, 104
Abdul-Malek Ibn Marwan, 136
Abel, 19
Abiathar, 128
Abijah, 156
Abimelech, 45
Abner, 121, 123–4
Abraham, 28, 30, 32–6, 53–4, 63, 64, 122
Absalom, 128
Abu Simbel, 69
Achan, 93
Achish, 121
Achshaph, 96
Adad-nirari III, 166
Adonijah, 130, 132
Adoram, 154
Aelia Capitolina, 125, 136, 228, 286
Aenon, 39n., 288
Agnes Scott College, Atlanta, 143
Ahab, 35, 37, 104, 106, 108–9, 111n., 133, 152, 155n., 160n., 163–4, 167–71
Aharoni, Yohanan, 95–7, 146, 147, 179–80, 204, 272
Ahaz, 105, 141n., 186–8
Ahaziah, 163
Ahijah (prophet), 149
Ahiram, 106
Ahmose, 68–9
Ai (=et-Tell?), 37, 44, 49–52, 89, 93
  sanctuary, 50–2, 101n.
Ain el Qudeirat (=Kadesh-barnea), 180
Ain-es-Sultan (spring), 29
Akhen-aton, see Amenophis IV
Akhet-Aton (=Tell el-Amarna), 70
al Muqayyar, 32
Alalakh, 143
Alalakh Tablets, 64
Al-Aqsa Mosque, 137
Albright, W. F., 18, 22, 28, 64, 92, 93, 94, 117–19, 149, 154n., 166n., 290
Alexander the Great, 13, 24, 214–17
Alexandria, North Africa, 14
Amalekites, 121–2
Amarna Letters, see Tell el-Amarna
Amaziah, 178–9
Amenemhet I, 62
Amenophis III, 13, 70, 73, 84, 85
Amenophis IV (Akhen-aton), 70–1, 73
American School of Oriental Research, 18, 44, 253, 262

Ammon, Ammonites, 116, 155, 179
Amon (king), 200
Amon (god), 158
Amorites, 43, 54, 59–60, 62, 63
Amphictyony, 114
Anath, 77–8, 82, 100–1
Anathoth, 82, 101
Antakya, 294
Antioch of Pisidia, 299–300
Antioch-on-Orontes, 293–6
Antonia Fortress, 226–9, 313
Aphek, 89
Aqabah, 146
Aqabah, Gulf of, 131, 132, 139, 146, 179
Arabah, 179, 181
Arameans, 44, 62
Araunah, 137, 144
Areopagus, 307–8
Arnon River, 85
Arslan-Tash (Hadatu), 104, 166
Arvad, 86
Asa, 153, 156–7, 160
Asher, 90
Asherah, 51, 80–1, 100–2
Ashkelon 87, 88
Ashtar (Ashtaroth, Ashtoreth), 77, 101
Ashurbanipal, 13, 16
Asshur-nasir-pal II, 14, 166, 167
Assos (Behram Koy), 312
Assuan, 69, 111n.
Assyria, Assyrians, 13, 27, 94, 141n., 145, 155, 167–8, 176–203
Astarte, 100, 105
Athaliah, 111n.
Athens, 13, 17, 292, 306–8
Attalia (Antalya), 299, 301
Avaris, 85
Avigad, N., 179
Azariah (Uzziah), 131n., 179–81

Baal, 30, 76–81, 103–5, 182, 184
Baal-Ammon, see Moloch
Baalath, 145
Baal-berith temples, 33, 91, 99
Baanah, 124
Baasha, 156–7
Bab edh-Dhra', 49, 53, 268
Babylas, St., 295
Babylon, Babylonians, 27, 94, 205–10
Baghdad, 28

Bar Kochba, 269, 272, 276
Barnabas, 296, 298, 301–2
Basra, 32
Bathsheba, 131
Baza, 158
Beeroth, 91
Beer-Sheba, 47, 66, 147, 148
Belshazzar, sister of, 13
Ben-Hadad I, 157, 158, 166–8
Ben-Hadad II, 166
Benjamin (tribe and territory), 90, 91, 117, 156, 157
Berlin Museum, 13, 70
Beroea, 306
Berytus, 86
Beth Anath, 82
Beth Anoth, 82
Bethany, 39n., 288
Bethel, 44, 66, 86, 93, 104, 154–5, 156, 157
Bethesda (Bethzatha), 288, 289
Beth-horon, 145, 159
Bethlehem, 38, 89, 255, 280–1
Beth-Omri (=Shemer), 161, 162
Bethsaida, 282
Beth-shan, 44, 50, 69, 87, 88, 90, 101, 116, 117, 120, 142, 143, 159
Beth-Shemesh, 130, 148, 159, 178
Beth-zur (Kirbet et-Tubeiquah), 219–20
Bezek, 116
Bithynia, 303
Black Obelisk (of Shalmaneser III), 176, 177
Blegen, C. W., 18
Boaz pillar, 140, 142
Boghazkoey Texts, 34, 64
Botta, Paul, 14, 16
Breasted, James, 33
Britain, Roman ruins, 17, 22
British Museum, London, 13, 28, 32, 311
British School of Archaeology, Jerusalem, 18, 92, 125, 127
Bronze Age, 19
  Early Bronze, 22n., 23, 29, 37, 46–54, 55, 56, 84, 92, 93
  Middle Bronze, 26, 30, 55–8, 63, 64, 65, 92, 118, 126, 142
  Late Bronze, 37, 58–60, 79, 84, 86, 92, 93, 122, 126, 142, 149
Bubastis (=Tell Basta), 158
Burrows, Millar, 253
Byblos, 44, 59, 62, 68, 86, 102